# Neoconservatives in U.S. Foreign Policy under Ronald Reagan and George W. Bush

# Neoconservatives in U.S. Foreign Policy under Ronald Reagan and George W. Bush

## Voices behind the Throne

Jesús Velasco

Woodrow Wilson Center Press
Washington, D.C.

The Johns Hopkins University Press
Baltimore

EDITORIAL OFFICES

Woodrow Wilson Center Press
One Woodrow Wilson Plaza
1300 Pennsylvania Avenue, N.W.
Washington, D.C. 20004-3027
Telephone: 202-691-4029
www.wilsoncenter.org


ORDER FROM

The Johns Hopkins University Press
Hampden Station
P.O. Box 50370
Baltimore, Maryland 21211
Telephone: 1-800-537-5487
www.press.jhu.edu/books/

Library of Congress Cataloging-in-Publication Data
Velasco Nevado, Jesús.
  Neoconservatives in U.S. foreign policy under Ronald Reagan and George W. Bush : voices
behind the throne / Jesús Velasco.
      p. cm.
  Includes bibliographical references and index.
  ISBN 978-0-8018-9549-4
  1. United States—Foreign relations—1981–1989—Decision making.   2. United States—
Foreign relations—2001–2009—Decision making.   3. Conservatism—United States—History—
20th century.   4. Conservatism—United States—History—21st century.   5. Reagan, Ronald.
6. Bush, George W. (George Walker), 1946–   I. Title.
  E876.V44 2010
  320.520973—dc22          2009047216

*To the memory of my mother, Martha Grajales*
*To Rodrigo, my son, my true joy*

# Contents

# Tables

# Preface and Acknowledgments

Let me start this book with an anecdote. In 1997, I spent nine months at the Institute of Public Policy at George Mason University conducting interviews with neoconservatives and searching out information for this book. During that time, I had frequent lunches and conversations with Seymour Martin Lipset, whom I had the good fortune to meet when I finished my BA. One day, he approached me: "Jesús, as you know, the American Political Science Association convention is currently in Washington, and a lot of my friends from different areas of the country are in the city now. So I am holding a party at my home tomorrow. Would you like to come?" Of course, I gratefully accepted his kind invitation. He asked me to be at his home at 7 PM, but I intentionally arrived at 8, because I wanted to be at his home when most of the people were already there.

When I arrived at Lipset's home, I was astonished at what I saw: a cordial gathering of some of the main leaders of the first neoconservative movement. In Lipset's living room, I saw Irving Kristol, Gertrude Himmelfarb, Ben Wattenberg, Joshua Muravchik, Peter Skerry, Max Kampelman, Jeane Kirkpatrick, and many, many others talking, laughing, eating, and drinking, in small circles of four or five people. I decided to walk around and stop for a few minutes with each group. What I noticed was that, in most cases, the conversations focused on political issues—American foreign affairs with respect to Israel, Bill Clinton's foreign policy, the new article in *The New Republic* or *Commentary*, and so on. I was fascinated, because I was able to listen to their conversations and arguments, see their attitudes and gestures, and observe their behavior. Sometimes, they looked at me, wondering "Who is this guy?" But they basically ignored me. The only one who paid a little attention to me was Nelson Polsby, who, after

Lipset introduced me to him, asked: "Why are you interested in the neoconservatives?" I responded: "Why not?" He did not like my answer, immediately ignored me, continued eating his copious dinner, changed the subject, and started talking to other people. Yet overall, I really enjoyed the party, because I was able to observe a social gathering of neoconservatives, my subject of inquiry.

When I left Lipset's home, I was fully convinced that neoconservatism is a living political and intellectual force. The neoconservatives were this small group of influential people who exchanged views, perceptions, and ideas. They were friends, or at least colleagues, who debated political issues, expressed their disagreements, applauded their coincidences, and frequently concurred in their judgments. They did not need to belong to a political party or hold a statement of principles to share a common perspective. Journalists and social scientists may have problems defining neoconservatives—I faced many in writing this book—but after Lipset's party, I did not have a single doubt that this movement exists, is there, fighting to spread its ideas, seeking to affect the course of American foreign policy.[1]

This book is about neoconservatism, but not as a stable and undeviating entity. On the contrary, the book sees neoconservatism as a living force, as an expression that has evolved throughout its history. It distinguishes between the first and the second neoconservative movements, and it contrasts both expressions. The first generation of neoconservatives came to prominence during the Ronald Reagan administration's first term. The second acquired relevance during the George W. Bush administration's first term. Both generations are very important, for at least two reasons. First, they represented an eminent intellectual expression—especially the first movement—that has highly influenced, with their ideas, American intellectual debate on foreign affairs during the last fifty years. Second, neoconservatism has been a very influential political expression that has shaped American foreign policy viewpoints in two important Republican administrations. To account for this intellectual and political history, I not only studied the historical context in which both neoconservative expressions emerged but also delved into their ideas, institutions—in particular, their think tanks and magazines—and interests. My aim was always to uncover the various interconnected facets of neoconservatism in order to present a comprehensive and accurate portrait of this movement.

The book claims that the ideas advanced by neoconservatives on human rights and on military buildups and defense influenced American foreign policy during the Reagan administration's first term. It also argues that neoconservatives influenced the American invasion of Iraq and the war on terror during the George W. Bush administration's first term. Thus, neoconservative ideas directly and indirectly shaped policy agendas and policy measures during the period of analysis, altering the route of American foreign policy. To analyze the period's events following this theme, I present a framework that combines realignment theory with historical institutionalism.

This book has been written with the tools of the historian. I have extensively consulted three archives and made good use of materials in another two. The use of archives as a source of information is not a common practice for political scientists, in particular rational choice scholars. In general terms, political scientists disregard the specific facts provided by archives because they do not supply information that can be tested and used to make generalizations. Political scientists want to "go beyond conventional history's preoccupation with historical particularity and aim for theoretical generalization."[2] It is not strange, therefore, that rational choice scholars such as Margaret Levi maintain that "rationalists are almost willing to sacrifice nuance for generalizability, detail for logic, a forfeiture most other comparativists would decline."[3]

I believe that archival work should be a central component of research in political science. Knowledge of particularities and aims for generalizations are not conflicting enterprises, contrary to what Levi asserts. We can confidently test hypotheses when we have exhaustively worked with data. In fact, the systematic study of primary sources is one of the most reliable bases for making accurate assertions, re-creating a historical episode, or offering a profound analysis. These sources provide us with the closest contact to our object of inquiry.

The information I encountered in the archives proved indispensable as I built my case studies, and it helped me to go deeper into the particularities of neoconservatism as an intellectual-political expression. I located information never mentioned by neoconservatives or revealed by any scholar. For instance, when I examined the financial records of the Committee on the Present Danger, I discovered its main sources of financial support. My work in the archives was also indispensable for finding out that Jeane Kirkpatrick's formulation in her essay "Dictatorships and Double Standards" emerged from ideas previously discussed in neoconservative circles. I found, for example, in the papers of the Coalition for a Democratic Majority that the organization had spent a significant amount of time debating these ideas. Kirkpatrick, therefore, became the voice for a general neoconservative view. Likewise, my work in the archives helped me to corroborate the information I collected in my interviews. I discovered a significant consistency between what neoconservatives told me during our conversations and what I found in the archives.

Contrary to what most scholars believe, I found that anecdotal information is not superfluous but rather offers important insights into the main concerns, motivations, and interests of neoconservatives. Anecdotes can be seen as a synthetic form of expression, a way to simplify complex events in a very accessible fashion. They often help reinforce previous observations, illustrating certain phenomena and assisting us to re-create a historical event. They are, in the words of Lionel Gossman, "a particular instance exemplifying and confirming a general rule or trend or epitomizing a large general situation."[4] Anecdotes, therefore, were not excluded from the material used in this study; they were incorporated into the general narrative.

I have been fortunate in my work with the archives I consulted. Peter Rosenblatt and William Van Cleave—the owners, respectively, of the papers of the Coalition for a Democratic Majority and of the papers of the Committee on the Present Danger—kindly granted me access to their archives, which until the time of writing this book were not available to the public. One of the main contributions of this book is that it offers an analysis based on information never before presented by any scholar.

As mentioned above, I also employed another tool commonly used by historians, sociologists, and anthropologists: interviews.[5] It is common for sociologists to talk with social actors. They interview social leaders, peasants, workers, businesspeople, and so on. In conducting interviews, they obtain firsthand information that they can systematize or use as a primary source. Historians and anthropologists employ similar strategies. In my conversations with neoconservatives, I collected their perspectives about the history of their movement and their influence on foreign policy. With these conversations, I tried to reconstruct a sort of oral history of neoconservatism.

The more than fifty interviews I conducted for this study proved valuable in three ways. First, they provided me with firsthand information that either confirmed what neoconservatives had said before or contained observations that had never been made public. Second, direct contact with the main actors of my study allowed me to observe their personal reactions. How did they behave when I asked them difficult questions? What facial expression or posture did they adopt when I criticized them? What were their main concerns? How did they evaluate their achievements and failures? How did they perceive themselves? Emotions and attitudes are very difficult to capture through written words. They can only be obtained through personal contact and observation. It was quite a different experience talking with the late Irving Kristol, a very bright intellectual who smoked like a chimney, speaking with passion about American politics and neoconservatism at the same time, than with Norman Podhoretz, whose every word breathes fanaticism, or with Michael Novak, an intelligent person who never loses his temper and always speaks in the same tone of voice.

Third and finally, these interviews allowed me to observe the settings in which neoconservatives work. Work settings reveal a lot about people's personalities and preferences. Richard Perle's home office—where magazines featuring his picture line the walls, small American flags decorate his desk, and photos of him with distinguished politicians like Ronald Reagan dominate the room—gave the impression that he is a powerful person who enjoys his power. My interview with Irving Kristol took place in a corner of the American Enterprise Institute's cafeteria reserved for him to smoke, a clear expression of his respected and influential position within the institute—one with significant privileges. These impressions added to the portrait I tried to construct of an important episode in American political and intellectual history.

In researching and writing this book, I combined my archival work and interviews with the study of printed information and the evaluation of think tanks and neoconservative magazines. For neoconservatives, think tanks like the American Enterprise Institute and the Project for the New American Century have been key institutions, where they have met influential politicians and businesspeople, have disseminated their views, have spread or censored ideas, and have linked policy analysis with politics. Think tanks have the ability to popularize unknown topics and to raise consciousness of subjects already in the media and public discussions. They have staffs with the skills to persuade politicians of the pertinence of policy measures and to educate congressional staffers and legislators about key subjects. Think tanks, therefore, have been main institutions in the dissemination of neoconservatives' ideas to political and business elites and to the educated public, in order to influence opinions. At the same time, neoconservatives have conveyed considerable respectability to think tanks. The intellectual credentials of neoconservatives—mainly those of the first generation—became a central element of think tanks' national and international reputations. In all, as one specialist asserted, "The appreciation of think tanks is helpful not just for understanding the political role of expertise and ideas in American policy making but for accounting for how ideology informs policy making."[6]

Neoconservatives of both generations were great believers in the power of magazines as vehicles for communication and instruments to influence policy debates. With their periodicals, neoconservatives created a sort of intellectual community where people with similar viewpoints exchanged opinions. In these magazines, neoconservatives published articles that became centerpieces of their perspectives, and sometimes influenced the policy views of politicians. Through think tanks and magazines, neoconservatives thus obtained widespread recognition. In this book, I carefully evaluate the role of neoconservative think tanks and magazines as important components in the development of neoconservative ideas and in their impact.

I am aware that I am doing political science with the instruments of history, as has often been the case for European or Latin American scholars, or the founders of American political science. Unfortunately, in the United States, this practice was relegated to relative disuse for a long time. However, since the end of the 1980s, we have witnessed the reemergence of American political history within the political science community. Today, many American scholars are interested in history and historical approaches, and they are using archival materials as an important source of information. I share their interest in the study of American political history and American political development because I believe that history and political science complement each other. In a way, this book is an attempt to show that history and political science can come together, and that their marriage is not only desirable but also often indispensable and fruitful.

While writing this book, I was very fortunate to have the encouragement and constructive criticism of several colleagues and friends. My deepest gratitude goes to Seymour Martin Lipset. He unconditionally supported my academic career from the days when I was an undergraduate student. Throughout all these years, until he passed away, he shared with me his extensive knowledge on political sociology, American politics, and American intellectual history. Regarding this book, he made substantial comments on the first drafts, helped arranged several interviews with neoconservative leaders, and made it feasible for me to stay at the Institute of Public Policy at George Mason University to conduct my fieldwork. In innumerable conversations, he kindly shared many stories about his relationships with neoconservatives and his personal views on this political and intellectual movement. He was a friend, a very generous person, and a great teacher for almost two decades. Without the help and guidance of this humble man and outstanding intellectual, this book would have never been possible.

Walter Dean Burnham was not only a superb teacher but also a good critic of the first draft of this book. He helped me to understand the relevance of studying American political development. His encyclopedic knowledge of American politics, his profound comprehension of American history, and the methodological meticulousness of his analysis helped me understand two important facts: first, that history and political science are not conflicting but complementary enterprises; and second, that no equation can replace deep and systematic historical research. My appreciation for him goes far beyond what could be expressed in words.

I have established close friendships and working relationships with Maurico Tenorio and Jean Meyer. I have spent long hours with Maurico conversing about American intellectual history, and we have discussed many of the ideas contained in this book. He read the entire manuscript and made very constructive comments. Throughout these years, he has been a severe critic, a great colleague, and, above all, an unconditional friend. Jean has highly encouraged my academic development. Although never formally my teacher, he has been my professor. His various comments on this work helped me revise my arguments.

Catherine Boone and Benjamin Ginsberg read the first version of this book and made great observations. Rodolfo de la Garza and Stephen Skowronek seriously criticized my theoretical chapter and made good suggestions for improving my arguments. Peter Trubowitz has been a kind critic of my work, an unconditional supporter of my academic career, and a superb friend. I am deeply grateful to Jorge Dominguez, who has supported my work during the last five years and decidedly backed my stay at Harvard University when I finished this book. Merilee Grindle, the director of the David Rockefeller Center for Latin American Studies at Harvard University, was not only a very cordial host during my stay at the Rockefeller Center but, above all, a person who fully understood my difficult circumstances during my last months at Harvard. For that, I am fully grateful to her. I am also indebted to Ambassador Andres Rosenthal and to Andrew Selee, who made possible my stay at the Woodrow Wilson Center.

My colleagues at the Division of International Studies at the Centro de Investigación y Docencia Económicas in Mexico City have been super persons and great supporters of my work. I offer special thanks to Jorge

Chabat, Guadalupe Gonzales, Antonio Ortiz Mena, and Jorge Schiavon. My appreciation is also extended to the director of the Woodrow Wilson Center Press, Joe Brinley, who was always very sympathetic and patient with my work and also supervised the development of this volume from beginning to end. Yamile Kahn and Alfred Imhoff made superb editorial comments. Finally, I acknowledge my debt of gratitude to my friend and teacher Luis Maira, who first opened my eyes to the relevance of studying American politics from within.

Neoconservatives in U.S. Foreign Policy under
Ronald Reagan and George W. Bush

# 1

# Introduction: An Analytical Framework

"Neoconservatism"—understood as a movement of intellectuals, politicians, and journalists of national reputation, with a particular historical trajectory, specific journals, and institutions, and a centrist liberal ideology (first generation) or conservative views (second generation)—has become a key term in understanding contemporary American politics. From the late 1970s to the present, scholars, media specialists, and politicians have repeatedly referred to the neoconservative movement in their speeches and analyses. After the September 11, 2001, terrorist attacks, the word "neoconservatism" invaded the pages of magazines, newspapers, and academic studies. The term is so popular that during the George W. Bush presidency, major newspapers tracked the neoconservative movement on a permanent basis.[1] In different ways, analysts have sought to uncover the impact of neoconservatism on contemporary American politics, in particular its influence on foreign policy.

Neoconservatism achieved significant influence at two particular historical moments characterized by the leadership of two Republican presidents, Ronald Reagan and George W. Bush. At these moments, neoconservatives were the voices behind the throne, the people giving advice to the "king" and persuading him to implement a particular foreign policy. With respect to these two moments, and overall, the neoconservative movement's first generation differed substantially from its second generation. As mentioned above, the first generation was characterized by a centrist liberal ideology, whereas the second is typified by conservative views. (In this book, I use "first and second neoconservative movements" and "first and second neoconservative generations" interchangeably.) The second neoconservative movement has a very different history, however, than its

1

predecessor. The second neoconservative movement has been characterized by different patterns of growth and surges in influence, and its members have different political origins, affiliations, and intellectual credentials.

This book is an attempt to shed new light on the significance of the
neoconservative movement for American politics. Three main questions
guide my inquiry in the following pages: How can we understand neoconservatism's political ascendancy? Under what historical conditions are
neoconservatives able to influence American politics? How can we explain
the influence of neoconservatives on American foreign policy? In answer-
ing these questions, I also explore the fundamental differences between
the first neoconservative movement of the 1970s through the 1980s and
the second neoconservative movement of the 2000s. I claim that the ideas
advanced by neoconservatives on human rights and military buildups and
defense influenced American foreign policy during the Reagan administration's first term. In the later chapters of this book, I argue that neoconservatives influenced the foreign policy of the George W. Bush administration's first term, in particular with regard to the American invasion of Iraq
and the war on terror. I maintain that neoconservatism was able to shape
American politics because of the confluence of several causal elements—
a suitable historical context, ideas, institutions, and interests—that together facilitated the influence of neoconservative ideas on American foreign affairs.

In the course of this book's analysis, I discuss the relationship among
ideas, institutions, and interests and their links to the policymaking process. In doing so, I use a framework based on both realignment theory and
the concept of historical institutionalism. In my use of the former, I build
on the work of Walter Dean Burnham, in particular his periodization
scheme and his later views on the nonpartisan realignment of the late
1960s. My analysis also builds on historical institutionalism, specifically
those efforts that integrate the analysis of ideas, institutions, and interests.
My analytical framework merges both theories, and, as I hope to illustrate
in subsequent pages, my framework helps explain how neoconservatives
shaped American foreign policy during the Reagan administration's first
term and the George W. Bush presidency's first term. I also aspire to show
that despite several criticisms of realignment theory, some of its basic principles possess great utility. Realignment theory can be a valuable tool for
analyzing macro issues of patterns of evolution in American politics, but it

is also useful in the micro study of concrete policy measures, especially when it is enriched by historical institutionalism.

## Setting Out the Problems

Studying the influence of the neoconservative movement on American foreign policy by using a framework that fuses realignment theory and historical institutionalism is relevant for four main reasons—two empirical, two theoretical. First, previous books on neoconservatism have fundamentally examined this movement as an intellectual expression without fully appreciating neoconservatives' influence on policy. Second, studying the neoconservative movement of the 1980s can help us to understand the current neoconservatism of the 2000s. Third, scholars of realignment have typically ignored the role of ideas on policy changes. Finally, there has been no previous attempt to integrate realignment theory with historical institutionalism.

Previous studies have emphasized an analysis of the neoconservative movement as an intellectual expression, examining the characteristics of neoconservatives' thought on foreign policy, social issues, and/or cultural subjects.[2] For instance, Peter Steinfels's 1979 history of the movement examines the thinking and political views of Irving Kristol, Daniel Bell, and Daniel Patrick Moynihan. His book was the first comprehensive analysis of neoconservatism, but because it was published before the appointment of neoconservatives to important positions in the Reagan administration, the influence of neoconservatives on particular policy decisions is largely absent. John Ehrman's intellectual history of neoconservatism from the late 1940s to the mid-1990s examines "the ideas and impact on American foreign policy of a small and influential group of cold war liberals who became known as neoconservatives."[3] Similarly, Gary Dorrien offers "a critical examination of neoconservatism's history, its argument, and its future prospects."[4] His work is also essentially an intellectual history with special emphasis on the work and ideas of four forerunners of the movement: Irving Kristol, Norman Podhoretz, Michael Novak, and Peter Berger. Analysts of the second neoconservative movement are more interested in the policy impact of neoconservative ideas. This is the case for Stefan Halper and Jonathan Clarke. However, they basically ignored the policy influence of the first generation, and although they make some compari-

4

INTRODUCTION: AN ANALYTICAL FRAMEWORK

sons, they do not fully contrast both generations.[5] Consequently, a book that studies and contrasts both generations' influence in foreign affairs is absent from the literature.

Although I am also interested in the intellectual history of the neoconservative movement and dedicate important parts of the book to this topic, my emphasis is on how this group of intellectuals and politicians influenced the decisionmaking process in four particular areas: (1) American foreign policy related to human rights; (2) the military buildup and defense policy during the Reagan administration's first term; (3) the war on terror; and (4) the invasion of Iraq during the George W. Bush administration's first term. My analysis moves the debate on neoconservatism from the field of intellectual history and political theory to the terrain of political history and public policy.

Studying the first generation of the neoconservative movement of the 1970s and 1980s promises to shed light on the second generation of neoconservatism of the 2000s. My analysis of the first neoconservative expression provides a way to contrast the same political movement in two different historical periods. This comparison allows us to identify patterns, observe how context affected the development of this expression, explore how and why neoconservatism changed, and determine the significance of that change.[6]

In spite of American political scientists' growing interest in ideas and the way they shape and change policy outcomes, critical realignment scholars have fundamentally ignored this theme. They have examined American political development in order to identify critical elections and realignment periods, linking them to parties, party coalitions, and changes in the nature and direction of public policy. Classic realignment theory—understood as the "significant and durable change in the distribution of party support over relevant groups within the electorate"[7]—has been largely concerned with the study of electoral politics, overlooking other elements of realignment that build *longue durée* American political eras.[8]

One exception is the work of Eldon Eisenach, who studies the role of ideas in the legitimization of political institutions. He has developed a methodology that (1) identifies a political group that establishes a new regime, and the "institutional form through which they mobilized and institute their regime"; and (2) analyzes the "forms of thoughts, traditions and rhetoric that shape their common political project." For Eisenach, studying realignment is an "inquiry into legitimization, into the way in which governing institutions and practice are justified."[9] In his analysis of the present regime (1952–present), he highlights three fundamental patterns: (1) pluralism and elitism; (2) internationalism, the Cold War, and presidential government; and (3) the Supreme Court and a new constitutionalism.[10]

Eisenach studies the ideas that legitimate political institutions, period. He also offers a general panorama of the prevailing ideas in a certain political era and those ideas that sustain a particular political regime. He makes a significant contribution to our comprehension of the role of ideas in political realignments by uncovering schools of thought in specific historical eras that are associated with particular institutions.

I diverge from Eisenach's approach in several ways. For him, the years from 1952 to the present constitute a single political era. In contrast, I agree with Burnham's argument that between 1968 and 1972, the United States experienced a nonpartisan realignment, and I see this period as marking the beginning of a new political moment characterized by a deep general crisis. The difficulties created by the crisis affected the interests and future of different political actors who sought to defend their interests. The neoconservative ascendancy to power is unintelligible without an evaluation of the impact of this general crisis on American politics. I am also fundamentally concerned with specific policy changes in a certain historical period. Thus, I present a case study, rather than a general picture of the phenomenon, in order to penetrate the intricacies of particular policy arenas and specific possible policy changes. Finally, despite several criticisms of realignment theory, I believe that it is a useful framework for analyzing important episodes of American political history.[11]

Some scholars have focused on realignment theory's failure to properly account for the status quo, in particular during the realignment of the late 1960s.[12] Karen Orren and Stephen Skowronek, who advocate a historical-institutionalist perspective, question realignment theorists' periodization, which they see as "overly rigid."[13] They suggest using a more flexible scheme, which functions over time and periods: "intercurrence." This term emphasizes that "institutions of a polity are not created or recreated all at once, in accordance with a single ordering principle; they are created instead at different times, in light of different experiences, and often for quite contrary purposes."[14]

Certainly talking about the existence of a classic realignment during these years is controversial. Many scholars argue in favor of "dealignment" rather than realignment. Other academics, however, have seen traditional partisan realignments between 1968 and 1972, the same historical period of Burnham's nonpartisan realignment.[15] Still others have found significant "changes in the regional balance of the major parties across six major regions of the United States."[16] Clearly, however, the United States experienced important economic, political, international, and cultural changes in the late 1960s. The transformations created by the general crisis that marked the period shaped important political tendencies at the macro level, structuring American politics in the years to come.[17]

For realignment scholars, the periodization of American political history through the recurrent cycles of crisis and stability is central. Without a framework of reference that differentiates regime change through the ascendancy of some political forces (parties or social groups) and the decline of others, there would be no realignment theory. Despite the implications of Orren and Skowronek's critique, realignment theory neither denies the survival of certain political elements from previous eras nor ignores the different trajectories and behaviors of institutions historically or within a particular political period.[18] Furthermore, I think it is possible to incorporate the concerns of historical-institutionalist scholars within the main framework of realignment theory. To do so, we have to admit that historical institutionalism and realignment are models that function on different levels of analysis but that can be integrated.

In this book, I am not dealing with the realignment/dealignment question, or puzzling over causes that provoked the realignment of the 1960s. Here, I assume that the United States experienced significant changes during those years (we can call it realignment, enduring shift, or sea change), and I use Burnham's notion of nonpartisan realignment as the basic matrix for my analysis.[19] In my schema, realignment theory operates in the background, placing my research in the proper historical context and highlighting the main tendencies of the historical-political period under analysis.[20] Historical institutionalism works at the front, guiding me into the intricate, overlapping worlds of ideas, institutions, and interests.

## How Can Realignment and Historical Institutionalism Be Synthesized in an Analytical Framework?

This book seeks to explain the rise and influence of the neoconservative movement with respect to American foreign policy for human rights and the military buildup during the Ronald Reagan administration's first term, and the influence of the second generation of neoconservatives on the Iraq war and the war on terror during the George W. Bush administration. I have selected these themes because they are central topics within the foreign policy literature, and, above all, because they constitute the core of American foreign affairs. Human rights is related to moral authority, to the historical effort of America to present itself as the defender of freedom and the world's unquestionable and honorable moral leader. Defense is related to military power, to the capacity of the United States to be the dominant authority by being the most powerful armed force in the world. And the Iraq war is, in a way, the fusion and materialization of these two elements of America's moral authority and its role as the world's dominant military power.

Together, these two elements constitute what Thomas Jefferson called the "empire of liberty," a notion that sees empire and liberty as compatible. According to John Lewis Gaddis, the origin of the expression "empire of liberty" lay "in the belief that the American system of government, unlike any other in the world at that time, assumed the universality of human rights, so that people living outside it would want to be included within it or, failing that, to emulate it. An empire expanding because of its own attractiveness would therefore, safeguard liberty." Likewise, the Founding Fathers believed that "the security of American institutions required their expansion. The liberty the republican experiment had produced could only flourish within an empire that provide safety."[21] Human rights, defense, and security are, therefore, part of the historical foundation of American international affairs. Neoconservatives, who are embedded in this tradition, have concentrated their efforts on affecting American foreign policy on human rights, defense, and international security.

Three main questions led my research: How can we understand the ascendancy of neoconservatism to power? Under what historical conditions do neoconservatives influence American politics? How can we explain the influence of neoconservatives on American foreign policy? I also explore the question of why the first neoconservative movement of the 1970s and 1980s differed from the second neoconservative movement of the 2000s. To answer these questions, I developed a methodological framework that combines realignment theory and historical institutionalism, to which I alluded above.[22]

At first glance, the fusion of these two theories seems absurd. However, if we understand that realignment and historical institutionalism move at different levels of analysis, and that the main goal of these two theories is diverse, we can use significant components of both of these approaches and blend them into a new one. Both approaches have something in common: They take history seriously.

I view realignment through the lens of Walter Dean Burnham's concept of nonpartisan realignment, which I alluded to above. In 1991, Burnham asserted that there are not one but two types of realignment: the partisan, or type A; and the nonpartisan, or type B. Realignments, he argues, occur when "politically decisive minorities of the relevant population at any given time, alter what they have traditionally been doing in politics (including participation or non-participation) rather suddenly, ushering in something very different."[23] His formulation of a type B, nonpartisan realignment allows him to explain the 1968–72 period as a critical time of realignment.

Burnham's nonpartisan realignment has its origins in the global crisis between 1968 and 1972, and it reflects the exhaustion of the New Deal order.[24] According to Burnham, the nonpartisan realignment of the late 1960s has four main characteristics in the formal, institutional domain: (1) the decline of political parties as organizations of collective action, (2) the emergence of the mass media as the organizers of political campaigns, (3) the "institutionalization" of the House of Representatives, and (4) divided government.[25]

These four characteristics of nonpartisan realignment—plus the notion of participatory democracy[26]—highlight the main trends of the historical-political time period I examine. Understanding these trends helps us comprehend the political behavior of certain social actors at a particular historical moment. It would be difficult to comprehend the mobilization of corporations and corporate and private foundations in favor of neoconservative ideas without taking the nonpartisan realignment of the late 1960s into account. Likewise, that mobilization in response to a general social crisis helps explain the impact of neoconservative ideas on foreign policy. Indeed, the neoconservative presence in academic journals, television, think tanks, and the press is in part explained by the growth of the mass media's influence on contemporary American politics.

Like Burnham, my conception of realignment goes beyond the traditional notion of electoral politics. I recognize a particular theoretical conception of history, look for patterns to explain change and continuity in American political developments, and utilize a form of periodization that enables me to understand events in their complexity, within an entire political era. "The periodization underlying realignment, or regime theory [in Stephen Skowronek's view]," asserted Elizabeth Sanders, "is a useful way to order American political history."[27] Building on Burnham's work, I view realignment theory as oriented not toward electoral politics but rather toward "eras politics." The notion of nonpartisan realignment helps to place my work in the proper historical context and also to be aware of the main political trends of the historical period under analysis.

Although realignment theory tell us a great deal about what happened in the late 1960s and early 1970s and the changes in American politics that followed, it only provides a general picture of a particular historical moment. To fully develop my case study, I need a framework that helps me to navigate the complexity of the issues under analysis. To achieve this goal, I build on the historical-institutional approach, which highlights the importance of examining the internal dynamics of institutions. It is built on six basic ideas. The first is the notion of path dependence and unintended consequences. The second idea is the relevance of historicizing the emergence of institutional arrangements and contextualizing the analysis of institutions within a particular historical period. The third is the study of how different institutions actually formulate policies. The fourth is Orren and Skowronek's concern for institutional trajectories, and the survival of political and institutional arrangements from previous political periods. The fifth is the notion of multiple orders existing simultaneously, with elements that move at different paces and have several areas of overlap. The sixth and final idea is how institutions permit or hinder the access (and eventual adoption) of ideas.[28] In a nutshell, realignment theory is a sort of canvas on which I paint my work. Historical institutionalism is the painting, the different brushstrokes, that portray my case study. The canvas and the painting are mutually dependent; they need each other to give life to a work of art.

Consequently, the analytical framework I employ operates at two different levels of analysis, the macro and the micro. The macro level consists of the basic features of the 1968–94 realignment period. At the micro level, specific policy changes are analyzed from a perspective that draws on historical institutionalism and considers the role of ideas in policy formulation. My goal is to correlate the macro and micro levels, showing how the main features of the realignment episode help us to understand concrete policy changes, and often (but not always) how particular policy changes are expressions of realignments. Attention to macro-micro interactions is important for building bridges between general and middle-range theories. Jeffrey Tulis asserts that "American political development can usefully be treated as a layered text."[29] I find Tulis's notion of superimposed strata a useful way to characterize my analytical framework. I thus refer to the distinct categories of my analysis as strata composed of structure, policy, and ideology—which are divisions consistent with the literature on ideas, institutions, and interests.[30]

### The First Analytical Stratum: Structure

I place factors associated with the economy—in particular, the behavior of American big business—in the first analytical stratum, structure. The economic crisis of the early 1970s affected American big business.[31] The decline of profits provoked corporate mobilization on four basic fronts.[32] One of these fronts was seeking the control of ideas through the economic support of think tanks and social organizations.[33] The neoconservative movement was a very well-financed political and intellectual expression that obtained its economic resources from corporations, corporate foundations, and private foundations. Consequently, neoconservatives had the economic resources to advance their views on foreign policy and other issues. It is in this particular stratum that we see a "marriage of convenience" between private corporations and neoconservatives. To reach their goals of gaining market share and generating profits, corporations need a political discourse capable of penetrating society with sufficient persuasion and intellectual legitimacy so that it will be embraced by important sectors of the population, especially decisionmakers. Neoconservatives need access to economic resources to fund the creation and maintenance of journals, publish books, and develop research projects. Private corporations fill this need.

Corporations and corporate leaders helped the flourishing neoconservative organizations,[34] because neoconservatives developed a political discourse that furthered their interests and protected them. Neoconservatives alerted business leaders, foundations, and corporations to the significance of financially supporting conservative causes. "Your philanthropy," asserted Irving Kristol in 1977, "must serve the long-term interests of the corporation. Corporate philanthropy should not be, cannot be disinterested."[35]

### The Second Analytical Stratum: Policy

I locate policy changes in the second analytical stratum. To properly understand policy shifts, we have to explore the internal dynamics of institutions and the behavior of their actors. We must know not only the nature of the policy initiative and its main proponents but also whether institutions enhance or inhibit the access of certain policies and particular ideas in the decisionmaking process. To properly assess the influence of neoconservativism on American foreign policy changes, it is necessary to understand both how American institutions shaped neoconservatives' political behavior and also the roles played by neoconservatives within American institutions. My analysis of this stratum considers the history, traits, and internal dynamics of policymaking institutions, in particular the State Department and the Department of Defense.

## *The Third Analytical Stratum: Ideology*

The periods of time selected for this study constitute an ideal time frame for examining ideological change. Today, the eclipsing of political parties has not only made the idea of a traditional partisan realignment problematic but has also made ideas a powerful agent of political change.[36] The evaporation of party politics opened up the system to ideological appeals. "Conservatives," asserts Sidney Blumenthal, "are replacing old party politics with an ideological politics in which the ideas order up the images."[37] In this historical context, neoconservatives—the main actors of my ideological stratum—found the proper ground to diffuse their ideas. They had the academic credentials to be recognized as experts in their respective fields.[38] They had (in particular the first generation) the vehicles for the diffusion of their ideas (books, journals, frequent op-ed contributions in some of the nation's most important newspapers) and the organizational backing necessary to penetrate crucial economic and political circles.

The third analytical stratum, ideology, deals with any significant changes in the set of ideas that legitimate policy changes. This is where we can observe the political struggle for the predominance of a particular perspective. We can also uncover the important activities of organizations dedicated to the diffusion of ideas, such as journals, newspapers, think tanks, and electronic media. Intellectuals—and, in Russell Jacoby's term, "public intellectuals"[39]—play a prominent role in these sorts of activities. Intellectuals, and in this specific case neoconservative intellectuals, are not only disseminators of discourses or interpreters of social reality but also suppliers of explanations and designers of political strategies. It is important to highlight that in times of ideological change, intellectuals can create a new set of ideas (e.g., Keynesianism in the 1930s) or refashion old or prevailing conceptions. Political ideas, which may be unsuccessful in one concrete historical context, do not necessarily disappear forever. On the contrary, they usually are shelved for future use. New or hidden ideas emerge with particular impact in times of crisis. The power of ideas increases when intellectuals form alliances with societal and state actors to defend their respective interests. They help create a perspective that legitimates structural and policy modifications.

## Reflections on the Strata and the Analytical Framework

The origins of the ideological changes evaluated in this study are frequently located before the structural changes and become evident only after the structural and institutional changes are under way. It is important to emphasize that the structural stratum operates primarily in the terrain of economic interests but also has important political elements. The policy stratum can be seen at work practically in the realm of institutions and ideologically in the sphere of ideas. Each stratum is dominated by a primary actor—private corporations in the structural stratum, politicians in the policy stratum, and intellectuals in the ideological stratum. Each has different goals and different capabilities, and each member contributes specific forms of capital to the coalition—private corporations provide economic capital, politicians provide political capital, and intellectuals provide cultural capital. The alliance I discuss was made possible by the impact that the global crisis of the late 1960s and early 1970s had on each set of actors. Table 1.1 summarizes my analytical framework.

How does one apply this framework to study the influence of the neoconservative movement on foreign policy changes? The first way is by using a historical approach. History, as I understand it, is not merely a way of describing events but also a systematic, analytical tool that lends itself to comparing one period with another.

*Table 1.1. An Analytical Framework for Realignment*

| Stratum | Realm of Action | Actors | Contribution |
|---|---|---|---|
| Ideology | Ideas | Neoconservative intellectuals | Cultural capital |
| Policy | Institutions | Politicians | Political capital |
| Structure | Interests | Private corporations | Economic capital |

Historical analyses are indispensable for reconstructing events and making sense of a particular phenomenon. History, as Stephen Jay Gould asserts, is "unique and complex. It cannot be reproduced in a flask." In his view, it is by digging in the past that we come to comprehend previous times, clarify concepts, judge previous questions, open new queries, and reconstruct the paths taken by other scholars and disciplines. "Once the path is traced," he argues, "we may be able to specify the causes that led history to follow this, rather than another, route."[40]

The historical explanation advanced here seriously considers contingencies. Contingencies, understood as "phenomena that do not form patterns, may include the actions individuals take for reason known only to themselves. . . . They can involve what the chaos theorist calls 'sensitive dependence on initial conditions,' situations where an imperceptible shift at the beginning of a process can produce an enormous change at the end of it."[41] Thus, the notion of contingency alerts us to historical moments when certain patterns stop following a particular direction and take a different route. The terrorist attacks in New York and Washington on September 11, 2001, changed the George W. Bush presidency significantly. The subsequent decisions made by the Bush administration, notably the invasions of Afghanistan and Iraq, sent the United States on a different foreign policy path. The citizenry's feelings of vulnerability produced a general institutional and policy shift in the conception and organization of American national security. The creation of the Homeland Security Department is the clear materialization of this phenomenon. Similarly, the terrorist attacks increased the relevance of neoconservatism as a political and intellectual expression. The idea of contingency is highly consistent with the historical-institutionalist perspective, in particular with the notion of path dependence.

This book is a sort of study of the genealogy of ideas. My aim is not to discover the most remote antecedents of a particular viewpoint but to find its early connections with the neoconservative movement. I follow the historical evolution of an idea until the time when it influences policy decisions. I also examine the role played by neoconservative organizations and journals in the diffusion of their conceptions of society and governmental institutions. The study of neoconservative organizations reveals three important characteristics of the neoconservative movement: (1) forms of operation, (2) strategies, and (3) relations with political and economic elites. I then analyze the historical conditions that made the emergence of a receptive audience for neoconservative views possible. Finally, I discuss how neoconservatives and their organizations interacted to diffuse these intellectuals' ideas.

I evaluate policy changes by considering significant policy modifications and analyzing the different institutions involved in each issue. Because institutions exist in a particular historical context, I analyze the evolution and main traits of the institutions involved in my case studies. I assess whether these institutions enhance or inhibit the influence of neoconservative ideas and interests during the decisionmaking process. Finally, in the structural stratum, I study the nexus between political and economic interests and the neoconservative movement. As Hugh Heclo points out, there is a codependency among ideas, institutions, and interests: "Interests tell institutions what to do; institutions tell ideas how to survive; ideas tell interests what to mean." In each realignment era, "ideas, institutions, and interests come together to form a distinctive order."[42]

This sort of analysis, like most studies of ideas, involves serious methodological problems. As Judith Goldstein and Robert Keohane observe, "A key problem is that students of the role of ideas must interpret what is in people's heads."[43] Furthermore, like historians, we must consider "how such events must have looked to those who participated in or were affected by them."[44] History has taught us that it is possible to undertake the scientific study of the past by conducting a hermeneutical analysis of the available evidence.

To increase the quantity of this available evidence, I conducted more than fifty interviews with neoconservative leaders, which provided me with firsthand information from participants in policy debates and institutional decisionmaking. In these interviews, I sought these leaders' perspectives about the origins and evolution of the neoconservative movement, its organizations, its relationship to think tanks, and its influence on American policy changes. I did not evaluate their answers passively. Instead, I analyzed their statements alongside neoconservative organizations' archival records and my own research. In other words, I tried to reconstruct a sort of oral history of neoconservatism—not only to obtain firsthand information or to fill gaps in my knowledge of the movement but also "to get a better history, a more critical history, a more conscious history which involves members of the public in the creation of their own history."[45] In all this work, I sought to immerse myself in the neoconservatives' complex world, with the sole purpose of gathering all possible information and viewpoints so as to be able to understand their perspectives and institutions and thereby offer the most accurate history and most informed inter-pretation of this political and intellectual expression.

In these ways, I have applied the analytical framework outlined here to the study of the neoconservative movement. In the next chapter, I examine the main features of this movement, one of the most important intellectual and political expressions in contemporary American politics.

# 2

# Who Is a Neoconservative?

It is certainly difficult to define neoconservatism. It is not a political party; nor is it a formal organization. Its members are not affiliated with a single party or organization. In 1979, Peter Steinfels asserted:

> We have no Neoconservative Manifesto, no neoconservative program for the seventies and the eighties, no statement issued from the National Association of Neoconservatives. . . . Indeed it may be that no neoconservative is the neoconservative; the center of gravity of a collection of individuals may rest somewhere between them and outside of any single person.[1]

It is just as difficult to classify neoconservatism in ideological terms. It is a current of thought that shares principles with New Deal liberalism—the first generation—and traditional American conservatism, often looking like a "syncretic intellectual" expression. However, like most U.S. conservative expressions, neoconservatism has a liberal matrix.[2] This hybrid quality makes understanding neoconservatism even more of a challenge.

"Neoconservatism" is often a misleading term. Some European scholars, for instance, have used the word to classify Margaret Thatcher's and Ronald Reagan's policies, to label the monetarist theory of Milton Friedman, or to characterize the social demands of the Moral Majority. From this perspective, Friedman, Jeane Kirkpatrick, and Jerry Falwell would be part of the same political phenomenon.[3] An American specialist on neoconservatism has even renounced defining the term, because of its ambiguous connotations.[4] Because of this terminology problem, Seymour Martin Lipset declared twenty years ago that "the concept of neoconservatism is irrelevant to further developments within American politics, . . . because it is a term which confuses, rather than one which helps further political discourse."[5]

How can we study neoconservatism when it is such an amorphous term, not to mention a slippery political phenomenon? How can we capture its essence without falling into generalizations and misleading classifications? There is no easy way to solve these puzzles. But identifying neoconservatives, and a historical analysis of neoconservatism's evolution and organization, can help us draw the boundaries of this intellectual and political expression and formulate a useful working definition of the term.

This chapter is divided into three sections. First, I identify the core members of the first generation of neoconservatives. Second, I examine four interconnected elements of the neoconservative movement: origins, organizations, publications, and ideology. My purpose here is to identify neoconservatism as a type of "intellectual community"—a group of people who share, in general terms, common origins; who participate in the same organizations; who write with analogous perspectives about similar topics; who are involved in the publication of several journals that disseminate their ideas; and who share a basic political ideology or worldview.[6] Third, I present some general characteristics of the second generation of neoconservatives. In addition to identifying the main figures of this second generation, I describe broad points of contrast between the first and second generations.

## Toward an Identification of the First Generation of Neoconservatives

One of the main problems with the term "neoconservatism" is the difficulty of identifying the primary advocates of what I refer to as an intellectual and political expression. Difficulties arise, for example, when the people most identified with the term "neoconservative" disavow the label. Daniel Bell describes himself as "socialist in economics, liberal in politics, and conservative in culture,"[7] and he vehemently rejects being classified as a neoconservative.[8] He considers himself "the oldest young Menshevik in America,"[9] and in 1984 he clearly expressed to Sidney Hook his animosity to some neoconservatives: "I do not trust Norman Podhoretz or Joe Epstein. I do not trust Irving Kristol, as I trust you. I disagree now very much with Irving politically, and undoubtedly to some extent with you, but I respect you and Irving. I do not respect Norman or Midge [Decter] or Epstein, etc."[10] Podhoretz maintains that Daniel Patrick Moynihan disliked being called conservative, and he asserts that Moynihan moved away from neoconservatism after his election as senator.[11] Kristol has called Lipset a "bumblebee" because it was hard to predict where he would land.

Likewise, the term "neoconservatism" is problematical because it "has never referred to a set of doctrines to which a given group of adherents subscribe."[12] Intellectual communities are typically hard to identify. As Charles Kadushin noted more than thirty years ago, intellectual circles (and other cultural circles) "have no clear boundaries and the dividing line between the center and the periphery is often arbitrarily drawn."[13] Despite this severe limitation, it is possible to offer a fairly clear picture of the main neoconservatives. To identify them, first it is important to establish the distinction between the first and second generations of neoconservatives. As I try to show throughout this study, although there are important links between these two generations, there are also significant differences between them. Here, I concentrate on the first generation, an expression that flourished between the 1960s and the 1980s. I offer some observations about the second generation, which I discuss more comprehensively in the later chapters of this book.

To properly situate the first generation of neoconservatives, I analyzed three journal articles written by these intellectuals about their movement, in order to create a list of people recognized by neoconservatives as part of this tendency.[14] To achieve this goal, I used a consensus method. If a person was listed in two of the three articles, I considered him or her a core neoconservative. Table 2.1 summarizes the results of this study by naming the authors of the three articles and then listing the people quoted in each respective article. The analysis reveals that ten persons who constituted the core of the first generation of neoconservatives. Nathan Glazer, Jeane J. Kirkpatrick, Hilton Kramer, Irving Kristol, Daniel Patrick Moynihan, Norman Podhoretz, and James Q. Wilson were quoted in all three articles. Daniel Bell, Seymour Martin Lipset, and Norman Podhoretz were cited in two, and each wrote one of the articles. (Michael Novak was also cited in two of the articles.)

My account is very consistent with the opinions of several specialists. Alexander Bloom[15] considers Moynihan, Kirkpatrick, Kristol, Podhoretz, Bell, Glazer, and Lipset to be the most prominent neoconservative figures. Robert Nisbet does not include Kirkpatrick on his list,[16] but he does name Samuel Huntington and James Q. Wilson. Peter Steinfels and Isidore Silver name more or less the same people.[17] Adam Wolfson lists Kristol, Glazer, Moynihan, Podhoretz, and Kirkpatrick as representative neo-

*Table 2.1. Neoconservatives Quoted in Three Crucial Articles*

| Author of Article | | |
| --- | --- | --- |
| Daniel Bell | Seymour M. Lipset | Norman Podhoretz |
| Neoconservatives Quoted in Article | | |
| 1. *Daniel Bell* | 1. Elliott Abrams | 1. William Barrett |
| 2. Joseph Epstein | 2. *Daniel Bell* | 2. *Daniel Bell* |
| 3. *Nathan Glazer* | 3. William Bennett | 3. John B. Bunzel |
| 4. Samuel Huntington | 4. Peter Berger | 4. *Nathan Glazer* |
| 5. *Jeane J. Kirkpatrick* | 5. Midge Decter | 5. Sidney Hook |
| 6. *Hilton Kramer* | 6. Chester Finn | 6. *Jeane J. Kirkpatrick* |
| 7. *Irving Kristol* | 7. *Nathan Glazer* | 7. *Hilton Kramer* |
| 8. *Seymour Martin Lipset* | 8. Carl Gershman | 8. *Irving Kristol* |
| 9. Robert Nisbet | 9. Gertrude Himmelfarb | 9. *Seymour Martin Lipset* |
| 10. *Daniel Patrick Moynihan* | 10. Max Kampelman | 10. *Daniel Patrick Moynihan* |
| 11. *Norman Podhoretz* | 11. *Jeane J. Kirkpatrick* | 11. Michael Novak |
| 12. *James Q. Wilson* | 12. *Hilton Kramer* | 12. *Norman Podhoretz* |
| | 13. *Irving Kristol* | 13. Diane Ravitch |
| | 14. William Kristol | 14. *James Q. Wilson* |
| | 15. Everett C. Ladd | |
| | 16. *Seymour Martin Lipset* | |
| | 17. Edward Luttwak | |
| | 18. *Daniel Patrick Moynihan* | |
| | 19. Michael Novak | |
| | 20. Richard Perle | |
| | 21. Richard Pipes | |
| | 22. *Norman Podhoretz* | |
| | 23. Diana Trilling | |
| | 24. Robert Tucker | |
| | 25. Ben Wattenberg | |
| | 26. Aaron Wildavsky | |
| | 27. *James Q. Wilson* | |

*Sources:* Daniel Bell, "The Cultural Wars: American Intellectual Life, 1965–1992," *Wilson Quarterly* 16, no. 3 (Summer 1992): 74; Seymour Martin Lipset, "Neoconservatism: Myth or Reality," *Society* 25, no. 5 (July–August 1988): 29–37; and Norman Podhoretz, "The Neo-Conservative Anguish over Reagan's Foreign Policy," *New York Times Magazine*, May 2, 1982, 30–33, 96–98. Two criteria were used to select these articles. First, the authors were commonly identified as neoconservative; and second, in these articles they broadly alluded to the advocates of this tendency. The authors who were quoted in all three articles are listed in italic type.

conservative thinkers.[18] The coincidence between the opinions of these scholars and the outcome of my analysis reinforces my claim that the ten persons mentioned above form the nucleus of the first neoconservative movement.[19]

A number of other intellectuals and politicians who can be classified as neoconservatives, or are at least sympathetic to this political and ideological tendency, cluster around these ten core thinkers. Lipset's list in table 2.1 is very revealing in this regard. Furthermore, Kristol maintained more than fifteen years ago—before the second generation of neoconservatives became relevant in American politics—that his son, William Kristol, as well as Peter Skerry, Suzanne Garment, and others, constituted a second generation of neoconservatives.[20] This second generation has consolidated during the last decade, creating a distinctive political tendency. Therefore, what we have is two political and intellectual movements, which differ ideologically and generationally but have some important points of nexus. Furthermore, the members of the first generation have played an important role in the activities of the second generation. As mentioned, later in this book I describe in more detail the differences between the first and the second generations of neoconservatives. Here, suffice it to say, the members of the second generation came from a different background, followed a different route in developing their ideological and political commitments, are significantly more conservative than the first generation, and are fully integrated within the Republican Party.

To include other neoconservative thinkers beyond the core group seems to be unavoidable. In including other neoconservatives in my study—without making inappropriate classifications—I want to establish what I call the periphery of the neoconservative movement. This periphery is composed of those people who are cited in Bell's, Lipset's, and Podhoretz's articles but who are not listed as members of the core group. The people included in the periphery group are individuals recognized by core neoconservatives as a part of the movement.

My analysis, therefore, deals with the people in both the core and periphery groups. Any additions to this list are considered only if, in my interviews with neoconservatives, they named other persons as advocates of the movement. Table 2.2 presents a list of the ten core and twenty-six periphery members who constitute the nucleus, but not the totality, of the neoconservative movement. Neoconservatism has an important political dimension frequently ignored by social scientists and journalists as well as by many neoconservatives themselves. In 1993, Kirkpatrick asserted that

*Table 2.2. The Core and the Periphery of the First Generation of the Neoconservative Movement*

| Core | Periphery | |
|---|---|---|
| 1. Daniel Bell | 1. Elliott Abrams | 14. Max Kampelman |
| 2. Nathan Glazer | 2. William Barrett | 15. William Kristol |
| 3. Jeane J. Kirkpatrick | 3. William Bennett | 16. Everett C. Ladd |
| 4. Hilton Kramer | 4. Peter Berger | 17. Edward Luttwak |
| 5. Irving Kristol | 5. John B. Bunzel | 18. Robert Nisbet |
| 6. Seymour Martin Lipset | 6. Midge Decter | 19. Richard Perle |
| 7. Michael Novak | 7. Joseph Epstein | 20. Richard Pipes |
| 8. Daniel Patrick Moynihan | 8. Chester Finn | 21. Diane Ravitch |
| 9. Norman Podhoretz | 9. Suzanne Garment* | 22. Peter Skerry* |
| 10. James Q. Wilson | 10. Carl Himmelfarb | 23. Diana Trilling |
| | 11. Gertrude Himmelfarb | 24. Robert Tucker |
| | 12. Sidney Hook | 25. Ben Wattenberg |
| | 13. Samuel Huntington | 26. Aaron Wildavsky |

*These neoconservatives were quoted in interviews.

"[Senator Henry] Scoop Jackson was the godfather of neoconservatives but in politics."[21] Charles Horner likewise stated his belief that "everything started with CDM [Coalition for a Democratic Majority]."[22] And Richard Schifter, Eugene Rostow, and Douglas J. Feith, three individuals who had important political functions at different periods, defined themselves as neoconservative more than fifteen years ago.[23] Thus, this study differs from most analyses of neoconservatism in the significant consideration that it devotes to the political branch of the neoconservative movement. Neoconservatism is both a political and an intellectual movement. These expressions interact and complement each other.

Those people who belonged to neoconservative organizations and were not included in the three articles mentioned above form the political sphere of neoconservatism. However, even with this criterion, I still have difficulty including the American Enterprise Institute (AEI) and the Committee for the Free World (CFW). At AEI, neoconservatives were a minority, and therefore we can find people who worked there and were not neoconservatives. And the CFW had several European intellectual members. To address this problem, I have used four main criteria to define the political branch of the neoconservative movement. First, a person had to belong to or work for one or more neoconservative organizations. Second, the main activity of that individual had to be not writing but politics. Third, he or she had to be concerned with the same topics as neoconservatives and share their perspective. Fourth, these people could not be cited in the three articles studied above. Several people satisfied these criteria, but only twelve were relevant for my analysis: Henry Fowler, Frank Gaffney, Fred C. Iklé, Henry Jackson, Penn Kemble, Paul Nitze, Peter Rosenblatt, Eugene V. Rostow, Albert Shanker, Richard Schifter, Maxwell D. Taylor, and Elmo R. Zumwalt Jr.

Thus, ten core, twenty-six periphery, and twelve political members constitute what, for the purposes of this study, I will consider the first neoconservative movement. Limiting my study to the political and intellectual activities of a concrete number of people helped me draw some boundaries around the often-nebulous term "neoconservatism," and established a frame of reference for my analysis. However, it is important to emphasize that this list is only the first step in the identification of the neoconservative movement.

## Elements of the Neoconservative Movement: Origins, Organizations, Publications, and Ideology

Broadly speaking, the history of neoconservatism as a political and intellectual tendency has had three main phases of development: First, its core thinkers belonged to young radical associations; second, they became members of a group of distinguished social scientists and writers who defended centrist liberalism; and third—without losing their importance as scholars—they became public intellectuals participating in think tanks and political organizations as neoconservative advocates.

To study neoconservatism, history is important, for three main reasons. First, gaining an understanding of the historical evolution of neoconservatism helps us to appreciate the response of this group of intellectuals to the main historical challenges faced by the United States throughout many decades. Second, having a view of neoconservative history is essential to comprehend the formation of this political expression. Thus, through an evaluation of the historical path taken by neoconservatives, we can detect and appraise the periods when neoconservatives formed or participated in important organizations, their nexus with Washington's circles of power, or their presence in the media. We can also identify the moments of change, the times when the neoconservative movement took a different path. Third and finally, history allows us to observe the evolution of neoconservatives' thought, the process of deradicalization, and the conformation of the neoconservative view. In other words, what I am doing here is using the notion of path dependence to evaluate neoconservatives' historical trajectory. The aim is to observe the critical moments, the junctures in neoconservative history, that help us to explain the moment when neoconservatives became a relevant political and intellectual expression.

Contrary to common understanding, neoconservatism is not necessarily a by-product of the 1960s.[24] Some neoconservative views have their origin in the 1930s. In 1936, almost all the main leaders of the October Revolution in Russia were charged with treachery, sabotage, and espionage against the Soviet state. These events, known as the Moscow Trials, provoked strong reactions among some American intellectuals and members of particular political circles, who seriously criticized the Soviet regime. Anti-Stalinist sentiment promptly flourished in the United States. In U.S. intellectual circles, it quickly became more acceptable to declare oneself a supporter of Leon Trotsky, whose radical ideology had not, seemingly, been depraved by bureaucracy and power. In 1936, the left-wing *Partisan Review*, perhaps the most influential literary journal at that time, broke relations with the Communist Party. After having been refunded in 1937 as an independent magazine, *Partisan Review* became an anti-Stalinist publication sympathetic to Trotskyist viewpoints. To a greater extent, Trotskyism provoked the emergence of the anticommunist left wing among New York intellectuals and became a clear symbol of radical opposition to Stalin. "Trotskyism made it possible for these rebellious intellectuals," asserts Alan M. Wald, "to declare themselves on the side of revolution . . . and yet also to denounce Stalin from the left as the arch betrayer of Lenin's heritage."[25]

Several intellectuals, who later were to be associated with neoconservatism, shared an antagonism to Stalinism in their youth. As students at the City College of New York, Irving Kristol, Daniel Bell, Nathan Glazer, Seymour Martin Lipset, and others presented a consistent critique of Stalinism. Some of them even became members of the Young People's Socialist League, a Trotskyist youth organization. Furthermore, by the late 1930s, one of them, Lipset, became chairman of this organization. Some neoconservatives, therefore, started their political journey as radicals and as leftist advocates and critics of the most extreme communist expressions.

City College, an institution with a very active political life, played a quite important role in the formation of neoconservative intellectuals. In the mid-1930s, during the Great Depression, several Jewish students, mainly young men from the Bronx and Brooklyn, enrolled at City College. During the late 1930s, leftist tendencies predominated among the highly politicized student body. Although the institution had a good academic reputation, students did not show significant deference for their teachers. "Except for a few cases," recalled Bell, "one didn't respect one's teacher; . . . by and large most of the teachers were all dodos and we educated ourselves."[26] In a similar vein, the radical thinker Irving Howe remembered his days in City College in this way: "The atmosphere was dingy— the place needed a paint job, the teachers were overworked, many of them were mediocre. It wasn't a very distinguished faculty at all. There were a few brilliant teachers like the legendary Morris Cohen. [But among the students] there was an atmosphere of perfervid, overly heated, overly excited intellectually, because the radicalism of the moment was essentially abstract."[27]

Political life at City College centered on two main alcoves where students gathered. One, known as Mexico City, or Alcove No. 1—because, at that time, Trotsky was living in Mexico—was filled with a variety of radical anti-Stalinists. The other, known as the Kremlin, or Alcove No. 2, was occupied by the Communists and Stalinists. These two alcoves were places of intellectual recreation and learning. "Students," asserts Lipset, "were there all day, talking, reading, arguing and eating. . . . For the anti-Stalinists, the alcoves were classrooms. The older, more knowledgeable taught the new recruits. They gave lectures, answered questions, explained passages in books by Marx, Lenin, or Trotsky."[28] In Alcove No. 1, students read the *New International* (a journal edited by Max Shachtman and James Burnham) and *Partisan Review*, and outside the classroom received "a peculiar intense undergraduate education in what is now called social science."[29] City College was, in a way, a training camp for these neoconservatives. Here they not only learned Marxism and became aware of domestic and international problems. The college also initiated them into their future careers—the world of political and intellectual debate.

During the 1940s, some neoconservatives started a personal and intellectual relationship with Sidney Hook. Hook was a professor, and he was a well-known figure in New York intellectual circles when most neoconservatives were still in high school. Neoconservatives shared a similar intellectual history with him. Like many neoconservative intellectuals, he was Jewish, had studied at City College, and had been a communist in his youth. He had participated in several Trotskyite organizations, became anticommunist in the late 1930s and 1940s, was involved in the American

Committee on Cultural Freedom (he was its first chairman), and, like some neoconservatives, eventually went on to support Ronald Reagan. President Reagan had a deep appreciation for Hook. In celebration of Hook's eightieth birthday, Reagan asserted: "You have been our global philosopher of freedom, through more than a half century's continuous struggle against totalitarian ideologies of left and right."[30]

For many neoconservatives, Hook was a sort of intellectual mentor, a person they truly respected and admired. Bell dedicated *The End of Ideology* to him. "I share most of his [Hook's] intellectual concerns," Bell wrote in the preface, "while disagreeing with some of his passions; but above all I admire his courage, personal and intellectual, which is expressed in his refusal to shirk a fight, however unpopular the cause, or abandon a friend. He is, as all who have heard him know, one of the great teachers of the generation." Twenty-five years later, Bell asserted in a similar fashion, "I accept the designation of being your [Hook's] student. . . . While never formally your student, I have learned in the best of ways, through the close collaboration in various intellectual and organizational efforts."[31]

Irving Kristol was also very close to Hook. He considered Hook his "intellectual daddy," and in 1961 and 1985 expressed his debt to Hook with these words: "It all began in 1936 with the time I literally plagiarized excerpts from your [Hook's] 'Toward the Understanding of . . . [Karl Marx]' and submitted them as the term paper to Krikorian. He gave me an 'A' and ever since then I have been profoundly indebted to my teacher—not my professor, but my teacher, Sidney Hook."[32] Midge Decter called Sidney Hook the "spiritual godfather" of the Committee for the Free World,[33] and Daniel Patrick Moynihan considered that Hook's "achievements as scholar and citizen have had the most profound effect upon our century. . . . We have learned," Moynihan added, "from your thoughts and deeds, and your influence upon more than two generations of scholars and those in public life cannot be exaggerated."[34] According to Gary Dorrien, Hook was a forerunner of neoconservatism: "He represented the aggressive, self-affirming, militantly anti-communist Americanism that modern liberals had abandoned."[35] Hook, therefore, had a significant influence on many neoconservatives, who remained close to him throughout his life.

In the late 1940s and early 1950s, many neoconservatives began to move from the left to the center of the ideological spectrum, rejecting both communism and fascism.[36] Their process of deradicalization was shaped by several domestic and international events. In the domestic sphere, their ideology was changed by their experience with American Communists in states like New York, Washington, and Minnesota, when communism was an important political force. In these states, neoconservatives such as Max Kampelman and Jeane Kirkpatrick strongly opposed communism. Likewise, the origins of the anticommunism of people like Henry Jackson can be placed in the 1930s, when Communists dominated the Washington State Democratic Party for a time.[37] In all, according to Seymour Martin Lipset, these people "were anti-Soviet not because of what was going on in the Soviet Union; they were anti-Soviet because of their experiences with American communists."[38] In the international arena, the Soviet invasion of Czechoslovakia in 1948, the blockade of Berlin, the Korean War, and the violation of human rights in the Soviet Union and Eastern Europe strongly affected and influenced their beliefs.

Disenchanted with the political left, in the 1950s neoconservatives became liberals—defenders of Franklin Delano Roosevelt, New Deal politics, and the American welfare state. However, their years at City College, their participation in radical journals such as the *New Leader*, and their leftist interests provided them with a significant knowledge on Marxism and leftist literature. Their expertise on Marxism was solid and sometimes amazing. "When I need a reference on Marx," asserted Lipset, "I just called Dan Bell; he has memorized everything."[39] Their knowledge about this topic allowed them to participate in debates and write academic essays or journal articles with a deep understanding of the relevant literature. Their interest in Marxism and leftist literature never disappeared. Furthermore, for some of them, like Bell and Lipset, Marxism and socialist politics and policy played a prominent role in their analysis. Lipset developed his entire academic career having in mind one central question—although not the only one—why communist governments have evolved into totalitarian regimes, and as an extension of this same question, the analysis of democracy and antidemocracy. Bell wrote a book on Marxism and socialism in the United States,[40] and Marxism remained an important frame of reference in his subsequent political analysis. This deep familiarity with Marxist literature is one significant difference between the first and second generations of neoconservatives. The second generation basically ignores Marxism.

For these first-generation neoconservatives, Marx and Marxism had played a significant role in their formative years. Their knowledge of Marxism served as an important point of contrast with socialist American politics. Rejecting totalitarianism because of its suppression of freedom of thought, some neoconservatives participated in the American Committee for Cultural Freedom, an organization of anticommunist intellectuals, which was affiliated with the international Congress for Cultural Freedom. Both these congresses were conceived to defend "intellectual and cultural freedom against the forces of totalitarianism both at home and abroad."[41] Irving Kristol became the American Congress's first executive director, and Daniel Bell participated as an officer. In 1953, Kristol cofounded, with Stephen Spender, *Encounter*, a London-based magazine sponsored by the Committee for Cultural Freedom and financially supported by the U.S. Central Intelligence Agency (CIA).[42] On many occasions, Kristol denied knowing about the financial support from the CIA. It is clear that at this juncture, neoconservatives were very well integrated into the mainstream of American society.

In 1950, in both public and academic venues, this group criticized anticommunism from the right, especially McCarthyism. According to neoconservatives such as Bell, Kristol, and Nathan Glazer, the anticommunism of Joseph McCarthy lacked any kind of sophistication and was a terrible problem for the United States. "If American liberalism is not willing to discriminate between its achievements and its sins," Kristol warned in 1952, "it only disarms itself before Senator McCarthy, who is eager to have it appear that its achievements are its sins." Similarly, a year later, Glazer asserted that it was "a shame and an outrage that Senator McCarthy should remain in the Senate."[43]

Their concern and disapproval of McCarthyism were expressed in their academic work and in their constant efforts to explain the rise of this political phenomenon on the American political scene. In 1954, Lipset, Bell, and Glazer held a faculty seminar at Columbia University with other distinguished groups of social scientists. The result of their deliberations was published a year later in *The New American Right*,[44] a book that was republished in 1963 under the title *The Radical Right, Expanded and Updated*.[45] Believing that McCarthyism had extensively damaged the fabric of democratic politics,[46] the authors of *The Radical Right*, especially Richard Hofstadter and Lipset, used the notion of "status politics" to explain the rise of extremist movements. Status politics "refer[red] to political movements whose appeal is to the not uncommon resentments of individuals or groups who desire to maintain or improve their social status."[47] For them, class politics arise in times of "economic depression, and status politics in periods of betterment." "In times of prosperity and general well-being on the material plane," asserted Hofstadter, "status considerations among the masses can become much more influential in our politics."[48]

Consequently, according to this group of scholars and thinkers, the growth of radical-right organizations is the result of the displacement of some sectors of the population from former positions of domination. When certain groups feel that they are "losing their power and status, they seek to reverse the direction of changes through political means." Radical-right expressions are, thus, mainly the reaction to the "loss of status and influence."[49] The concept of status politics was used to explain McCarthyism, because this political expression emerged in a period of great economic bonanza. For Lipset, radical-right movements are marginal expressions of discontent that do not threaten the U.S. democratic process.[50]

In the 1940s and 1950s, another branch of the neoconservative movement emerged. This branch was composed of individuals who were associated with the Democratic Party and lacked the radical past of the New York intellectuals like Bell, Kristol, and Lipset. They were sympathetic to the hard-line anticommunism of Harry Truman, and they thus supported Hubert Humphrey around 1948 when the people of Minnesota elected him to the Senate. According to Richard Schifter, this group has maintained a liberal Democratic position throughout the ensuing decades.

Therefore, they were in favor of a "strong liberal position, opposition to all forms of totalitarianism, support for civil liberties across the world, advocacy of human rights, and democracy."[51] This branch of neoconservatism included figures like Jeane Kirkpatrick and Schifter. Likewise, during those years, Paul Nitze, a politician close to neoconservatism, became a prominent political figure after the elaboration of National Security Council Report 68, known as the NSC-68 report, "the most famous strategy document of the Cold War era."[52]

The 1960s and early 1970s were another critical juncture for the neoconservative movement. During those years, neoconservatives moved from some of their previous liberal positions—for instance, they never abandoned their positive view of the welfare state—to neoconservative views on some issues. Thus, the 1960s and early 1970s were crucial years for neoconservatism. First, the U.S. experience of the global crisis during that time greatly accentuated some political and ideological tendencies previously manifested by neoconservative advocates. Neoconservatives were highly affected by three main events: the Vietnam War, the students' revolt, and the growth of the New Left. Their reactions to these and other events of the time showed more conservative positions. These were the years when the term "neoconservatism" was conceived.

Second, this period marked the neoconservatives' transition into the role of public intellectuals, a process that gained momentum in the 1970s. Most observers agree that a global crisis flourished at that time.[53] In the United States, the breakdown laid bare the end of the Roosevelt New Deal project and the appearance of a profound political, economic, international, and cultural crisis. This general crisis fractured the vital center of American society. Increasing polarization made the maintenance of consensus a difficult task. Different versions of relevant political issues were in vogue: prowar and antiwar expressions; pro–civil rights movements and racist organizations; associations in favor of women's liberation and groups against women's emancipation; people sympathetic to the students' protests and citizens against their antiestablishment and antiauthority tendencies; New Left intellectuals and academics antagonistic to New Left ideas. American society was badly divided; the divisions were evident in almost every single manifestation of U.S. political life.

Neoconservatives tended to be against the changes taking place in American society. They criticized the New Left for calling for guerilla action "in the field of culture,"[54] and for being "left-wing 'intellectual Poujadisme,' of a backlash opposition to systematic and quantitative social science, to the large scale of social research, to the very conception of the utility of efforts at value-free objective scholarship in policy relevant fields."[55] For Norman Podhoretz, the New Left resembled the Stalinism of the 1930s; he said its adherents "constitute a 'new class' that has taken over the universities and the publishing, public service, and cultural industries of the United States."[56]

Neoconservatives opposed the student movement for its confrontational strategies. To them, the students' main goal was the destruction of authority itself,[57] the "destruction of what was most distinctive and most valuable in universities—the ability to distance themselves from immediate crisis, their concern for the heritage of culture and science, their encouragement of individualism and even eccentricity."[58] Some of them considered the prolife movement "one of the greatest human rights programs"[59] and argued that radical blacks had destroyed the civil rights movements of the early 1960s.[60] For them, the crisis of those years was the product of the emergence of a counterculture, which is to say, a "rebellion against established moral, social, and aesthetic values of the 1960s."[61]

Because many of the neoconservatives had established scholarly reputations in the social sciences, the academic and political communities paid close attention to neoconservative commentaries on the social protests of the 1960s. It is worth noting that with the publication of *Political Man*, Seymour Martin Lipset gained recognition as an advocate of modernization theory, American exceptionalism, and the end of the ideology movement. In that same year, 1960, Daniel Bell published perhaps his most famous book, *The End of Ideology*, arguing the exhaustion of ideology in the West.[62]

In 1963, Nathan Glazer and Daniel Patrick Moynihan issued *Beyond the Melting Pot*, a controversial study of five ethnic groups in New York. And five years later, Samuel Huntington published *Political Order in Changing Society*. Huntington criticized classic modernization theory, highlighting the superiority of American values, institutions, and processes. His analysis became very influential in American political science, and, in 1988, his book was the one most required by graduate professors in the core course of comparative politics.[63]

Politically speaking, neoconservatives were mainly in the center of the Democratic Party. The crisis of the 1960s cracked the party alliances that had been created during the political realignment around the New Deal. Vietnam and the social issues that emerged during those turbulent years divided the party into two main factions. One faction, represented by Eugene McCarthy, George McGovern, and Robert Kennedy, moved to the left, rejecting the war and favoring arms control negotiations with the Soviet Union. Old New Dealers and heads of labor unions belonging to the AFL-CIO, who remained anticommunist and prowar, made up the other faction. This group, whose leaders included Lyndon Johnson, Hubert Humphrey, and Henry Jackson, won Johnson the 1968 presidential nomination. However, four years later, the revolts against the war and the social issue cleavages led to the triumph of George McGovern as the party's presidential candidate. By 1972, it was clear that the party was badly split.

It is within the anticommunist, prowar faction of the Democratic Party that we find a significant number of neoconservatives. At that time, they were mainly Democrats who voted for Humphrey in 1968. Some of them voted for Richard Nixon in 1972, but mainly as a way to oppose McGovern.[64] "In 1972, Irving [Kristol] and I," Bell recalled, "had agreed not to endorse any candidate for President so as not to have the magazine [*The Public Interest*] identify in a partisan way. But Ronald Berman, under pressure from the White House to get 'intellectuals' to come out for Nixon, persuaded Irving (and Shils and Oscar Handlin) to speak out for Nixon. For that reason, I told Irving that I would announce I was voting Democrat."[65]

Considering that McGovern exemplified the erosion of the traditional principles defended by centrist Democrats, neoconservatives participated in 1973 in the creation of the Coalition for a Democratic Majority, an organization dedicated to returning the party to the center. Ben Wattenberg, Midge Decter, Max Kampelman, and Jeane Kirkpatrick were involved in the organizing committee for the CDM. Daniel Bell, Nathan Glazer, Seymour Martin Lipset, Michael Novak, and Norman Podhoretz were founding sponsors, and Moynihan and Jackson were cochairs of the organization. (A more detailed analysis of the CDM is presented in the following chapters.)

Also by the late 1960s and early 1970s, a group of young activists associated with the Socialist Party joined the neoconservative movement.[66] People such as Carl Gershman, Penn Kemble, and Joshua Muravchik became followers of Max Shachtman, a socialist activist and thinker. In the 1920s, Shachtman was a member of the Communist Party. In the 1930s, he became a follower of Trotsky, whom he discarded in late 1939 because of his support of the Soviet invasion of Finland. After that time, Shachtman sought to develop a new socialist trend: socialist anticommunism. His criticism of the Soviet Union as a "bureaucratic collectivist state," his search for a more democratic socialism, and his hard-line position on foreign affairs captured the attention of young anti-Stalinists.

During the early 1970s, the Socialist Party faced an internal political battle between the Shachtmanites and the followers of Michael Harrington. Central to their dispute was each group's position on the Vietnam War and the New Left. Harrington's faction was against American intervention in Southeast Asia and sympathetic to New Left ideas, while the Shachtmanites supported the war and "considered the New Left as the most 'disorienting and self-defeating phenomenon of the period.'"[67] The Shachtmanites also favored changing the party's name to Social Democrats USA. Gershman, Kemble, and Muravchik were among the young Shachtmanites who led and won the struggle against Harrington. In the 1972 election, the Shachtmanites supported Jackson, and soon some of them (especially Kemble and Muravchik) became actively involved in the CDM and started writing for neoconservative journals.

By the early 1970s, a variety of political expressions had converged to form the neoconservative movement. Three are most relevant. First, neoconservative intellectuals, people who had been socialists in their youth, had moved to the center of the ideological spectrum in the 1950s and to a neoconservative position in the 1960s and 1970s. Second, politicians with nonradical pasts associated mainly with the Democratic Party and held a strong anticommunist position. Third, young socialists affiliated with the Socialist Party and later with the Social Democrats USA had strong contacts with the labor movement and had an anticommunist and anti–New Left position. These three groups shared a viewpoint: They were anticommunists, defenders of a hawkish position in foreign affairs, and critics of America's 1960s social movements.

By the 1980s, part of the neoconservative movement participated actively in the Reagan administration, especially in the field of foreign policy.[68] Richard Perle, Jeane Kirkpatrick, Elliott Abrams, and Max Kampelman were appointed to major positions in the State and Defense departments. Richard Pipes worked for the National Security Council. Norman Podhoretz and Ben Wattenberg participated in Reagan's national communication apparatus. Michael Novak became ambassador to the United Nations Human Rights Commission, and Richard Schifter became his deputy.[69] Likewise, neoconservatives formed an alliance with the Social Democrats in their fight against international communism. Gershman worked with Kirkpatrick at the United Nations; Kemble became head of Friends of the Democratic Center in Central America (PRODEMCA), an influential pro-Contra lobby; and Tom Kahn was appointed director of the International Affairs Department of the AFL-CIO.[70]

The 1960s also marked the neoconservatives' consolidation as a group of important public intellectuals. In the previous decades, neoconservatives like Bell, Glazer, and Kristol had engaged in important activities as public intellectuals. In the early 1940s, Bell became the managing editor of *The New Leader*, a socialist publication. Glazer became the assistant editor of *Commentary* and wrote very often for other magazines as well. Kristol wrote for *Commentary* and *The New Leader*, became assistant editor of *Commentary*, and cofounded *Encounter*. By the 1960s, however, these neoconservatives were playing a more prominent role as public intellectuals, consolidating their status in the eyes of ample sectors of informed Americans as authorities on political, social, and international issues. In 1960, Podhoretz assumed the directorship of *Commentary*, giving a clear neoconservative perspective to this journal. Five years later, Kristol and Bell founded *The Public Interest*, and neoconservatives began publishing articles in magazines and newspapers with wide circulation.

In the 1970s, an important number of neoconservatives arrived at think tanks.[71] In these institutions, they founded journals to spread their ideas to a general and educated audience and obtained an institutional base to support their role as public intellectuals. There were neoconservatives at the Center for Strategic and International Studies; the Hoover Institution for War, Revolution, and Peace; and the Institute for Contemporary Studies. But according to Kirkpatrick, the centerpiece of the neoconservative movement was the American Enterprise Institute.[72] Neoconservatives have always been highly involved in AEI's activities, and their participation in this organization has been very important in their relationship with political power in Washington, a relationship that is addressed below.

## Toward an Identification of the Second Generation of Neoconservatives

Identifying and defining the second generation of neoconservatives, as with the case of the first generation, is a complicated task. There are at least three main obstacles to arriving at a proper classification of the second neoconservative movement. First, Elliott Abrams, Douglas Feith, Joshua Muravchik, Richard Perle, and Norman Podhoretz, among others, played an important role in both the first and second neoconservative expressions. Consequently, it is often difficult to distinguish between the first and the second generations. Second, as with the first generation, several figures associated with the second reject the "neoconservative" label. Third, since the late 1980s and early 1990s, neoconservatism has been fully assimilated into the Republican Party. As a result, it is sometimes difficult to differentiate neoconservatism from other conservative political tendencies. What is more, according to Francis Fukuyama, the main neoconservative principles "have been widely shared not only by neoconservatives but by other important groups across the spectrum of political life."[73]

Despite these challenges, here I attempt to identify the most important neoconservatives of the second generation by examining three texts written by figures often recognized as second-generation neoconservatives. Using a consensus method, I aim to create a list of the main protagonists of the current neoconservative movement. I also trace some general distinctions between the first and the second generations. My aim here is to develop additional criteria that will help me to properly identify second-generation neoconservatives. A more detailed account of the differences between the two generations of neoconservatives is given in the later chapters of this book.

Some figures identified by others as neoconservatives reject the term. David Frum rejected my request for an interview, asserting categorically: "I am not a neoconservative." Gary Schmitt asserted that at the Project for the New American Century (PNAC), "we call ourselves neo-Reaganites because . . . [there] was not an agreement among neoconservatives about what to do in the post–Cold War era."[74] According to Douglas Feith, the "term neoconservative has become so widely used and so changed in its meaning, and in particular in its political connotation, that I am not sure you can even compare how the term is used now, which tends to be very loose and very negative, with the way the term was used before Iraq."[75] Other people commonly identified with the second generation of neoconservatives have a more sympathetic perspective. "I didn't use the term 'neoconservative' about myself," declared William Kristol. "I thought it was a generational phenomenon." The term, he continued, was reinvented in the 1990s and "applied to [Robert] Kagan and me and the hawks in the late 1990s, especially after 9/11." Kristol does not oppose the label; on the contrary, he likes the term and affirms, "I am happy to be associated with the original neoconservatives."[76]

No single document defines second-generation neoconservatism. We have information about neoconservative organizations such as the PNAC, but no neoconservative manifesto. Despite this serious constraint, it is possible to gain a comprehensive view of the second generation of neoconservatives by studying three texts written by major second-generation neoconservative figures. If a person is listed in two of the three documents, I considered him or her a core neoconservative. Others made up a group at the periphery of the neoconservative movement. Table 2.3 lists these people.

Again, table 2.1 summarizes the results of my analysis, naming the authors of the three articles and then listing the people mentioned in each article. My analysis yields the names of nine people—Elliott Abrams, Douglas Feith, Robert Kagan, William Kristol, Charles Krauthammer, Richard Perle, Norman Podhoretz, Paul Wolfowitz, and James Woolsey—who I argue compose the core of the second generation of neoconservatives. The three articles used in this work all cited Robert Kagan, William Kristol, and Charles Krauthammer. These intellectuals can be considered active members of the current neoconservative movement. Muravchik cited Max Boot and Francis Fukuyama, who each wrote at least one text cited. As

*Table 2.3. The Core and the Periphery of the Second Generation of the Neoconservative Movement*

| Core | Periphery |
|------|-----------|
| 1. Elliott Abrams | 1. John Bolton |
| 2. Douglas Feith | 2. Linda Chavez |
| 3. Robert Kagan | 3. Christopher DeMuth |
| 4. Charles Krauthammer | 4. Francis Fukuyama |
| 5. William Kristol | 5. Lewis "Scooter" Libby |
| 6. Richard Perle | 6. Gary Schmitt |
| 7. Norman Podhoretz | |
| 8. Paul Wolfowitz | |
| 9. James Woolsey | |

*Note*: Two clarifications are needed here. First, the authors listed in this table also name other neoconservatives, like Irving Kristol and Jeane Kirkpatrick, whom I have cited at the beginning of this chapter as members of the first generation. Consequently, I have only listed those people whom I consider part of the second generation. Second, near the time of this book's publication, Francis Fukuyama renounced his association with neoconservatism. He had, however, been a neoconservative for a long time and is very knowledgeable about the movement. For instance, Irving Kristol published Fukuyama's article "The End of History" in *The National Interest* after Gary Schmitt rejected it, Fukuyama was close to people like Paul Wolfowitz and studied with William Kristol at Harvard University, and Fukuyama published in neoconservative journals such as *Commentary, The National Interest, The Public Interest,* and *The Weekly Standard.* When he broke with neoconservatives after a strong disagreement with Charles Krauthammer, he became involved in the publication of *The American Interest.*
*Sources*: Max Boot, "Think Again: Neocons," *Foreign Policy*, January–February 2004, http://www.foreignpolicy.com/users/login.php?story_id=2426&URL=http://www.foreignpolicy.com/story/cms.php?story_id=2426; Max Boot, "What the Heck Is a 'Neocon'?" *Wall Street Journal*, December 30, 2002; Francis Fukuyama, *America at the Crossroads: Democracy, Power and the Neoconservative Legacy* (New Haven, Conn.: Yale University Press, 2006), chap. 2; Joshua Muravchik, "The Neoconservative Cabal," *Commentary*, September 2003, 26–33.

with the first generation, it also seems important to acknowledge peripheral members of the movement. This periphery is composed of those people quoted by Boot, Fukuyama, and Muravchik but not listed as members of the core group. Six people—John Bolton, Linda Chavez, Christopher DeMuth, Francis Fukuyama (at least until 2006), Lewis "Scooter" Libby, and Gary Schmitt—constitute this peripheral group.

Many of the key neoconservative figures active in the second generation were also active in the late 1970s and 1980s, when the first generation became prominent. This was the case with Abrams, Chavez, Feith, Muravchik, Perle, Podhoretz, and Wolfowitz. Some of them were young people who in the 1980s were just beginning their political or academic careers—Abrams, Feith, and Muravchik—whereas others—Podhoretz and Wolfowitz—were already important politicians or intellectuals. This group of neoconservatives constituted a transitional group, a cluster of people who were very active historically and who built bridges between the first and second generations of neoconservatives. They have remained active and have become important promoters and defenders of neoconservative principles.

The list offered in table 2.3 is consistent with the names cited by various scholars of neoconservatism. Murray Friedman considered Abrams, Feith, Perle, and Wolfowitz important Jewish neoconservatives within the George W. Bush administration. Friedman also included journalists and writers, such as David Brooks, Kagan, William Kristol, Krauthammer, Muravchik, and Podhoretz.[77] Stefan Halper and Jonathan Clarke maintained that Kagan, William Kristol, Muravchik, Perle, Wolfowitz, and "others had assumed the leadership role that had long been held by Nathan Glazer, Irving Kristol, Daniel Patrick Moynihan, and Norman Podhoretz."[78] Gary Dorrien argued that after the end of the Cold War, several neoconservatives such as Wolfowitz, Perle, Krauthammer, Wattenberg, Muravchik, Frank Gaffney, Midge Decter, Michael Ledeen, and Zalmay Khalilzad were the first to promote the view "of [an] American-dominated world order."[79]

Finally, it is also important to include several people who participated in neoconservative organizations and therefore were at least sympathetic to neoconservative viewpoints. Here I would place people like Gaffney, who was a close collaborator with Feith and Perle during the Reagan administration. In 1988, he founded and then headed the Center for Security Policy, a neoconservative organization. Though his analyses are often more conspiratorial and simplistic that the views of people like Kagan, Kristol, and Muravchik, he shares their neoconservative perspective. Khalilzad is another example. Like Wolfowitz, he studied at the University of Chicago with Albert Wohlstetter, worked with Wolfowitz at the State Department during the Reagan years, was a signatory of the PNAC's Statement of Principles, and published a handful of articles in neoconservative journals. He was the U.S. ambassador to Afghanistan and Iraq and was the U.S. ambassador to the United Nations from April 23, 2007, until the end of the George W. Bush presidency.

Perhaps the two most complicated examples I have not included in this list are former vice president Richard Cheney and former secretary of defense Donald Rumsfeld. Neither Cheney nor Rumsfeld followed a neoconservative trajectory. Rather, they were both traditional Republican hawks who were sympathetic to neoconservative views. Cheney was a signatory of the PNAC's Statement of Principles, and he was one of the main players in bringing neoconservatives into the Bush administration. For a long time, Rumsfeld has been close to neoconservatives like Midge Decter, collaborated with Wolfowitz and Perle, signed the PNAC Statement of Principles, and was considered a moral leader by some neoconservatives. Although neoconservatives like William Kristol criticized his performance as secretary of defense, Muravchik called Rumsfeld the "leading patron of neocons in the [George W. Bush] administration." Rumsfeld, Muravchik added, was "sort of the bridge by which some of the neoconservatives got into the administration. So even though Rumsfeld was not part of us we were part of him, we were part of the Rumsfeld team."[80]

My analysis thus has identified nine core and six peripheral members of the second generation of neoconservatives. Other important elements of second-generation neoconservativism, such as the movement's political trajectory and ideological perspective, are examined in the later chapters of this book. To properly understand neoconservatism, it is necessary to study neoconservative organizations. In the following chapter, I consider the role played by neoconservative organizations in the movement's development and political impact.

# 3

# Neoconservative Organizations as
# a Vehicle for an Ideological Crusade

Organizations "define the framework within which human interaction takes place."[1] Organizations also often reflect a set of ideas that represent the interests of particular social groups. Neoconservative ideas and intellectual perspectives have been filtered and diffused through the different organizations in which they operate. These organizations have facilitated the formation of a prominent political and intellectual movement, heightening the influence of neoconservatism on public policies.

Neoconservative organizations have four main functions. They:

1. promote the dissemination of neoconservative ideas,
2. coordinate neoconservatism's political network,
3. operate as centers of political organization and advice for political and economic elites, and
4. serve as hubs for political and intellectual deliberation.

In short, these organizations have been, and continue to be, the framework that facilitates interaction between neoconservatives and American political and economic elites, between neoconservatives and U.S. society, and among neoconservatives themselves.

In this study, I focus on four neoconservative organizations that emerged from the first generation of neoconservatives:

1. The Coalition for a Democratic Majority (CDM),
2. The American Enterprise Institute (AEI),

3. The Committee on the Present Danger (CPD), and
4. The Committee for the Free World (CFW).

Two additional important organizations emerged from the second generation of neoconservatives: the Project for the New American Century, and the Center for Security Policy. Here, I focus first on the organizations of the first generation, leaving those of the second generation for discussion in a section later in this chapter.

I selected these organizations based on an examination of published information and direct inquiries with key informants. Through an analysis of published information, I detected the participation of neoconservatives in several key organizations, among them the Center for Strategic and International Studies, the Institute for Contemporary Studies, the Hoover Institution, the Heritage Foundation, the National Endowment for Democracy, the Democratic and Republican parties, the Ethics and Public Policy Center, Freedom House, and Social Democrats USA. The participation of neoconservatives in any of these institutions does not automatically make them neoconservative organizations. Thus, my second step was to compare the analysis of printed information with the opinions of neoconservative leaders.

Seymour Martin Lipset, Joshua Muravchik, Charles Horner, Richard Schifter, and Richard Perle all considered the CDM to be a neoconservative organization—especially, but not exclusively, during the early years of the movement, which is to say the 1970s.[2] Max Kampelman, Norman Podhoretz, and Midge Decter regarded the CPD similarly. And Jeane Kirkpatrick, Michael Novak, Joshua Muravchik, Suzanne Garment, William Kristol, and Peter Skerry regarded AEI as neoconservative.[3] Finally, Midge Decter, Norman Podhoretz, and Lipset also believed that the CFW was a neoconservative association. Thus the four organizations mentioned above were most cited by neoconservatives as their own.

Neoconservative organizations fall primarily into the categories of political and educational bodies. Applying Douglass North's system of classification, political bodies can include, for instance, political parties, the U.S. Senate, a city council, or a regulatory agency. Educational bodies denote institutions such as schools, universities, and vocational training centers.[4] More precisely, the four neoconservative organizations on which this study focuses can be categorized as a faction within a political party (CDM), a pressure group (CPD), a think tank (AEI), and an intellectual association (CFW). Each one has a specific political target. Together, they complement each other.

These organizations also present several peculiarities. First, none of them is *exclusively* neoconservative. Instead, a cluster of social groups that share common political interests and similar ideological orientations constitutes them. Second, they differ in their structure and basic form of organization. The CDM is essentially a faction within the Democratic Party and therefore emphasizes, among other activities, political relations and, to a lesser extent, grassroots work. AEI is a think tank that markets ideas to an educated audience, mainly political and economic elites. The CFW is an intellectual association. The CPD is a pressure group in the area of foreign and military affairs whose main target is elites, especially decision-makers. Despite their differences, all share one commonality: Their main battles are in the terrain of ideas. "What rules the world," asserted Irving Kristol, "is ideas, because ideas define the way reality is perceived."[5] These organizations present and defend a particular viewpoint. Their "intellectual lobby" is conducted to persuade common people but is primarily directed toward elites—to convince them that the implementation of their perspective will solve political problems. In brief, their political fight is fundamentally (but not exclusively) in the realm of ideas rather than in the field of political praxis or electoral politics.

Over the years, the CDM and AEI have changed and evolved substantially. The CDM evolved from a party faction with important ties to the labor movement and its general concerns to a group detached from workers' interests that concentrates almost exclusively on foreign affairs. AEI moved from being a small economic research organization with a limited budget to a wealthy and influential think thank (despite experiencing serious financial trouble in the mid-1980s) with research interests in social, political, economic, international, and religious issues. The CPD and CFW altered their focus over time, too, but not to the same degree. Both were in existence for shorter periods of time, and both had very specific goals, which diminished internal disagreements and inconsistencies.

With the exception of AEI, neoconservatives founded these organizations and played significant roles in their development and orientation. Likewise, each institution shares a neoconservative perspective and ideology, each has had extensive contact with other neoconservative organizations (this is especially true of contacts between the CDM and CPD), and, most important, each has been recognized by neoconservatives as a neoconservative organization.

## The Coalition for a Democratic Majority

The CDM, which was created in 1972 after George McGovern won the Democratic Party's presidential nomination, can be understood as a reaction to the political changes of the 1960s and early 1970s and the ascendance of the most liberal factions of the Democratic Party. For the CDM's founders and followers, the election of McGovern exemplified the success of the "New Politics movement,"[6] comprising those political expressions that questioned American participation in the Vietnam War as immoral and imperialistic, decried racial discrimination against blacks and other minorities, and questioned the prerogatives of the "Washington establishment."

McGovern represented a political faction that had worked to successfully modify Democratic Party rules. With the purpose of making the party more open and participatory, the Democrats' Commission on Party Structure and Delegate Selection—known as the McGovern-Fraser Commission—changed the nomination process for the party's presidential candidate in a fashion that undermined the power of the party's traditional elites. According to Ben Wattenberg, a neoconservative and CDM founder, the CDM was created to "provide a platform for Democrats who strongly reject the politics of the New Left" and to promote "the traditional democratic formula of liberalism at home, firmness abroad and defense preparedness sufficient to deter armed attack and to support our foreign policy."[7]

In a statement published December 7, 1972, in the *New York Times* under the headline "Come Home America," the CDM's forerunner announced the organization of a group made up of politicians, academics, professionals, and business and labor leaders. In this declaration, the founders of what would soon become the CDM asserted that the Democratic Party was coming under the influence of "forces and ideas unrepresentative to the democratic tradition." They expressed their discomfort with dominant Democratic views on foreign policy (which included national security policy and defense issues) and social issues such as racial and gender quotas. They saw party reform as necessary to restore the organization to "its rightful role as spokesmen for the majority of the American people, as the party of progress, freedom, and security for all." Their battles with the most liberal sectors in the party showed, once again, the difficulties faced by the Democratic Party in maintaining the New Deal's political coalition decades after Franklin Delano Roosevelt's ascendance to the White House.

Members of the CDM particularly objected to McGovern's interpretation of American foreign policy as expansionist and immoral and instead proposed more active involvement in international affairs. The organization's position was based on the perception that the United States was engaged in a life-and-death struggle with the Soviet Union. This battle was viewed as a confrontation of civilizations—between the free world, represented by the United States, and the totalitarian world, exemplified by the Soviet Union. According to Peter Rosenblatt, the CDM's former president, "it was necessary to recognize that the Soviet Union was immersed in a world-wide effort to undermine the interests of the United States." At the time, he believed that the United States must start an "ideological struggle and increase its military capabilities."[8] At a moment when there seemed to be no consensus on foreign policy in postwar America, the CDM emerged as the defender of a strong Cold War perspective.

Another issue that rankled the CDM's members was quotas. As a result of the civil rights movement, Americans have been engaged in an ongoing debate about different ways to create a fairer society. The policy of affirmative action, which was begun as an instrument to reduce structural inequality, was one of the most controversial strategies to emerge from these debates. The CDM's basic position was that the principle of individual merit should not be replaced by race, sex, or group origin. For the CDM, the implementation of affirmative action had several negative implications. Jeane Kirkpatrick, a founding member of the CDM and a core neoconservative, argued that such measures violated the "widely shared beliefs of just reward and the traditional relationship between State and society," and "commit[ted] government to use coercion to impose new practices on a reluctant society." Finally, she claimed that governmental interference in such matters was an "unwarranted use of regulatory power which progressively narrows the scope of individual freedom, undermines the society's most basic values and intrudes government's heavy hand into many subjects remote from its appropriate concerns."[9]

The issue of quotas also accentuated divisions within the Democratic Party. The McGovern-Fraser Commission ordered each state delegation to the national convention to include women, young people, and minority groups in "a reasonable relationship to the group's presence in the population of the state." As a result, interest group caucuses grew. Caucuses representing different minorities would "deal with the candidate's organization as virtually equals."[10] These modifications to party procedure irritated the members of the CDM because they felt displaced from former positions of domination. Rosenblatt expressed this perception of disempowerment:

> One had to be at the Miami convention in 1972 to understand how far this process had gone. I spent most of my time with the New York State delegation, and I found that it was a zoo. Before the New York State delegation met, it first had some meetings with various groups, ranging from blacks to Hispanics, from women to homosexuals, and just about every other group that was represented by more than one individual in New York State and the convention itself. We understood that the decision about the allocation within the party would be made on the basis of memberships in one of these groups. We felt that all of this was simply out of keeping with our democratic tradition and with any kind of rational way of running a society.[11]

The party, according to the CDM, had become an organization contrary to Cold War liberal policies and to the legacies of Franklin D. Roosevelt, Adlai Stevenson, John F. Kennedy, Lyndon B. Johnson, and Hubert H. Humphrey. Centrist liberals had three alternatives: to create a third party, to move to the Republican camp, or to fight in the Democratic Party for the reestablishment of moderate policies. In the 1970s, the CDM took the third path, becoming a dissenting voice within the Democratic Party. By the 1980s, some of the organization's main adherents had left for the Republican Party, demonstrating the deep fissures that had emerged.

Before that happened, the CDM perceived the election of Jimmy Carter as an opportunity to participate in the decisionmaking process at the highest levels of government. Fifty-three members of the organization—including Nathan Glazer, Kirkpatrick, Rosenblatt, Penn Kemble, and Wattenberg—publicly offered to serve in the new government. Carter, however, had a different perspective. "We were completely frozen out," remembered Elliott Abrams; "we got one unbelievably minor job. It was a special-negotiator position. Not for Polynesia. Not Macronesia. But Micronesia. The Carter administration turned out to be ideological, a New Left administration,"[12] a version of "McGovernism without McGovern."[13] By this time, the CDM had relegated domestic affairs to second place. Racial and gender quotas and other domestic policy issues formed part of its political discourse but not its daily efforts to affect the course of American politics. Instead, foreign policy emerged as its dominant concern.

The face of the CDM changed substantially. The organization moved from being a political faction with global concerns and general views about the state and society to a single-issue faction within the Democratic

Party. Its perspective on international affairs was advanced via several task forces on foreign and defense policy.[14] These task forces took up four recurrent themes:

1. assisting movements struggling against tyrannies from the left or from the right;
2. viewing the Soviet Union as the "gravest threat to freedom, peace, and progress in the world";
3. maintaining American military capacity; and
4. rebuilding the worldwide alliance of free nations.

These issues would occupy the attention of the CDM until its disappearance in the early 1990s.

Although its members were a small minority in the Democratic Party, the CDM was a useful organization for the neoconservative movement. In fact, its peculiarities and form of operation contributed to the degree of influence neoconservatism has had on American politics. Its geographic location was a definite advantage. From its founding, the CDM operated primarily in Washington and had satellite groups in other cities like Los Angeles, New York, and Chicago. Of the decline of the organization, Rosenblatt would later say, "We either did not have the internal abilities or the resources to become a mass membership organization. None of us was a competent fundraiser. We did not have the time to go out and get the money. . . . Our contacts were also in Washington."[15]

The CDM was not only Washington-centered but also congressionally oriented.[16] The affiliation of leading members of Congress such as Henry "Scoop" Jackson, Thomas Foley, and Daniel Patrick Moynihan with the CDM and its friendly relationships with other legislators such as Lloyd Bentsen, James Exon, David L. Boren, Ernest Hollings, Sam Nunn, Les Aspin, Larry Smith, and Bill Richardson permitted it to constantly communicate with Congress. All of them—but especially Jackson, who was cochair of the CDM—spread neoconservative ideas in the legislature. The Bipartisan Commission on Central America, suggested and promoted by Jackson and the neoconservative leader Kirkpatrick, is one example. The CDM also worked hard to help Moynihan get elected and to promote the political success of other members of Congress.

The CDM's strong relationship with leaders of the labor movement— such as Peter Bommarito, Sol Chaikin, and William Doherty Jr.—gave the organization a social base and a connection to everyday people and their interests. The labor movement also provided considerable financial support to the group. The CDM and its analogous neoconservative institution, the CPD, each had significant labor components. Some scholars have interpreted this as a clear indication of the CDM's social democratic tendencies.[17]

Neoconservatives constituted the CDM's intellectual nucleus; it expressed the viewpoints of these intellectuals at the same time that they gave it a coherent ideological shape. Kemble, its executive director, described this relationship in a letter to Charles McGuire of the Merrill Lynch Effective Government Association, who had requested information about the CDM. "Our main sponsors in the intellectual community," Kemble wrote, "are magazines such as *The Public Interest* and *Commentary*," and "two of our main intellectual mentors are Daniel Bell and Norman Podhoretz."[18] Neoconservatives also helped construct important relations with other journals like *The New Republic* and forged connections to the academic community in general as well as think tanks.

The CDM remained a fundamentally elite organization. Though the CDM worked hard to build grassroots support, its composition limited its success in this sphere. Its contacts and influence were built on the achievements of its renowned members. People like Max Kampelman, Jackson, Zbigniew Brzezinski, Eugene Rostow, Bommarito, and Leon H. Keyserling, to mention but a few, connected between the CDM and American centers of power. In its heyday, the organization worked more as an interest group than as a faction within a political party. Its members concentrated their efforts on the diffusion of neoconservative principles, especially as related to foreign policy, to American political elites.

The CDM used the infrastructure of the Democratic Party to coordinate the political network of the neoconservative movement. Through the CDM, neoconservatives released messages to Congress and the president, lobbied for policy measures or in favor of candidates to public posts, and established political relationships with influential politicians. Consequently, the CDM became an important launching pad for the political careers of several neoconservatives. Figures associated with the CDM like Perle, Schifter, Abrams, and Kirkpatrick were renowned during Ronald Reagan's administration. The political network established by the CDM and other neoconservative organizations helped them to build their political careers. It is interesting to highlight that some neoconservatives of both the first and the second generations started their professional careers working with Jackson (Perle) or with Moynihan (Abrams and Gary Schmitt).

The CDM collapsed in 1992 after a last attempt by its leaders to fuse the organization with another moderate faction in the Democratic Party, the Democratic Leadership Council (DLC).[19] Having been created in 1985 by Bill Clinton, Al Gore, and other prominent Democrats, the DLC concentrated its work on domestic policy. Because the DLC had no foreign policy focus, the CDM believed that a merger between the two groups would be ideal. According to Rosenblatt, "This never happened because of the opposition of Al Fromm, president of DLC." In Rosenblatt's view, "In terms of ideas, there is no distinction between what DLC stands for . . . and [our group]. In fact, the existence of DLC is one of the reasons we decided that there was no longer any need for CDM."[20] For the leaders of the CDM, the ascent of Clinton to the White House exemplified the CDM's triumph. Clinton incorporated some CDM members and, more important, the CDM's basic principles into his administration. "Since our major concern was to bring the Democratic Party back to basic principles," asserts Rosenblatt, "we were no longer an opposition. Our party and our president have embraced our ideas. With Clinton in the presidency, we have nothing further to say."[21]

This proved to be untrue, but the CDM had had a significant impact on American politics. John Ehrman has argued that the CDM "was ultimately ineffective" because it was not able to roll back reforms within the Democratic Party, particularly those regarding delegate selection.[22] However, the CDM played an important role in American politics, Democratic Party politics, and the neoconservative movement, in three principal ways. First, starting in the early 1970s, the CDM was one of the main promoters of the moderate policies that in the late 1980s and 1990s dominated both political parties, but particularly the Democratic Party. Currently, the foreign policy positions of the extreme left of the Democratic Party seem to be losing traction. In contrast, the positions of the radical right of the Republican Party became increasingly relevant during the 1990s and flourished during the George W. Bush administration.

Second, the CDM can be understood, to a certain extent, as the antecedent of moderate tendencies within the Democratic Party, represented mainly by the DLC and the Clinton administration. "If we [the DMC] had not been there," asserted Rosenblatt, "we would have to be invented to justify the changes in the party's foreign policy position. To a certain extent we are being invented; we have been recreated by people like Madeleine Albright, who never mention us by name, but who wanted it to be known that she was always on our side."[23]

Third and finally, and this is perhaps the most important legacy of the CDM, some of its most active members implemented their ideas— especially in foreign affairs—during the Reagan administration. People like Kampelman, Kirkpatrick, Perle, Schifter, Abrams, and Rostow helped to build American foreign policy during the Reagan years. Neoconservative Democrats associated with the CDM were the architects of the Republican foreign policy during the 1980s.[24] Likewise, some of the important figures of the current neoconservative movement had their political origins in the CDM.

The birth of the CDM represented both the consolidation of an important political institution and the beginning of the breakdown of the consensus among neoconservatives. In 1972, many neoconservatives were active Democrats working to defend the "vital center" of American society. In the 1980s, the predominance of more liberal tendencies in the Democratic Party and the adoption by the Republicans of some concerns of the CDM provoked disagreements among them. Schifter, Perle, Kampelman, Wattenberg, Lipset, Glazer, and others remained Democrats during this period. Others, like Abrams, Podhoretz, Decter, and Kirkpatrick, moved to the Republican Party.

Neoconservative fragmentation was especially visible with regard to domestic affairs. For example, the CDM members disagreed about the prudence of adopting supply-side economics as a model to solve American economic problems. It was much easier to maintain harmony on foreign policy, where the fight against communism was a unifying theme. Of course, there were differences on international matters like the disputes that Podhoretz had with Lipset and Glazer over Israel, particularly U.S. foreign policy on Israel, but anticommunism was such a central issue for them that it preserved the alliance for most of the 1970s and part of the 1980s. The move of Podhoretz, Decter, and Abrams to the right of the Reagan administration was a tangible expression of the rupture among neoconservatives. In subsequent years, divisions among neoconservatives on party preference and policy issues have declined substantially. Few neoconservatives, especially those of the first generation, remain in the Democratic Party, allowing those with the neoconservative tendency to maintain a strong, united foreign policy position. However, some neoconservatives do maintain a nominal affiliation with the Democratic Party. "I still register as a Democrat," Wattenberg recently asserted, "but I do not remember when was the last time that I voted for a Democrat."[25] Others, a significant number of the first generation and the entire second generation, have moved to the Republican Party, making neoconservatism a political ideology that is primarily associated with the Republicans.

## The American Enterprise Institute

If the CDM was the political institution of neoconservatism, the American Enterprise Institute was the organization most responsible for the dissemination of neoconservative ideas. Among the more than one hundred think tanks operating in Washington in the late 1980s,[26] AEI was the principal home of neoconservatism. Lewis Brown, president of the Johns-Manville Corporation, founded the American Enterprise Association in 1943. In the 1950s, the organization had five full-time employees and a number of research programs, focused primarily on economics. In 1960, the organization was renamed the American Enterprise Institute for Public Policy Research and obtained public recognition for its economic studies. Four years later, AEI's president, William J. Baroody Sr., became well known for advising and writing speeches for Barry Goldwater. Baroody was explicitly committed to creating an academic institution to oppose liberal think tanks like the Brookings Institution. In the 1950s and 1960s, he brought distinguished economists such as Milton Friedman, Gottfried Haberler, Paul McCracken, and G. Warren Nutter onto AEI's board of academic advisers. But AEI continued to be a small organization. In 1970, its budget was around $1 million, and in 1972 it hosted seventeen adjunct scholars.

In May 1972, AEI's relationship with neoconservatives became public. The second issue of its newsletter, *AEI Memorandum*, reprinted some passages from Irving Kristol's critique of American journalism—*Press, Politics and Popular Government*—a book published by AEI.[27] Two issues later, *AEI Memorandum* announced the creation of a major project to analyze the coverage of the 1972 presidential campaign. The project established a general advisory committee whose members included the core neoconservatives Kristol, Lipset, and Moynihan. In the same issue, the editors published excerpts from Lipset and Ladd's work, *The Divided Academy: Professors and Politics*.[28]

At the time, U.S. society was highly divided on political, social, economic, and cultural issues, and AEI considered itself enmeshed in a public battle. AEI claimed that the competition of ideas is fundamental to a free society. A free society, if it is to remain free, cannot permit itself to be dominated by one strain of thought. Public policy derives from the ideas, speculations and theories of thoughtful men and women. Policy makers themselves rarely originate the concepts underlying the laws by which people are governed. They choose among practical options to formulate legislation, governmental directives, regulations and programs. If there is no testing of ideas by competition, public policy decisions may undermine rather than bolster the foundations of a free society.[29]

During those years, the relationship between neoconservatives and AEI remained rather informal. AEI found interesting interpretations of American politics in the work of neoconservative intellectuals. The organization published excerpts of neoconservative works or invited intellectuals to collaborate on events or as advisers to different projects. The participation of Kristol, Lipset, and Peter L. Berger in the Lecture Series on the American Bicentennial and the publication of excerpts of Lipset's work illustrate this tendency toward informal involvement.[30] From the very first collaborations, it was evident that a strong ideological coincidence existed between AEI, a moderate think tank, and centrist liberal intellectuals.

In 1974, Lipset became the first neoconservative to be formally associated with AEI. Two years later, Kristol and Kirkpatrick become resident scholars at the organization. In 1976, AEI established the Center for the Study of Government Regulations "to develop and communicate a better understanding of the role of legal and political institutions in decision-making in our economy and society."[31] Kristol served as a chairman of the advisory council, and three other neoconservatives—Max Kampelman, Aaron Wildavsky, and James Q. Wilson—served as council members.[32] According to the scholars Martha Derthick and Paul Quirk, AEI and Brookings influenced the regulatory policy of both the Carter and Reagan administrations,[33] and, at least in the beginning of the regulation program at AEI, neoconservatives had a tremendous influence on the organization and development of this project.

In June 1976, the same year that the CPD was formed, AEI created the Public Policy Project on National Defense.[34] In 1976, AEI organized the roundtable "Who Is First in Defense, the United States or Russia?" with the participation of former defense secretary Melvin R. Laird, Paul Nitze, and senators Thomas McIntyre and Charles Mathias. Two years later, the

CPD published "Is America Becoming Number Two?" The titles of the roundtable and paper show how similar the concerns of the two organizations were at the time.

Furthermore, the leaders of AEI and the CPD maintained ongoing, informal contact. In June 7, 1976, Richard Allen of the CPD met with his friend Baroody to talk about AEI's project on national defense. In this conversation, Baroody informed Allen that AEI was concluding a two-year program on energy problems. This program was to be replaced by a national security and foreign policy project, with Laird as chair. According to Allen, Baroody saw "no conflict at all in our [CPD's] objectives and his, and in fact we both agreed that our efforts would be mutually reinforcing." Likewise, Allen suggested to Eugene V. Rostow that Bill Baroody and perhaps his son Joe Baroody would be ideal candidates for the CPD Board.[35] Subsequently, Joe Baroody became a member of the CPD. With few formal relations, neoconservative organizations such as AEI, the CPD, and the CDM kept in constant contact, coordinated some of their activities, and initiated projects of mutual influence.

By 1976, AEI had begun to emphasize neoconservative issues. It reproduced passages of Lipset's lecture in Dearborn, in which he "cautioned against the trend in American society toward equality of opportunity for groups, as differentiated from America's earlier conception of equality of opportunity for individuals."[36] In a similar vein, it published the work of Thomas Sowell—who has been frequently associated with neoconservatism but is not included as such in this study—titled *Affirmative Action Reconsidered: Was It Necessary in Academia?* which criticized affirmative action in higher education.[37] Likewise, AEI organized a debate between senators Bill Brock and Edmund Muskie about the wisdom of increasing the American defense budget.[38]

By the mid-1970s, neoconservatives had joined forces with conservative economists. AEI was a natural place for neoconservative scholars because of its ideological moderation, especially when compared with center-right think tanks like the Heritage Foundation and those of the center-left like Brookings. Likewise, enlisting Democratic neoconservatives like Lipset, Wattenberg, and Kirkpatrick (who were also members of the CDM) proved important in building a reputation for balanced excellence. By 1980, AEI had grown into an organization with a budget of $10.4 million and a staff of 135. In 1981, the organization was considered "the leading source of conservative intellectual firepower."[39]

Neoconservatives continue to be very active within AEI. Gertrude Himmelfarb, Samuel Huntington, and James Q. Wilson were members of AEI's council of academic advisers during the 1990s, and Wilson was also a member of its board of trustees. Wattenberg and Lipset were the coeditors of *Public Opinion*, while Kristol and Kirkpatrick sat on its editorial board. The editor of *Regulation* was Anne Brunsdale, and Kristol and Kirkpatrick served on the editorial board. Neoconservatives also promoted the creation of journals within the organization. The publication of *Regulation*—a journal concerned primarily with deregulation—was Kristol's idea.[40]

Neoconservatives have performed at least five important functions for and within AEI. First, they have given the organization academic recognition. As distinguished intellectuals, its members are capable of defending their viewpoints in a scholarly fashion. In the "war of ideas," they have presented intellectual arguments against what they consider the "adversary culture." According to Kristol, "neoconservatives have demonstrated to the media, the intellectual and political community that conservatism could be intellectually respectable. Bill Buckley can be dismissed, but we cannot be dismissed."[41] "Neoconservatives," concurs Peter Skerry, "played a critical role in the development of AEI. I do not think that AEI would be what it is without Irving Kristol and the subsequent arrival of people like Michael Novak or Ben Wattenberg."[42] Moreover, neoconservatives have translated complicated research into a language accessible to politicians and the public alike.

Second, within AEI and more generally, neoconservative intellectuals have brought together different conservative trends. Neoconservatives believed that the "New Politics" movement and the policies promoted by the "new class" had seriously affected the economy. They also argued that only capitalism could guarantee the survival of a civilized culture. Thus, Kristol judged that "neoconservatives . . . built the bridge between economic conservatives and cultural conservatives." According to Kristol, "cultural conservatives were mainly religious, and economic conservatives were all agnostic. Through the emphasis on social policy, we have been able to some degree to bridge that gap, which is very important, because that is the future of the Republican Party, to reach that gap."[43]

Third, neoconservatives have mobilized conservative foundations in support of conservative publications and organizations such as AEI. Important figures, such as Kristol, established strong relationships with important philanthropic leaders, thus obtaining economic resources that supported a spectrum of neoconservative projects. According to William Simon, the president of the Olin Foundation, the goal of his association with Kristol was "to form a partnership that would bring together businessmen and right-thinking intellectuals in common cause. . . . We want to persuade businessmen to make the commitment to compete and win on the battlefield of ideas and to support their friends rather than foes in this battle."[44] Kristol participated in the three-year campaign established in 1978 by AEI to raise $60 million for an endowment. Kristol and Novak called upon business leaders, foundations, and corporations to financially support conservative causes in the "war of ideas." "Your philanthropy," asserted Kristol in 1977, "must serve the long-term interests of the corporation. Corporate philanthropy should not be, cannot be disinterested."[45] Until recently—before the vanishing of the first generation's neoconservative journals—conservative foundations financed three of the main neoconservative publications: *The Public Interest*, *The National Interest*, and the *New Criterion*.

Fourth, neoconservatives have used the language of social science to target a political enemy. In their diagnosis of the main problems faced by the United States, they refer to the so-called new class as the main protagonists of the U.S. crisis. Formed by a range of professionals, this new class rejects the basic values of American society and culture, creating what neoconservatives call the "adversary culture." Fifth, AEI has used—especially during the 1970s—forms of communication not commonly employed by other think tanks. AEI televised public affairs programs, which presented national figures debating relevant topics, and published (before its liberal counterpart, the Brookings Institution) several widely circulated journals. In 1973, AEI broadcasts were carried by 270 television stations in the United States, in addition to being distributed on videocassette and audiocassette.

Thus, the permanent participation of think tank neoconservatives in conferences, briefings, and luncheons to discuss policy issues with politicians, the mass media, and leaders of the business community, often on TV, has transformed these academics into public intellectuals. For example, in March 1992, Wattenberg organized a conference at AEI titled "New Global Popular Culture" with the participation of the core neoconservatives Michael Novak, Walter Berns, and Robert A. Goldwin. The lecture was broadcast nationally by C-SPAN. Kirkpatrick commented on the August 1991 Soviet coup at AEI's press briefing. Richard Perle organized the

"Gulf Crisis," a videotaped made-for-television conference, and Wattenberg discussed the 1992 presidential primaries on CNN. More recently, on January 9, 2004, Perle and David Frum presented their book *An End to Evil* at AEI. On April 15, 2004, Novak participated as a commentator on Jonathan Rauch's book *Gay Marriage*. Finally, on February 10, 2004, Charles Krauthammer, a journalist often associated with the second generation of neoconservatives, received the Irving Kristol Award, AEI's highest annual honor.

AEI exemplifies the importance of think tanks to the consolidation of the neoconservative movement. In general, think tanks perform several important functions for these intellectuals. First, they serve as a base of operations. In Washington, a city where politicians often turn to think tanks rather than to universities when they seek policy advice, neoconservatives' association with think tanks increases the possibilities of establishing relationships with influential political and economic figures. Kristol describes Washington as an intellectual center for public policy research that is dominated by social scientists. In his words, many of the best and the brightest "congregate in that extraordinary Washington institution, the think tank."[46] To create webs of influence in the centers of power, neoconservatives must win and maintain the institutional support of think tanks.

The name of the most important award offered by AEI is that of one of the most important figures within the neoconservative movement. Among the recipients of this award—until 2002 known as the Francis Boyer Award, and since then as the Irving Kristol Award—have been neoconservative leaders such as Jeane Kirkpatrick (1985), Irving Kristol (1991), James Q. Wilson (1997), Michael Novak (1999), and Norman Podhoretz (2002). AEI's appreciation for Irving Kristol—and in a way for neoconservatism—was expressed on February 26, 2003, by Christopher DeMuth, AEI's president, with these words: "No one had more profound influence on the work of the American Enterprise Institute, or on American political discourse, than Irving Kristol. Combining philosophical depth with intense practicality and constant good cheer, he has, as president [George W.] Bush declared, 'transformed political debate on every subject he approached from economics to religion, from social welfare to foreign policy.'"[47] Thus the link between AEI and neoconservatives has been extremely strong for more than thirty years. AEI sells ideas, and neoconservatives would not be able to disseminate their products to a nationwide audience without its help.

Think tanks support the notion of neoconservatism as an intellectual-political movement. Think tanks concentrate people with similar ideological tendencies in a concrete organization. These institutions facilitate the external perception of neoconservatism as a political movement and reinforce neoconservatives' image as a group of "public intellectuals," a community of articulators and disseminators of political discourse. Within the walls of AEI, neoconservatives reinforce each other as well as create the image that this is not the activity of just one person expressing his or her viewpoints but an identifiable current of opinion.

Since its beginnings, AEI has sought to affect the decisionmaking process. In 1974, it clearly expressed its belief that its published materials "serve[d] as a bridge between scholars and those who make our public policies."[48] It has nurtured this focus by serving as a meeting place for neoconservatives and political elites. For example, it organizes an annual Public Policy Week, which culminates in a Public Policy Dinner. In 1983, among the distinguished guests at this dinner were President Ronald Reagan, former president Gerald Ford (who in February 1977 became a distinguished fellow of the organization), Helmut Schmidt, Martin Feldstein, Paul Volcker, Mario Cuomo, George Deukmejian, and Brent Scowcroft. At the dinner, President Reagan took the opportunity to praise the organization, saying, "I can't overstate the debt of this administration to you at AEI. You did so much of the intellectual groundwork for our policies, and to help put those policies in place, you have given us over two dozen outstanding men and women to work in the administration."[49] In summary, as a highly visible institution, AEI has contributed significantly to both the diffusion of neoconservative ideas and the solidification of the relationships between neoconservative intellectuals and American political elites. Like the Coalition for a Democratic Majority, AEI has helped neoconservatives establish their political network.

## The Committee on the Present Danger

The Committee on the Present Danger has been, perhaps, the most important neoconservative pressure organization. The CPD became a public organization on November 11, 1976, just a few days after Jimmy Carter's election to the presidency. In contrast to the Coalition for a Democratic Majority, which was a faction of the Democratic Party, the CPD was a bipartisan association founded by an important group of intellectuals, politicians, and business and labor leaders. The CPD emerged out of the disintegration of the postwar consensus on foreign policy. After World War II, there had been a basic, bipartisan agreement about the United States' international objectives. Democrats as well as Republicans supported the goals of globalism, anticommunism, and containment of the Soviet Union. This bipartisan consensus permitted the successful management of U.S. interests during the Cold War and encouraged continuity and consistency in decisionmaking from one administration to another. During the mid-1960s and the beginning of the 1970s, however, this consensus began to break down. The United States' failure in the Vietnam War marked the end of the agreement on foreign affairs, which had been predicated on the national goal of containing communist expansion. Vietnam demonstrated to both the world and American society the inability of the United States to achieve this goal.

Two political factions grew out of this fracture: critics of American interventionist policy and Cold War hard-liners. The first group judged American foreign policy as imperialistic and immoral. The second argued that the Soviets continued to represent a significant menace to the United States. These contrasting views struggled for political dominance beginning in the late 1960s. Critics of American global intervention dominated during the Nixon years, while hard-liners held sway during the Reagan administration. The CPD was perhaps the most enthusiastic and well-organized expression of the hard-line Cold War view held by politicians like Hubert Humphrey and Henry Jackson and organizations such as the CDM.

The CPD grew directly out of the work of "Team B."[50] In 1976, President Ford asked Central Intelligence Agency (CIA) director George H. W. Bush to name a group of experts to evaluate CIA data on Soviet military capabilities. This group of experts—"Team B"—was composed of seven members, four of whom—Richard Pipes (chair), Paul Nitze, Foy Kohler, and William Van Cleave—later became members of the CPD. The selection of Pipes as head of the group "insured that Team B would take a pessimistic view of Soviet intentions. His predisposition was shared by the team members he picked."[51] The overlapping of hard-line members between Team B and the CPD assured that both groups would engage in similar discourse. Indeed, in its report, Team B asserted that "the ultimate intention of Soviet strategic aims was to develop forces capable of impeding merchant vessels, denying raw materials to the West, disrupting fuel supplies, defeating the 'projection of power from sea to land' by Western forces, and developing strategic forces that would ultimately have a superior first-strike capability."[52] Studies based on the declassification of Team B reports have shown that Soviet military spending "began to slow down precisely at the time that Team B was writing" about a steadily increasing Soviet military buildup.[53] In retrospect the "rearm[ing]" of the United States was, perhaps, unnecessary.

A few months after Team B presented its report, Eugene Rostow's brainchild, the CPD, came to life. Rostow had been particularly affected by the limited impact of CDM in the Democratic Party and the media[54] and by his disagreements with Henry Kissinger on American foreign policy. In 1974, the CDM appointed Rostow as the head of its Foreign Policy Task Force. In his report, issued in the summer of the same year, Rostow and the CDM presented a major criticism of the United States' détente policy with regard to the Soviet Union. Kissinger fundamentally objected to the task force's views.[55] Disappointed with Kissinger's reaction, Rostow decided to push the CDM's hard-line foreign policy perspective through another organization that went beyond the confines of party politics.

Thus, in 1975 Rostow spoke with a number of different people about the feasibility of establishing the CPD. On March 12, 1976, an initial organizational meeting took place with the participation of Richard Allen, Lane Kirkland, Paul Nitze, David Packard, Eugene Rostow, James Schlesinger, Charles Tyroler II, Charls Walker, and Elmo Zumwalt.[56] George Ball, Karl Bendetsen, Peter Dominick, Henry Fowler, Max Kampelman, Arthur Metcalf, Donald Rumsfeld, and Dean Rusk were also consulted. "Our goal," wrote Rostow to Rumsfeld on April 5, 1976, "is a bipartisan, non-partisan committee to help alert the country to the present danger, and rally public opinion to a sensible and adequate foreign and defense policy." Rostow noted that conversations about the CPD had remained within the original circle of organizers, but he said that soon those core members would reach out "with special emphasis on youth, women, and some dovish but not hopeless Democrats."[57]

To undertake these activities, the CPD needed money. To obtain it, Charls Walker and John B. Connally organized a luncheon with select businessmen and public figures in Houston to "discuss a project that may prove vital to the future of this nation, if not the entire Free World." In the invitation letter, the CPD wrote that "although reference is made to 'a' committee, the project will actually run on two tracks. One track will involve policy statements. . . . The second track will involve lobbying, as pure as simple."[58] At that event the CPD collected $50,135.28—not $37,000, as David Callahan has asserted[59]—from twenty-six people in contributions that varied from $150 to $16,235.28. The major donors included Lloyd H. Smith, who gave $16,235.28 and remained a key donor throughout the organization's history. Bay Houston Lowering Company gave $7,500, James A. Elkins gave $5,000, Cecil R. Hayden gave $2,500, and Stewart Stevenson gave $2,000.[60] Similar fund-raising events were planned in other cities like Chicago,[61] although I have not found documentation related to these events in the CPD archives. Additional money came from important CPD members, such as David Packard, who donated $10,000. By December 7, 1976, Rostow reported to its Board of Directors that the CPD "had only $76,000 in hand as we started operations, and perhaps $25,000 more in reasonable prospect. Our first budget is $500,000, exclusive of newspaper advertisements and of special projects."[62]

The CPD initiated its activities with a press conference at the National Press Club in Washington. There, it presented its founding statement, "Common Sense and the Common Danger." Written by Rostow, the statement was originally titled "Challenges to Freedom," subsequently "A Time for Change," and finally "Common Sense and the Common Danger," at the suggestion of Nitze.[63] According to the political scientist Simon Dalby, the document was revised thirteen times during 1976, the same period that Team B was conducting its intelligence review.[64]

Representatives from radio, TV, and newspapers were at the National Press Club to report on the birth of the CPD. After reading the statement, Rostow, Kirkland, Nitze, Packard, Walker, and Fowler answered questions during a press conference that lasted an hour. "All of us there," Rostow informed the CPD's Board of Directors in December 1976, "felt that our venture was well and truly launched, and that we had made a good beginning."[65] Despite their presence, however, the press virtually ignored the event.

In its policy statement, the CPD emphatically declared that the United States was the victim of a conspiracy. The United States was in danger, and that "danger was increasing." According to the CPD, the Soviet Union and its ambitions for dominance, based "upon an unparalleled military buildup," threatened to "destroy the world balance of forces on which the survival of freedom depends." To confront the enemy, the CPD suggested that the United States "restore an allied defense posture capable of deterrence at each significant level and in those theaters vital to our interests." The reestablishment of American military might was essential, because "without a stable balance of forces in the world, . . . no other objective of our foreign policy is attainable." The organization aspired to "build a fresh consensus to expand the opportunities and diminish the dangers of a world in flux."[66] "The purpose of the Committee," recalled Kampelman, a founding member of the organization, "was simple and straightforward—to alert American policy makers, opinion shapers, and the public at large to the ominous Soviet military buildup and its implications, and to the unfavorable trends in the U.S.-Soviet military balance. We were all convinced that international stability and peace with freedom required a strong America— one that could and would deter Soviet adventurism and aggression."[67]

In a way, the CPD popularized Team B's findings with the aim of shifting public opinion and, in particular, elite perceptions about the "Soviet nuclear threat."[68] The CPD rejected from membership all political parties, political candidates, government officials, representatives of the defense industry, and individuals who were working full time in government. Clearly, the CPD had decided to present itself as an unbiased, pluralistic association unrelated to any political or economic interests. For Kampelman, these provisions "emphasized the Committee's true bipartisan membership and nonpartisan attitude" and "kept us free of the charges that we were the voice of the defense contractors who were profiting from large Pentagon budgets." With this membership clause, the CPD sought to achieve credibility, which its members considered "the essential ingredient in the process of persuasion."[69] Yet, in spite of these efforts to cultivate bipartisanship, the CPD became an organization fundamentally opposed to Carter's foreign and military policy and those favoring détente.

The CPD was also explicitly conceived and organized as an elite association. Its membership was restricted to its Board of Directors, which was originally limited to 100 members but eventually expanded to 150. Of those 150, 60 percent were Democrats and 40 percent Republicans.[70] The limit on membership was established to avoid internal difficulties and achieve significant harmony. The board agreed to make the CPD a nonprofit research and educational association rather than a lobbying group. This decision was fundamentally economic because "under IRS regulations, contributions to the Committee could be deducted for Federal Income Tax purposes."[71] According to one study, the CPD's budget was relatively small: "$90,000 in 1977, $200,000 in 1978, and $300,000 in 1979."[72]

Nine months after its launch press conference at the National Press Club, the CPD's leaders met with President Carter. Apparently, the meeting, called by Hamilton Jordan, Carter's chief of staff, took CPD members by surprise. The idea, according to McGeorge Bundy, was to "sustain a dialogue between hawks and doves, and his concern over the fact that the Administration was staffed almost entirely by pronounced doves."[73] According to a confidential report presented by Rostow to the CPD's Executive Committee, a group of CPD members gathered with the president on August 4, 1977. In that meeting, Nitze and Rostow offered opening statements, presenting an overview of the CPD's main concerns and views on foreign and defense policy, and expressing their opinion that the United States needed to increase its military spending. Carter spoke on different "aspects of SALT [Strategic Arms Limitation Talks] and of the Soviet-American relations." In Rostow's account of the reunion, the president wanted to have the advice of the CPD on foreign and defense policy and "where we could give it, our support." President Carter asked CPD members "to meet regularly with Secretaries Vance, and Brown, and Mr. Brzezinski to review and evaluate the complex data on the basis of which he must reach his decision." The CPD and the Carter administration differed on SALT and other foreign policy issues, but President Carter thought "regular meetings might narrow differences and make it possible for our Committee to support his policies in the years ahead." Henry H. Fowler and David Packard assured the president that the CPD "desired and intended to be helpful and meet with him and with Secretaries Vance, Brown, and Dr. Brzezinski whenever they wish us to do so; and also that we would feel free, at his kind invitation to request such a meeting when we thought they might be helpful to us in our own work."[74] This meeting with the president was kept confidential and never discussed with the press.

Despite the fact that the CPD wanted to keep the meeting with President Carter confidential, the *Christian Science Monitor* and the *Washington Post* both reported the gathering. The *Christian Science Monitor* related the main views of the CPD and noted that its members were "convinced that they made progress with Carter." The *Washington Post*, in contrast, reported that a "mood of exasperation dominated the one-hour meeting that left everybody ill at ease."[75] On August 23, Rostow sent a private letter to the CPD Board of Directors highlighting the publication of the two newspaper articles, and stressing that the CPD would follow the policy of "no comments." Likewise, Rostow summarized the letter previously sent to the Executive Committee on August 10.[76] In these confidential documents to the CPD membership, Rostow presented a positive view of the meeting with President Carter. In a memorandum for the organization's files, however, he presented a more pessimistic account of the meeting. There, he asserted that in that meeting "the President's personality and style came through as pathetic, almost painful."[77]

It was evident that President Carter wanted the support of the CPD, and either tried to convince its members to support his policies or at least show to the public that he had considered the opinions of the organization. The CPD and a few members of the Carter administration were convinced that Carter needed to be tough. A dialogue with the president and some of his primary Cabinet members was perceived as a step in the right direction. Ultimately, however, it became clear that Carter and the CPD held opposite views on America's foreign and defense policy. As a consequence, Carter's attempt to persuade the CPD to support his initiatives was a complete failure.

In the late 1970s and early 1980s, the American political environment was rife with conservative expressions. As a result of the decline of the New Deal, these tendencies found fertile soil in which grow. Conservative organizations that sought to preserve the status quo challenged the "New Politics" movement, and radical-right expressions defended a backlash ideology. Within the Republican Party, the defeat of Nelson Rockefeller, the last Republican candidate who described himself as a liberal, marked the beginning of the alienation of liberal sectors and the consolidation of conservative factions. In 1980, liberals made up 6 percent of the Republican Party. By 1988, that figure had declined to 3 percent.[78] What is more, other groups emerged, including the so-called New Right and the Christian Right. The New Right played an important role in fund-raising, but it was even more instrumental in mobilizing popular support in favor of Reagan's candidacy. Neoconservativism became the intellectual bedrock of Reagan's campaign and an important base of support during his first four years in the White House.

The move toward conservatism also manifested itself in the business sector's political activities. Economic crisis and the state's growing tendency to intervene in the economy mobilized the private sector to dedicate both economic and human resources to political affairs.[79] Seeking to recuperate their previous position of influence, corporations strengthened their direct relations with the government, reinforced their involvement in congressional lobbying, increased their participation in political action committees, created corporate umbrella organizations like the Business Roundtable, and provided economic resources to organizations working to modify both intellectual and public opinion. Private corporations sought to influence the American government both directly and indirectly through these activities.

Besides finding a welcoming conservative political climate, the CPD was able to advance neoconservative views through its structure and form of operation. First, it had no formal ties to political parties or business groups. This characteristic helped it to position itself as an organization devoted to the promotion of the well-being of the nation and not the self-interests of political or business organizations. Second, its highly selective membership of intellectuals, politicians, and business and labor leaders formed a network with sufficient political and economic power to penetrate the decisionmaking process.

The participation of neoconservative intellectuals—such as Norman Podhoretz, Midge Decter, Jeane Kirkpatrick, Seymour Martin Lipset, and Nathan Glazer, as well as Nobel Prize winners like Saul Bellow, Eugene Wigner, Robert Mulliken, and W. F. Libby—both lent the CPD intellectual capital and gave it a presence in the academic world. The membership of important labor leaders—such as Lane Kirkland, John Lyons, and Albert Shanker—who constantly defended anticommunist positions, fostered the establishment of meaningful connections between the CPD and labor unions and facilitated the diffusion of its neoconservative ideas in workers' circles. Business executives such as Packard, Nicolas Thomas, Arthur Temple, and William Franklin guaranteed a close connection between the CPD and the business community. This connection was essential, especially for obtaining funding. Finally, the membership of renowned former diplomatic, military, and political figures—such as Randolph Burgess, Lyman Lemnitzer, Leonard Marks, George McGhee, Robert McNair, William Colby, John Connally, and C. Douglas Dillon, to mention but a few—contributed to the links between the CPD and influential political circles in Washington.

The membership of prominent intellectuals, business executives, and former politicians gave the organization considerable clout. The CPD was able to promote alliances with analogous groups and mobilize them in favor of concrete political measures. SALT II is an interesting case in this regard. The Coalition for Peace Through Strength, the American Security Council, and the Conservative Caucus were some of the organizations operating under the CPD that spent more than $7 million to stop the treaty. According to the *Christian Science Monitor*, opponents of SALT II spent about fourteen times as much money as did treaty supporters. In all, the "CPD became the umbrella organization for many groups trying to increase military spending and restart the Cold War."[80] Anti-SALT organizations had distinct advantages over their opponents—religious organizations, unions, professional associations, and the Carter administration. These advantages included unity, resources, and effective means of influencing public opinion. They published more editorials and position pieces than their adversaries, thereby keeping their views in the public eye.[81]

The CPD was established as an educational association, and as such, worked to affect the opinions of political and business leaders and the public in general. The CPD used its well-placed position in the media to advance its views. A substantial number of its directors were owners or held important positions in media outlets, such as the Evening News Association, *Reader's Digest*, and Time Incorporated. Likewise, some of its members were editors or major contributors to journals like *Commentary* or *The National Review*. For example, Richard Pipes published his influential article "Why the Soviet Union Thinks It Could Fight and Win a Nuclear War" in *Commentary* in 1977. Two years later, in the same journal, Jeane Kirkpatrick published the essay "Dictatorships and Double Standards," which paved the way for her to become a prominent political figure and a central influence on the design of American human rights policy during the Reagan administration.[82]

The CPD also used the influence of its members who were politicians to promote its policies in the U.S. Congress and the White House. The nomination of Paul Warnke illustrates both the CPD's mode of operation in the executive and legislative branches and its canny use of the mass media. A few weeks after Carter won the presidency, he announced the nomination of Warnke to run the SALT negotiations and serve as a director of the Arms Control and Disarmament Agency. Warnke's nomination disturbed CPD members because of his involvement in the 1972 campaign of George McGovern, whose platform had promoted a vast reduction in military spending. In short order, the CPD started a political campaign to derail Warnke's nomination.

The CPD worked together with the CDM (demonstrating both the relationship between these two organizations and the common strategies used by some neoconservative organizations) and the Emergency Coalition against Unilateral Disarmament, an organization created specifically to fight the Warnke nomination. This coalition had been formed by the CPD and CDM, several New Right organizations, the American Conservative Union, Young Americans for Freedom, the Committee for the Survival of a Free Congress, and a traditionally conservative group, the American Security Council. Together, these groups sent more than 600,000 letters asking the public to express its opposition to the nomination.

One of the coalition's first activities was to distribute an anonymous memorandum criticizing Warnke's views and his abilities as a negotiator. The memo, which was distributed to members of Congress and the media, received a great deal of public attention. The memo itself had been conceived and written by Joshua Muravchik in the CDM's offices.[83] Muravchik argued that "it is hard to see how the American side in SALT can be effectively upheld by someone who advocates as Warnke does the unilateral abandonment by the United States of every weapons system which is subject to negotiations at SALT."[84] Other activities—such as a letter from Paul Nitze to Senator John Sparkman, chairman of the Foreign Relations Committee, criticizing Warnke's nomination; Nitze's testimony before the Senate; and the permanent vocal protest of CDM leader Henry Jackson in the same chamber—complemented the memo. Although Warnke was later confirmed by a vote of fifty-eight to forty, the CPD and CDM sent a very clear message: "Warnke could not go out and negotiate a SALT treaty of his own preference."[85]

The Warnke case demonstrates the CPD's mode of operating and political power. First, the case reveals the CPD's capacity to use the media to diffuse its political viewpoints. Second, it demonstrates how neoconservative organizations worked together to advance their perspectives. Third, it highlights the ability of neoconservative organizations in general, and the CPD in particular, to penetrate Congress to lobby in favor of or in opposition to concrete policy measures. The affiliation of distinguished members of Congress with the CDM guaranteed a permanent voice for the CPD and other neoconservative organizations in the legislature. Finally, it shows how the CPD's leadership could mobilize analogous groups in support of its views.

The CPD's favored tactics become clear if we examine some figures. In 1979, during the hearings on SALT II, CPD "members testified 17 times before Congress; Paul Nitze's SALT II paper was updated 11 times; Executive Committee and Board members participated in 479 television and radio programs; press conferences, debates, and public forums were given for citizen leaders; and 400,000 copies of pamphlets and reports were distributed."[86] In the 1980s, the CPD changed substantially. It shifted from being a pressure group to—when the Reagan administration appointed thirty-three of its members to his administration—actually holding a great deal of political power in an administration that embraced the organization's hard-line neoconservative perspective in its foreign policy program.

## The Committee for the Free World

Like the CPD, the Committee for the Free World, the brainchild of Midge Decter, was a nostalgic association. Both tried to revive, in slightly different fashions, political institutions created in the 1950s. The CPD was a 1970s version of a movement with the same name and goals that had existed during the Truman years. Similarly, in the early 1980s the CFW attempted to resuscitate the basic principles and aspirations of the Congress for Cultural Freedom, an international organization of the postwar era. According to Peter Coleman, the CFW "was a sort of partial regrouping of Congress intellectuals."[87]

The CFW was an unequivocally neoconservative institution. Of the four organizations included in this study, the CFW had the highest number of neoconservative associates. Midge Decter worked as the executive director. The twenty-nine members of its Board of Directors included eight declared neoconservative members: William Barrett, William Bennett, Carl Gershman, Jeane Kirkpatrick, Hilton Kramer, Irving Kristol, Seymour Martin Lipset, and Norman Podhoretz. The members of its General Committee included neoconservatives such as Elliott Abrams, Chester E. Finn, Suzanne Garment, Nathan Glazer, Gertrude Himmelfarb, Sidney Hook, Samuel Huntington, Max Kampelman, Michael Novak, Richard Perle, Richard Pipes, Ben Wattenberg, and James Q. Wilson.

In its founding statement, the CFW defined itself as an intellectual association formed by a group of "writers, artists, editors, trade unionists, scientists, teachers, publishers, and others who live in various countries." With a pronouncement similar to the one delivered by the CPD, the CFW declared that "free societies are coming increasingly under attack." This threat, the "rising menace of totalitarian barbarism,"[88] was exemplified by the Soviet Union. The organization also believed that "freedom had been threatened by the spread of ideas hostile to it." As in the case of the CPD, this conflict was framed as being between Western civilization and the totalitarian, Soviet-led world. To safeguard the free world, it was necessary "to conduct a world-wide ideological defense of freedom."[89]

The CFW declared three main purposes: first, "to reaffirm that Western democratic society provides the best model known to mankind of just and human social order"; second, "to rouse the unconcerned to the recognition that whatever diminishes freedom anywhere in the world diminishes their own freedom as well"; and third, "to oppose the influence of all those, both from outside free society and within, who have made themselves the enemies of the democratic order."[90] The CFW decided to fight this war in the realm of ideas. The organization contended that the "struggle for freedom may in the end be won or lost not in the battlefield but in books, newspapers, broadcasts, classrooms, and in all public institutions where the determination to remain free is enhanced or undermined."[91] The CFW believed that it could make an impact because intellectual energy was on its side.[92] To that end, it served as an intermediary for both neoconservative and conservative writers. It became, in the words of Decter, "an informal literary agency, placing books and articles with likely publishers."[93]

To win the "struggle for freedom," the CFW required sufficient financial resources. Its donations came primarily from individuals, from corporations, and in large measure from foundations. Its relationship with corporations and conservative foundations provided a link between those wealthy conservative groups with particular ideological and political interests and the neoconservative movement. The CFW enjoyed the unconditional support of important conservative foundations such as the John M. Olin Foundation, the Smith Richardson Foundation, the Carthage Foundation, and to a lesser but important extent, the Coors and Harry Bradley foundations. These philanthropic organizations shared the CFW's views and concerns, and Decter herself had friendly relationships with and direct access to these foundations' chairmen and key members.[94] These foundations were not only charitable associations supporting "scientific research or humanitarian causes"; they were also political organizations dedicated to supporting, although not exclusively, conservative causes and making conservative thinking available in order to affect American public opinion.

This orientation can be seen in the exchanges between foundation officers and the CFW. In a letter from Leslie Lenkowsky, director of research at the Smith Richardson Foundation, to Midge Decter, Lenkowsky highlighted the foundation's support for American strong national defense policy and adherence to neoconservative views:

We [the Smith Richardson Foundation] are concerned that the antinuclear movement is apparently having an effect—perhaps even with the Reagan administration—in weakening support for strong foreign

and defense policy. We are even more concerned about the seeming inability of sound and realistic ideas about nuclear war to make much
headway in the current climate of opinion.[95]

Lenkowsky organized a "gathering of a select group of our friends" to
study the issue. That meeting started with a panel discussion featuring
three neoconservatives (Kristol, Podhoretz, and Robert Tucker) and two
conservative thinkers (Edward Luttwak, who was sometimes associated
with neoconservatism, and Herman Kahn). The basic goal of this encounter was to "have a thorough discussion of what 'our side' might think, say,
or do to respond more effectively to this last version of the peace movement." At these sorts of events, neoconservatives not only debated ideas
and shared viewpoints on particular issues but also designed strategies and
agendas that were subsequently implemented by conservative foundations.

Likewise, the Smith Richardson Foundation clearly expressed its political conservatism in its decision to support the "Oxford Afghanistan Ex-
pedition." In 1986, the CFW sent a proposal to the foundation requesting
financial aid for a group of journalists and photographers based in England
to visit Afghanistan. On July 22, 1986, Devon Gaffney sent an interdepartmental memo to Randolph Richardson recommending approval of this
project. According to Gaffney, the purpose of this grant was "to report on
Soviet atrocities" in Afghanistan and to "increase Western media coverage
of Soviet human rights violations" in that country, a central topic for neoconservatives. Gaffney felt the report would have a significant impact on
public opinion.[96] On July 28, 1986, the grant was approved.

Smith Richardson was not alone. Other foundations showed similar in-
clinations in favor of neoconservative views. In 1984 Jack Brauntuch, executive director of the JM Foundation, argued the "importance of the Committee's informal network of public opinion leaders who are dedicated to a
renewed sense of American honor, duty, and love of country."[97] "We are
delighted," the Olin Foundation's William Simon wrote to Midge Decter
in 1989, "to continue our support of the Committee's excellent work, and,
in this way, to join in your resolute defense of freedom."[98] An ideological
empathy existed between CFW-style neoconservatism and American conservative foundations. This empathy was a precious resource, carefully
cultivated by neoconservatives. The affinity created projects, opened
doors, attracted the attention of elites, and sold ideas.

Cannily, Decter used her contacts with foundations to promote the
study and promotion of conservative perspectives. She negotiated with

Michael Joyce of the Lynde and Harry Bradley Foundation for a $25,000 grant to support the work of Vladimir Bukovsky, who would be CFW's (and, by extension, the neoconservative movement's) European-Soviet consultant.[99] She also interceded with the Smith Richardson Foundation in favor of support for Mauro Lucentini's conservative Italian newsletter, *Lettra di New York*, and with the Carthage Foundation to support the conservative thinker Rachel Ehrenfeld's research on narco-terrorism.[100] The CFW also received the support of several individuals, smaller philanthropic organizations, and a number of corporations (for more on these, see the section below on financial support).

In addition, several well-known individuals either helped to spread neoconservative views or worked as liaisons between neoconservatives and political and economic elites. Packard and Dillon supported the committee. Republican New York State Representative Jack Kemp endorsed, promoted, and peddled CFW and its ideas. Robert Bartley, editor of the *Wall Street Journal*, had a friendly relationship with Decter, and Kenneth L. Adelman was willing to help in any possible way the CFW. Richard Allen of the CPD congratulated Decter "on the splendid work that the CFW is doing,"[101] and Donald Rumsfeld participated directly in the organization, serving as a liaison between the CFW and American corporations.

In particular, Rumsfeld functioned as an intermediary between the CFW and the defense corporation Northrop. In 1983 Stanley Ebner, Northrop's senior vice president for governmental relations, answered a letter from Rumsfeld. In this communication, Ebner agreed with the former secretary of defense "that there is a real need for an organization such as CFW to wage a war of ideas in defense of the United States against false political arguments and misrepresentation of facts. . . . I would certainly recommend careful consideration of [*sic*] Northrop of a formal proposal of its support."[102] The CFW archives offer no indication that Northrop actually supported the organization. Ideologically speaking, however, Northrop's corporate board agreed with neoconservative principles. Journalists and scholars writing on the influence of neoconservatism on American foreign policy during the George W. Bush administration's first term have frequently asserted that Rumsfeld is not a neoconservative, but the evidence indicates that he was quite happy to support at least some neoconservative initiatives.

The CFW quickly became a forum for neoconservative debates and discussions. *Contentions*, its monthly bulletin, was "devoted to questions and arguments currently being agitated within the political and cultural community." Likewise, the bulletin had a special section titled "Where the Money Goes." Here, the CFW dedicated space to presenting the "way in which some of the major foundations have elected to distribute certain of their funds."[103] The bulletin often reprinted neoconservative writings, such as Kristol's piece in the *Wall Street Journal* about the Timerman affair. The CFW also published newspaper pronouncements in favor of American foreign policy in El Salvador or against congressional opposition to the "Nicaraguan resistance."[104] It distributed the documentary films *KGB Connection: An Investigation into Soviet Operations in North America* and *Agents of Deception*. The latter film was sold to more than seventy colleges and universities. The CFW also ran its own publishing imprint, the Orwell Press, and served as "a kind of unofficial agency for recommending or providing radio and television panelists."[105] What is more, the CFW held five international conferences,[106] at which neoconservatives debated American foreign policy and, to a lesser extent, domestic and cultural issues. According to Decter, the CFW helped to spin off the National Association of Scholars,[107] advised conservative foundations, and cultivated permanent relationships with some important sectors of the so-called New Right.[108]

The CFW played a modest but very important role in the neoconservative movement. It ceased its activities in 1990 because of the "worldwide demise of the Communist, and with it the socialist-collective idea" and declared itself the winner in the battle against the Communist world. Throughout its years of existence, the CFW created a forum in which political and intellectual figures met to debate important political issues. In these meetings, disputes often arose between neoconservatives, such as the disagreement between Peter L. Berger and Hilton Kramer about the influence of American culture in the world. New issues arose—such as multiculturalism, an issue on which some neoconservatives concentrated their analysis in the post–Cold War era. Likewise, the CFW publicized neoconservative views, gave national and international recognition to neoconservative ideas and organizations, and facilitated relationships between neoconservatives and international communities of conservative intellectuals.

## Neoconservatives' Financial Support

A central component in the emergence of neoconservatism as an important political and intellectual expression was the economic support received from private hands. The link between private sources and neoconservatives becomes clear from an analysis of the financial contributions from corporations, corporate foundations, and foundations to the American Enterprise Institute, the Coalition for a Democratic Majority, the Committee on the Present Danger, and the Committee for the Free World.

Since its origin in the 1940s, AEI, which was founded by Lewis Brown, president of the Johns-Manville Corporation, had been closely tied to the business community. Beginning with the leadership of William J. Baroody Jr. in 1977, AEI worked to increase contributions from the business community. With the support of private corporations and the fund-raising activities of Irving Kristol, AEI grew from a budget of around $1 million in 1970 to $10.6 million in 1983.

AEI's leadership reflected its relationship to the business community. In the mid-1980s, at the apex of its political influence, its Board of Trustees included important business leaders such as Wallace Abbott, senior vice president, Procter & Gamble; Robert Anderson, chairman of the board and chief executive officer, Rockwell International Corporation; Richard M. Morrow, chairman of the board and chief executive officer, Standard Oil Company; Paul F. Oreddice, president and chief executive officer, Dow Chemical Company; and Roger Smith, chairman of the board and chief executive officer, General Motors.[109]

In addition to the financial support of corporations, in the early 1960s, AEI president William J. Baroody Sr. obtained the economic aid of some conservative organizations such as the Earhart, Falk, Kresge, Pew, and Sloan foundations. In the 1970s and particularly in the 1980s, AEI also received grants from the Olin and the Henry Luce foundations. By the 1980s, its budget was largely made up of funds from corporations, corporate foundations, and private foundations. To cite but one example, in 1982 and 1983, it received 25 percent of its total income from corporate foundations, 30 percent from private foundations, and 32 percent from corporations.[110]

Neoconservative intellectuals and AEI eagerly furnished a rationale for the activities of corporations. Kristol argued that corporations were the new defenders of American democracy,[111] and that AEI's "views on economic policy appeal[ed] to the business community." AEI, he continued, "has been the citadel of free-market economics." John Post, the Washington representative of the Business Roundtable, recalled, "It used to be that practically every policy committee [of the Roundtable] meeting would talk about making contributions to support AEI."[112] Thus, AEI and its neoconservative staff worked successfully to obtain the support of the large business community.

Neoconservatives also received significant amounts of money from conservative foundations—especially from the so-called four sisters: the Bradley, Olin, Smith Richardson, and Scaife Family foundations. Although liberal-leaning foundations have historically given more economic resources to support and develop projects, the four sisters tend to act in agreement, backing more or less the same kinds of projects. According to Leon Howell, in 1993 the four sisters made grants of $57 million, a small figure in comparison with the grants of $290 million made by the Pew Charitable Trusts and the Lilly Endowment that same year. "But those [liberal] foundations," Howell writes, "unlike the four sisters, on the whole do not funnel money directly to the front lines of the intellectual battlegrounds."[113] These foundations have also invested heavily in disseminating the work that their funding produces. From 1990 to 1993, four conservative journals—*The National Interest*, *The Public Interest*, *The New Criterion*, and the *American Spectator* (the first three are neoconservative journals)—received a total of $2.7 million from conservative foundations. In contrast, during the same period, four liberal and radical journals—*The Nation*, *The Progressive*, *In These Times*, and *Mother Jones*—received just one-tenth of this amount ($269,500) from liberal foundations.[114] The conservative foundations effectively promoted, supported, and helped disseminate a particular viewpoint.

The Coalition for a Democratic Majority has a slightly different history. At its inception, the CDM's yearly budget never exceeded $250,000. It obtained its financial resources primarily from member contributions, private corporations, the organization of political events, and, especially, the labor movement. In reviewing the CDM's archive, I found out that only one foundation, the Scaife Family Foundation, funded the CDM, for the purpose of publishing a series of position papers.

A snapshot for fiscal year 1973–74 shows the CDM's various sources of funding. That year, it generated revenue of $98,017. Of this, $11,255 came from contributors, $39,700 from labor contributors, and $6,025 from memberships (new and renewed) and other activities and events. Some of its members were associated with corporations such as Mannkraft, Lilly-Ann, American Income Life Insurance, Continental Telephone, and Allied Chemical. Its main individual contributors in the 1970s were Bernard Rapoport, chairman of the board and chief executive officer of the American Income Life Insurance Company, and S. Harrison Gogole, of the Global Security System Incorporated.[115]

In the 1980s, the CDM began to attract contributions from corporations for luncheons, receptions, panel discussions, and special events. For instance, in 1985 it organized the "Henry M. Jackson 1985 Friends of Freedom Award Dinner" to honor Ambassador Max Kampelman, Senator Sam Nunn, and Representative Les Aspin. The sponsors of this event included some of the most important corporations associated with the military-industrial complex, such as AVACO, General Dynamics, Lockheed, and Northrop.[116] "Our relationships with military corporations," Ben Wattenberg would assert later, "was a marriage of convenience. We were saying we want stronger defense, McDonnell Douglas wanted stronger defense. . . . These guys knew how to make airplanes and guns, but they did not know how to say Western civilization is under threat. They learned the rhetoric of these things from us."[117] The CDM's discourse helped military-related corporations legitimize the American military buildup.

The other main economic supporter of the CDM, especially in its early days, was the labor movement, notably the United Steel Workers and the AFL-CIO's Committee on Political Education (known as COPE). According to Wattenberg, labor was "in favor of CDM because they were fundamentally anti-McGovern. They thought that the left wing was taking over the Party. They felt that this [CDM] was useful for them in the war of ideas. . . . So we got money and very important support."[118] This relationship reflects the strong ties of the CDM and neoconservatives such as Penn Kemble, Josh Muravchik, and Carl Gershman with the Social Democrats USA, and by extension with organized labor. Although the CDM was receiving financial support from big business, especially during the 1980s, and while important military-related corporations were sympathetic with the CDM's activities and ideas, its main source of income at a crucial historical moment was the labor movement. The reader might find it strange that the CDM received financial support from groups with such opposing views. Business, however, only began to support the CDM when it began to focus more on foreign policy.

The Committee on the Present Danger was formed by a group of businessmen, academics, ex-politicians, and leaders of the labor movement. Businessmen, however, played a large and important role. The CPD's founding board members included important corporate leaders from the Potomac International Corporation, Allied Chemical, Caterpillar Tractor Company, the Digital Recording Corporation, Hewlett-Packard, and the Paraffine Oil Corporation, as well as Citibank and Prudential Insurance.

The CPD's financial support came from six different sources. First, wealthy individuals made large contributions, such as Shelby Cullom Davis, C. Douglas Dillon, Henry H. Fowler, Paul Nitze, Peter O'Donnell, David Packard, Horace Chapman Rose, Frank Sinatra, Lloyd H. Smith, and Elmo R. Zumwalt Jr. Second, people sympathetic to the CPD made small donations (less than a thousand dollars). Third, corporations made donations, such as the Adolph Coors Company, American Financial Corporation, Bay Houston Lowering Company, Howell Corporation, Merrill Lynch, and Texas Instruments. Fourth, corporate and conservative foundations made significant grants, such as the Scaife Family Charitable Trusts and the Carthage, Smith Richardson, O'Donnell, Samuel Robert Nobel, and Packard foundations.[119] The labor movement, especially the AFL-CIO, and a military-related corporation made up the last two sources of funds.[120] Clearly, the CPD enjoyed great access to economic resources.

Donations to the Committee for the Free World came primarily from individuals, corporations, and foundations. Though it is impossible to obtain a complete list of main sponsors of the CFW throughout its whole existence, surveys of its main benefactors in 1982 and 1989 give a sense of its supporters; these are listed in table 3.1.

The CFW also received support from a long list of people and organizations, including William Brady, Shelby Cullom Davis, Lewis E. Lehrman, Lloyd H. Smith, C. Douglas Dillon, the Heritage Foundation, the Nobel Foundation, the Omsur Foundation, the Scaife Family Charitable Trusts, the Vernon K. Krieble Foundation, Allegheny International Incorporated, Baxter Traveral Laboratories, Cavenham Holdings Incorporated, G. D. Searle & Company, Mercantile–Safe Deposit and Trust Company, Mobil, Vulcan Materials, and Sears Roebuck and Company. These and many other small donors constituted its basic financial sponsors.

The evidence also indicates that the CFW cultivated a friendly relationship with military-related corporations. Donald Rumsfeld, the former secretary of defense, was a key figure in that relationship. Though not a neoconservative, in the 1970s and 1980s, as well as today, he has maintained close ties to important figures in the neoconservative movement. He was close to people involved with the CPD and CFW and maintained close relationships with key neoconservative figures such as Paul Wolfowitz, Jeane Kirkpatrick, Richard Perle, and Midge Decter.[121] During the George W. Bush administration's first term, most academics, journalists, and politicians saw Rumsfeld as a traditional hard-line Republican. However, due to his long relationship with many neoconservatives, he was considered by Joshua Muravchik as the "leading patron of neocons in the administration."[122]

*Table 3.1. Selected List of Contributors to the Committee for the Free World, 1982 and 1989*

| Name | Date | Amount (dollars) |
| --- | --- | --- |
| *1982 Contributions* | | |
| W. H. Bradley Foundation | September 25 | 10,000 |
| Carthage Foundation | February 23 | 100,000 |
| Carthage Foundation | November 24 | 30,000 |
| Adolph Coors Foundation | August 23 | 5,000 |
| Earhart Foundation | June 15 | 2,500 |
| Hewlett Packard Company | October 20 | 5,000 |
| Ingersoll Foundation | November 16 | 5,000 |
| Jewish Community Foundation | March 1 | 1,000 |
| JM Foundation | September 30 | 25,000 |
| Joyce Mertz–Gilmore Foundation | May 10 | 6,000 |
| O'Donnell Foundation | July 26 | 25,000 |
| John M. Olin Foundation | April 7 | 15,000 |
| John M. Olin Foundation | April 13 | 15,000 |
| John M. Olin Foundation | December 14 | 25,000 |
| J. Howard Pew Freedom Trust | November 2 | 25,000 |
| Pfizer Inc. | March 8 | 3,500 |
| Reader's Digest Association | March 5 | 10,000 |
| Reader's Digest Foundation | July 1 | 15,000 |
| Henry Salvatori | June 21 | 10,000 |
| Smith Richardson Foundation | December 27 | 50,000 |
| *1989 Contributions* | | |
| Lynde and Harry Bradley Foundation | June 12 | 10,000 |
| W. H. Bradley Foundation | August 4 | 5,000 |
| Carthage Foundation | August 29 | 35,000 |
| Vernon K. Krieble Foundation | August 4 | 5,000 |
| Nobel Foundation | February 20 | 5,000 |
| John M. Olin Foundation | February 2 | 45,000 |
| Smith Richardson Foundation | March 10 | 35,000 |

*Source:* Committee for the Free World Collection, Hoover Institution on War, Revolution, and Peace, Stanford, Calif., boxes 55, 59, and 63.

Rumsfeld has served as a broker between neoconservatives, business organizations, and politicians. For example, in the 1970s and 1980s, he functioned as an intermediary between the CFW and the arms corporation Northrop.[123] Clearly, a structural nexus existed between big business, American military-related corporations, and the neoconservative movement. One way or another, directly or indirectly, corporations became the beneficiaries of neoconservative ideas, which legitimated their interests.

I am not arguing that neoconservatives consciously developed their ideas with the sole objective of obtaining economic support. Neoconservatives defended the American military buildup beginning in the postwar period, when weapons manufacturing was not a high priority for the U.S. government. However, in the historical context of the late 1960s, a "marriage of convenience" between military-related corporations and the neoconservative movement became possible. The economic breakdown of the late 1960s mobilized the business sector on different fronts. The business lobby experienced some success during the Carter administration, but it was during the Reagan years that the tax cuts and military buildup that benefited corporations were implemented. These policies originated not in the late 1970s but in the late 1960s. The significant changes of that period provoked structural modifications that reverberated in the relationship between neoconservatives and business organizations and foundations.

Neoconservative organizations such as the CDM, AEI, the CPD, and the CFW were vital to the formation and consolidation of the neoconservative movement. They were central instruments of neoconservativism's ideological crusade. In times when public policy was constantly separated from any base of popular support and political power was increasingly concentrated in the hands of a few, neoconservatism emerged as a movement capable of affecting the decisionmaking process by influencing political and economic elites.

The nature and activities of different neoconservative organizations reveal why this movement has had its biggest impact in foreign affairs. With the exception of AEI, which focused primarily on domestic policy issues, neoconservative institutions dedicated most of their time to the defense of Cold War foreign policy. These organizations ensured that the views of their adherents on this issue would penetrate circles of political power. Thus, neoconservative organizations matter because they provided an institutional framework for neoconservative ideas and systematically opened avenues for the diffusion of neoconservative views to those most directly involved in the political decisionmaking process.

## The Neoconservative Organizations
## of the Second Generation

One of the main similarities between the first and second generations of neoconservatives is that both generations conferred a similar role on organizations and their journals. At both historical moments when neoconservatism emerged, neoconservatives constructed institutions and created publications to disseminate their views. As previously discussed in this chapter, neoconservative organizations paved the way for the dissemination of neoconservative views to decisionmakers and the educated public.

The second generation of neoconservatives became politically and intellectually active in the 1990s. These neoconservatives created two think tanks—the Project for the New American Century, and the Center for Security Policy—and one publication, *The Weekly Standard*. Through these institutions, the second-generation neoconservatives were able to penetrate American society and, most important, circles of power.

### The Project for the New American Century

Though there was little demand for neoconservative politicians in the 1990s, neoconservative intellectuals continued to press the Clinton administration to modify its foreign policy. In particular, they criticized the isolationist foreign policy that had been adopted by the United States, which in their view could damage America's world primacy. In 1997, with these concerns in mind, neoconservatives launched the Project for the New American Century (PNAC), which demanded active involvement on the part of the United States in foreign affairs. During its existence, and especially after the arrival of George W. Bush in the White House, the PNAC's ideas and policy recommendations seriously influenced American foreign policy. The PNAC became the most important organization of the second neoconservative movement.

According to Gary Schmitt, who was for a long time its executive director, the PNAC was a direct result of the publication of Robert Kagan and William Kristol's article "Toward a Neo-Reaganite Foreign Policy."[124] "In theory," Schmitt remembered, the idea of that article was "to lay out a vision of foreign policy for Bob Dole. They [Kristol and Kagan] had no expectations that Bob Dole was going to win, so it was mostly an intellectual exercise, but the result of that was that a number of foundations came to us and said you know this looks like a good idea to follow through on . . . and that eventually led to why don't we set up a small think tank to promote that strategic vision."[125]

Schmitt also considered the creation of the PNAC the outcome of an internal debate within the Republican Party. In his opinion, Republicans

then had a substantial disagreement about the most convenient international strategy for the United States. "Conservatives," he opined, "had either slipped into being realist or various forms of neo-isolationists. The
neo-isolationists were either the moral types like Buchanan or the libertar-
ians . . . who were against big foreign policy because it would increase big
government. . . . Now what struck us about that was that the most serious
realists, the Kissingers, the Scowcrofts," considered "that the U.S. need
not play a larger role internationally, unless its vital interests were at stake.
. . . In practical terms the conservatives had an agenda of pulling the U.S.
away from the world. For a variety of reasons, we thought that was un-
healthy."[126] In a way, the members of the PNAC tried to modify the dominant tendencies within the Republican Party, offering a view that recuper-
ated important components of Ronald Reagan's foreign policy and the
ideas of their predecessors, the first generation of neoconservatives. But
the PNAC did something more: It adapted some first-generation neoconservatives' views to the postcommunist era.

From Schmitt's perspective, the different statements published by the
PNAC were elaborated internally, without the advice of any signer of the
documents. "All we did," asserted Schmitt, was to "write up our statements and send them out to people's offices and say sign if you want, don't
sign it if you don't and that's it. None of the people that sign any of these
things [were] in any fashion or form part of the organization."[127] It is difficult to agree with Schmitt's account. Politicians with the experience of
Dick Cheney, Donald Rumsfeld, or Paul Wolfowitz do not sign any "Statement of Principles," like that of the PNAC, without carefully consulting
with the authors of the text. Distinguished signers of such documents typically ensure that their views are included and clearly stated.

In contrast to this alleged situation vis-à-vis the PNAC documents, according to my research, the writing of the CPD's Statement of Principles
and the recruitment of that organization's members had four main phases.
First, a statement of principles was drafted. Second, the draft was circulated among organizers and discussed, and new drafts were generated.
Third, the organization's leadership personally solicited additional prominent supporters. Fourth, a letter was sent to those who would become the
associates of the organization. In all, eighteen months were spent setting
up the organization, several of which were dedicated to elaborating its
Statement of Principles.[128] Therefore, it is highly unlikely that the PNAC
was careless in the establishment of the organization, and that its State-

ment of Principles was written without incorporating the suggestions of some of its signatories.

New technologies have changed how neoconservative organizations operate. Letters and telephone conversations have been replaced by faxes and e-mails. According to Schmitt, the PNAC operates in the following way: When we see something important in the paper, "we write one or two pages and we fax out or e-mail that out to 2,000 of my closest friends, . . . which include reporters, congressional staff, other think tanks, and the like." Thus, the dissemination of neoconservative ideas to influential people and organizations is virtually instantaneous. After some time, Schmitt observed, the PNAC's views were making their way onto some newspapers' op-ed pages. "Our success," he said later, "was largely just getting our strategic vision as a part of the debate."[129]

The first generation of neoconservatives very rarely wrote op-eds or letters to the editor.[130] Their thoughts were instead published in books, academic journals, and magazines for the informed public. Their readers included scholars, the well informed, and politicians. Perhaps the only exception was Irving Kristol, who wrote an op-ed column in the *Wall Street Journal*. The members of the second generation of neoconservatives, however, did not have the academic credentials of their predecessors, and their goal was to influence the political circles of Washington with the aim of shaping public opinion. The Center for Security Policy (CSP), another neoconservative organization, expressed this position clearly (see below for more on the CSP). The CSP's constituency is "the U.S. security policy-making community, corresponding organizations in key foreign governments, the press, the global business and financial community and interested individuals in the public at large."[131]

The PNAC was closely connected with other significant neoconservative organizations, in particular AEI and the CSP. The PNAC's headquarters are located in the building that has housed AEI for many decades, and there has been a certain mobility of personnel between the two organizations. When Schmitt resigned as the PNAC's executive director, AEI immediately hired him. The two organizations have not only shared ideological affinities but also some neoconservative figures, such as Dick Cheney and Richard Perle, who have played a role in both institutions. A similar relationship can been seen between the PNAC and the CSP, which was founded and directed by Frank Gaffney.[132] Gaffney signed the PNAC's Statement of Principles, and James Woolsey, a former director of the CIA, and Senator Jon Kyl are honorary cochairmen of the National Security Advisory Council (NSAC, previously known as the CSP Board of Advisors), a group within the CSP. The NSAC has counted among its members other well-known neoconservatives and people sympathetic to the movement, including William Bennett, Devon Gaffney Cross (Frank Gaffney's sister, who for a long time helped to find financial support for the first generation of neoconservatives), Midge Decter, Stanley Ebner (who also participated in the CDM), Charles Fairbanks (former deputy assistant secretary of state and a politician close to Perle), Charles Horner (former associate director of the U.S. Information Agency and a researcher at the Manhattan Institute), Fred C. Iklé (undersecretary of defense and an important member of the CPD), Jeane Kirkpatrick, Charles Kupperman (former executive director of the General Advisory Committee on Arms Control and a member of the CPD), John Lehman (former secretary of the Navy and a member of both the CPD and CDM), Richard Perle, Edward Teller, and William R. Van Cleave (all of the CPD). As with the first generation of neoconservative organizations, the second generation includes individuals who share an ideological perspective and participate in more than one organization.

Among the signers of the PNAC's Statement of Principles, we find many neoconservative politicians or people sympathetic to neoconservative views that held high-level positions in the George W. Bush administration's first term, such as Elliott Abrams, Cheney, Iklé, Rumsfeld, and Paul Wolfowitz. Others—like Bennett, Decter, Gaffney, Kagan, Kristol (chairman), and Podhoretz—are neoconservative intellectuals or politicians. In the early 1980s, distinguished members of the CPD were hired by the Reagan administration to work in the defense policy area. Twenty years later, in a similar fashion, another neoconservative organization, the PNAC, played the same role, supplying the National Security Council and the Defense and State departments of the George W. Bush administration with employees and advisers.

Arguably, the primary architect of the relationship between Bush and the neoconservatives was Cheney, who was not only a vice presidential candidate but also the person in charge of building Bush's team. "Early in the process," asserted Donald F. Kettl, "Bush delegated to Dick Cheney the job of sorting through candidates for Cabinet positions. Cheney and his team interviewed leading candidates and made recommendations."[133] Cheney was familiar with neoconservatism long before he became Bush's running mate. He had a close working relationship with Wolfowitz, undersecretary of defense for policy when Cheney was secretary of defense for George H. W. Bush. During those years, Wolfowitz was intimately involved in the planning of the Gulf War and, together with Perle, criticized George H. W. Bush for not taking Baghdad. Cheney, like Donald Rumsfeld, also signed the Statement of Principles of the PNAC. Rumsfeld had a long-standing relationship with first-generation neoconservatives such as Dec-ter. He even used his connections to find financial support for Decter's CFW.

The web of connections among those neoconservative politicians who later had important positions in the defense and foreign policy teams of the George W. Bush administration's first term is complicated and long standing. Wolfowitz and Perle were old friends. Albert Wohlstetter and Paul Nitze introduced both to Washington circles. Wohlstetter, a professor of the University of Chicago who specializes in nuclear strategy and had been Wolfowitz's dissertation adviser, significantly influenced both. Perle had met Wohlstetter long before. Perle was a classmate of Wohlstetter's daughter, Joan, at Hollywood High School. Once Joan invited Perle to his home and introduced him to her father at the swimming pool. On that day, Wohl-stetter gave Perle a copy of his article "Delicate Balance of Terror," which had been published in *Foreign Affairs*. Wohlstetter became a mentor and friend of Perle. "Almost everyone who got to know Albert," stressed Richard Perle in 2002, "became his student formally or informally. . . . He was teaching all the time; . . . what he taught us to do was to think hard about difficult issues."[134]

When Cheney chose people for George W. Bush's defense and foreign policy teams, it was natural that he turned to neoconservative politicians, especially to the PNAC's founding members. Cheney was a key protag-onist in the appointment of Abrams, Richard I. Armitage, John Bolton, Rumsfeld, Wolfowitz, and many others. In this regard, Cheney played the same role that Richard Allen had played in 1980 with the first generation of neoconservatives: Both were the political entrepreneurs, highly sensible to the role of ideas that linked neoconservatives with presidential candidates. Both were, as John W. Kingdon said more than twenty years ago, "people willing to invest their resources in return for future policies they favor."[135]

## *The Center for Security Policy*

The Center for Security Policy is the second major organization of the current neoconservative movement. Created by Frank Gaffney in 1988, the CSP is a think tank dedicated to the analysis of foreign and defense policy. Its mission, clearly asserted in several of its documents, is "the promotion of international peace through American strength," a statement quite similar to the CPD's principles. The CSP openly declares that it is "loosely modeled" on the CPD, and several members of its National Security Advisory Council worked in the George W. Bush administration. Cheney is a member of the CSP's Board of Advisors, and in 1998 former secretary of defense Rumsfeld received its Keeper of the Flame Award, its highest form of recognition.

In accord with the times, the CSP concentrates its work on the analysis of "Islamic extremism, the war on terror, homeland security, space and missile defense, Asian and hemispheric security issues, . . . and unconventional warfare with emphasis on political and information warfare and the 'war of ideas.'"[136] Gaffney started his professional career working, like Perle, on the staff of the former senator from Washington and leader of the CDM, Henry "Scoop" Jackson. There Gaffney became familiar with missile defense, a subject that in the early 1990s was a quite relevant policy issue. It was natural that when Gaffney established his own think tank, he put special emphasis on this topic. Furthermore, according to William Hartung, the list of CSP associates looks like the "Star Wars Hall of Fame."[137]

For a long time, neoconservative organizations like the CPD carefully avoided any association with military industries. Several CPD documents state quite clearly that the organization would not accept donations from military-related corporations. The CSP is the first neoconservative organization to openly show its nexus with military industries. For instance, its Board of Directors includes Charles M. Kupperman, vice president for strategic integration and missile defense systems of the Boeing Company. Likewise, Amoretta M. Hoeber, who has worked as a consultant for several major defense companies (including DynCorp, Rockwell Defense, and Jaycor), is member of the National Security Advisory Council.

As is the case with most organizations of the second neoconservative movement, the CSP does not aspire to be an academic institution but rather a political institution dedicated to influencing the decisionmaking process. According to Gaffney, "The Center specializes in the rapid preparation and real-time dissemination of information, analyses, and policy recommendations via e-mail distribution; computerized fax; its exciting, redesigned

Web site; published articles, and the electronic media. The principal audience for such materials is the U.S. security policy community (the executive and legislative branches, the armed forces and appropriate independent agencies)."[138]

The CSP also has, as one of its missions, the mobilization of the U.S. population in support of different political causes. In this regard, the CSP has actively worked to increase the number of constituents that will be willing to support the war on terror and the war in Iraq. To achieve this goal, the CSP has dedicated significant time to making the population aware of the war on terrorism. Gaffney's campaign is aimed at generating popular support for two main issues: supporting the ongoing war in Iraq, and creating a "national-security-minded constituency that will be needed to sustain the large Pentagon and Homeland Security expenditures made necessary by the war on terror."[139] In other words, the CSP is a political organization dedicated to the dissemination of a particular conservative perspective rather than generating scholarship aimed at comprehending, from a conservative point of view, current international affairs.

In this regard, there is a very interesting difference between the think tanks of the first and second generations of neoconservatives. Among the more than one hundred think tanks that operate in the Washington metropolitan area, there are small and large entities; conservative, liberal, and radical ones; and academic-oriented and policy-oriented bodies. As I have pointed out previously in this chapter, during the late 1970s and early 1980s, AEI was the main neoconservative think tank. Since its founding, AEI has been perceived as an academic think tank—although, throughout the years, it has become slightly more policy oriented—the conservative counterpart of the Brookings Institution. AEI's form of organization, main publications (most, but not all), and form of operation resemble those of Brookings rather than other policy-oriented think thanks. No doubt, AEI is an organization that has had and still has a significant impact on different policy issues. Part of its organizational structure is dedicated to the diffusion of ideas. Although the second-generation neoconservative movement maintains strong ties to AEI and it remains a central component of the current movement, the two think tanks created by the second generation of neoconservatives (the PNAC and CSP) are policy-oriented organizations, resembling the Heritage Foundation more than AEI.

## The Weekly Standard

As with the first generation of neoconservatism, organizations continue to play a major role in the dissemination of neoconservative ideas. Today, the PNAC is the most important neoconservative think tank in developing foreign policy for the postcommunist era. The perspectives of the second generation of neoconservatives have not, however, only been disseminated through its think tanks, articles on op-ed pages, and books authored by adherents; they have also been presented to a broader public in the magazine *The Weekly Standard*. Neoconservatives also published in other neoconservative journals such as *Commentary*. (In 2007, John Podhoretz, son of Norman Podhoretz and Midge Decter, became the editor of *Commentary*, providing a continuity to the journal. *Commentary* continues to be a neoconservative journal for the second generation.)

There is a famous old joke credited to Irving Kristol: "If you want to do something, start a magazine."[140] Faithful to family tradition, Irving's son William, together with John Podhoretz and Fred Barnes, established *The Weekly Standard*. The magazine's first issue hit the newsstands in September 1995—a propitious moment. Under the leadership of Newt Gingrich, the Republican Party had mobilized around the Contract with America to resuscitate the Republicans' role in the House of Representatives after forty years of Democratic dominance. "It was a new moment for Republicans," asserted William Kristol in September 2005; "they need constructive criticism, they need defense sometimes, and we thought it was a good time to start a magazine."[141] In his view, the neoconservative movement needed a weekly, and not another journal that would compete with *Commentary* or *The Public Interest*.[142] In the words of Jeane Kirkpatrick, *The Weekly Standard* "is a good magazine, a little more journalistic, . . . a little more popular and a little more newsy on the neocon side. . . . Bill Kristol and Fred Berns did a good job."[143]

The members of the first generation of neoconservatives, especially Irving Kristol, were great believers in the power of print. The second generation shares this perspective. For both generations of the neoconservative movement, magazines and journals have played a central role in the dissemination of ideas. In the words of William Kristol, *The Weekly Standard* has a "certain point of view, a certain persuasion, as my father would have said." But the magazine has also played another important role; it has been the gathering place of neoconservative thinkers. "If you look at the history of these kind of intellectual/political movements," Kristol argued, "they need a kind of focus—an institution, a magazine, a think tank, or all of the above. . . . So I think maybe in this respect, *The Weekly Standard* was a kind of magnet. Look at the people who came to *The Weekly Standard.* I didn't know Max Boot much, and Max Boot started to write more for us because he agreed with us. . . . Having one place, one publication helped build a group."[144]

According to William Kristol, *The Standard* was never conceived to be a neoconservative magazine. "I don't think," he argued, that "you could find the world 'neoconservative' anywhere in the founding documents or issues of *The Weekly Standard.* . . . We [never] intended to be at all self-consciously neoconservatives."[145] However, the magazine soon became identified with neoconservative thought. The reason: William Kristol and John Podhoretz were the sons of two distinguished neoconservatives of the first generation, Irving Kristol and Norman Podhoretz, who had in their own time edited major neoconservative journals—*Commentary*, *The Public Interest*, and *The National Interest*. William Kristol and John Podhoretz were familiar with this type of activity, but they needed someone with significant experience editing a magazine. Fred Barnes, who had spent ten years as an editor of *The New Republic*, became the ideal collaborator.

Starting a periodical is typically a complicated task, especially because it is difficult to find financial support for such an expensive enterprise. In the case of *The Standard*, the story was different. Rupert Murdoch, the Australian mass communications magnate, contributed $3 million to launch the magazine.[146] Though the magazine was openly established as a conservative journal, Kristol was fully aware of the need to obtain credibility across the board. In May 1995, he asserted, "If we don't occasionally upset conservatives, we won't be doing a good job."[147] In its fifteen years of existence, *The Standard* has become well known for being a controversial magazine and even for criticizing conservative figures like President George W. Bush, Colin Powell, and Donald Rumsfeld. It has also published disagreements among neoconservatives, such as the divergent opinions of John Podhoretz and Bill Kristol regarding Rumsfeld's performance as secretary of defense.

For neoconservatives of both generations, the large circulation of their magazines has never been a priority. According to Midge Decter, "There is no correlation between the size of a magazine's circulation and its influence."[148] In 2001, the circulation of *The Weekly Standard* was around 65,000,[149] a number far away from the distribution of other weeklies such as *Time*, with about 4 million, or *Newsweek*, with 3 million.[150]

Since the beginning, the *Standard* has been conceived as a magazine targeting Washington's circles of power. Barnes recalled that while he was at *The New Republic*, "Reagan's White House in the beginning and then the Bush's White House couldn't wait to get *The New Republic* magazine every week." In his view, what was lacking was a "weekly conservative view from Washington on politics and policy."[151] Likewise, the magazine was designed to be provocative and humorous. The idea of publishing caricatures of its contributors was indeed innovative. By the same token, its last pages are fundamentally satirical, often publishing fake memorandums. "It's surprising," asserts Kristol, "how parody-able, if that's the word—how easy it is to make fun of so much of America, as it is the case."[152]

Even before the publication of its first issue, several periodicals reported the coming appearance of the *Standard*.[153] Later on, when George W. Bush arrived in the White House, and especially after September 11, some observers highlighted the political relevance of the magazine. "The neoconservative *[The] Weekly Standard*, is reportedly required reading for Vice-President Dick Cheney's aides."[154] In a similar vein, Scott Sherman wrote in the pages of *The Nation* that "Dick Cheney does send over someone to pick up thirty copies of the magazine *[The Standard]* every Monday. . . . And *The Washington Post* has reported that Kristol meets regularly with Karl Rove and Condoleezza Rice."[155]

However, Kristol downplayed his influence over the Bush administration. In 2004, he asserted that with the exception of Wolfowitz, nobody in the administration shared his viewpoints. According to Kristol, to be influential, you have to persuade the people at the top tier. Before September 11, Bush, Cheney, Rumsfeld, Rice, and Powell did not share his views. But after the collapse of the Twin Towers, "Bush and Condi, I think, really came to this kind of view." Kristol was close to Rice, with whom he got together on a regular basis. In his own words, "I see Condi every three or four months, very casual. What's on your mind? Tell me what things we are doing wrong? I would say not a detailed consultation. . . . I know other people in the White House better actually from my political days, speech writers, people on the political side."[156] Despite his denial, it seems apparent that Kristol and his magazine shaped American foreign affairs during the Bush administration's first term.

*The Standard*'s influence became evident after September 11, 2001. The weekly was a longtime advocate for the removal of Saddam Hussein from power. In 1997, the same year as the PNAC's founding, *The Standard* published an issue under the title "Saddam Must Go." In an article by

Paul Wolfowitz and Zalmay Khalilzad, under the title "Overthrow Him," these authors maintained that the United States must work to remove Hussein from power.[157] Later on, Wolfowitz and Khalilzad became important members of the Bush administration, with the political power to introduce their ideas to President Bush and his closest associates.

The terrorist attacks on September 11 became windows of opportunity for neoconservatives. In its October 1, 2001, issue the magazine's cover featured the word "WANTED" and pictures of Saddam Hussein and Osama bin Laden. The accompanying article hypothesized that Hussein and bin Laden could have worked together in the terrorist attacks. Starting in the fall of 2001, *The Standard* and other neoconservative publications strongly promoted the idea of invading Iraq. Neoconservative ideas became a central point of reference for the George W. Bush administration. Furthermore, significant aspects of neoconservatives' views were implemented during the Bush administration's first term. In many ways, neoconservative organizations were the stepping-stones that catapulted neoconservative figures and ideas into American circles of power.

# 4

# Ideas, Institutions, and Interests: The Influence of Neoconservatism on Reagan's Human Rights Policy

Ronald Reagan's ascent to the White House marked an important shift in America's human rights policy. Jimmy Carter, Reagan's predecessor, was politically committed to human rights and assigned them a central role in the formation of U.S. foreign policy. He promoted a policy grounded in a congressional mandate and based on moral considerations. For Carter, the United States' commitment to human rights was rooted in unalterable American moral values. In contrast, Reagan conceived of human rights as a part of his global geopolitical strategy and as a central component of his struggle against the Soviet Union and international communism. Neoconservatives, as I discuss in this chapter, were the main intellectual architects of this policy. Their ideas, combined with the fundamental characteristics of the institutions involved—primarily Congress and the State Department—and the special interests behind this policy, were essential to the substantial shift in the place of human rights in foreign affairs.

I contend that neoconservative ideas, American political institutions, and interest groups worked together in the conception, development, and implementation of Reagan's foreign policy on human rights. The particular historical context of the 1980s, the mobilization of certain economic interests, and the concrete traits of some institutions facilitated the influence of neoconservative ideas. I have divided this argument into three sections. First, I present the origins and development of neoconservative ideas on human rights and explore how these ideas were expressed by different neoconservative organizations. I examine how a particular concept evolved out of "civil society," made its way into the American government, and was subsequently integrated into the government's policymaking apparatus. Second, I look at the particularities of the U.S. Congress and the State

Department from the late 1960s to the early 1980s, to determine to what extent these characteristics opened "windows of opportunity" for neoconservative ideas. Finally, I analyze the links between political and economic interests and neoconservative ideas.

## Neoconservative Ideas on Human Rights

A defining characteristic of neoconservative thought on human rights is its differentiation of totalitarianism from authoritarianism. Hannah Arendt developed this distinction in her book *On the Origins of Totalitarianism*, published in 1951. In the 1970s, neoconservatives who were familiar with her work—and that of other thinkers on totalitarianism—and had been deeply affected by the postwar fear of fascism and communism that dominated the United States, reworked her basic argument and applied it to the field of foreign policy.

In 1979, Jeane Kirkpatrick published "Dictatorships and Double Standards" in the neoconservative journal *Commentary*. In this essay, she presented a general critique of President Jimmy Carter's foreign policy and asserts that in formulating that policy he had overlooked the centrality of the East/West conflict. She writes, "Although there is no instance of a revolutionary 'socialist' or Communist society being democratized, right-wing autocracies do sometimes evolve into democracy. . . . Traditional authoritarian governments are less repressive than revolutionary autocracies, they are more susceptible to liberalization and they are more compatible with U.S. interests."[1] Consequently, she surmises, the United States must give preferential treatment to authoritarian allies over communist adversaries. According to the Coalition for a Democratic Majority (CDM) leader Penn Kemble, Kirkpatrick was writing out of a leftist tradition that Arendt had initiated almost thirty years earlier.

Kirkpatrick's *Commentary* essay had a significant impact on both her professional career and American politics, especially Reagan's presidential campaign and his first four years in office. "This article changed my life," she asserted in 1998. "I have never received so many letters from all over the world, especially from the Soviet Union."[2] Reagan read the article and was very impressed with her ideas. Richard Allen, Reagan's first national security adviser, and his associate since his time as governor of California, brought the article to his attention. "I was in an airplane reading *Commentary*, and I read this remarkable article and marked it up for Reagan," Allen remembers, "It happened to be that Reagan was in Washington and was going back to California, and I said, 'Read this article on the way.' When he got to Los Angeles, he called me and said, 'I read this article you gave me; who is this guy Jeane Kirkpatrick?' and I said, 'Well, it's not a guy, it's a woman, and I think you ought to meet with her.' 'Yes, I would be happy to do it.' Then Reagan wrote her a letter."[3] Allen arranged a meeting between Reagan and Kirkpatrick in Washington. She began working on Reagan's campaign and became not only the American ambassador to the United Nations but also a very influential figure in the Reagan administration's first term.[4] Her thesis thus influenced American public policy because of, first, the historical context of the late 1970s; second, the personal experiences of neoconservatives and their analysis of this topic; and third, the dissemination of totalitarian ideas within neoconservative institutions. In the final analysis, Kirkpatrick developed, systematized, and published ideas previously discussed in neoconservative circles at the right moment.

The late 1970s had been difficult for the United States. The Carter administration faced serious economic problems, including inflation, a decline in real income, the failure of the nation's energy policy, and considerable debt. In international affairs, the revolutions in Iran and Nicaragua meant the loss of two traditional friends and allies in the Middle East and Central America. The Soviet intervention in Afghanistan and the hostage crisis in Iran demonstrated the decline of the United States' power abroad. The United States' international position was a serious concern for neoconservatives. "I was watching U.S. foreign policy," asserted Kirkpatrick, "and I thought Carter's foreign policy was a disaster."[5]

This political context proved fertile ground for political discourse, such as that contained in Kirkpatrick's essay, promising the rehabilitation of the American economy and the reestablishment of its international power. Kirkpatrick's thesis provided a rationale for Reagan's attack on Carter's foreign policy. As Allan Gerson noted in his study of Kirkpatrick's career at the United Nations, her essay supplied "exactly what Ronald Reagan was looking for in order to hold the Carter administration responsible for replacing an authoritarian regime in Nicaragua (that of Sebastian [Anastasio] Somoza) with the totalitarian rule of the Ortega brothers."[6]

Reagan's adoption of Kirkpatrick's thesis represented the culmination of an idea's journey from civil society to the American government. Although it is difficult to describe this journey systematically, I identify four basic phases: (1) theoretical knowledge and the personal experiences of neoconservatives, (2) discussion in neoconservative organizations, (3) diffusion of the idea within governmental institutions, and (4) persuasion of the Republican candidate.

Neoconservatives had been aware of the distinction between authoritarianism and totalitarianism since the 1950s. They were deeply immersed in Cold War politics and in the postwar political culture that rejected fascism and communism. The political sensitivity of that time is reflected in the historian Arthur Schlesinger's book *The Vital Center*, in which he condemned totalitarianism from both the right and the left.[7] Neoconservatives loathed Stalinism, and many, as Jews, had been especially touched by the Holocaust. According to Daniel Bell, "Stalinism and the Holocaust had been 'traumatic' experiences that affected his generation."[8] Both Bell and Kristol were involved in the American Committee for Cultural Freedom, an expression of centrist politics in the postwar era. It was during this period that neoconservatives initiated their critique of both radical-right and radical-left movements. In *The New American Right*,[9] published in 1955, these scholars began using the concept of extremism to defend the unique character of American liberalism.

As part of the New York intellectual community, neoconservatives were acquainted with Arendt and her work. As a contributing editor at *Commentary*, she worked with Irving Kristol, Daniel Bell, and Nathan Glazer. Kristol considered her text *On Revolution* a "very profound book, . . . to which I am much indebted."[10] Norman Podhoretz, in turn, recognized that he was "overly influenced by Hannah Arendt and other theorists of totalitarianism."[11] In this regard, Podhoretz recalled the significant impact that *The Origins of Totalitarianism* had on him. "It would be impossible to overstate," he wrote, "the effect this book had on me. Reading it threw me into so fevered a condition of intellectual exhilaration that I had to keep putting it down every few pages in order to regain the composure to go on."[12] As a college student, Kirkpatrick was likewise persuaded by Arendt's arguments and by a whole body of literature on totalitarianism. "One of my principal teachers," she remembered in a conversation with me, "was Franz Neumann. He was a social democrat, a left social democrat and very much involved in the Frankfurt group, with that circle of professors. I think that I first read her [Arendt] with him and in relation with him. . . . I was interested in Hannah Arendt as an undergraduate, I read *The Origins of Totalitarianism* as soon as the book appeared.[13] At the apex of the Cold War, Arendt's 'thesis on totalitarianism' served as a key foundation for the emerging liberal anticommunist ideology of the postwar years."[14]

Other neoconservatives such as Michael Novak noted that the difference between authoritarianism and totalitarianism was the "most important distinction of the twentieth century, and it was best formulated by Hannah Arendt."[15] In April 1978, Novak, a member of the CDM, used Kirkpatrick's arguments to criticize Carter's policy on human rights. Novak asserted that Carter's administration had misjudged when it declared that "nations erred against human rights more or less equally." "No distinction was made between totalitarian nations and authoritarian nations," writes Novak. "There are many cases of authoritarian nations that have become democratic. There are no cases of totalitarian nations that have become democratic."[16]

In the 1970s, the distinction between authoritarianism and totalitarianism was widely discussed within neoconservative organizations. Kirkpatrick's formulation impressed both the Committee on the Present Danger (CPD) and the CDM, whose members had used a variant of this framework in their analysis of human rights policy in the United States. Their attention to these ideas preceded the publication of Kirkpatrick's article, revealing a previous popularization of this framework within neoconservative organizations.[17] On August 21, 1977, the CDM's executive director, Joshua Muravchik, sent a memorandum to the CDM's Executive Committee in which he asserted that members of the organization had "been discussing, formally and informally, ideas about CDM's program." In such discussions, Penn Kemble had accepted the organization's invitation to write a proposal on "how the human rights issue would be incorporated as the principal focus of our activity."[18]

In his memo, Kemble argued that it was necessary for the CDM to formulate a powerful conceptual framework like containment or détente. He suggested that the foundation for such a conception could be found in several articles published by Daniel Patrick Moynihan in *Commentary*, in which the senator affirmed that "human rights [is] a political component of American foreign policy, not an humanitarian program." Kemble recommended writing a manifesto emphasizing that "communist nations [are] the chief violators of human rights in the world," and encouraging the development of specific "proposals to the Executive or Congress for implementing a political and ideological campaign against the totalitarian threat to human rights."[19]

Even at this early moment, Kemble's proposal had some of the same themes that could be found in Kirkpatrick's essay "Dictatorships and Double Standards" two years later. First, human rights was understood as a primary component of the general struggle against communism and, as such, was an important factor in the United States's hostility toward the Soviet Union. Second, the proposal integrated the topic into a broader analysis of U.S. foreign policy by making the issue of human rights central to foreign affairs. Finally, Kemble connected this framework to the current situation by using the term "totalitarianism" to describe present-day communism.

In the course of formulating this manifesto, the CDM consulted Walter Laqueur, Norman Podhoretz, Elmo R. Zumwalt Jr., Midge Decter, Tom Kahn, Max Kampelman, Michael Ledeen, Richard Perle, John R. Richardson (Freedom House), and the office of the House of Representatives' majority leader, Jim Wright. The document highlighted the advantages of framing human rights as an issue capable of influencing international affairs. From the CDM's perspective, the topic was morally unquestionable and therefore could help launch both an ideological assault on perceived enemies of the United States and restore popular support for American foreign policy at home and abroad. After criticizing the single standard of the Carter human rights policy, the CDM considered it necessary to move beyond détente and containment and to add a "political and ideological strategy, built on the principles of human rights," to the country's political and economic strategy.[20]

Finally, the CDM offered an argument that paralleled the one presented by Kirkpatrick. "We cannot overlook," asserted the Executive Committee, "the fact that no society which has undergone totalitarianization under communist rule has ever succeeded in evolving beyond or breaking out of the totalitarian mold, while societies ruled by right-wing authoritarian or military governments do so frequently."[21] As a member of the CDM, it was highly unlikely that Kirkpatrick was unaware of the debate on human rights within the organization or the existence of this document. In 1977, the framework she would make popular was already circulating within the CDM. She needed only to refine it and apply it to the U.S. international crisis and the foreign policy failures of the Carter administration. Her "impartial," academic analysis of the concept was considered the ideal way to launch these ideas.

Something similar happened within the CPD. On May 18, 1978, the CPD distributed a draft written by Robert Conquest to its special Subcommittee on Human Rights. In this document, Conquest placed human rights at the core of the American struggle against the Soviet Union. He distinguished "between injustices occurring sporadically and unsystematically, and states whose entire principle of rule [was] founded on the denial of human rights." The Soviet Union fell into the second category and, according to Conquest, should be considered the main threat to the United States "and to human rights as a whole." Like the CDM and Kirkpatrick, Conquest argued that "the extreme denials of human rights in fact take place far less in reactionary or military dictatorships than under radical totalitarian regimes such as Hitler's and Stalin's, whose raison d'être included not merely the suppression of political enemies but the annihilation of whole races or social classes."[22]

Thus, by the mid-1970s, neoconservative organizations were working to incorporate human rights into their global strategy against the Soviet Union. Arendt's framework had become a useful rhetorical and political tool that could be used to defend the supremacy of American values over those of communist countries on "moral grounds." The dissemination of neoconservative ideas about human rights was essential in the promotion of these concepts within the political community.

The CDM's position paper was widely distributed within the U.S. Congress, because the CDM's allies in Congress worked hard to ensure that legislators heard these ideas. Dick Olson, special assistant to Majority Leader Wright, commented extensively on Kemble's proposal, which he admired.[23] On April 3, 1978, Kemble sent a letter to Senator Moynihan requesting his comments on the draft and inviting him to participate in a press conference with Senator Henry Jackson, during which the document would be officially presented to the media.[24] Later, these ideas would reach the White House. At the beginning of 1980, when the United States was facing difficult foreign policy issues, President Carter requested the assistance of one of his most strident critics, the CDM. Among other things, Carter was looking for advice on how to improve his relations with Congress, increase defense expenditures, promote human rights, and restore public confidence in the Central Intelligence Agency.[25] Before the official meeting with Carter, the CDM sent a letter to the president. In it, the organization praised Carter's foreign policy measures after the "brutal Soviet seizure of Afghanistan." In addition, it criticized the expansionist policy of the Soviet Union and asserted that the USSR must be defeated in "ideological warfare." To achieve this goal, the CDM considered it necessary to activate a new foreign policy, complete with a new strategy and a new team.

The CDM recommended the reformulation of the International Communications Agency to respond to Soviet propaganda and suggested an active policy on human rights based on the distinction developed by Kirkpatrick. "No Communist government," claimed the organization, "has ever been replaced by a liberal regime, while the number of right-wing authoritarian governments has steadily declined. No right-wing government presents a serious military or political threat to the democratic government. In fact, some right-wing governments, however distasteful, may at certain times provide the only available obstacle to the advance of Soviet power." The organization also argued that all these initiatives must be "backed by a long-term effort to rebuild America's military superiority."[26]

Using policy-speak rather than the academic-journalistic language of Kirkpatrick, the CDM suggested a formula to rebuild American foreign policy. In some respects, Carter followed the advice of the CDM, moving American foreign policy to the right during his last year as president. But his political performance was so questioned and the political and economic difficulties of the period were so intense that Reagan easily defeated him in the 1980 election. By that time, neoconservative ideas on human rights could be found in the media and were circulating in both political parties, Congress, and the White House. The political arena was primed for the convergence of ideas and politicians. Thirty years after it began its journey from civil society in the early 1950s, a political concept had made its way into governmental circles of power.

The incorporation of this distinction—separating totalitarianism from authoritarianism—into American foreign policy represented a substantial change in the U.S. approach to human rights in international affairs. However, the exposure of decisionmakers and political elites to these ideas would not have been possible without institutions that maximized the influence of neoconservative ideas. In the next section, I study the role of Congress and the State Department in the advancement of neoconservative ideas on human rights.

## Congress and the State Department in the Advance of Neoconservative Ideas on Human Rights

To understand the influence of neoconservatism on U.S. foreign policy on human rights, it is necessary to study the two political institutions involved in the decisionmaking process: Congress and the State Department. Institutions matter, because their forms of organization and structures can facilitate or block the circulation of certain ideas in government circles. Beginning in the late 1960s, Congress was characterized by what I will call "unchallenged revitalization." During this period, the legislature began to take an active role in the decisionmaking process in foreign policy, without seriously impugning the primacy of the executive branch. The State Department was similarly characterized by "unchallenged revitalization" and a certain degree of flexibility, which likewise facilitated the introduction of neoconservative ideas to decisionmakers.

## Congress

The historical context of the nonpartisan realignment in the late 1960s coincided with the reemergence of Congress as a central force in the construction and implementation of American foreign policy.[27] As a result of the consolidation of the "imperial presidency" in the hands of Richard Nixon, the U.S. failures in the Vietnam War, and the association of the United States with the repressive governments of South Vietnam and Chile, Congress had become very concerned with the nation's activities abroad.

In 1973, the House Subcommittee on International Organizations and Movements (later renamed the Subcommittee on Human Rights and Humanitarian Affairs), presided over by Donald M. Fraser, organized a series of hearings on the relationship between human rights and foreign policy. At the end of these hearings, Congress decided to construct human rights–related foreign policy around two basic principles: "the promotion of human rights abroad and the dissociation of the United States from repressive regimes."[28] Toward this end, Congress made several decisions restricting military, economic, and financial assistance to open violators of human rights. These measures had two shortcomings, which neoconservatives used to advance their political views. First, the laws typically permitted the president to exert significant influence on the application of the legislation, and thus they left open the possibility that the chief executive would conduct policy in accord with *his* political perspective. Second, the laws established a legal framework to encourage certain political and strategic policies but not necessarily one that would promote human rights.

The legislation's limitations help explain why, under the same legal constraints, Carter's and Reagan's policies on human rights differed substantially. Among other changes, Congress revised Section 502B of the Foreign Assistance Act of 1961, which made security assistance (military aid and arms sales) to any country engaged in violations of human rights conditional upon the president's certifying in writing to Congress the existence of extraordinary circumstances warranting the provision of such assistance. This provision explicitly linked U.S. security assistance to human rights. Under this law, Congress has the right to adopt a "joint resolution terminating, restricting, or continuing security assistance for such country." In the eyes of some, this legislation created a deep, inherent conflict between the "pursuit of morality and the pursuit of national security."[29]

Although Congress had substantial control over this provision, the president still possessed a broad mandate to oversee American foreign policy. Examples from both the Carter and Reagan administrations illustrate this point. The Carter administration, which sometimes even ignored the law, never used the category of "gross violator" or certification under the clause of extraordinary circumstances. For example, Carter advocated for military assistance to El Salvador in 1980, even though violations of human rights were evident in that country. Congress did not react to Carter's initiative, suggesting that when there is a perception of a possible threat to U.S. national security, the legislature is reluctant to contradict presidential decisions. Reagan increased security assistance to anticommunist regimes without any consideration of their human rights records. Congress never challenged Reagan under the provision of Section 502B.

National security remained at the core of neoconservative political thought, despite interest in human rights. According to neoconservatives, the United States had to respond to the Soviet threat, and thus reinforce its national security. Thus, there was no inconsistency between American national security interests and making a distinction between authoritarian and totalitarian regimes. Neoconservatives argued that totalitarian regimes were structurally organized to repress, and, therefore, they represented a permanent menace to the interests and values of the United States. The nature of authoritarian governments, conversely, was basically transitory. Because, according to neoconservatives, these regimes did sometimes evolve into democracies, their ephemeral character made them more desirable as allies of the United States. This view not only established the moral superiority of pro-Western, nondemocratic regimes over their communist counterparts but was also an argument against Soviet expansionism.

According to neoconservatives, this was a realistic human rights policy. William Clark, assistant for national security affairs to President Reagan, expressed the neoconservative position clearly when he argued that the "administration believes that a strong America—an America whose national security is assured—is good for personal liberties throughout the world,"[30] a statement in tune with the views of the second generation of neoconservatives. Similarly, the CDM expressed its support for the increase in military spending to safeguard American national security and to meet its "responsibility to defend the democratic idea worldwide."[31] The Kirkpatrick thesis was, as David Forsythe writes, "Reagan policy with regard to Section 502B. . . . No security assistance was cut, much less terminated, by the Reagan administration for human rights reasons during the 1981–1984 period. . . . Security assistance was up some 300 percent by 1984, compared to 1980."[32] What is more, a struggle within the State Department limited the law's implementation. With the creation of the Bureau of Human Rights and Humanitarian Affairs within the State Department (which I analyze in detail later in the chapter), a dispute developed between Foreign Service officials and the new human rights office. This conflict was the result of two different visions of American activities abroad. The Foreign Service leaned toward maintaining friendly relations with other governments, while the bureau understood its charge to be the implementation of Section 502B.[33]

Through the so-called Harkin Amendment, Congress also tied development assistance to respect for human rights. The law limited economic help to repressive governments "unless such assistance will directly benefit the needy people in such a country."[34] Again, the last clause rejected the elimination of the president's power in the conduct of American foreign policy on this topic and provided a legal mechanism to support authoritarian regimes that were violating human rights. Accordingly, Reagan refused to suspend economic aid to anticommunist regimes in the name of human rights.

With the International Financial Assistance Act of 1977, Congress asked the Office of the Executive—that is, the president—to use its voice and vote in international financial institutions to oppose countries that violate human rights. During the Reagan administration, the United States supported right-wing regimes and opposed left-wing adversaries through multilateral financial institutions. This becomes evident when we contrast the behavior of the Carter and Reagan administrations. From 1977 to 1980, the Democratic administration abstained or voted 104 times against loans proposed by international financial institutions because of human rights considerations. In a similar period of four years, from 1981 to 1984, the Reagan administration voted against such proposals a mere 23 times.[35]

Another congressional measure that served neoconservative interests was the Jackson-Vanik Amendment.[36] In the context of a general trade agreement between the United States and the Soviet Union, the neoconservative leader of the CDM, Henry Jackson, together with Representative Charles Vanik, introduced an initiative to adjust Section 402 of the 1974 Trade Act. This legislation forbade the granting of most-favored-nation status to nonmarket economies that unreasonably restricted the right of immigration. The measure had a significant impact on Jackson's political career and reflected important ideological components of neoconservatism. For Jackson and the CDM, the amendment was an attempt to mobilize their core constituencies for Jackson's presidential campaign. They sought to obtain the support of the Jewish community and the labor movement by showing the pro–human rights, pro-Jewish, and anticommunist leanings of neoconservatism.

Finally, in 1976, Congress established of the Bureau of Human Rights and Humanitarian Affairs in the State Department. Congress designated a coordinator with the rank of assistant secretary, who was responsible for preparing reports about human rights conditions in countries receiving American aid and making recommendations to the Agency for International Development on continuing assistance, among other duties. The creation of this office within the executive branch and its organizational structure facilitated the establishment of Reagan's policy on human rights based on neoconservative principles.

## The Department of State and the Human Rights Bureau

Fragmentation has been one of the main characteristics of the State Department since World War II. This fragmentation is evident in both the internal conflicts among different offices within the State Department and the participation of agencies originally created to address domestic problems in designing foreign policy. The bureaucratic structure created to combat drug trafficking clearly illustrates this point. "At least 15 Federal agencies," the Senate Judiciary Committee declared at the end of the Reagan administration's first term in 1984, "play a role in the regulation of commerce of dangerous drugs. . . . These agencies are located in six different departments. Under such circumstances, it is inevitable that divergences as to priorities will arise and that there will be conflicting interpretations of national policy."[37]

The Department of State differs from most departments and agencies in the executive branch. Perhaps more than any other Cabinet-level agency, it is closely tied to the chief executive. Since the establishment of the Constitution, the secretary of state has been held responsible for formulating and conducting American foreign policy under the oversight of the president. This arrangement gives the president more influence in foreign affairs than other policy areas. Unlike other departments, the State Department is exempt from notifying Congress about its activities. What is more, under the doctrine of executive privilege, the State Department has the right to refuse congressional requests for information if the president considers that the release of facts might affect American national security.[38]

During the 1980s, academics and politicians criticized the State Department on four main counts. First, many observed that the department was highly resistant to change or innovations. Second, the technical competence of its staff was considered inferior to that of new and more specialized agencies. Third, its ideological biases seemed to distort its perspective and policy recommendations. Finally, it was critiqued for being in favor of the status quo.[39] These criticisms conveyed the image of a highly fragmented, rigid institution with ideological biases and structural links to the chief executive. It was these very characteristics that enabled neoconservative ideas to influence the process of making foreign policy in the State Department. In the 1980s, the department's ideological emphasis on anticommunism mirrored Reagan's own anticommunism. This ideological coincidence between the president and the State Department led to a consistent American foreign affairs stance on human rights. The State Department did not have to change to support Reagan's views.

The strategic use of institutions that favor neoconservative interests was exemplified when the State Department's Bureau of Human Rights—which had been founded during the Gerald Ford administration—provoked an intra-agency struggle during the Carter administration that involved Foreign Service officials and the bureau's personnel. Foreign Service officials typically pursue the promotion of good and harmonious relations with other countries. Economic aid or military assistance are seen by the Foreign Service as a means of achieving cordial relationships with foreign nations. Sometimes, career bureaucrats identify more with the interests of other states rather than with the national interests of the United States. They see foreign nations as "clients."[40] The Bureau of Human Rights, in contrast, is committed to promoting and defending American human rights policy. Its duties sometimes clash with the political behavior of other nations. The bureau has the right to participate in all decisions on security assistance and has its own sources of information. In addition, the bureau's staff is often composed of "outsiders" with no foreign affairs experience. The relative autonomy of this bureau in relation to other divisions in the State Department is an "invitation to struggle." The "Humanitarian Affairs Bureau," asserted Howard Warshawsky, was "seen by some within the State Department to be headed and staffed by 'do-gooders' who probably had little real understanding of foreign policy."[41]

These intra-agency conflicts vis-à-vis the Human Rights Bureau were greater during the Carter administration than during the Reagan years, perhaps because of the individuals each president assigned to the bureau and the way they understood its function. Carter appointed Patricia Derrian, a southern civil rights advocate with a limited background in foreign affairs and no experience in Washington, to head the bureau. She staffed it with people who had been active in human rights advocacy but were seen by the Foreign Service personnel as "outsiders." In a series of interviews with members of the Foreign Service, Edwin S. Maynard learned that some State Department personnel found Assistant Secretary Derrian and Senior Deputy Assistant Secretary Mark Schneider "to be uncompromising and confrontational."[42] Derrian believed that one of the main functions of the bureau was to challenge other bureaus and departments (Defense, Commerce, and Treasury) to give more attention to human rights. Her perspective on human rights created several conflicts with the regional bureaus in the State Department. For example, the relationship between Derrian and the assistant secretary for East Asian affairs, Richard Holbrooke, was overtly hostile, and her perspective on human rights in Argentina differed from that of the Bureau of American Regional Affairs. Overall, there was little cooperation between the Human Rights Bureau and the regional bureaus.[43]

However, the role that the Human Rights Bureau played in the Reagan administration minimized intra-agency conflict. Reagan staffed the bureau with neoconservatives who shared his broad political perspective. But above all, he integrated human rights into his geopolitical strategy of confrontation between the United States and the Soviet Union. "When confronting the human rights situation in Somoza's Nicaragua or today's El Salvador," wrote the neoconservative Elliott Abrams, "we need to think not simply about the internal situation but about how the country in question fits into the framework of East-West relations." In agreement with Jeane Kirkpatrick's thesis, Abrams maintained that the United States "will at times support regimes which abuse human rights because we think that their replacement would be much worse for the cause of human rights, and because we think that American (and others') pressure can greatly improve these regimes over time." The primary goal of the United States, he continued, should be "to prevent virtually any country from being taken over by communist regimes tied to the Soviet Union." "In my view," he concluded, "resistance to the expansion of communism is essential to a human rights policy."[44] In this framework, the bureau lost autonomy but acquired status as an important actor in the general design of American foreign affairs.

Ernest Lefever was Reagan's first choice to preside over the Human Rights Bureau. Lefever had been the director of the Ethics and Public Policy Center, a think tank highly sympathetic to neoconservative views.[45] A number of neoconservatives were members of the center's Board of Directors. He maintained cordial relationships with neoconservative leaders such as Midge Decter, Norman Podhoretz, and Irving Kristol and contacts with members of the CPD. In a way, he considered himself a forerunner of neoconservatism. "Why am I always before my time?" he asked Decter in 1982. "I anticipated Jeane Kirkpatrick's views on the United Nations in 1957, and most of the neo-conservative agenda of analysis and ideas fifteen years before the term was born."[46] In 1978, he had argued that the Carter administration had "confused our foreign policy goals and trivialized the concept of human rights." Even before Kirkpatrick drew the distinction between totalitarian and authoritarian regimes, Lefever asserted that "human rights are more honored in Chile than in Cuba," and that "human rights as we know them in the United States . . . can be eroded or even obliterated from within by acquiescing to willful men who seek to capture the reins of power for their own narrow ends or from without by the totalitarian regimes determined to extend their domains." Carter's policy on human rights, he thought, was "unwise" and could end in disaster.[47]

During his confirmation process in the Senate, Lefever faced strong opposition, prompting him to withdraw his nomination in June 1981. His withdrawal, although expected, represented a failure for the Reagan administration. "It is with the greatest regret," said President Reagan, "that I accept the decision you and your wife have taken to withdraw your name from consideration for Assistant Secretary of State for Human Rights and Humanitarian Affairs." "You have my deepest personal sympathy," the president added, "for the ordeal you have gone through. . . . I can only thank you for your perseverance, in the face of hostile and often willfully uncomprehending criticism, in explaining to the public and the world the foundation of our new human rights policy. Your contribution to our common endeavor has been an invaluable one; I fully intend to build on it."[48]

Lefever did not, however, disappear from the political arena; on the contrary, he maintained strong ties to the Reagan administration. In July 1981, a month after he withdrew his nomination for the Human Rights Bureau, he became a paid consultant to the Office of the Secretary of State, obtaining for a few days of work the same honorarium and privileges as for the assistant secretary of state. He also served, without remuneration, on two of the advisory committees of the U.S. Information Agency and remained in personal communication with President Reagan.[49]

Reagan waited almost a year to appoint a neoconservative, Elliott Abrams, to the Human Rights Bureau (Lefever was sympathetic to neoconservatives but not a neocon).[50] Between the withdrawal of Lefever and the designation of Abrams, neoconservatives worked to secure control of the bureau. Even before Lefever's withdrawal, Irving Kristol argued in favor of Kirkpatrick's double standard and for the incorporation of human rights criteria into U.S. military aid programs, economic aid programs, cultural exchange programs, and so forth.[51] Michael Novak wrote praising the Reagan administration for keeping alive the American historical tradition in defense of human rights.[52] *Commentary* published a symposium on human rights, whose contributors stressed both the relevance of incorporating human rights into American foreign policy and the advantages of the Kirkpatrick thesis.[53]

Neoconservatives engaged in a similar battle within the State Department and the White House. According to Abrams, after Lefever's withdrawal there was "anger within the administration," and a confusion over "what we [were] going to do. . . . The first reaction was to shut down the bureau, but that was impossible for legal considerations."[54] "I decided to get the job," Abrams recounted in an interview. "Paul Wolfowitz and Bill Clark asked me about the bureau and about names. I went back to them and said, 'The person to do the job is me.' And they said, 'That is terrific, but let's be very clear.' So I wrote this memo, the Clark-Kennedy memorandum. To me, [the memo] was announcing a neocon human rights policy. Clark, to my gratification, read it and said, 'This is it.'"[55]

In this memo—in a way, a polished version of Lefever's ideas— Abrams contended that "human rights are at the core of American foreign policy. Human rights are not something we take on to our foreign policy but its very purpose: the defense and promotion of freedom in the world." For some scholars, that memo marks "the beginning of a new phase in the Reagan human rights policy."[56] Essentially, it was the culmination of a long process in which neoconservatives sought to gain control of this sphere of American foreign affairs. According to Abrams, the State Department did not have "any idea of what to do with human rights policy, so I gave them a policy. The policy, from their point of view, might seem very brilliant and original. From my point of view, it was a straight neocon dogma."[57]

Abrams had limited experience in foreign affairs but was considered an "insider." He had served as assistant secretary of state for international organizations, which gave him some experience in day-to-day management. Within the State Department, he was judged to be "extremely competent and influential,"[58] as well as a skillful negotiator. Contrary to Derrian, who saw her activities as a guardian of human rights—regardless of the perspective of other agencies and departments—Abrams conceived of his role as that of being a team player, and the Human Rights Bureau as a key protagonist in the U.S. global struggle against communism. Abrams rarely challenged the State Department's geographic bureaus and maintained the sympathy of Congress. With the exception of its opposition to the nomination of Lefever, Congress "had little influence over how the Bureau was managed."[59]

Reagan's commitment to anticommunism permeated the executive branch, in part through his careful selection of political appointees and strategic use of career bureaucrats. The president believed that one of the "primary tools for transforming political goals into public policy" was the designation of loyal collaborators at different levels of the bureaucracy.[60] E. Pendleton James, head of Reagan's recruiting team, claimed that these people have to "function as 'team players' without a personal or political hidden agenda."[61]

Three criteria were used to choose these executive branch personnel. "One, was he a Reagan man? Two, a Republican? And three, a conservative?" With these criteria, Reagan sought to "ensure that conservative ideology was properly represented."[62] An analysis of the Nixon, Carter, and Reagan White House staffs revealed that Reagan was more conservative than Nixon and Carter, and the "consensus in the Reagan White House [was] substantially greater than either the Carter or the Nixon White House."[63] People appointed for jobs received training to sensitize them to Reagan's viewpoints. In terms of the relationship between the Executive Office of the President and the Human Rights Bureau, Reagan's and Abrams's ideological affinity helped in developing a harmonious and consistent policy.

Congress, the State Department, and the Human Rights Bureau all

helped to legitimate American foreign policy during the Reagan adminis-
tration. Congress did not challenge the president's role as the main actor in
U.S. foreign policy. This enhanced his control over human rights policy.
Similarly, the State Department's historically close ties with the White
House and the role that Reagan conferred on the department's Human
Rights Bureau were central to the defense and promotion of his view-
points. That is, the institutional features of Congress and the State Depart-
ment enabled the advancement of neoconservative ideas on human rights.

## The Links between Political and Economic Interests and Neoconservative Ideas

The issue of special interests in relation to President Ronald Reagan's
human rights policy must be addressed in two different registers: neoconservative political and personal concerns about human rights issues, and
the economic benefits that accrued to segments of the private sector because of the neoconservative ideas implemented during the Reagan years.
Neoconservatives' personal and political concerns with human rights have
been described in different sections of this book. To briefly recapitulate,
neoconservatives were largely second- or third-generation immigrants.
Their family histories are full of references to repression, economic difficulties, and genocide in their native countries. As Jews, many of them
were familiar with racial, religious, and political discrimination, and some
of them had personally suffered from different forms of intolerance. Likewise, as intellectuals, they had seen the rise and decline of fascism and
had become disenchanted with communism and the Soviet Union, especially due to its violations of human rights. It was a small wonder, then,
that neoconservatives were very concerned with this issue.[64]

At first glance, it seems paradoxical to talk about the economic interests behind neoconservative ideas on human rights, because human rights
are supposedly beyond material concerns. However, a careful reading of
neoconservative views on human rights reveals that they can be easily interpreted as part of a broad geopolitical strategy. Making a distinction
between totalitarian and authoritarian regimes implies that totalitarian
governments are contrary to American economic and strategic interests.
Following this logic, authoritarian governments are, then, sympathetic to
American values. Although undemocratic, they provide the necessary stability for economic growth and, according to their supporters, sometimes

evolve into democracies. In the late 1970s, neoconservatives feared that authoritarian regimes were in danger of being replaced by revolutionary movements. Therefore, it was imperative for the United States to contend with communism and to promote and protect democracy by supporting economically and militarily authoritarian regimes.

The same logic can be seen at work in arms sales. After World War II, arms sales were conceived as an integral component of American foreign policy. Before the 1970s, during a time of bipartisan consensus on foreign policy, arms transfers were an uncontroversial issue—a part of America's global efforts to contain communism. In the late 1960s, President Nixon bucked that historical trend. The Nixon doctrine declared that the United States ought to diminish its presence overseas but continue to offer military aid and economic assistance to other countries. Foreign governments, Nixon added, had to assume "the primary responsibility of providing the manpower for [their] defense."[65]

The Nixon doctrine modified the nature of American military assistance. In the aftermath of World War II, U.S. arms transfers were regulated under the Military Assistance Program, which had been established by the Mutual Security Act of 1951. Transactions were arranged in the form of grants or loans and supplied mainly outmoded or overstocked weapons. In 1968, at the beginning of the nonpartisan realignment, Congress enacted the Foreign Military Sales Act. Under this act, transfers were made in the form of "direct payments or loan repayment grants," and from 1976 to 1980, they accounted "for almost 80 percent of total military transfers."[66] As an expression of the resurgence of the legislature in the decisionmaking process in foreign affairs, Congress banned arms sales to governments that violated human rights.

The Carter administration, in contrast to the general trend of American politics, sought to stop the growing sales of arms abroad. Carter declared that the United States "would view arms transfers as an exceptional foreign policy implement, and considered arms transfers as a major cause of instability around the world."[67] Although Carter's stance was often more of a rhetorical exercise than a firm policy position, his administration implemented preconditions, such as respect for human rights, for the selling of American weapons and adhered to stricter criteria than previous administrations, which had often been quite flexible. But despite Carter's best efforts, security considerations continued to prevail over human rights concerns.[68]

Reagan revived the general tendency initiated by Nixon. The Reagan administration considered arms sales a "vital and constructive instrument of American foreign policy."[69] To face the communist threat, the United States not only had to reinforce its military capacity but also had to help its friends and allies defend themselves against communism "through the transfer of conventional arms and other forms of security assistance."[70] Table 4.1 summarizes the distinct policy arguments about arms transfers mobilized by the Carter and the Reagan administrations.

Although the United States had been an arms supplier since the late

*Table 4.1. U.S. Arms Transfer Policy under Jimmy Carter and Ronald Reagan*

| Carter's Basic Guidelines | Reagan's Basic Guidelines |
|---|---|
| The Carter administration attempted to control U.S. arms sales abroad:<br>• The United States would reduce the dollar volume of new commitments.<br>• The United States would not introduce newly developed advanced weapons systems into a region until they were operationally deployed with U.S. forces.<br>• An effort would be made to promote respect for human rights in recipient countries, and the economic impact of arms transfers to countries receiving U.S. economic assistance would be considered.<br>• The United States would not permit the transfer of American weapons, equipment, and major components.<br>• The United States would not permit coproduction agreements for significant weapons, equipment, and major components.<br>• An attempt would be made to remove the economic initiatives for arms sales, such as lower per unit costs for Defense Department procurement on similar terms.<br>• An attempt would be made to reduce international arms traffic through multilateral negotiations. | The Reagan administration viewed arms transfers as an "essential element of its global defense posture and an indispensable component of its foreign policy":<br>• To help deter aggression by enhancing the preparedness of friends and allies.<br>• To improve military effectiveness by improving America's ability in conjunction with its friends and allies "to project power in response to threats posed by mutual adversaries."<br>• To support efforts that foster the ability of U.S. forces to deploy and operate with those of U.S. friends and allies, thereby strengthening mutual security relationship.<br>• To demonstrate the enduring interest that the United States has in its friends and allies and that it will not allow them to be at a military disadvantage.<br>• To foster regional and internal stability, thus encouraging the peaceful resolution of disputes and evolutionary change.<br>• To help enhance U.S. defense production capabilities and efficiency. |

*Source:* Roger P. Labrie et al., *U.S. Arms Sales Policy: Background and Issues*, Studies in Defense Policy 359 (Washington, D.C.: American Enterprise Institute, 1982), 11–15.

1960s for economic reasons—as a way to relieve its unfavorable balance of payments in the international economy—neoconservative arguments legitimated a geopolitical rationale for Reagan's arms sales abroad. Neoconservatives elaborated a reasonable argument that justified the marketing of weapons to authoritarian countries. "If the accusation is that we justify the marketing of weapons to authoritarian countries," Elliott Abrams recalled, "the answer is: absolutely. Communism was worse, so our mission was to stop communism. In essence, we did justify."[71]

In January 1981, the business magazine *Fortune* properly captured the mood of the time when it published an article titled "Happy Days Are Here Again for the Arms Makers." Military-related corporations were the primary beneficiaries of Reagan's implementation of neoconservative ideas on human rights at the policy level. Military contractors' profits increased considerably during the Reagan years. In fiscal year 1984 alone, "the Pentagon paid American businesses $124.9 billion for work performed in the United States, a 3.2 percent increase, after inflation, over the year before." The same year, "twelve companies received prime contract awards totaling more than $2 billion each."[72]

Eleven of the leading companies had sales of $12.4 billion during the Carter years and $13.2 billion during the Reagan administration's first term. A closer examination of particular cases offers even more insight. Northrop, an exported-oriented company, had sales of $2.2 billion during the Carter administration and $3.7 billion in the first Reagan term, an increase of $1.5 billion in four years. Sales under the Foreign Military Sales Act grew from $369 million during the period 1976–80 to $571 million between 1981 and 1985. General Electric's sales bloomed from $674 million to $887 million during that period. But some companies' profits decreased during the period. For example, General Dynamics reported sales of $3.3 billion during the Carter administration and $2.6 billion during the Reagan administration's first term.

It is important to bear in mind that the American arms buildup began not during the Reagan administration but in the Carter years, specifically the years 1978–79. General Dynamics, for example, generated the most sales revenue in 1978. In fact, the majority of companies reported significant percentage sales increases during this period. Sales under the Foreign Military Sales Act grew from –8.45 percent in 1978–79 to 258.42 percent in 1979–80—General Electric's from –42.61 to 74.26 percent, General Dynamics' from –64.91 to 91.70 percent, General Motors' from 59.38 to

113.73 percent, and Lockheed's from –52.19 to 4.93 percent. Northrop was the only company to report negative growth during the late 1970s, but it registered an increase of 1,157 percent in the years 1980–81.

The U.S. government was the most important client of American military contractors, but arms contractors also sold significant amounts of products to foreign countries. Paul Hammond asserts that "key electronic, communications, and transportation industries depend upon military exports a great deal. In 1977 the top ten U.S. contractors depended for an average of 12 percent of their total sales on arms exports. Northrop depended upon arms exports for 25 percent of its total sales."[73] Several companies' profits derived from foreign sales increased substantially in the 1980s. In 1976, General Motors' foreign military sales were less than $100 million; but by 1980, they were approximately $200 million, and by 1986, they were close to $300 million. In 1977, General Electric's sales were around $250 million, and in 1979, they had declined to approximately $150 million. But then General Electric experienced a permanent increase, with sales of nearly $600 million in 1986. McDonnell Douglas's sales were about $450 million in 1977, declined to $250 million in 1978, and surged to $500 million in 1979. In 1980, the company's sales soared to $850 million, and in 1982 reached more than $900 million, a high that would be followed by a significant decline.

Northrop is another interesting example. In the first two years of the Carter administration, when the tendency was to control military transfers, its sales fell from $900 million in 1977 to $250 million in 1978. In 1979, the Carter administration moved to the right and adopted a quite conservative position in foreign affairs. In 1979, the company's sales were around $600 million. By 1980, its sales had fallen again, to $450 million. In 1986, it achieved its highest sales in a decade, around $1.6 billion.

Military contractors warmly welcomed both the popularization of the neoconservative distinction between authoritarian and totalitarian governments, and the active policy of arms sales initiated by Carter and strengthened by Reagan. Following neoconservative thinking, Reagan implemented a human rights policy based not on humanitarian considerations but on geopolitical concerns. "The Reagan administration," wrote former secretary of state George P. Shultz, "came to office with a critical view of the way President Carter had approached human rights issues. I, too, was critical of what I called 'light-switch diplomacy,' an effort to turn trade and investment on and off in order to try to influence a country's human rights

*Table 4.2. Jeane Kirkpatrick's Distinction between Authoritarian and Totalitarian Regimes in Practice*

| Country or Group | Type of Government | Law Ignored | Type of Aid | Particular Justification |
|---|---|---|---|---|
| South Africa, South Korea, Turkey | Right-wing authoritarian regimes | Section 502B of the Foreign Assistance Act | Security assistance increased 300 percent from 1980 to 1984 | The United States confronted a present danger from the USSR and its allies, so preparation was necessary. |
| Nicaragua | Leftist regime | International Financial Institutions Act of 1977 via Section 701 | The administration lobbied the multilateral development banks and Western European governments to stop giving loans and aid | The aid was restricted because the administration believed that the Sandinistas were devout Marxist-Leninists and saw a Sandinista-led Cuba working as a proxy for the USSR to spread revolution throughout Central America. |
| Chile | Authoritarian regime | International Financial Institutions Act of 1977 via Section 701 | Loans and military assistance; the administration voted for a loan to Chile from the Inter-American Development Bank in spite of a clear pattern of human rights violations by Pinochet's dictatorship | In accordance with the double standard thesis, the policy in the multilateral banks was characterized by voting for loans to right-wing allies but voting against loans to certain left-wing regimes. |

| | | | | |
|---|---|---|---|---|
| El Salvador | Authoritarian regime | Section 502B of the Foreign Assistance Act | Military assistance program and economic aid | The Reagan administration rejected claims that large numbers of abuses were occurring and instead blamed the rebels for the political violence; El Salvador represented a textbook case of Communist aggression |
| Haiti | Authoritarian, pro-U.S. regime | Section 502B and the Harkin Amendment of the Foreign Assistance Act; in 1981, an amendment to the act established that U.S. aid to Haiti could be provided only if the president certified that Haiti was making progress on human rights | Military assistance and economic aid increased significantly, from $27.1 million in 1980 to $34.6 million in 1981 and $55.6 million in 1985 | The administration put forth ostensible evidence of positive advances and progress on human rights and downplayed the negative in its annual Human Rights Certification |
| Romania | Communist regime | Jackson-Vanik Amendment, or Section 402 (a) (b) of the 1974 Trade Act | Granting of most-favored-nation status in trade | It was applied to certain countries with "reasonable emigration procedures" |

*Source:* Compiled from David P. Forsythe, *Human Rights and U.S. Foreign Policy: Congress Reconsidered* (Gainesville: University of Florida Press, 1988); and Thomas Carothers, *In the Name of Democracy: U.S. Policy toward Latin America in the Reagan Years* (Berkeley: University of California Press, 1991).

practices. A guide text for the Reagan administration had been an article by Jeane Kirkpatrick in the November 1979 issue of *Commentary* distinguishing between totalitarian regimes . . . and authoritarian regimes."[74] Thus, authoritarian governments, like those of Argentina, Guatemala, Turkey, South Korea, and El Salvador, received American military and economic support. Totalitarian regimes such as Nicaragua and Cuba received condemnation and blockades. In the case of Nicaragua, the United States supported the military forces that worked to overthrow the Sandinistas. Table 4.2 presents some of the cases in which the Kirkpatrick thesis was applied. What is more, the proactive foreign policy of the late 1970s and 1980s increased the profits of American military contractors.

In sum, changes in the direction of American human rights policy were made possible through the convergence of structural, political, and ideological factors. In the late 1960s and early 1970s, Congress reemerged as a central actor in the decisionmaking process, but it created flexible institutions that in due time were used by neoconservatives and the president to implement their political agendas. Neoconservatives produced frameworks for analysis and popularized ideas that were then taken up by politicians. American defense corporations benefited from this diffusion of neoconservative ideas and institutional changes that encouraged the promotion of neoconservative politicians' views. In the late 1970s, ideas, institutions, and interests came together to provoke a significant policy shift in the area of human rights.

# 5

# Ideas, Institutions, and Interests: The Influence of Neoconservatism on the U.S. Military Buildup

From the beginning of his presidential campaign, Ronald Reagan emphasized the decline of American hegemony and the worldwide spread of communism. The Republican Party shared his concerns. "For the first time," read the 1980 Republican platform, "the Soviet Union is acquiring the means to obliterate or cripple our land-based missile system and blackmail us into submission. Marxist tyrannies [are] spread[ing] more rapidly throughout the Third World and Latin America. . . . At the start of the 1980s the United States faces the most serious challenge to its survival in two centuries of its existence."[1] To face this perceived danger, the Republicans advocated increasing the U.S. military budget.

Reagan and the Republican Party appear to have captured the public mood. According to the National Opinion Research Center, 17 percent of the people interviewed in 1974 considered American defense spending too low. By 1978, that figure had increased to 27 percent; and by 1980, it was 56 percent.[2] When, in 1981, President Reagan proposed and Congress approved a substantial increase in the military budget, the measure had significant popular support. The increase represented not only the largest peacetime military buildup in American history but also a significant partisan change. The new policies that favored American high-technology companies and punished other important economic sectors—steel, automobiles, textiles, and so forth—represented an industrial policy change as well.[3] Neoconservatives were the main ideological architects of this sea change. Their ideas, their economic interests, and the institutions they sought to influence—mainly Congress, the Pentagon, and the Defense Department—were the key to a substantial policy shift in American foreign affairs.

In this chapter, I analyze the interaction among neoconservative ideas, political institutions, and interest groups in the conception, development, and implementation of Reagan's defense policy. First, I introduce the origins and diffusion of neoconservative arguments favoring an American military buildup. Second, I look at the role of Congress, the Pentagon, and the Defense Department in formulating defense policy in order to evaluate these institutions as fertile ground for neoconservative ideas. Third, I analyze the connections between political and economic interests and neoconservative ideas. Fourth and finally, I examine interplay of these three variables in order to better explain the Reagan administration's policy changes in foreign affairs.

## The Neoconservative View of the Military Buildup

At the end of World War II, the two main political parties reached an accord concerning the nation's international objectives. Democrats and Republicans alike supported the goals of internationalism, anticommunism, and containment of the Soviet Union. This bipartisan consensus was a decisive factor in the successful management of U.S. interests during the Cold War. It gave strong continuity and consistency to decisionmaking from one administration to another. In the late 1960s, however, the United States' failure to succeed in Vietnam marked the end of the postwar consensus on foreign policy. Vietnam demonstrated both to the world and to American society the inability of the United States to contain communist expansion.

The breakdown of the postwar bipartisan consensus divided internationalists into liberals and conservatives. Conservative internationalists were pro-interventionists, defenders of the Cold War position, and skeptical about the effectiveness of détente. Often, they held a Manichean view of the world: democracy versus dictatorship, capitalism versus communism, freedom versus repression. In contrast, liberal internationalists were the product of the post-Vietnam era. Prodétente and antimilitary, they saw the world in global terms and rejected a hegemonic role for the United States in world affairs.[4]

Though concentrated in the Republican Party, conservative internationalists were also active within the Democratic Party, mostly as part of the neoconservative Coalition for a Democratic Majority (CDM). "For me, the essence of liberalism," declared the distinguished neoconservative thinker and CDM member Max Kampelman, "requires hostility to communism, so I do not see it as a unique conservative approach. . . . Wilson, Roosevelt, Truman, Kennedy, Humphrey, and Jackson are all liberals, which is why I do not feel that the isolationists in the Democratic Party had a right to identify themselves as a part of the liberal tradition of American politics. I think they distorted the tradition."[5] This bipartisan character gave internationalism a broader legitimacy than it might otherwise have enjoyed. Though not all conservative internationalists were neoconservatives, neoconservatives played a prominent role in articulating and spreading internationalism.

In large measure, Reagan shared the conservative internationalist perspective. Hard-line statements on foreign affairs filled his campaign rhetoric. Some neoconservatives, like Jeane Kirkpatrick, even considered Reagan the first neoconservative. He had been a member of the Committee on the Present Danger (CPD), and he acknowledged in a letter to the CPD's board that he had "benefited greatly from the work of the Committee."[6] As a member of the CPD, Reagan became acquainted with neoconservative thought. When he reached the White House, it seemed natural that some neoconservatives would find a place in his administration. Indeed, a significant number were named to committees and offices that dealt with defense policy. There, they promoted a strong anticommunist position and advocated a military buildup. Their appointment to the Republican government shifted their role from that of intellectuals setting the tone of political debate to that of decisionmakers affecting the direction of American foreign affairs.

Neoconservatives' views in favor of American military buildup were just one element of their anticommunism. Although they had become anticommunists in the late 1940s, most of them did not advocate an increase in military spending at that time. In the aftermath of World War II, they focused on dissociating themselves from both their socialist past and radical-right anticommunist expressions. They concentrated on elaborating a centrist view—a liberal anticommunist argument that would be acceptable to both the elite and the general public.[7]

Beginning in the 1950s, however, neoconservatives began working to promote an increase in the American military budget. For instance, as director of the Policy Planning Staff of the State Department from 1950 to 1953, Paul Nitze, who was a member of both the CDM and the CPD, drafted the now-famous National Security Council Report 68, known as NSC-68.[8] This document, written a few weeks before the outbreak of the Korean

War, was a comprehensive review of American national security policy. Nitze's report warned U.S. policymakers about Soviet ambitions and called for a "rapid and sustained build-up of the political and military strength of the free world."[9] Samuel F. Wells Jr. found that the "real significance of NSC-68 was its timing—the tocsin sounded just before the fire."[10] Zara Steiner saw NSC-68 as the "culmination of a long term effort to secure the resources needed to back an ambitious foreign policy."[11] Daniel Yergin declared NSC-68 as important as "Kennan's Long Telegram and the Truman Doctrine in the postwar history. . . . It provided the rationalization not only for the hydrogen bomb but also for a much-expanded military establishment."[12] For Jerry Sanders, it transformed George Kennan's original notion of containment and marked the beginning of "containment militarism."[13]

In the midst of Stalinism, the Berlin blockade, the expansion of communism in Eastern Europe and China, McCarthyism, and the Korean War, NSC-68 received the support of important politicians.[14] Henry "Scoop" Jackson, the influential senator from Washington State and leader of the CDM, declared that it was the "first comprehensive statement of a national strategy."[15] Dean Acheson considered the document a bible for the Cold War era and asserted that NSC-68 laid out the "conflicting aims and purposes of the two superpowers: the priority given by the Soviet rulers to the Kremlin's design for world domination, in contrast with the American mind and environment, in which a free society could exist and flourish. Throughout 1950, the year my immolation in the Senate began, I went about the country preaching this premise of NSC-68."[16] Except for Kennan and Charles Bohlen, there were few major dissenters.

The American Enterprise Institute (AEI) was the first neoconservative organization to become concerned with U.S. national defense and the military buildup. In October 1972, about the same time the CDM was formed, AEI organized a defense policy conference that was broadcast on television. The main speaker, Caspar W. Weinberger, director of the Office of Management and Budget, presented views that were highly constrained by his administrative post and quite different from what his position would be in the 1980s. He credited President Richard Nixon and the Pentagon for making substantial cuts in defense spending possible during Nixon's first term. However, he balanced his position by arguing that it was necessary to "keep the nation sufficiently strong to deter aggression against ourselves and our allies."[17] Other invitees, such as Admiral Gene LaRocque and Murray Weidenbaum, shared this perspective.

AEI clearly had the capacity to convene influential people and disseminate ideas. In the early 1970s, it had started a public affairs telecast, which offered discussions on public issues. These programs were available on one-hour videocassettes and audiocassettes, as well as 16-millimeter films, and were transmitted by "270 television stations, by many radio stations, and by more than 100 cable television systems."[18] AEI's printed materials were sent to bureaucrats and legislators. In 1973, "96 United States senators and 391 congressmen were receiving AEI publications."[19]

Defense continued to be a major theme at AEI. In May 1974, it organized a debate on the defense budget between senators Edmund Muskie and Bill Brock. Muskie argued in favor of significant cuts in defense spending. He presented figures to disclaim neoconservatives' arguments about Soviet military expansion. Since the 1970s, he claimed, the United States had produced 758 additional missiles, in contrast to 492 by the Soviet Union, and 4,850 nuclear weapons, in contrast to 572 by the Soviet Union. When Senator Brock spoke, he argued that in the aftermath of the Vietnam War, defense spending had been reduced in "excess of $25 billion," and as a proportion of the national product, it had been reduced from 9 to less than 6 percent.[20]

Soon, other neoconservative organizations joined AEI in its concern about defense spending. In 1974, the CDM created a Foreign Policy Task Force, which was headed by Eugene Rostow. Other members included Henry Fowler, former secretary of the Treasury; Max Kampelman, former counsel to Vice President Hubert Humphrey; John P. Roch, former special assistant to President Lyndon Johnson; Norman Podhoretz, editor of *Commentary*; Albert Shanker, president of the American Federation of Teachers; and professors Jeane Kirkpatrick, Lucian Pye, and Paul Seabury. The task force produced a document that circulated in elite political circles. An abstract of the document, written by Rostow, was also published in the *Wall Street Journal*.[21] This dual method of distribution of CDM members' views—on the one hand, ensuring that their views reached influential elites, and on the other, using the mass media to reach the general public—characterized neoconservative strategies for disseminating ideas.

Rostow's article in the *Journal* criticized the Nixon-Kissinger policy of détente, arguing that Nixon had substituted "negotiation for confrontation." What is more, détente—an endless goal of American foreign policy—had not been accomplished. According to the CDM task force, Soviet policy had not changed since 1945, and thus by the 1970s its power was superior. In a highly conspiratorial tone, the CDM asserted that Soviet expansionism threatened American interests in different ways: "Our interest in access to raw materials; in strategic naval and space communication; and in the balance of power itself through Soviet or Soviet proxy threats to nations whose political independence is vital to our own security, and nations to whose future we are committed for even deeper reasons of history, kinship, and honor."[22] The CDM stressed that while Soviet military power was growing an average of 5 percent a year in real terms, American forces were in decline. According to Rostow and his colleagues, U.S. defense expenditures had fallen to their lowest point since the late 1940s. Moreover, the United States was advocating unilateral disarmament. Rostow maintained that the United States should build up its military capabilities "in order to avert a catastrophic military imbalance." The Soviet military buildup ought to be opposed by increases for the "Navy, for our ready forces, and for research and development." The CDM recommended an increase of about $10 billion.

Correspondence between Secretary of State Henry Kissinger and Rostow illustrates neoconservatives' ambitions to affect the views of political elites. Rostow was not only an influential member of the CDM but also a well-known politician with easy access to the inner circles of Washington. Taking advantage of this position, he sent a letter and the CDM task force document to Henry Kissinger. The letter had three main purposes: first, to establish a permanent dialogue with the secretary of state about détente and related issues; second, to affect and, if possible, to modify the opinions of Kissinger and other important politicians; and third, to spread the CDM's ideas among influential decisionmakers.

In his response to Rostow's letter, Kissinger argued that he shared the CDM's goals but differed with it on the "means to their achievement." Contrary to Rostow, he expressed his belief that "restraint and cooperation with ideological adversaries" were possible. He maintained that U.S. policy had been realistic. "We have sought to foster changes in Soviet behavior," he wrote, "by stressing our mutual stake in a wide spectrum of efforts to normalize our relations." Likewise, Kissinger stated his belief that the U.S. policy was flexible. "When the Soviets have threatened American interests," he argued, "we reacted strongly." Finally, he emphasized that in the strategic area, "we frankly see no evidence of a Soviet 'headlong drive for first strike capability in both nuclear and conventional arms.'"[23]

In his reply, Rostow's main disagreement with Kissinger was on the issue of détente. Whereas, for Kissinger, the relaxation of tensions in the international arena was evident, for Rostow détente did not exist. Rostow claimed that it was "not only wrong, but dangerous to lull Western public opinion by proclaiming the end of the Cold War." He also differed with Kissinger regarding Soviet military expenditures, which he considered much larger than those of the United States. He claimed that the Soviets were ahead in "sensitive categories of arms" and in important areas of "military technology." Finally, Rostow expressed the CDM's desire to develop a bipartisan consensus on foreign policy.[24] This sort of exchange with influential political elites complemented the insertion of the CDM task force report into the *Congressional Record.* On November 18, 1975, Representative Daniel Flood introduced into the Records of the House an article published on June 20, 1975, in *Tactics* that summarized the document.[25]

The dissemination of neoconservative ideas within political institutions was an important step in the process of spreading these views to a wider audience. This approach not only made congressional leaders aware of neoconservative views but also facilitated the interaction of neoconservative ideas and political institutions, paving the way for the policy changes that occurred during the Reagan administration.

Events in the international sphere also helped set the stage for such changes. The U.S. economy languished following the devaluation of the dollar in 1971 and the oil embargo in 1973. The American defeat in Vietnam and ongoing rapprochement with Communist China challenged a country that had considered itself undefeated and anticommunist. American covert interventions in Chile, the funding of right-wing activists in Italy, and other similar activities provoked congressional and public dissatisfaction with U.S. foreign policy. Norman Podhoretz described the mood of the time as a "culture of appeasement," a culture characterized by "self-doubt, self-criticism, self-loathing."[26]

The years 1976 and 1977 turned out to be important ones for the development of neoconservative institutions and the diffusion of neoconservative ideas. During those years, neoconservatives helped to shape the foreign policy section of the Democratic Party's platform, participated in the creation of the CPD, and helped AEI start its program on defense policy. Together, these institutions launched a significant campaign to redirect American foreign policy toward the Soviet Union and to support a U.S. military buildup.

In 1976, neoconservative ideas began to have a significant impact on the U.S. government. That year, President Gerald Ford approved the establishment of Team B to evaluate the diagnosis of Soviet military capabilities made by the Central Intelligence Agency (CIA). Team B—which was headed by a neoconservative, Richard Pipes, with the collaboration of three future CPD members, Paul Nitze, Foy Kohler, and William Van Cleave—disseminated its straightforward conclusions just before President Jimmy Carter took office. These conclusions were that the Soviets were engaged in a massive military buildup, and that the USSR had surpassed American military forces and was even ready to win a limited nuclear war. To solve this security problem, Team B recommended that the United States start its own military buildup.

The neoconservative magazine *Commentary* served as a medium for a broader diffusion of Team B's perspective; in July 1977, Pipes published "Why the Soviet Union Thinks It Could Fight and Win a Nuclear War." In this article, he observed that whereas in the USSR, nuclear weapons were conceived of as a means of attack, in the United States they were seen as deterrent weapons. Consequently, American policymakers were naive to believe that the Soviets would embrace mutual deterrence.[27] With this and other similar ideas, Pipes contributed considerably to neoconservative views on the USSR. Gary Dorrien argues that Pipes established *Commentary's* "line on the Soviet threat,"[28] and Jerry Sanders writes that Pipes was "perhaps second only to Nitze in formulating the [CPD's] strategic views."[29]

The CDM initially supported Henry Jackson in the 1976 presidential campaign. After Jackson's defeat in the Pennsylvania primary, the CDM worked to introduce its ideas about American foreign and defense policy into the Democratic platform. Members of the CDM wrote a draft platform, in which they argued that it was insufficient to endorse vigorous domestic policy without a firm international posture. This faction criticized the policy of détente, calling it "a program of veiled concessions to Soviet interests, conducted for political advantages at home rather than to safeguard our interests and ideas abroad." Finally, the CDM advocated a significant increase in defense spending in order to confront Soviet military superiority.[30]

For Stephen S. Rosenfeld of the *Washington Post*, the foreign and defense policy chapters of the Democratic platform reflected "to a striking degree" the "particular combination of toughness and idealism of Scoop Jackson, his political ally Daniel Patrick Moynihan, the Jackson-oriented Coalition for a Democratic Majority, and some of the contributors to *Commentary* magazine." Rosenfeld maintained that the Jackson faction was involved in the writing of early versions of the platform and was able to include some important amendments, and that the result was a "document that firmly (though not exclusively) asserts the basic Jackson & Co. principles."[31] Table 5.1 summarizes the influence (or presence) of the CDM's ideas on the Democratic platforms of 1976 and 1980. The table shows that the CDM's neoconservative ideas had successfully infiltrated relevant political institutions and even helped shape the platform of the Democratic Party.

The presidential election of 1976, when both the presidency and a particular ideological viewpoint were at stake, increased the possibilities for neoconservatives to affect the course of American foreign policy. The CDM and AEI endorsed different candidates. The CDM, as a faction within the Democratic Party, backed Carter after the defeat of Jackson in the primaries, while AEI backed Ford, who had been highly sympathetic to AEI during his administration. (After his defeat by Carter, Ford became a distinguished fellow at AEI.) Yet the two organizations coincided in their ideas on defense policy, and both worked to put American defense issues at the top of the political agenda.

In the early 1970s, the Watergate scandal affected the Republican Party's prospects of staying in the White House. Accusations of corruption within Richard Nixon's administration and the resulting crisis of confidence in American institutions only strengthened the Democrat Jimmy Carter's candidacy. Against the backdrop of a significant economic recession, Carter conducted a campaign that emphasized his honesty and moral credentials. For a Democratic Party divided by George McGovern on the left and George Wallace on the right, Carter's centrist position was the best means of recuperating the southern vote and reconciling conflicting interests and factions. Though Carter gave anticommunist fears a low priority during his presidential campaign, several neoconservative organizations were ready to ensure that defense became a top priority once he came into office.[32]

In the months leading up to the 1976 election, neoconservatives continued to draw attention to defense issues. In June, AEI organized a roundtable with former defense secretary Melvin Laird, CDM leader and former Strategic Arms Limitation Talks (SALT) delegate Paul Nitze, and senators Thomas McIntyre and Charles Mathias. Laird claimed that the Soviets were ahead of the United States in some weapons, such as the number of tanks, whereas the United States surpassed the Soviets in antitank weapons. For Laird, however, the Soviets had a significant advantage because "they are able to devote a great amount of their resources to defense, twice

Table 5.1. Influences of the Coalition for a Democratic Majority on the 1976 and 1980 Democratic Party Platforms: Convergences and Divergences on Issues Related to Policy Objectives

| Policy Area | Coalition for a Democratic Majority | Democratic Party, 1976 | Democratic Party, 1980 |
|---|---|---|---|
| Foreign policy | • To conduct their affairs with the knowledge of the American people. Foreign policy must be open, without secret negotiations and agreements with foreign governments.<br>• To restore American influence and strength to meet the rising dangers.<br>• To restore domestic vitality. | *Convergence:* The security of the nation must depend first and foremost on the internal strength of American society.<br><br>*Convergence:* To formulate and execute basic policy with public understanding and support. | *Convergence:* To strengthen the military security of the United States and to consult closely with our allies to advance common security and political goals. |
| Defense policy | • It is necessary to assure an efficient system of national defense by guaranteeing significant increases in the defense budget.<br>• To restore American influence and strength to meet rising dangers. | *Convergence:* The defense budget is considered the primary measure to deter, and if necessary, outfight, potential adversaries. Military expenditures must be consistent with the real security needs of the American people.<br><br>*Divergence:* To reduce defense expenditures by about $5–7 billion. | *Convergence:* To establish a commitment to increase the defense budget by at least 3 percent a year is crucial for the maintenance of allied consensus. |

| | | |
|---|---|---|
| Human rights | • To use their moral and economic influence to encourage the recognition of human rights in countries with dictatorial governments. | *Convergence:* To reaffirm the fundamental American commitment to human rights across the globe.<br><br>*Convergence:* To encourage the observance of human rights in those countries which receive American aid. | *Convergence:* To be vigilant about human rights violations in any country in which they occur.<br><br>*Convergence:* To support the leadership role taken by the U.S. in the area of human rights. |
| Democratic purposes | • To rebuild influence with movements of democratic change in developing countries.<br>• Strong emphasis in reviving the democratic ideal around the world. | *Convergence:* To restore the democratic tradition of friendship and support for third-world nations. | (Topic does not appear.) |
| Military aid | • Military aid is required to be cut in the repressive governments such as Chile, Spain, and South Africa. | *Convergence:* Not to provide aid to any government which uses secret police and torture.<br><br>*Convergence:* To significantly limit conventional arms sales and reduce military aid to developing countries. | *Convergence:* To deny assistance to governments that violate fundamental human rights. |

121

*Source:* Coalition for a Democratic Majority, "The Platform of the Democratic Party," July 1976, LBJ Library and Museum, Austin, containers 14, 71, 73, 75, 76.

as much as we are in terms of measurement in gross national product."[33] Similarly, Nitze expressed the need to improve experimental research and development.

Senators Mathias and McIntyre challenged the position of Nitze and Laird from different angles. Mathias asserted that the Russians were facing economic difficulties and were interested in reaching "some accommodation." He added that the United States was ahead technologically. McIntyre called for a more realistic budgetary position by the Pentagon, maintaining that on defense matters, the United States was ahead of the Soviets.

Only a few days later, AEI organized a debate between representatives Les Aspin and Jack Kemp on "how much defense spending is enough." Aspin called for a "'rational' policy for U.S. defense," and he asserted that neither cutting the defense budget nor increasing it substantially would restore the credibility the United States enjoyed in the 1950–60 period. He argued that it was possible to match the USSR's real growth and still cut the president's request from 7 to 2 percent. Kemp's position was simple and quite clear: The military balance favored the Soviet Union.[34] The same year, AEI published *Detente and Defense: A Reader*, edited by Robert J. Pranger, which presented contrasting views on the subject of Soviet military power.

The campaign to spread the idea that the Soviet Union continued to be a threat was enhanced in 1976 by the establishment of the CPD, which "grew out of the work of Team B" and was conceived, fundamentally, to alert Americans about the Soviet military buildup and its implications for global stability.[35] Using alarmist rhetoric, the CPD concluded that the United States was "in a period of danger." Therefore, it was necessary to reinforce its military and economic capabilities and to "assure peace with security." According to the CPD's leadership, its main activity was to be educational, to "inform public opinion before it can reach considerable judgment."[36] Originally, the CPD was composed of 141 private citizens who "not only had access to the elites of American foreign policy, but were themselves members of the foreign policy establishment."[37] They would be some of the main actors in making U.S. foreign policy during the postwar years.

The CPD's position on foreign policy was reinforced in articles published by neoconservative intellectuals associated with the group. Less than a year after the CPD's founding was publicly announced, Norman Podhoretz published "The Culture of Appeasement" in the October 1977 issue of *Harper's Magazine.* Podhoretz argued that the Vietnam War had damaged American society and that "naive pacifism" was "the dangerous legacy of Vietnam." The increased popularity of pacifism, which he equated with anti-Americanism, had changed American views toward communism and made it difficult to maintain high levels of military spending. "While the Soviet Union engages in the most massive military buildup in the history of the world," he wrote, "we haggle over every weapon."

Considering the Soviet Union "the most dangerous enemy of liberty, democracy, and human rights on the face of the Earth," Podhoretz expressed a clear affinity with neoconservative organizations, maintaining that only a "few individuals like Henry Jackson, Paul Nitze, and Elmo R. Zumwalt, and the few small groups like the CPD and the CDM keep trying to alert American public opinion to unprecedented dimensions of the Soviet military buildup." "The democratic world was under siege," he declared, and "American power [was] indispensable to its defense."[38]

The CPD's influence on American foreign and defense policy can be seen most clearly in the negotiation of the SALT II Treaty, which took place in the winter of 1976. In his inaugural address, Carter openly declared that he wanted to eliminate nuclear weapons from the Earth. The statement provoked a strong reaction from the CPD and other neoconservative organizations. A mere two weeks after the inauguration, Senator Jackson, the leader of the CDM and an opponent of the SALT negotiations, visited the White House. In his meeting with the president, Jackson criticized SALT I, saying that it had left "Soviet forces intact." The senator also argued against the Vladivostok accord and Henry Kissinger's January 1976 proposal. Carter asked Jackson to expand on his ideas in a written statement.[39]

Jackson asked the neoconservative Richard Perle, one of his closest advisers, to draft a memorandum to the president. In this document, he objected to the position Kissinger had taken in the SALT negotiations and called for reductions in both Soviet intercontinental and intermediate-range ballistic missiles. He also suggested a redefinition of "heavy" intercontinental ballistic missiles. If the Soviets were reluctant to accept the United States' proposal, "it would be defensible to replace the interim agreement with a new interim accord which would at least codify the basic numerical equality and MIRV [multiple independently targetable reentry vehicle] limitations of Vladivostok as long as it were made clear that this accord would be replaced within a relatively short period of time by a more satisfactory resolution to the bomber and throw-weight issues." The memo "unquestionably reinforced the instincts of Carter, Brown, Brzezinski, and Aron to seek more than a mere consummation of the Vladivostok Accord."[40]

Through the Jackson-Perle memorandum, neoconservative ideas influenced the viewpoints of President Carter and his closest collaborators. But the memo was only one among many tactics used by neoconservatives to affect American foreign and defense policy. After the CDM and CPD opposed the nomination of Paul Warnke to lead the SALT negotiations and to serve as director of the Arms Control and Disarmament Agency, the CPD published "Where We Stand on SALT."[41] According to Max Kampelman, at that time "the principal preoccupation of the Committee"[42] was to prevent the ratification of SALT II.

The CPD believed that the U.S. population was misinformed on the SALT negotiations. It argued that the "Soviet objective has been to extend its gains in a relative posture while encouraging maximum restraint upon U.S. programs."[43] The proposal offered by the Carter administration in March 1977—calling for substantial, mutual reduction in forces—was, they wrote, "unfavorable for the United States."[44] The CPD also disseminated the so-called window of vulnerability argument in the essay "Is America Becoming Number 2?" According to the CPD, the Soviet goal was to obtain a "visible preponderance of military power," and only a strategic initiative could restore the credibility of the United States' ability to maintain "second-strike deterrent capability."[45] In the CPD's eyes, the SALT II treaty was an "expression of American acquiescence in the Soviet drive for overwhelming military superiority."[46]

Although it is difficult to measure the CPD's impact on the SALT II negotiations with exactitude, a sample of the organization's public activities in 1979 provides a sense of the extent to which its ideas circulated in the media and in political circles:

1. During the hearing on SALT II, the CPD's Executive Committee and board members testified by invitation on seventeen different occasions before the Senate Foreign Relations and Armed Services committees, more than all other critics of the treaty put together.

2. During the negotiations, Paul Nitze's famous comprehensive paper on SALT II was updated eleven times, approximately once each month.

3. The CPD's Executive Committee and board members participated

in 479 television and radio programs, press conferences, debates, public forums, briefing conferences of citizen leaders, and major speeches on SALT and the military balance.

4. The CPD distributed more than 200,000 copies of its pamphlets and reports.[47]

While the CPD was working to influence the SALT II negotiations, AEI initiated a project on national defense and began the bimonthly publication of *AEI Defense Review*, which in 1979 changed its name to *AEI Foreign Policy and Defense Review*. The birth of *AEI Defense Review* was an important step in the growing influence of neoconservative ideas on defense policy. AEI became an important forum for the socialization of political, business, academic, and media players interested in defense issues, as well as a powerful disseminator of neoconservative ideas among people with political and/or economic influence.[48]

The advisory council for AEI's project on national defense reflected the power of AEI to bring together people with important ties to Washington's inner circles and demonstrated an ideological tendency to support a hard-line perspective. Former secretary of defense Melvin Laird was chairman, and General Bruce Palmer, former vice chief of staff of the Army and chairman of the Defense Manpower Commission, was a consultant to Laird. Other members of the council included such conservative figures as former CIA director William Colby, Arizona senator Barry Goldwater, New York representative Jack Kemp, former deputy secretary of defense Paul Nitze, and former secretary of defense Clark Clifford, who had a well-known hawkish reputation. The council also included corporate leaders like R. E. Kirby, chairman of Westinghouse Electric Corporation, and Thomas Murphy, chairman of the board of General Motors Corporation. Other members were drawn from the military, such as General Leonard F. Chapman Jr., U.S. Marine Corps (retired), commissioner of the Immigration and Naturalization Service; Admiral Thomas Moorer, U.S. Navy (retired), former chairman of the Joint Chiefs of Staff; General Bernard A. Schriever, U.S. Air Force (retired), and principal shareholder in Schriever and McKeen, Incorporated; and Lieutenant General George Seignious, U.S. Army (retired), president of the Citadel.[49] Seignious had replaced Paul Warnke as director of the Arms Control and Disarmament Agency in 1979, just as the Carter administration was shifting to the right in foreign policy.

The president of AEI, William J. Baroody Sr., maintained permanent contact with some members of the CPD, especially, informally, Richard V. Allen. Baroody and Allen coordinated the efforts of both organizations to influence American political and public opinion on defense issues. As previously mentioned, in the summer of 1976 Allen went to see William Baroody to learn about the different activities and programs developed by AEI in the area of international affairs. In their conversation, Baroody described AEI's new program on foreign policy and national security and stated that both the CPD and AEI should continue to work on those issues and to explore possible avenues of collaboration. The friendly relationship between the two neoconservative organizations remained over the years.

In 1978, AEI began a second major project called "The Future Conduct of American Foreign Policy," which complemented its program on defense. The project's advisory council was headed by George H. W. Bush and by two moderate liberal Democrats, Senators Gary Hart and William Fulbright. The project's director, Donald Hellmann, a CPD member, gave a conservative orientation to the project. That same year, AEI published *Grand Strategy for the 1980s*, a volume that strongly supported the American military buildup and featured contributions from five important former military officers, among them Elmo R. Zumwalt Jr., a member of both the CDM and the CPD, and Maxwell D. Taylor, also a member of the CPD.[50]

In 1978 and 1979, international events, economic failures, and internal pressures provoked substantial changes in Carter's domestic and foreign policies. Pro-American regimes in Iran and Nicaragua were in turmoil in 1978; respectively, the governments of the shah and Anastasio Somoza were in the middle of popular insurrections that resulted in Ayatollah Khomeini and the Sandinistas gaining power. The president's energy program was in complete disarray, and by the end of 1978 oil companies were predicting a rise in American oil imports. Rumors of a possible devaluation of the dollar circulated in financial and political circles, while neoconservatives, New Right organizations, and defense industries pushed the president to increase the military budget. In late 1979, Carter promised a real increase in military expenditures of 5 percent over the next five years. And by 1981, public opinion had shifted strongly to favor higher defense spending following the Soviet invasion of Afghanistan in 1980—considered by conservative internationalists as the irrefutable sign of the USSR's imperialist ambitions—and a neoconservative campaign to alert policymakers to the Soviet threat (table 5.2).

From 1978 to 1980, AEI's concern with defense issues grew. The anal-

*Table 5.2. Public Opinion on U.S. Defense Spending, 1974–81 (percentage of survey participants)*

| Opinion | 1974 | 1976 | 1977 | 1979 | 1981 |
|---|---|---|---|---|---|
| Too little | 12 | 22 | 27 | 34 | 51 |
| Too much | 44 | 36 | 23 | 21 | 15 |
| About right | 32 | 32 | 40 | 33 | 22 |
| None | 12 | 10 | 10 | 2 | 12 |

*Source:* Daniel Wirls, *Buildup: The Politics of Defense in the Reagan Era* (Ithaca, N.Y.: Cornell University Press, 1992), 27.

ysis generated during that period reflects a shift to a more emphatically conservative position. In 1978, AEI published a debate between Fulbright and Taylor on the SALT agreement, as well as the opinions of Les Aspin and Jack Kemp titled "The Reality of the Soviet Threat." (The title reflected the state of alarm that prevailed within AEI.) In 1979, AEI published *The SALT Handbook: Key Documents and Issues, 1972–1979*, which included statements by the negotiations' main protagonists and provided comprehensive coverage of the negotiations. *The Problem of Military Readiness*, by Melvin Laird and Lawrence Korb, was issued by AEI in 1980. In accord with the outlook of the CDM and the CPD, they believed that the United States was threatened by Soviet military superiority. In the "major categories of the conventional arms balance," they argued, "the USSR leads the United States in total military manpower by 220 percent (4.4 million to 2.0 million), in tanks by nearly 500 percent (50,000 to 10,500), in artillery by over 200 percent (40,700 to 18,000), in tactical aircraft by 4 percent (4,350 to 4,116), and in major warships by 200 percent (523 to 260)."[51] By the mid-1980s, these types of publications were being complemented by AEI events, such as "U.S. Defense: What Can We Afford," a panel with Paul Nitze, Jack Kemp, Patricia Schroeder (D-Colo.), and Sanford Gottlieb.[52]

In the 1980s, AEI's analysis of defense issues exhibited two basic characteristics: first, clear opposition to Carter's military budget; and second, the belief that the United States was in danger because of the military superiority of the Soviet Union and its expansionist ambitions. This view of the United States as a besieged fortress was key to obtaining the endorsement of political and economic elites and the population in general for an American military buildup. Knowing it was an ideal time to spread its views, the CDM organized an informal and off-the-record meeting on the "Finlandization of America" to evaluate what the impact on the daily lives of the American people would be if the Soviets became the main military power in the world. In this way, neoconservative organizations sought to use the American public's greatest fears about personal and family life to mobilize them against the Soviet Union.

As was noted in the previous chapter, on January 31, 1980, the CDM's leaders met with President Carter at the White House. Before this official meeting, the CDM had sent a letter to the president in which they stated that they recognized what they considered improvements in Carter's foreign policy and argued that it was necessary to start "a long-term effort to rebuild America's military superiority. To this end," the letter stated, "we must move promptly to guarantee our strategic forces against attacks, to restore our naval power to undisputed command of the sea, to assure adequate military manpower in the event of crisis, and to provide a sufficient military presence throughout the world to regain the confidence of our allies."

The corollary to this neoconservative offensive was Norman Podhoretz's article "The Present Danger." He not only echoed the name of the Committee on the Present Danger in the title but also made use of the sense of alarm felt by neoconservatives since the late 1960s in crafting his argument. He compared the Soviet Union to Hitler's Germany—both governments that "wish[ed] to create a new international order." He argued that the United States must resist Soviet imperialism if it did not want to be subjected to Soviet political control. He explained that he considered Soviet imperialism a "threat to the United States," not merely because the Soviet Union was a "superpower bent on aggrandizing itself" but also because it was, as the heroic Russian dissident novelist Aleksandr Solzhenitsyn had said, a "Communist state, armed to the teeth and dedicated to the destruction of free institutions that are our heritage and glory." He concluded: "We are fighting for freedom and against communism, for democracy and against totalitarianism."[53]

Indeed, Carter's foreign policy moved to the right, following conservative internationalist views. The president withdrew SALT II, resumed the military draft registration program, implemented a grain embargo against the Soviet Union, boycotted the Soviet Olympics, and promoted increased defense spending. "In the dangerous and uncertain world of today," asserted Carter in early 1980, "the keystone of our national security is still military strength—strength that is clearly recognized by Americans, by our allies, and by any potential adversary."[54] From the perspective of neoconservatives, American foreign policy had shifted in the proper direction.

To achieve the complete transformation they desired, it was only necessary to find a new leader.

Neoconservatives believed that they had found this leader in the former California governor, Ronald Reagan. By the late 1980s, many neoconservatives had come out in support of Reagan.[55] "In Ronald Reagan," Podhoretz would later write, neoconservatives had "found a political force capable of turning things around."[56] Richard Allen was the person who built the bridges between neoconservatives and Reagan. Allen had become familiar with neoconservatives in the mid-1970s, when he had been instrumental in the creation of the CPD. He convinced Reagan to join the CPD, and in early 1978, when the former actor decided to run for the presidency, Allen deliberately brought neoconservatives into the Reagan camp. "My task," Allen recalled, "was to overcome the obvious bias that they would have against a person like Reagan because not only the main media but many of the intellectuals considered him to be a second-rate, maybe a third-rate, movie actor; probably too lazy and ignorant, certainly divisive, and maybe reactionary. By late 1978 and 1979, I was absolutely convinced that neoconservatives were headed our way." Allen continues: "Neoconservatives who care deeply about national security and about revising the trends of the Cold War could be brought to Reagan if they met him, so I began to introduce Reagan to some of them. Most of the strategy was done by Charles Tyroler, who, among other things, arranged dinner for Reagan at Paul Nitze's house with Eugene Rostow and others. . . . My primary objective . . . was to expose [Reagan] to the essential fact that neoconservatives were very close to him on a wide range of issues and that he needed to sit in a dialogue."[57] Allen believed that neoconservatives could be convinced that they belonged in the Reagan camp.

During Reagan's presidential campaign and later during the transition to the start of his administration, the CPD and its members played important roles. Throughout the campaign, the CPD advised the Republican candidate on foreign policy issues. Once he had been elected, several CPD members worked on the Reagan transition team on defense and foreign policy. Richard Allen and Fred C. Iklé coordinated defense and foreign policy working groups, each of which was populated by CPD members. For example, Kenneth Adelman, W. Glenn Campbell, Iklé, and Richard Pipes were involved with the group on goals and overall strategy for U.S. foreign policy, and Adelman, Jeane Kirkpatrick, and Nathan Glazer participated in the group on instruments of foreign policy pertaining to information and communication.[58] Finally, a CPD member, William Van Cleave, became the overall coordinator of the defense transition team, while Iklé, Charles Kupperman, John Lehman, Van Cleave, and Donald Rumsfeld participated in the subgroup on strategic forces.

Similarly, several neoconservatives were asked to suggest names for positions in the new Reagan administration. In a letter to Tyroler, Nitze proposed William D. Rogers, a partner in the Arnold & Porter law firm; Albert Fishlow, director of the Concilium on International and Area Studies at Yale University; Francis L. Mason, vice president of Chase Manhattan Bank; Martha T. Muse of the Tinker Foundation; and Riordan Roett, director of the Center for Brazilian Studies at the School of Advanced International Studies at Johns Hopkins University.[59] Nitze also suggested Rumsfeld or Henry Jackson for secretary of defense; Lehman for secretary of the navy; and James Woolsey, Marshall Turner, or Amoretta Hoeber for secretary of the army.[60] These recommendations were made with the idea of advancing neoconservative views on foreign policy. When CPD member Iklé recommend Lehman as secretary of the navy to Anne Armstrong, he told her that "[the] smartest move I made during my entire four years as a director of the Arms Control Agency was to induce John Lehman to serve as my Deputy." According to Iklé, Lehman possessed an important "sense of loyalty and [his] sense of proportion." He would make an ideal secretary of the Navy, Iklé continued, because he "knows the Navy in all aspects, . . . [his appointment] would be a very cost-effective way to get a badly needed improvement in morale; he [has] excellent relations with Congress, and [has] an enviable reputation with the serious people in the media and in industry."[61] Above all else, Iklé felt that "our national security will be better off" if Lehman were appointed.

When Reagan reached the White House, he staffed his foreign policy team with a significant number of neoconservatives. Thirty-two members of the CPD (in addition to the president) were named to positions in foreign and defense policy offices. In their capacity as federal bureaucrats, they were able to advance a strong anticommunist position and advocate for an increase in military spending. The relationship between Reagan and neoconservatives continued throughout the early years of his administration. In 1982, in the context of the Strategic Arms Reduction Treaty negotiations with the Soviet Union, he responded to a letter sent by Charls E. Walker, chairman of the CPD. Reagan wrote that he "greatly appreciate[d] the support of the Committee on the Present Danger." He agreed with Walker that what he called "our approach" contained "the hope of breaking free from the fallacies that subverted SALT. . . . Certainly, this will not be an easy or quick negotiation. . . . Because of this, the value of your Committee's support will become even more essential in buttressing that resolve as time passes." Reagan maintained that his proposal included "all the significant elements of the strategic equation—with significant reduction in ballistic missile warheads, the missiles themselves, and a throw weight in the initial phase and with further reductions, possible inclusion of other systems, and equal limits on throw weight, below U.S. levels, in the later phase." Finally, the president expressed his gratitude to Walker and the CPD and concluded his letter, "I am counting on your valuable support."[62]

In February 1984, Reagan wrote to Walker again, saying that "as a result of continued Soviet intransigence, we will face increasing pressure to make progress in nuclear arms control." The president maintained that the purpose of our arms control policy is to "ensure overall U.S. security even as we seek to enhance stability and to reduce the risk posed by nuclear forces." For Reagan, the fundamental goal of U.S. foreign policy was "security and stability." Reagan once again thanked Walker for the "valuable support you and the Committee on the Present Danger have provided in the past; . . . we will count on your invaluable support in the future."[63]

Clearly, Reagan valued the support and advice of the CPD. He was aware that neoconservatives in general, and the CPD in particular, would be important allies in the promotion and support of his policy initiatives. Unsurprisingly, during his administration's first term, a degree of consistency between the actions of neoconservatives in the government and the views and arguments of neoconservatives outside the administration could be observed. Again, as in the past, institutions facilitated the introduction and penetration of those ideas into the decisionmaking process. In particular, the Defense Department and Congress served as important conduits for neoconservative ideas about defense policy.

## The Roles of Congress and the Defense Department in Advancing Neoconservative Ideas on the Military Buildup and Defense Policy

Major coordination problems and interbureaucratic struggles among the numerous federal agencies are primary characteristics of the process of making U.S. foreign policy. This difficulty derives, in part, from the nature of the U.S. political system and, in part, from the complexity of American foreign policy since World War II. With regard to the nature of the U.S. political system, a number of elements seem to contradict each other. First, there exists a "constitutional system that shares formal powers among separate institutions,"[64] and in which "government power is fractionalized within the executive branch, within Congress, and between the two."[65] Second, there is a redundant and overlapping approach between Congress and the executive branch.

Constitutionally, the president is designated to implement policies, and Congress can accept, modify, or reject the executive branch's decisions. The political scientist Edward Crowin considers this structure an "invitation to struggle for the privilege of directing American foreign policy."[66] Although the struggle has often been acute, according to Crowin, the president "almost always win[s]." As commander in chief of the armed forces, the president has historically conducted American military affairs with significant freedom and quite often has ignored Congress. The explanation for this fact must be found in the structure and behavior of the three branches of the U.S. government. Usually, the president has taken the initiative in foreign policy, Congress has accepted his decisions, and the Supreme Court has supported his actions.[67]

The War Powers Resolution (WPR), passed in 1973 over Richard Nixon's veto, clearly illustrates this dynamic. The WPR was designed to diminish the power of the president in international affairs by preventing the executive office from unilaterally sending armed forces abroad without congressional authorization. To date, it has been the strongest expression of congressional participation in the war-making process. However, it presented so many deficiencies in its design—mainly consultation and reporting provisions[68]—that it neither improved the role of Congress in the process of declaring war nor prevented—as its sponsors wished—the president from involving the United States in military operations without congressional approval. Furthermore, with the clear endorsement of the WPR, the president could invade any nation with only the requirement to remove the troops in sixty days (as was done in Grenada). In short, even after congressional approval of this important law, Congress continued to delegate authority to declare war to the president, who continued to be the central figure in U.S. military affairs. "The formula implanted by the Framers in the Constitution—of Congress as the initiator of war and the president as its conductor"—asserted Louis W. Koenig, "has been all but reversed, with the president becoming both the initiator of war and its conductor."[69]

The centralization of military decisionmaking power in the presidential office, worked, however, to facilitate the transmission of neoconservative ideas to decisionmakers. Neoconservatives needed to deal mainly with political elites; they had to persuade only the president and his closest collaborators. Their access to the wielders of power was even more notable during times of crisis. In normal situations, though the notion of centralizing the decisionmaking process prevailed, it was more common to observe the struggle within the bureaucratic apparatus for the predominance of a particular viewpoint. At moments of crisis, however—when decisions needed to be made immediately—the president was more likely to rely on advice that came directly from trusted advisers.

The overlapping of functions in the executive branch was also the result of the proliferation of international issues. The emergence of the United States as a leader of the capitalist world in the late 1940s made its insertion in the international arena more complex. Thereafter, the United States enhanced its economic relations with other nations, mainly in Europe, and started or expanded its political, military, and cultural contacts with other countries. The postwar international system provoked a situation in which "no less than forty government agencies [had] a hand in foreign policy."[70] This new global leadership position complicated the bureaucratic management of American domestic and international affairs.

In the area of defense policy, the situation was equally intricate. Not only were there interbureaucratic struggles among the different departments and agencies of the executive branch, but there was also a strong rivalry within the Defense Department itself, mainly between its military and civil sectors. This conflict was the result of the Defense Reorganization Act of 1947, which conferred supremacy on the civilian secretary of defense over his military counterpart. This law and its subsequent modifications during the 1950s greatly facilitated the access of neoconservative ideas to decisionmakers. I will proceed to the analysis of the main features of the American defense apparatus.

### The Structure of the American Defense Policy Apparatus

Before World War II, the president alone—or at times together with the secretaries of state, war, the navy, and the Joint Chiefs of Staff (JCS)—was in charge of American defense decisions. However, after that international conflagration, President Harry Truman considered the creation of a unified Defense Department indispensable. The idea provoked an intense debate within government offices. Two positions dominated the dispute.

On one hand, the War Department "advocated a centralized defense establishment focused on military policy and strategy."[71] On the other, the Navy Department proposed a decentralized defense organization and suggested the creation of two institutions: a military committee (the JCS) and a civilian council (which later became the National Security Council).

With the National Security Act of 1947, Congress attempted to reconcile both positions by establishing a Defense Department directed by the secretary of defense (as the army wanted) with separate subdepartments for the navy, army, and air force. The law stipulated that the secretary of defense was "the principal assistant to the President in all matters relating to the national security . . . and the Secretary was in charge of the overall operation of the Defense Department."[72]

This same act established a new office, the JCS—as the navy demanded—within the Defense Department. This office's main tasks were to be to prepare strategic and logistical plans and to serve as the main advisory body to the president, the secretary of defense, and the National Security Council on military affairs. The members of the JCS, who were to be appointed by the president, could present their military views to Congress, giving them significant influence on topics such as arms control and the military budget.[73] With the insertion of the JCS within the Defense Department, under the secretary of defense, the secretary obtained unprecedented powers placing him just below the president in terms of defense issues. His powers were strengthened by amendments to the National Security Act in 1949, 1953, and 1958.

The act also created the CIA and established the National Security Council (NSC), as the Navy demanded. Taking the British Committee of Imperial Defense as the model, the NSC was established to "advise the President with respect to the integration of domestic, foreign, and military policy relating to the national security so as to enable the military service and other departments and agencies of the government to cooperate more effectively in all matters involving the national security."[74]

The establishment of the NSC with the specific purpose of advising the president on military affairs further reinforced the chief executive's leadership on defense and military matters. Originally, the NSC was made up of the president; the secretaries of state, defense, the army, the navy, and the air force; the chairman of the National Security Resources Board; and other members who were to be designated by the president. By 1980, however, the NSC was made up of just the president, the vice president, the secretaries of state and defense, and other people selected by the chief executive. The director of the CIA and the chairman of the JCS served as statutory advisers. Thus, the main offices within the U.S. government involved in military issues were under the control of the president.

Scholars are divided about the evolution of the NSC into two main phases; the first was its creation to meet the crisis of American foreign policy in the late 1960s, and the second began after the breakdown of the postwar bipartisan consensus in the late 1960s. During the first period, the president used the NSC in different ways, but Truman, Eisenhower, Kennedy, and Johnson made their main decisions independently of the NSC. According to Frederick Hartmann and Robert Wendzel, from its creation in 1947 to the end of the Johnson administration, the NSC "rarely was a major forum for the determination of decisions affecting major security interests and only infrequently provided a forum for effective coordination of advice and action in political and military policies."[75]

During the first years of the Nixon administration, the NSC achieved some relevance, but it soon fell back to its previous unimportant status. Henry Kissinger, of course, played a prominent role as national security adviser, but his prominence was related more to his personal abilities and prestige than to the influence of his office. During the Ford years, the NSC continued to be more or less irrelevant, and although Carter sought to reinforce its activities in the design and implementations of policy, the organization did not function as a major decisionmaking forum. As had been the case with Nixon and Kissinger, Carter relied heavily on his national security adviser, Zbigniew Brzezinski.

Reagan, however, deliberately reduced the functions of Richard Allen, his first national security adviser, and conferred leading roles in defense policy on the secretaries of defense and state and on the director of the CIA. The NSC and its head accepted their new low profile and worked as facilitators rather than promoters of a particular view. Thus, national security advisers William Clark and Robert McFarlane had significant influence in designing and implementing Reagan's defense policy. The Iran-Contra affair demonstrated that John Poindexter was highly involved in foreign policy decisions. National security advisers became team players in the general design of Reagan's foreign and military policy.

It seems evident that the NSC only sporadically played the role its founders intended. Since its creation, it has neither advised the president on security matters nor coordinated the cooperation of the different agencies involved in national security. On the contrary, the NSC has often provoked conflicts between the national security adviser and the secretaries of state and defense. Different presidents, according to their particular interests, have used the agency in various ways. This has made the NSC a nonautonomous group closely tied to the president, who, in general terms, has used it to promote his policies.

Subsequent reforms to the National Security Act in 1949 and again in 1958 enhanced the power of the secretary of defense. The 1949 reform enlarged the Office of the Secretary of Defense, and the modifications of 1958 gave the secretary of defense significant independence in the management of defense resources and strengthened the secretary's control over research and development. In the 1960s, Robert McNamara introduced the planning, programming, and budgeting system (PPBS) to deal with the problem of interservice rivalry. Its "purpose was to provide a more rational process for decisions on force structure, strategic programs, and weapons systems."[76] Every spring, the JCS would present a strategic plan to the secretary of state to help the secretary then outline a five-year program. According to Samuel Huntington, "PPBS was an effort to tie together planning and budgeting, to look at programs 'horizontally' across service lines, to determine in a comprehensive manner the true cost that might be associated with new programs."[77] These were important measures in the efforts of different politicians to improve the functioning of the Defense Department.

The defense reorganization of 1947 and its successive modifications established a Defense Department in which two opposite forms of organization coexisted within the same office: a centralized civilian system, and a decentralized military system. As noted above, the reorganization also conferred supremacy on a civilian secretary of defense over his military counterpart. "A policy framework," asserted writer and journalist James Roherty in 1970, "is set by the Secretary of Defense, much of the data base is provided by the Secretary, judgments are invited by the Secretary, and decisions are made by the Secretary."[78]

The centralization of the decisionmaking process for military affairs in an office closely tied to the president facilitated the access of neoconservative ideas. On a structural level, the organization of the political system, in general, and the defense apparatus, in particular, was such that decisionmaking was concentrated in a small group of governing elites. The notion that the president and secretary of defense were the main actors and promoters of different initiatives marked the direction in this policy sphere. Neoconservatives did not have to penetrate into the different corridors of Washington; access to a few key people was enough to make their ideas resonate within the Reagan administration.

The structural features of Congress also contributed to the influence of neoconservative ideas on the American arms buildup and defense policy. Reforms during the 1960s and 1970s substantially changed the inner workings of Congress. Before those decades, the congressional system was designed to privilege committee chairmen, who had almost absolute control over committee resources, especially staff, and could influence committee agendas and "shape policies" and "outcomes through their dominance over subcommittees."[79] Likewise, negotiations in the legislature were closed, and the chairmen had control over the time of debate for bills. In this "democratic system," the chairman had become a sort of indisputable monarch.

The congressional reforms modified this distribution of power. Senior committee chairmen were given less power, and subcommittees obtained "independent status and authority." The reforms no longer allowed the chairman to "structure the subcommittee, to pick its chairman and members and control the jurisdiction and staff." Resources were expanded to all legislators, allowing subcommittee chairs to hire their own personal staffs. A specialist wrote: In "1965, standing committees employed 571 people in the House and 509 in the Senate, an average per committee of 28 and 32 respectively. By 1979, a couple of years before the beginning of the Reagan administration, the standing committee employed 1,959 in the House and 1,098 in the Senate, an average per committee of 89 and 73 respectively."[80] Additionally, committee debates were opened to the public, and House and sometimes Senate sessions were televised. Overall, these reforms resulted in a Congress that was less centralized and more democratic.

The reforms accentuated the division of labor within Congress. Its segmentation into committees and subcommittees often caused most congressional committees to be involved in some aspects of foreign policy, producing an inevitable overlapping of functions. Thus, as Kissinger described the work of congressional committees: "During the first session of the 99th [Congress] (1985), the Senate had sixteen standing (or permanent) committees, and nearly all of them claimed jurisdiction over some aspects of foreign policy. The situation is similar in the House. In the drafting of a trade bill in 1986, six different standing committees played a significant part." Consequently, Congress was frequently divided and inconsistent on important issues related to U.S. foreign policy. This is the case of its policy toward Nicaragua during the Reagan administration. Here, congressional ambivalence "provided neither continuity nor criteria to which even the most scrupulous administration could orient itself."[81] Thus, the way congressional labor was divided made foreign policy decisionmaking difficult at best.

In the area of defense policy, the reforms reinforced the role of subcommittees. In the case of the House Armed Service Committee (HASC), subcommittees played a dominant role because they "marked up the entire annual defense authorization bill and had the right to schedule hearings on virtually any subject."[82] Some figures highlight the subcommittee's policy relevance. In the 91st Congress (1969–71), the HASC referred only 12 percent of its legislation to subcommittees, in contrast to the 99 percent of legislation referred to subcommittees by the HASC of the 96th Congress (1979–80).[83] The situation in the Senate Armed Services Committee (SASC) was somewhat different. Although the "SASC continued to mark up the procurement account," its chair preserved the right to arrange hearings and meetings, and the "committee staff remained more centralized than in the House." Because of its small size, most of SASC's subcommittees "included nearly half of the full committee members."[84] The decentralization of power and new degree of influence of subcommittees facilitated the access of neoconservative ideas to the legislature, because it made it more likely that different perspectives would be heard in Congress.

Neoconservative ideas on military issues were further reinforced by the fact that members of the armed services committees of both chambers of Congress were often tied to military interests. Legislators joined these committees because of the relevance of military installations and defense industries in their districts or states. This constituency-based interest often coincided with the strong conservative positions of its members. "The [SASC]," asserted the political scientists Steven Smith and Chris Deering, "attract[s] a large contingent of members with significant state connections to the defense establishment who also have personal policy interests in the committee's activities."[85] A similar phenomenon occurred in the House. As former House Armed Services Committee Chairman L. Mendel Rivers expressed it to the new secretary of defense in 1969: "I am sure you know, better than anybody, that this committee is the *only* official spokesman for the [Department of Defense] on the floor."[86] Additionally, during the Reagan administration's first term, the SASC's membership was made up mainly of conservatives. Among them were found such advocates of the New Right as Strom Thurmond and Jeremiah Denton; such traditional conservatives as Barry Goldwater, Dan Quayle, and John Tower (the committee's chair); and the neoconservative leader Henry Jackson, who was also a member of the subcommittees on military construction, preparedness, and strategic and nuclear forces (this last subcommittee also being a bastion of neoconservatism). Other legislators, like Daniel Patrick Moynihan in the Senate and Jack Kemp in the House, were highly sympathetic to neoconservatism. Together, these members of Congress introduced neoconservative ideas on defense policy, brought neoconservatives to testify in different hearings, and facilitated the diffusion of their viewpoints in the legislature.

The ongoing correspondence between neoconservative thinkers and the leaders of neoconservative organizations illustrates the intimacy of their relationship with congressional leaders. For instance, in May and July 1978, Eugene Rostow, a neoconservative leader of the CDM and the CPD, exchanged correspondence with Edmund Muskie, chairman of the Senate Budget Committee. The language used by Rostow and Muskie demonstrates that the two men had a familiar and even friendly relationship. In one letter, Rostow communicated that he was "disappointed" by the Senate Budget Committee's recommendation on defense spending. To this complaint, Muskie replied: "But Gene, let me point out that the Committee was higher in its recommended military funding total for fiscal year 1979 than either the Committee on Armed Services or Appropriations and, of course, the President in his request." Unsatisfied with Muskie's answer, Rostow argued in a subsequent letter that the Senate has "not done enough to deal with the situation as it is. A quick and visible turnaround now is urgently needed. It would be far more effective, and much cheaper, than a slow buildup over the next few years."[87]

Neoconservatives like Rostow had direct, personal access to congressional leaders. Members of Congress did not necessarily implement neoconservative views, but they did respond to the demands and inquiries of this group of intellectuals and politicians, who worked to pressure Congress with the aim of altering the direction of American military policy. Their ability to influence Congress would have been stymied, however, had it not been for the structure of Congress and the executive branch, which gave them direct access to important decisionmakers.

### *The Defense Department and the Role of Neoconservatives in Arms Control Policy*

Although the National Security Council tended to dominate military and defense decisionmaking, and thus drew the attention of neoconservatives, the presence of members of the Committee on the Present Danger in the

Defense Department ensured that neoconservative views circulated there as well (table 5.3). In the aftermath of the SALT I agreement, Senator Henry Jackson worked to affect the composition of the Arms Control and Disarmament Agency (ACDA). At Richard Perle's suggestion, Fred C. Iklé became the director and John Lehman became his deputy. Their personal relationships and their ideological affinity facilitated teamwork. Later, Lehman would become secretary of the navy, Iklé would become undersecretary of defense for policy, and Perle would become the assis-

*Table 5.3. Members of the Committee on the Present Danger with Defense-Related Appointments in the Reagan Administration*

| Name | Position(s) |
| --- | --- |
| Richard V. Allen | Assistant to the president for national security affairs |
| W. Glenn Campbell | Chairman, Intelligence Oversight Board and member, President's Foreign Intelligence Advisory Board |
| William Casey | Director of Central Intelligence |
| John B. Connally | Member, President's Foreign Intelligence Advisory Board |
| Joseph D. Douglass Jr. | Assistant director, Arms Control and Disarmament Agency |
| John S. Foster Jr. | Member, President's Foreign Intelligence Advisory Board |
| Amorell M. Hoeber | Deputy assistant secretary of the Army for research and development |
| Fred Charles Iklé | Undersecretary of defense for policy |
| Max M. Kampelman | Chairman, U.S. Delegation to the Conference on Security and Cooperation in Europe |
| Geoffrey Kemp | Staff, National Security Council |
| John F. Lehman | Secretary of the Navy |
| Clare Boothe Luce | Member, President's Foreign Intelligence Advisory Board |
| Paul H. Nitze | Chief negotiator for theater nuclear forces |
| Peter O'Donnell Jr. | Member, President's Foreign Intelligence Advisory Board |
| Richard Perle | Assistant secretary of defense for international security policy |
| Richard Pipes | Staff, National Security Council |
| Eugene Rostow | Director, Arms Control and Disarmament Agency |
| Paul Seabury | Member, President's Foreign Intelligence Advisory Board |
| R. G. Stilwell | Deputy undersecretary of defense for policy |
| Charles Tyroler II | Member, Intelligence Oversight Board |
| William R. Van Cleave | Chairman-Designate, General Advisory Committee, Arms Control and Disarmament Agency. |
| Seymour Weiss | Member, President's Foreign Intelligence Advisory Board |
| Edward Bennett Williams | Member, President's Foreign Intelligence Advisory Board |

*Source:* David Shrebman, "Group Goes from Exile to Influence," *New York Times*, November 23, 1981.

tant secretary of defense for international security policy. All were positioned to spread neoconservative perspectives *and* put them into action.

Neoconservatives' presence in the Department of Defense's bureaucratic structure allowed them to influence defense policy in general and arms control policy in particular. Iklé oversaw the offices of International Security Policy, International Security Affairs, and Planning and Resources. These units were in charge of nuclear weapons policy, politicomilitary issues both within and outside Europe, and the planning of international security affairs. Iklé was also responsible for integrating the various plans and policies related to national security and overseeing military planning.[88] Thus, he was actively involved in arms control policy.

Since its creation in 1953, the office of the assistant secretary of defense for international security policy, led during the Reagan administration by Perle, has coordinated the Defense Department's participation in all foreign policy issues.[89] Although the influence of this office in the planning and decisionmaking process had varied from administration to administration, under Reagan it was expanded, reorganized, and renamed the Office of International Security Policy (ISP). These changes in ISP's structure facilitated the direct involvement of the Defense Department in American foreign affairs.

Likewise, as director of ACDA, Eugene Rostow represented the neoconservative perspective on arms control within the State Department. Established in 1961, ACDA was conceived of as part of the executive branch. Its main purpose was to serve as the principal advisory agency to the president and secretary of state on arms control and as a civilian counterweight to the military sector. Historically, the agency faced serious structural problems that limited its influence on American arms control policy. During the Reagan administration, as Barry Blechman and Janne Nolan assert, "The inter-agency mechanism for formulating arms control seems to [have] be[en] dominated by the Secretary of Defense and its subordinate. . . . The director of ACDA has hardly been present, much less decisive, in the Reagan administration."[90]

ACDA's minimal involvement in decisionmaking became less an obstacle than a means of promoting neoconservative views. ACDA became, in essence, a conservative pressure group that balanced the position of the State Department, whose top posts Alexander Haig had filled with some of the most important liberal and conservative establishment professionals, including Lawrence Eagleburger, Thomas Enders, and John Holdridge from the Foreign Service, and Richard Burt and Chester Crocker from the policy community. Together, they formed a moderate enclave of American foreign policy within a conservative administration. Caspar Weinberger, on the contrary, filled his subordinate positions with hard-liner political appointees.[91]

ACDA became an important place to press for the modification of the State Department's views on arms control. According to one scholar, Rostow got the job of ACDA director "because he was seen as more likely to counterbalance Haig's suspected softness on the issue."[92] According to Rostow, "There were some idealists in the State Department who opposed my view, but I took advantage of my position as the senior Democrat in the Reagan administration. Most of the time, I was respected." At ACDA, he continued, "we pushed strongly in the direction of an American military buildup. . . . We were able to speak about nuclear threat." He also had "cordial relations with the people of the Defense Department. I talked to them, and I tried to present the points jointly."[93]

Finally, the appointment of Paul Nitze—at Rostow's suggestion—as Intermediate-Range Nuclear Forces (INF) negotiator was a way both to help Rostow counterbalance Haig's position and to guarantee the presence of neoconservative views in negotiations with the Soviets. For Rostow, one of the biggest accomplishments of ACDA during the Reagan administration was promoting "a position about [the] INF treaty."[94] Rostow and Nitze shared ideological and political perspectives as well as a strong personal friendship. If, bureaucratically speaking, ACDA was irrelevant, it was nevertheless quite important for the promotion of neoconservative ideas.

Under Reagan, foreign affairs decisionmaking was organized in what the president called a "Cabinet government." Responsibility for making policy decisions was to occur within "Cabinet-level agencies." Under this scheme, the Department of State gained considerable control of interdepartmental groups. These groups were organized to "coordinate foreign policy planning and the operation of many government agencies involved in one or another way in foreign policy matters."[95] The State Department's Bureau of Political-Military Affairs coordinated the interdepartmental group on arms control. The other departments and agencies involved included the office of the assistant secretary of defense for ISP, ACDA, the JCS, the Arms Control Intelligence Staff of the CIA, and the NSC.

Among these agencies, the Bureau of Political-Military Affairs and ISP played a prominent role in developing arms control policy. Richard Burt, a former reporter for the *New York Times*, was in charge of the Bureau of

Political-Military Affairs. Perle headed the ISP. Burt was a moderate, pragmatic voice who worked to reconcile differences with the Soviet Union. In contrast, Perle was not only a leading neoconservative politician but was also considered by *Time* to be "the most influential Assistant Cabinet Secretary in 25 years."[96] He was highly suspicious of arms control and objected to any compromise with the Kremlin. A *Newsweek* article reported that Burt and Perle "fought a legendary bureaucratic war, with position papers and news leaks as their principal ammunition. Each man's objective was to win the inattentive mind of Ronald Reagan."[97]

Perle was politically well connected in Congress and the executive branch. As a former aide of Senator Henry Jackson, he had extensive experience in dealing with the legislature and defending neoconservatives' perspectives on arms control. He was also close to Caspar Weinberger, who trusted him. Young lieutenants, such as the deputy assistant secretaries Frank J. Gaffney and Douglas J. Feith, who shared Perle's viewpoints, also supported him. "My basic analysis," asserted Feith, who defined himself as a neoconservative, "was in line with [Perle's] basic analysis. He trusted me to make the right decisions."[98] Perle also brought others who shared his views to the Department of Defense. They, in turn, found that other neoconservatives already formed "part of the permanent government."[99] Neoconservatism had moved from intellectual and political circles and inserted itself into the Reagan administration's bureaucracy.

Perle and other neoconservatives worked on different fronts to introduce their ideas into American government. They were convinced that a more satisfactory arms balance was a prerequisite for feasible arms negotiations. Arms control was, they believed, the only way to restrain the Soviet nuclear threat. According to *Newsweek*, Perle—and I would add neoconservatives in general—"spearhead the administration's main initiatives—to deploy medium-range nuclear missiles in Europe, abandon the unratified SALT II agreement, and reinterpret the Anti–Ballistic Missiles treaty to permit the development of the Strategic Defense Initiative."[100] Thus, neoconservative ideas, institutions, and individuals such as Perle, Ikle, Nitze, Rostow, and Jackson influenced arms control policy.

## *Economic Interests*

Economic interests motivated the neoconservative ideas that influenced the U.S. military buildup and defense policy. Starting with his 1980 electoral campaign, Ronald Reagan proposed increasing American defense spending to confront the Soviet military threat. As Daniel Wirls has observed, "Reagan sustained the largest buildup in peacetime history, which by many measures exceeded spending during the Korean and Vietnam wars."[101] As table 5.4 shows, national defense spending in 1965 was $56.3 billion. By the beginning of the Carter administration in 1977, it had grown to $115.3 billion. Revolutions in Iran and Nicaragua, the Soviet invasion of Afghanistan, and constant pressure from neoconservative and other conservative organizations convinced Carter to increase the budget

*Table 5.4. The U.S. National Defense Budget, 1962–88*

| Year | Total Dollar Outlay (billions) | Outlay in Current Dollars (billions) | Outlay in Constant Dollars (billions) | Percentage of Gross National Product |
|---|---|---|---|---|
| 1962 | 58.0 | 52.3 | 202.2 | 9.4 |
| 1963 | 58.9 | 53.4 | 197.2 | 9.1 |
| 1964 | 60.4 | 54.8 | 198.8 | 8.7 |
| 1965 | 56.3 | 50.6 | 181.4 | 7.5 |
| 1966 | 64.0 | 58.1 | 197.9 | 7.9 |
| 1967 | 78.2 | 71.4 | 235.1 | 9.0 |
| 1968 | 89.0 | 81.9 | 254.8 | 9.6 |
| 1969 | 90.1 | 82.5 | 243.4 | 8.9 |
| 1970 | 90.4 | 81.7 | 225.6 | 8.3 |
| 1971 | 88.7 | 78.9 | 202.7 | 7.5 |
| 1972 | 89.9 | 79.2 | 190.9 | 6.9 |
| 1973 | 88.7 | 76.7 | 175.1 | 6.0 |
| 1974 | 92.7 | 79.3 | 163.3 | 5.6 |
| 1975 | 103.1 | 86.5 | 159.8 | 5.7 |
| 1976 | 108.1 | 89.6 | 153.6 | 5.3 |
| 1977 | 115.3 | 97.2 | 154.3 | 5.0 |
| 1978 | 123.5 | 104.5 | 155.0 | 4.8 |
| 1979 | 136.3 | 116.3 | 159.1 | 4.8 |
| 1980 | 155.2 | 134.0 | 164.0 | 5.0 |
| 1981 | 180.5 | 157.5 | 171.4 | 5.3 |
| 1982 | 209.3 | 185.3 | 185.3 | 5.9 |
| 1983 | 234.7 | 227.4 | 211.3 | 6.2 |
| 1984 | 253.0 | 252.7 | 230.0 | 6.4 |
| 1985 | 279.0 | 252.7 | 230.0 | 6.4 |
| 1986 | 299.7 | 273.4 | 244.0 | 6.5 |
| 1987 | 308.8 | 282.0 | 251.0 | 6.4 |
| 1988 | 319.8 | 290.4 | 252.8 | 6.1 |

*Source:* U.S. Office of Management and Budget, *Budget of the U.S. Government* (Washington, D.C.: U.S. Government Printing Office, various years).

to $155.2 billion in 1980. By 1982, the Reagan administration was spending $209.3 billion; and by 1988, $319.8 billion.

Reagan's emphasis on the American military buildup becomes clear if contrasted with other items of the general annual budget during his first term. From 1981 to 1985, Reagan allocated the largest share of federal expenditures to Social Security and welfare. In 1981, the president designated $235.5 billion. In 1984, this figure increased to $282.9 billion. Second only to welfare was defense. Expenditures for defense were higher than those for education, health, housing, and community and social services combined. In 1984, the Reagan administration spent $218.9 billion on defense, while expenditures on community and social services were $2.62 billion; on education, $16.3 billion; on housing, $22.7 billion; and on health, $97.4 billion.

This emphasis on defense spending was in large part the result of the mobilization of business in general and defense-related corporations in particular. As noted, in the late 1960s the members of the American business community mobilized politically to increase their profits in the face of government regulations and economic stagnation. They established organizations, founded political action committees (PACs), and financially supported think tanks. Defense corporations were part of this general tendency. The resurgence of anti-Soviet sentiments and American militarism was in part, I suggest, the consequence of the new political strategy of the defense business sector. According to Thomas Ferguson and Joel Rogers, the economic crisis that the United States began to experience in the late 1960s and early 1970s prompted American banks and industries to invest overseas.[102] The normalization of U.S.-Soviet relations, the size of the USSR, and the USSR's political stability augured well for investments in the Soviet Union. Pepsi-Cola, Chase Manhattan Bank, Caterpillar Tractors, and Control Data Corporation were some of the larger firms that invested in Lenin's land. As one might expect, neoconservatives criticized the attitude of the business community. "The American business community has disgraced itself," asserted Norman Podhoretz. "No one expected it—except Lenin—that they would be leading the parade."[103]

But soon, especially after the oil embargo and the recession of 1973–74, the members of the business community realized that the Soviet Union was not the paradise they thought. At the same time, the gross domestic product of developing countries grew. Opportunities for foreign investment in the developing world soon attracted business to those countries. "The existence of alternative investment and credit outlets," assert Ferguson and Rogers, "lowered the cost of disrupting U.S.-Soviet relations. Increased economic exposure in the Third World produced simultaneous demands for a 'liberalization' of U.S. attitudes toward the region and enhanced capacity for discrete military intervention within."[104] These changes in the patterns of foreign investment of U.S. corporations, together with American domestic opposition to détente, created significant support for an American military buildup.

Beginning in the early 1970s, U.S. defense contractors started to engage in broad political activities to defend their economic interests in the domestic arena. Among the most significant of these activities was the formation of defense industry PACs. The birth of defense PACs started in 1974 after the approval of financial electoral laws. Previously, campaign contributions from defense firms came via individuals. In 1968, according to Gordon Adams, individuals connected to defense companies made "federal campaign contributions of $1.2 million, concentrated primarily in Republican candidates."[105] Between April 1976 and February 1978, each of the eight major defense contractors at that time—Boeing, General Dynamics, Grumman, Lockheed, McDonnell Douglas, Northrop, Rockwell, and United Technologies—created PACs. From 1976 to 1980, "these defense contractors had total expenditures of $2.1 million."[106] In 1984, the political activities of defense-related corporations increased considerably. Total contributions to PACs by the "20 largest military contractors," the *New York Times* reported in 1985, "rose from $1,819,298 in 1980 to $3,636,587 in 1984, an increase of almost 100 percent. Of the twenty members receiving more than $15,000 from those PACs, 17 voted last week to approve the President's request for $1.5 billion to build more MX missiles. Thirteen of the 14 senators who received more than $30,000 backed Mr. Reagan on MX."[107] Defense-related PACs also contributed large sums to the 1986 congressional elections.[108]

Generally speaking, defense industry PACs, like many other PACs, focused on supporting incumbents. According to Larry Sabato, the "aerospace and defense industry PACs . . . typically support incumbents of both parties, especially from districts where major plants are located."[109] Sabato's assertion coincides with Adams's findings, which show that defense companies donated funds to the campaigns of members of Congress who either represented districts or states where the company had plant locations or were members of committees relevant to the interests of the defense industry and had the political power to affect the decisionmaking

*Table 5.5. Contributions of Defense Industry Political Action Committees to Members of Key Congressional Committees, 1976–80*

| Member | Dollar Amount of Donation | Number of Political Action Committees |
|---|---|---|
| *Senate Armed Services Committee* | | |
| Strom Thurmond | 14,300 | 8 |
| John Tower | 13,125 | 7 |
| John Warren | 11,000 | 7 |
| Sam Nunn | 9,000 | 5 |
| Barry Goldwater | 7,800 | 4 |
| *Senate Defense Appropriations Subcommittee* | | |
| Ernest Hollings | 13,000 | 8 |
| Warren Magnuson | 12,400 | 6 |
| Jack Gran | 5,500 | 4 |
| Edward Brooke | 5,300 | 5 |
| Daniel Inouye | 5,100 | 5 |
| *House Armed Services Committee* | | |
| Charles Wilson | 12,925 | 6 |
| Jim Lloyd | 11,650 | 8 |
| Mendel Davis | 10,100 | 8 |
| Bob Wilson | 9,700 | 7 |
| Richard Ichord | 9,925 | 8 |
| William Dickinson | 8,500 | 8 |
| David Price | 6,020 | 3 |
| Robert Daniel | 5,900 | 5 |
| Floyd Spence | 5,800 | 7 |
| Donald Mitchell | 5,200 | 7 |
| *House Defense Appropriations Subcommittee* | | |
| Joseph Addabbo | 10,800 | 6 |
| Robert Giaimo | 7,700 | 7 |
| Jack Edwards | 7,250 | 8 |
| Bill Chappell | 6,400 | 6 |
| Bill Burlison | 6,200 | 6 |
| John McFall | 5,990 | 7 |
| Elford Cederberg | 5,800 | 7 |
| Norman Dicks | 3,775 | 6 |
| Jack Kemp | 2,100 | 2 |
| James Robinson | 1,700 | 4 |

*Source:* Gordon Adams, *The Politics of Defense Contracting: The Iron Triangle* (New Brunswick, N.J.: Transaction Books, 1982), 117–18.

process in the legislature. As table 5.5 shows, the eight PACs mentioned above gave the most to members of key committees.

These giving patterns highlight two facts. First, a significant number of those members of Congress who received economic support from defense contractors were well-known conservative political figures. Legislators like John Tower, Barry Goldwater, Jack Kemp, and Bob Wilson advocated a strong military posture. The ideological consonance between the Reagan administration and members of these defense-related committees facilitated the approval of Reagan's defense policies.

Second, defense contractors' contributions to campaigns created political links between legislators and defense industries and between the public sphere and private economic interests, which had political implications and economic consequences. Because success in electoral campaigns currently depends considerably on politicians' ability to obtain economic resources, defense-related corporations are crucial in helping congressional and presidential candidates obtain public posts. Their financial support becomes a reward for those politicians who are sympathetic to their interests and a punishment for those who do not share their views.

During the Reagan administration, defense industries were able to parlay their influence into substantial contracts with the Department of Defense. From 1982 to 1984, the top twenty companies together gained contracts worth a total of $148 billion. In the same period, McDonnell Douglas was awarded contracts worth $19 billion; General Dynamics, $19 billion; Rockwell International Corporation, $13 billion; General Electric, $13 billion; and Lockheed, $12 billion (table 5.6).

The defense industry also invested heavily in conservative political organizations and think tanks. Big corporations in general, and the defense industry in particular, gave significant amounts of money to these institutions with hopes of influencing decisionmakers. Beginning in the late 1960s, neoconservatism had become perhaps the best-financed conservative expression in the United States. Wealthy corporations and neoconservative foundations supported neoconservative journals, institutions, and academic posts, giving neoconservatism a strong presence in the American public arena. For example, the American Enterprise Institute was primarily financed by large corporations. In its 1982–83 *Annual Report*, AEI declared that 32 percent of its total income came from corporations and 25 percent from corporate foundations. Among its corporate sponsors were Eli Lilly and Company, Ford Motor Company, Reader's Digest, and Procter & Gamble. AEI also received major donations from the Pew Charitable

Table 5.6. Top Contractors of the U.S. Department of Defense, 1982–84

| Company | Total Sales (millions of dollars) | | | Contract Awards (millions of dollars) | | | Contractor Rank | | |
|---|---|---|---|---|---|---|---|---|---|
| | 1982 | 1983 | 1984 | 1982 | 1983 | 1984 | 1982 | 1983 | 1984 |
| AVCO Corp. | 1,223 | 1,514 | 1,528 | 668 | 676 | 873 | 28 | 29 | 27 |
| Beech Aircraft Co. | 568 | 642 | 723 | 167 | 156 | 116 | N.A. | N.A. | N.A. |
| Boeing Co. | 9,035 | 11,129 | 10,354 | 3,239 | 4,423 | 4,564 | 6 | 5 | 5 |
| Cessna | 832 | 524 | 694 | 7 | 2 | 8 | N.A. | N.A. | N.A. |
| Ex-Cell-O Corp. | 1,027 | 954 | 1,141 | 60 | 36 | 44 | N.A. | N.A. | N.A. |
| FMC Corp. | 3,187 | 3,247 | 3,338 | 1,371 | 1,236 | 3,338 | 14 | 17 | 18 |
| Ford Motor Co. | 37,067 | 44,455 | 52,366 | 897 | 1,072 | 1,184 | 20 | 22 | 20 |
| General Dynamics | 5,890 | 6,799 | 7,291 | 5,891 | 6,818 | 5,951 | N.A. | 1 | 3 |
| General Electric | 26,500 | 26,797 | 27,947 | 3,654 | 4,518 | 4,514 | 4 | 4 | 6 |
| General Motors | 60,026 | 74,582 | 83,890 | 689 | 893 | 1,019 | 26 | 23 | 23 |
| Grumman Corp. | 2,057 | 2,255 | 2,604 | 1,900 | 2,298 | 2,419 | 11 | 11 | 11 |
| HARSCO Corp. | 979 | 839 | 1,101 | 102 | 139 | 233 | N.A. | 95 | 75 |
| Honeywell Inc. | 5,386 | 5,667 | 6,073 | 1,217 | 1,114 | 1,354 | 16 | 21 | 17 |
| Hughes Aircraft Co. | 4,386 | 4,938 | 4,925 | 3,141 | 3,240 | 3,231 | 7 | 9 | 7 |
| Lockheed Co. | 5,613 | 6,490 | 8,113 | 3,499 | 4,006 | 4,967 | 5 | 6 | 4 |
| McDonnell Douglas Corp. | 7,331 | 8,111 | 9,663 | 5,630 | 6,143 | 7,684 | 2 | 2 | 1 |
| Raytheon Co. | 5,217 | 5,631 | 5,996 | 2,262 | 2,728 | 3,093 | 9 | 10 | 9 |
| Rockwell International Corp. | 7,395 | 8,098 | 9,322 | 2,691 | 4,545 | 6,219 | 8 | 3 | 2 |
| United Technologies Corp. | 12,510 | 13,327 | 14,826 | 4,208 | 3,867 | 3,206 | 3 | 7 | 8 |
| Westinghouse Corp. | 9,745 | 9,533 | 10,265 | 1,492 | 1,778 | 1,943 | 13 | 14 | 13 |

*Note:* N.A. = not applicable.
*Source:* Compiled from Paul L. Ferrari, Raul Madrid, and Jeff Knopf, *U.S. Arms Exports: Policies and Contractors* (Cambridge, Mass.: Ballinger, 1988).

149

Trusts, the Smith Richardson Foundation, the Olin Foundation, and the Alfred P. Sloan Foundation. In 1987, AEI received corporate donations from three of the top twenty defense contractors: General Electric, General Motors, and Rockwell International.

The neoconservative Coalition for a Democratic Majority, while not significantly supported by defense-related corporations, is another interesting case. The CDM's income came primarily from small personal donations and contributions from the labor movement. Important CDM *events* were, however, funded by defense-related corporations. In 1985, private citizens and organizations underwrote the CDM's Henry M. Jackson Friend of Freedom Award Dinner. Among the thirteen event sponsors were three of the top twenty defense contractors: General Dynamics, Lockheed, and Northrop. Other patrons of this event included defense companies such as AVCO and United Technologies Corporation.[110]

The Committee on the Present Danger presents another model. The CPD's rhetoric and political discourse were extremely useful for defense contractors. At the time of its creation, the CPD stated quite clearly that it would not accept contributions from "companies or persons who derive substantial portions of their income from the defense industry."[111] This provision did not, however, exclude financial contributions from corporate foundations tied to defense industries.[112] Nevertheless, I found no evidence of economic links between the CPD and the defense industry. Moreover, I found several instances of defense contractors offering money to the CPD and the organization openly rejecting their donations. Defense corporations certainly benefited from the CPD's discourse, but, at least according to my research, these benefits were free of economic charge.

Thus, corporations and, in particular, the defense industry helped to convert neoconservative ideas into public policies. Of course, the military-industrial complex did not—could not—*invent* neoconservative ideas. As I have shown, neoconservatives expressed these ideas long before the mobilization of the corporate community in the late 1960s. However, the economic crisis of the 1970s made a marriage of convenience feasible between neoconservatives and defense-related corporations. As Douglas Feith points out, "When you have people who independently, and intellectually, and honestly, and philosophically come up with an argument that America needs to be strong, it should not surprise anybody that as these people are putting out these ideas, people who have an economic reason for supporting those ideas might find ways to support them."[113]

# 6

# The Second Neoconservative Movement

In 1996, Norman Podhoretz announced the collapse of the neoconservative movement. It had become difficult, he declared in an article published in *Commentary*, to distinguish the movement from other political expressions.[1] But history would prove him wrong. George W. Bush's ascent to the White House marked the return of neoconservatives to high-level positions in the U.S. government. Indeed, from the beginning of the new Republican administration, neoconservatism became the leading voice in foreign affairs. The terrorist attacks on September 11, 2001, strengthened this new generation of neoconservatives' position in both government and society. For years, neoconservatives had worked hard to construct a view that helped the U.S. government justify its unilateral position in foreign affairs. After the collapse of the Twin Towers, they were once again able to implement their foreign policy perspectives. Understanding neoconservative ideas, I assert, is a prerequisite to understanding the logic behind the American war against Iraq and the dominant tendencies of American foreign policy during the George W. Bush administration's first term.

In this chapter and the remaining chapters of this book, I turn to this second generation of neoconservatives. I do not attempt to offer an exhaustive account of this political and intellectual expression; others have done that accurately and well.[2] Rather, I compare and contrast the first and second generations of neoconservatives. In doing so, I seek to explain how and why the first neoconservative movement differed from the second. In the process, I highlight the main characteristics of the members of the second neoconservative movement and their convergences with and divergences from the first generation, by concentrating on the second neocon-

servative movement's history, organization, ideology, and political influence on the war on terrorism.

## Drawing Distinctions: Second-Generation Neoconservatives in the Shadow of the First

Stephen Skowronek convincingly argues that in the United States, presidential accomplishment is fundamentally connected to the historical context in which a president acts.[3] The historical context also helps us comprehend the behavior of other social actors. Neoconservatism achieved
significant influence at two particular historical moments characterized by
the leadership of Republican presidents Ronald Reagan and George W.
Bush. At these moments, neoconservatives were the voices behind the
throne, the intellectuals giving advice to the "king" and persuading him to
implement a particular foreign policy. The second neoconservative movement has a very different history, however, than its predecessor. The
second movement has been characterized by different patterns of growth
and surges in influence and has different political origins, affiliations, and
intellectual credentials than the first generation of neoconservatives.

The 1980s and the first decade of the twenty-first century were very
different periods in American history. As I have mentioned in previous
chapters, by the end of the 1960s and early 1970s, we observed the exhaustion of the New Deal order and the emergence of what Walter Dean
Burnham has called the nonpartisan realignment, which, as I have discussed, was characterized by the decline of political parties and the increasing importance of the mass media, the emergence of candidate-
centered campaigns, the professionalization of Congress, and divided
government. These structural features provided the broad historical context in which Ronald Reagan—and to a lesser extent George W. Bush—
emerged and governed.

In specific terms, Reagan achieved power in 1981 after defeating the
incumbent president, Jimmy Carter. The ascent of Reagan was, to a significant degree, the outcome of Carter's poor performance. The arrival of
Carter in the White House and his four years in office can be described
with two words: hope and disappointment. Carter represented hope because, at a time when corruption and scandals were common in Washington, he emerged onto the national political stage as someone uncontami-
nated by dirty politics. Because he was aware of the historical conditions

of his time, his campaign for the White House was based on open criticism of the Washington establishment. This "country deserves," he asserted, "a government as good as its people." In a way, he was the Democratic Party's answer to the general crisis of those days. But he was also a disappointment, because he left the presidency with a highly questionable record. During his administration, several economic, political, and international problems emerged. By 1980, inflation had reached 13 percent, and his energy program was in disarray. His administration was so criticized that by June 1979, only 29 percent of the population approved of his performance as the chief executive. This figure mirrors George W. Bush's approval rating a few months before he left the White House.[4]

The Carter presidency coincided with the growth of the United States' "global crisis," which was variably termed a "crisis of consensus," a "crisis of democracy," or a "crisis of the state." The power and legitimacy of political institutions such as political parties and the presidency declined, troubles in coordination between government bodies and the management of public policy became evident, and citizens began to display open distrust of their leaders. Academics such as James Sundquist and James McGregor Burns and politicians such as Lloyd Cutler and C. Douglas Dillon openly talked about America's governability crisis and even proposed the adoption of a parliamentary system.[5] As Walter Dean Burnham put it, "By the 1980s, 'ungovernability' was very much in the air."[6]

Throughout the years of the Carter administration, the United States remained immersed in the ideology of the Cold War. America was fighting an old enemy, an antagonist ideology, a strong international rival, and an adversary state. Soviet communism was not only the American rival in the international scene; it was also an opposing economic, political, social, and cultural model. Communism was the antithesis of the United States. In a way, during this period American identity was defined in opposition to an unacceptable "other": Soviet communism. Thus, Carter faced serious problems in international affairs.

In 1979, with the revolutions in Iran and Nicaragua, the United States lost two important allies in the Middle East and Central America. In Iran, Americans not only saw the collapse of a conservative regime sympathetic to U.S. views but also experienced the seizure of American Embassy personnel in Tehran. U.S. citizens perceived the capture of American hostages as a clear expression of vulnerability. "The long, humiliating Iranian hostages crisis," wrote the historian Alonzo Hamby, "left the nation with a sense of futility and impotence; perhaps more than any other issue, it was responsible for Carter's downfall."[7] The United States was likewise confronted with the Soviet invasion of Afghanistan and the spread of communist regimes in different parts of the world. By the time of the presidential election of 1980, it was clear that Carter's reelection was in danger. On November 4, 1980, Ronald Reagan obtained 51 percent of the popular vote to 41 percent for Carter and 7 percent for John Anderson. Reagan won 489 electoral votes. Carter received only 49. Reagan took 44 states, while Carter won only 6. By any criterion, this was a landslide victory.

It was in this historical context, marked by a perception of the Carter administration's weakness, failure, and vulnerability, and the growing threat of international communism, that Reagan and neoconservativism emerged as an alternative. Both Reagan and the leading neoconservative thinkers had once been associates of radical leftist organizations. Now, however, most were members of the neoconservative organization the Committee on the Present Danger. Adamantly anticommunist, they saw that America's power on the international scene was deteriorating. They also believed that the United States needed to reemerge as the indisputable leader of the "Free World." Very much products of their historical time, they believed the Soviet Union could be defeated. Reagan had the political power and rhetorical skills to promote policies that accorded with his ideological perspective. But he did not have solid arguments to back his general views. The neoconservatives, however, had what Reagan needed: a distinguished intellectual reputation and a set of clear, consistent, well-argued ideas. In the late 1970s and early 1980s, Reagan and the neoconservatives formed a marriage of convenience to promote neoconservative views on foreign affairs.

By 2000, the United States did not have a competitive rival in the world—at least in military terms. The decline of the communist world, dramatically symbolized by the collapse of the Berlin Wall in 1991, left the United States the sole world power. The absence of a significant threat substantially altered the place of the United States in the world and the nature of American foreign policy. Since the early 1950s American foreign policy had been constructed around containment, the idea of restraining the communist world. "The absence of serious threats to American security," Kenneth Waltz wrote in the early 1990s, "gives the United States wide latitude in making foreign policy choices. A dominant power acts internationally only when the spirit moves it."[8]

Thus, when Bill Clinton arrived at the White House, he had no enemy to fight, no rival to struggle against, and no foe to fear. He had to reinvent

American foreign policy at a time when the electorate was indifferent to international events. He presented a moderate program highly consistent with the principles of the Democratic Leadership Council, a centrist organization that he had helped to create. He privileged international trade issues, brokering trade pacts such as the North American Free Trade Agreement and the General Agreement on Tariffs and Trade, and participating actively in the World Trade Organization. His administration intervened in major wars in Europe, East Asia, and the Middle East, worked to remove Slobodan Milošević from Yugoslavia, promoted peace in Ireland, and helped to organize peace negotiations between Israel and Palestine. Clinton also worked to dissuade North Korea from acquiring nuclear weapons, and he supported China's entry into the World Trade Organization. But his foreign policy record was also marked by significant failures. His administration failed in its humanitarian efforts in Bosnia, Somalia, and Rwanda, and the United States' relationship with Russia deteriorated substantially. Yet he worked to reduce weapons of mass destruction, favored a more open world economy, and tried to build a world order in harmony with American values, emphasizing the promotion of democracy and respect for human rights in the world. In all, as Stephen M. Walt has asserted, "The foreign policy of the Clinton administration has been well suited to an era when there is little to gain in foreign policy and much to lose."[9]

Foreign policy was not a central issue in the 2000 presidential campaign. As Norman Ornstein asserted, when Americans were asked, "What is the most important problem facing the country today?" only 4 percent chose international issues and foreign affairs.[10] In studies of the 2000 election, foreign policy was barely addressed and in some cases was not noted at all.[11] Americans were more concerned about domestic issues, in particular the state of the economy, than with international affairs.

During the 2000 presidential campaign, neither George W. Bush nor the Democratic candidate, Al Gore, had to present a general strategy to combat international communism. Of course, there were in fact many important international issues that affected the presidential election. The emergence of China as an important world economic power, security in the Middle East, and missile defense preoccupied many Americans. But foreign policy was not a major concern at either the presidential or the congressional levels. Ronald Reagan's campaign had been built on a harsh critique of Carter's weak foreign policy, and his candidacy was presented as the only hope for the renaissance of American supremacy in the world. The Bush campaign was based on a critique of the liberal position of the

Clinton administration at a time when the United States was the undisputed dominant world power.

At the beginning of the 2000 presidential campaign, the relationship between Bush and the neoconservatives was strained. The neoconservatives supported John McCain's candidacy, generally considering Bush a second-class politician. During the election, William Kristol went so far as to call "getting in bed with Bush" a mistake.[12] The neoconservatives' distrust of Bush came primarily from the intellectual branch of the movement. The political branch, in contrast, cultivated a relationship with Bush. Several neoconservative politicians, including Richard Perle and Paul Wolfowitz, became quite close to Bush when they were brought in as his advisers. "Paul Wolfowitz," Joshua Muravchik later recalled, "wanted to be secretary of defense. He campaigned very hard for that position. . . . It was kind of a surprise when Bush and Cheney brought Rumsfeld back from retirement and gave Paul a consolation prize."[13] Perle later remembered that Bush "didn't know very much . . . [but] had the confidence to ask questions that revealed he didn't know very much. . . . He was eager to learn. . . . . You got the sense that if he believed something, he'd pursue [it] tenaciously."[14] Wolfowitz considered Bush "the 'new Scoop Jackson.'" According to Wolfowitz, Bush "wanted to be told what needed doing and how it should be done."[15] Thus, in Bush, the neoconservative politicians found an ideal candidate. He was willing to pay attention and be trained; he was a politician who could be influenced by the neoconservatives' viewpoints. He became the channel used by the neoconservatives to regain their influence on American foreign policy.

Upon his election, Bush appointed several neoconservatives to important positions in the Defense and State departments. The neoconservatives' influence on foreign affairs became particularly evident after the September 11, 2001, terrorist attacks. "The underlying principles that some of us were pushing," asserted Gary Schmitt, "became more relevant after 9/11."[16] Contingency made an obscure president—appointed after a disputed election—and a well-known group of politicians and intellectuals central figures in the development of American foreign affairs.


## Ideology

The ideological principles of the second generation of neoconservatives differ from those of the first generation. This is due not only to the different historical context in which each expression flourished but also to the historical trajectory each traveled. Some of the main leaders of the first neoconservative generation had been leftists in their youth, and they were familiar with Marxist principles. Most of them were Democrats who were against the nomination of George McGovern. Later, they founded the Coalition for a Democratic Majority, and, still later, moved to the Republican Party. Some people, like Ben Wattenberg and Peter Rosenblatt, remained affiliated to the Democratic Party, although Wattenberg no longer voted Democratic. In contrast, the second generation has always been Republican and conservative, having absorbed neoconservative views over decades.[17] "I have never been a Trotskyite, a Maoist or even Democrat," asserts Max Boot, "but I've always identified with the Grand Old Party. The same might be said of the other standard-bearers, even those (like Bill Kristol and John Podhoretz) who are the offspring of famous neocons. They, too, have been right from the start."[18] This helps explain, at least partially, the radical nature of the second neoconservative movement. They have turned neoconservative views into an ultra-neoconservative vision, and they have incorporated new, even extreme ideas that in some ways are contrary to traditional neoconservative perspectives.

Needless to say, there is a strong nexus between some members of the first and the second generations. This connection has three primary manifestations. First, there are personal connections between members of the two generations. Norman Podhoretz, Irving Kristol, and Richard Perle maintained close relationships with John Podhoretz, William Kristol, Douglas Feith, and Frank Gaffney. In two cases here, they were even fathers and sons.

Second, the members of the first generation have collaborated with the members of the second. This was the case for Paul Wolfowitz, Richard Perle, Norman Podhoretz, Joshua Muravchik, and the late Jeane Kirkpatrick, although some of them had significant differences with the second generation, particularly Kirkpatrick and Irving Kristol.

Third, the first generation has influenced the second, particularly with regard to theoretical frameworks. The first generation was full of scholars who were well recognized in their academic fields. Many of them were professors who dedicated their life to teaching and research at elite American universities. Some had their books issued by important publishing houses and had their articles appear in peer-reviewed journals. Scholars like Seymour Martin Lipset, Samuel Huntington, Gertrude Himmelfarb, Nathan Glazer, and James Q. Wilson, to mention but a few, received many accolades for the quality of their research. The members of the second generation, in contrast, are less oriented toward the academy. They are fundamentally dedicated to journalistic activities rather than social science research, and they thus write for broader audiences and are committed to influencing the decisionmaking process. Though more practical-minded, the second-generation neoconservatives nonetheless have adapted the theoretical frameworks generated by their forerunners to build their own policy views. This is particularly evident with regard to foreign policy. Some of Huntington's books and articles, for example, form the heart of current neoconservative thinking. They were used—and sometimes modified—to construct the argument in favor of the invasion of Iraq.

# 7

# Second-Generation Neoconservatives and Foreign Policy

Current neoconservative foreign policy views are fundamentally related to the downfall of the communist world. The collapse of the Berlin Wall left neoconservatives in a political void. As Seymour Martin Lipset maintains, neoconservatives have been linked by their "past involvement in the struggle against communism as anti-Stalinists in radical movements or as liberal opponents of communist-dominated factions in sections of the Democratic Party where the communists were once strong, e.g., the states of Washington, Minnesota, and New York."[1] Thus, with the end of the Cold War, neoconservatives lost their enemy and, in a certain sense, the reason for their existence.[2]

In the 1990s, neoconservatives criticized the isolationist foreign policy adopted by the United States. For instance, William Kristol and Robert Kagan maintained that "the lack of a visible threat to U.S. vital interests or world peace has tempted Americans to absentmindedly dismantle the material and spiritual foundation on which their national well-being has been based."[3] The late Harvard political scientist Samuel Huntington observed that the United States had constructed its identity in contrast to an undesirable other. He wrote: "The United States, perhaps more than most countries, may need an opposing other to maintain its unity."[4] Finally, the late Irving Kristol, in accord with Huntington's perspective, asserted nine months before September 11 that "with the end of the Cold War, what we really need is an obvious ideological and threatening enemy, one worthy of our mettle, one that can unite us in opposition."[5]

## Theoretical Influences: Leo Strauss and Samuel Huntington

Two distinguished scholars, Samuel Huntington and Leo Strauss, have allegedly influenced current neoconservative thought. The two had quite different backgrounds. Huntington (1927–2008) was a generation younger than Strauss. He was an American citizen who lived almost his entire life in the United States, primarily in New England. Strauss (1899–1973) was a German Jewish immigrant who came to the United States fleeing Nazism and became an American citizen in 1944. As with many mid-twentieth-century European immigrants, his experience of Nazism marked his entire life. Huntington was a political scientist who worked primarily in the fields of comparative and American politics, whereas Strauss was a political philosopher who specialized in the classics.

Huntington was frequently associated with the first generation of the neoconservatives, whereas Strauss, although admired by some neoconservatives of the first generation, was noted as an influence on a handful of second-generation neoconservatives. Huntington addressed many topics with direct policy and political consequences, whereas Strauss's policy influence was more indirect. The implications of Strauss's works must be deduced from his texts. Huntington's influence on neoconservatism has not been controversial, because journalists and scholars frequently considered him one of them, whereas Strauss's impact on the second generation of neoconservatives has been the object of considerable criticism. Some neoconservatives have openly rejected his influence. In a nutshell, Huntington had an impact on second-generation neoconservatives' foreign policy, but Strauss's influence on neoconservatism is doubtful.

Huntington's books—*American Politics: The Promise of Disharmony* (1981) and *The Clash of Civilizations and the Remaking of the World Order* (1996)—provided an important intellectual framework for neoconservatives' political views. First, Huntington argues, as mentioned above, that Americans have built their identity in contrast to an unacceptable "other," such as international communism. Second, he posits the existence of a "clash of civilizations" between the West and the rest of the world. Finally, he asserts that the United States and Western Europe are at war with virtually all forms of Islamism.[6]

Journalists of all stripes and neoconservatives have applied Huntington's views to explain the terrorist attacks of September 11, 2001, on the World Trade Center and the Pentagon. As Ervand Abrahamian observed, the "mainstream media in the USA automatically, implicitly, and unanimously adopted Huntington's paradigm to explain September 11."[7] Similarly, neoconservative thinkers frequently based their analysis of the events of September 11 on Huntington's thought, though they did not always credit him. Norman Podhoretz, for example, has asserted that in countries like Iraq and Iran, the United States is identified as the "Great Satan." According to his perspective, the hostility of these countries toward the United States is the product not of what "we have done wrong but of what we have done right. To them our democratic polity, and the freedom that goes with it, is as corrupting as our economic system. They want to destroy all of this, first in the Middle East itself, and then in as much of the world as they can, so that the way of life they believe is commanded by Allah can rise up again in all sacred purity from out of the degenerated rubble."[8] Finally, Huntington himself explained that "the "making[s] of a general clash of civilizations exist. Reactions to September 11 and the American response were strictly along civilization lines."[9] Huntington's ideas seemed to predict what happened on September 11, thereby legitimizing neoconservative perspectives on foreign policy. He also offered an academic explanation for the tragic events experienced by the United States. Above all, September 11 supplied the ideological enemy that he claimed the United States needed.

Strauss's influence on the second generation of neoconservatives has been more controversial, in at least six ways. First, for scholars like Catherine and Michael Zuckert, the alleged nexus between Strauss and George W. Bush's foreign policy is a very weak one. In the view of these scholars, the fact "that some of those in Washington who have been involved with Bush policy once studied with Strauss or with students of Strauss, or once knew someone who shook hands with a cousin of someone who studied with Strauss, is not sufficient reason to identify that person as a 'Straussian' or to connect his or her policies activities with Strauss." In their perspective, "the media vision of Strauss and the Straussians bears little relation to reality. . . . The policies of neoconservatives . . . show little influence [from Strauss] and certainly do not derive from Strauss's political thinking."[10] Contrary to this view, other analysts, like Seymour Hersh of *The New Yorker*, maintain that Abraham Shulsky at the Pentagon was, essentially, a student of Strauss. Hersh argues that Shulsky and Gary Schmitt, formerly at the Project for the New American Century (PNAC), were applying certain Straussian principles to criticize the intelligence community.[11]

Second, Strauss very rarely wrote on contemporary public policy, American politics, or foreign policy. He was a philosopher, and his "thought does not easily translate into policy directives."[12] Consequently, it is very difficult to establish clear connections between Strauss and neoconservatives. His lessons on American politics and foreign policy have to be inferred from his texts. Third, Strauss is well known for his complicated writing style. According to Earl Shorris, "Leo Strauss is more difficult to read than almost anyone including Wittgenstein, Heidegger, and Joyce." Shorris emphasizes that Strauss "did not want to be understood by any but the few, his disciples."[13]

Fourth, most neoconservatives never studied with Strauss and are not familiar with his work. Many never even encountered him in print. Max Boot observed that "Strauss's views inspired some of early neocons; few read him today, contrary to all the articles asserting that . . . Strauss is the neocons' mentor."[14] But even those neoconservatives who studied with Strauss denied the nexus. Paul Wolfowitz, who studied with Strauss at the University of Chicago, remembers taking "two terrific courses from Leo Strauss as a graduate student. One was on Montesquieu's spirit of laws, which helped me understand our Constitution better. And one was on Plato's laws. The idea that this has anything to do with foreign policy is just laughable."[15] Thus, whereas for some neoconservative intellectuals of the second generation like William Kristol, Strauss is seen as the inspiration for Bush's foreign policy, for other neoconservative politicians like Wolfowitz, this idea is patently ridiculous.

Fifth, some scholars argued that Straussian neoconservatives had transformed the original views of their mentor.[16] Thus, neoconservative visions do not represent Strauss's actual perspective. Sixth, with some exceptions, many neoconservatives, especially those involved in direct policymaking, are not interested in classical political philosophy but rather in political action. In a nutshell, it is important not to overrate Strauss's influence on neoconservatism.

Strauss certainly had an impact on some first-generation thinkers and politicians such as Irving Kristol and Wolfowitz. Kristol recalled, "Strauss's work produced the kind of intellectual shock that is a once-in-a-lifetime experience. He turned one's intellectual universe upside down."[17] Some second-generation neoconservatives were also familiar with Strauss's thinking. Among them we find William Kristol, Gary Schmitt, Robert Kagan, Lewis Libby, and John Podhoretz.[18] William Kristol learned about

Strauss through Harvey Mansfield, a conservative scholar of political theory at Harvard University, and was impressed. Sometimes Kristol cites Strauss to support his arguments in favor of the Bush Doctrine.[19] He even coauthored an article on Strauss's work with Steven Lenzer. In that essay, the authors claim that the philosopher had influenced the political action of the Bush administration. They write, "President Bush's advocacy of 'regime change'—which avoids the pitfalls of a wishful global universalism on the one hand, and a fatalistic cultural determinism on the other—is a not altogether unworthy product of Strauss's rehabilitation of the notion of regime."[20]

The notion of regime, highlighted by Kristol, is an important concept in Strauss's work. It is also the main idea used by journalists to establish the links between neoconservatives and this German American philosopher. Strauss considered the nature of regimes essential to understand politics. For him, the political regimes of his time—liberal democracy, communism, and fascism—were qualitatively different. He judged that liberal democratic regimes were the best possible regimes, and he considered the United States the bulwark of freedom. Finally, he argued that the preeminence of liberal democracy over its adversaries, communism and fascism, "is intelligible only as a reflection of the superiority of the political thought underlying liberal democracy, the natural rights doctrine."[21] For Strauss, therefore, liberal democracy was the alternative to totalitarianisms from the left and right.[22]

Perhaps the best way to evaluate the influence of Strauss on neoconservatism is to understand that the implications of his "teachings were almost always indirect."[23] In my view, the importance of Strauss' work for some and only some neoconservatives, if any, can be summarized with these ideas: (1) Communism and fascism are evil, which easily translates as Islam is also evil; (2) democracies operate in fundamentally different ways than tyrannies; and (3) the United States needs "[a] leader, especially strong in his actions, firm in his beliefs and willing to go against the grain to combat tyranny."[24] The first two points—in different expressions—have been central elements of conservative thought, as has the conviction that strong leadership is crucial.

Undeniably, however, the second generation of neoconservatives has promoted ideas that can be traced to both Huntington and Strauss—ideas such as the clash of civilizations; the importance of regimes, and a proper evaluation of the natures of regimes; and the value of promoting democracy in non-Western countries. Neoconservatives have considered these principles, and then have transformed them to create their own foreign policy perspective.

## Preemptive Attack, Regime Change, and the Promotion of Democracy

According to Francis Fukuyama—an often-cited neoconservative advocate who a few years ago broke with the movement—the core foreign policy views of the second generation of neoconservatives are "regime change; benevolent hegemony; unipolarity; preemption; and American exceptionalism." These main principles became, in the words of Fukuyama, the "hallmarks of the Bush administration's foreign policy."[25]

Although these ideas can be traced throughout the course of American history, neoconservatives have resurrected and reconfigured them in a new, comprehensive fashion. Robert Kagan, for example, has tried to legitimize neoconservative foreign policy views by maintaining that the United States is a fundamentally neoconservative state. He has asserted that the "tendencies associated these days with neoconservatism are more deeply rooted in American tradition than the critics care to admit, which means they will not so easily be uprooted, even by the coming epochal presidential election."[26] Elliott Abrams has similarly asserted, "People can say, 'Well, this theory [neoconservatism] has been disproved.' I would say, 'Come back in five years, and you will see [that] the next president of either party is pursuing essentially the same policy.' If not, you do not have foreign policy."[27]

Neoconservatives explicitly regard themselves as the heirs of Ronald Reagan's foreign policy views.[28] Despite the fact that Norman Podhoretz criticized Reagan severely, neoconservatives "[have] discover[ed] no good ground for abandoning the hard line they took during the Cold War."[29] In 2004, Jeane Kirkpatrick asserted, "President Reagan gave us a strong, steady policy that paved the way for a renaissance of freedom in the United States and the world.[30] Indeed, neoconservatives such as Abrams, Frank Gaffney, and Joshua Muravchik share Kristol's and Kagan's neo-Reaganite label.[31] "We seem to have forgotten," maintain the signers of the PNAC's Statement of Principles, "the essential elements of the Reagan Administration's success: a military that is strong and ready to meet both present and future challenges; a foreign policy that boldly and purposefully promotes American principles abroad; and international leadership that accepts the United States' responsibilities."[32] William Kristol declares, "In the pantheon of modern Republican heroes, he [Reagan] stands alone."[33] Neoconservatives consider themselves guardians of the Reagan tradition and followers of ideas crafted by the first generation of neoconservatives.

## Preemptive Attack

The notion of preemptive attack, defined "as the initiation of military action in anticipation of harmful actions that are neither presently occurring nor imminent,"[34] is frequently associated with neoconservatism. However, as John Lewis Gaddis has shown, the idea has a long history and constitutes a central element of American foreign policy history.[35] Gaddis is not alone in this judgment. Several years ago, Melvyn P. Leffler wrote, "Preemptive strikes to eliminate threats are a strategy nearly as old as the United States."[36] Before George W. Bush, American presidents contemplated the possibility of preemptive attacks against the Soviet Union and the People's Republic of China, and American foreign policy toward Latin American at the beginning of the twentieth century had a clear preemptive component. As Leffler wrote, "When Theodore Roosevelt justified intervention in the Caribbean and Central America, it was explicitly a preemptive form of intervention."[37] The Bill Clinton administration considered the option of prevention as a foreign policy strategy and was close to deploying a preemptive attack against Afghanistan to capture Osama bin Laden.

Preemption was neither a new concept nor a neoconservative creation. Neoconservatives have resurrected and popularized the concept and, what is more, integrated preemption into a comprehensive foreign policy framework for the post–Cold War era. The logic underlying this structure is perfectly suitable for a country that feels threatened by a powerful enemy. September 11 created a historical context in which preemptive attacks became a viable policy alternative. Thus neoconservatives, with their aggressive and often conspiratorial arguments, were able to persuade President Bush to implement a preemptive attack against Iraq.

The implementation of the preemptive strike as a foreign policy tool can be directly attributed to the activities of neoconservatives. First, neoconservatives disseminated their views on preemption through their publications, articles on op-ed pages, political statements, and interviews—all of which inserted the idea of preemption into American public debate on foreign policy. Second, neoconservatives held important positions in the George W. Bush administration's first term. People sympathetic to neoconservatism such as Dick Cheney, Donald Rumsfeld, and Zalmay Khalilzad, and neoconservatives such as Richard Perle, John Bolton, Lewis I. "Scooter" Libby, Paul Wolfowitz, and many others, supported neoconservative perspectives on foreign policy. It has been documented that Wolfowitz played a central role in persuading President Bush to launch a preemptive attack on Iraq.[38] The emergence of a new threat made Bush a popular president, and neoconservatives' ideas became relevant policy considerations.

However, neoconservatives started talking about preemption long before the beginning of the George W. Bush administration and the terrorist attacks on September 11. This view emerged when the United States faced no rivalry, when communism was fading, when the United States had become the hegemonic global power. From a neoconservative perspective, preemption is a tool to maintain the supremacy of the United States in the international scene. "The United States was a weak country at that time [in the past]," asserted Robert Jarvis. "Now the preemptive war doctrine is based on strength, and on the associated desire to ensure the maintenance of American dominance."[39]

Preemption is a concept that embraces five ideas. First, it reveals American military power. The United States has no rival in military affairs; consequently, it has the means to impose its will. Because of its hegemonic position in international affairs, the United States can and should behave distinctively. In a way, this was corroborated by the fast defeat of Saddam Hussein's military forces in Iraq. Second, it assumes that previous military strategies, like containment or deterrence, are not useful for facing current foreign policy threats. Terrorists do not negotiate; they are extremists, they are willing to die, and they cannot be persuaded. Third, the United States prefers to launch a preemptive attack multilaterally but is willing to act alone. Fourth, the use of forces is necessary to make the world safer from dangerous enemies. Therefore, the employment of preemptive forces is acceptable, because it advances noble causes such as the end of tyrannical governments and the promotion of democracy. Fifth and finally, the United States has the undeniable right to launch a preemptive attack, and it does not require the consent of international organizations. In a nutshell, as John Gerald Ruggie has asserted, "the use of American power abroad is entirely self-legitimating, determined solely by U.S. interests, neither requiring nor welcoming any form of external accountability."[40]

The origins of contemporary neoconservatism's views on the concept of preemptive attack can be traced to 1990, when distinguished neoconservative politicians like Richard Perle started talking about the need to take military action to avoid an international crisis. From Perle's perspective, there were times when military attacks were better than inaction. On September 24, 1990, less than two months after Hussein's invasion of Kuwait, Perle asserted: "Even without further provocation, we would be justified in attacking Iraq for taking American citizens hostages. Massive air strikes to destroy Iraq's chemical and nuclear facilities and its missiles and aircraft would be an appropriate response to Hussein's threats to use weapons of mass destruction. In short, we should feel free to strike when and where we choose." For Perle, the United States should not have been afraid of going to war with Iraq, because for him, "the only thing worse that angering the Arab world by destroying Hussein's military power would be failure to do so."[41]

During those years, Perle had three main concerns: First, Saddam Hussein was a threat, a dangerous dictator who could inflict serious damage not only on Iraq and the Middle East but also on the United States; second, Hussein possessed weapons of mass destruction that he could use at any time to kill civilians and affect American interests in the region; and third, Hussein was not trustworthy. According to Perle, diplomatic negotiations with Hussein were worthless. Under the circumstances, the United States had to destroy Hussein's military capabilities or remove him from power.[42] In 1991, neoconservative views were ignored when President George H. W. Bush, advised by Colin Powell, decided not to send American troops to Baghdad. Most neoconservatives never absolved the first president Bush for what they considered "a serious mistake."[43]

A year later, in 1992, another neoconservative talked about preemption. As undersecretary of defense for policy, Wolfowitz was in charge of preparing a new foreign policy strategy for the post–Cold War era. In a document that was leaked to the *New York Times*, he outlined what would later become some of the main foreign policy themes of the George W. Bush Doctrine. In this text, Wolfowitz maintained that the United States should play an active role as the sole leader of the world. He advocated the use of "military force, if necessary, to prevent the proliferation of nuclear weapons and other weapons of mass destruction in such countries as North Korea, Iraq, some of the successor republics to the Soviet Union and in Europe." Similarly, he asserted that the United States should be prepared to stop the development of weapons of mass destruction. "Those steps could include pre-empting impending attacks with nuclear, chemical or biological weapons."[44]

Later, during the Clinton administration, the PNAC outlined the notion of preemptive attack. "The history of the 20th century," it maintained, "should have taught us that it is important to shape circumstances before crises emerge, and to meet threats before they become dire."[45] Frank Gaffney used inflammatory language to reassess the relevance of preemption for American foreign policy: "In a world in which Islamofascists and their state sponsors and allies can reasonably be expected to have access to weapons of mass destruction, a proactive, offensive, and where necessary preemptive American strategy is indispensable. Nothing less is at stake than our survival as a free, democratic and secular nation."[46] Finally, Douglas Feith maintained that preemption would continue to be a central component of American foreign policy:

> I do not think that there is any government—certainly not the U.S. government, but also any government in the world—that would say, given that technology is the only way self-defense can work, to wait until somebody attacks you. The idea that states are going to protect themselves by attacking extremely great threats before they actually get hit, that [idea] is not going away.[47]

The notion of preemption did not constitute part of the conceptual framework of the intellectual branch of the first generation of neoconservatives. On the contrary, some neoconservative leaders like Irving Kristol and Jeane Kirkpatrick were against this type of thinking. In 1990, Kristol maintained that with "the end of the Cold War, an era of American foreign policy has come to a close. We won the war." Kristol wondered, "What is our foreign policy now about?" In his view, the only novel idea was that of the promotion of democracy. "This is a superficially attractive idea," he argued, "but it takes only a few moments of thought to realize how empty of substance (and how full of presumptions!) it is."[48]

Kirkpatrick was similarly in favor of an American military response to the terrorist attacks of September 11, but she disliked the way the Bush administration has conducted the war with Iraq.[49] She did not agree with the views of people like Wolfowitz and Feith who were, especially Wolfowitz, some of the main promoters of an American preemptive attack on Iraq. In 2004, when I asked her if she agreed with the thinking of Wolfowitz and Feith, she responded, "I don't think I can answer that question very satisfactorily because they are not people I have ever particularly identified; I haven't felt that our intellectual views are, comprehensively speaking, very close."[50] And she not only disagreed with Wolfowitz and Feith but also opposed the American invasion of Iraq. In the same conversation, she claimed:

> I would like us to get out of Iraq, frankly. I haven't said this on television; I haven't said it to a newspaper or to any journalists. . . . I have frankly had very deep misgivings about our Iraqi engagement from the very beginning, even before we actually went into that war. I'm not sure I'm right, and I've never felt sure I was right, but my misgivings about it have been quite strong and quite persistent because Iraq is a strong country. . . . I, by the way, think I know that Bea Kristol [Gertrude Himmelfarb] and Irving Kristol feel the same way about this war. I didn't want to see us go into [Iraq]. I would like to see us get out as soon as we can. I think that wars are costly and very dangerous. . . . People get killed. . . . I think the people we are fighting in Iraq today are dreadful. I was afraid we might make things worse. . . . Saddam Hussein was one of the big-time mass murderers of our century, but Iraq, on the other hand, was not the most violent of the Arab countries, and I was aware of the fact that the Iraqis, for example, educated women. They had a number of educated women in the government. It's another way of saying that they were not traditionalist Islamists.

Kirkpatrick believed that Hussein was moving in the direction of what she calls traditional Islamism, had developed weapons of mass destruction, and had established important ties with terrorist organizations. However, she emphatically declared, "I would have preferred to see us go along with further inspections, for example."[51]

Nathan Glazer also opposed the notion of a preemptive attack and the war with Iraq. He thought that after September 11, the United States should have behaved cautiously in international affairs. He judged that the United States had several alternatives before launching a war against Iraq. "It was a point of view presented at the time," he recalled, "that I felt most close to, and that was the viewpoint of Michael Walzer." Here, Glazer had in mind Walzer's views published in the *New York Times* just before the beginning of the war. Walzer proposed the idea of a little war as an alternative to the invasion.[52] Likewise, Glazer was convinced that the second generation of neoconservatives—especially journalists—did not have enough knowledge about the world beyond Europe. His argument against the war with Iraq was twofold. First, the Bush administration had alternatives, and thus could have avoided the war. Second, neoconservatives did not have enough knowledge about Iraq to evaluate the consequences of launching an attack.

Thus, some important figures of the first generation of neoconservatives were against the views promoted by the second generation. For almost forty years, neoconservatives had lived in a world in which their main rival, the Soviet Union, was as powerful as the United States. Any attempt to launch a military attack could have deadly consequences. So prudence became a characteristic of some neoconservative foreign policy. Of course, not all neoconservatives of the first generation were against preemption or what would become known as the Bush Doctrine. Besides Richard Perle and the politicians in the government, we find figures like Norman Podhoretz, Joshua Muravchik, and Michael Novak, among others. Novak even developed an argument that Catholic doctrine supports the use of force in exceptional circumstances.[53] In all, it is difficult to establish a clear-cut divide between the first and second generations of neoconservatives on all topics. It is, however, possible to assert that some distinguished members—though perhaps a minority—of the first generation were against preemption or the policies promoted by the second.

Although several countries have launched preemptive strikes in the recent past, it is a strategy that contravenes the United Nations Charter and, therefore, the international agreements established at the end of World War II. At the conclusion of that war, the United States played a central role in the founding of several international organizations committed to multilateral concords, such as the World Bank, the International Monetary Fund, and, of course, the United Nations. The George W. Bush administration, however, reversed this tendency by emphasizing unilateralism over multilateralism. As William Galston has asserted, "A global strategy based on the new Bush doctrine of preemption means the end of the system of international institutions, laws and norms that we have worked to build for more than a half of century. What is at stake is nothing less than a fundamental shift in America's place in the world. Rather than continuing to serve as first among equals in the postwar international system, the United States would act as a law unto itself, creating new rules of international engagement without the consent of other nations."[54]

Historically, neoconservatives have been against international institutions, in particular the United Nations. Daniel Patrick Moynihan called the United Nations a "dangerous place," and Jeane Kirkpatrick considered it an institution in which the United States was "smacked" by developing countries. In 1993, Irving Kristol asserted: "The U.S. will surely want to, and need to, remain an active world power, but this activity will not be within the confines prescribed by the United Nations or NATO or whatever. In the post–Cold War era, those organizations are on their way to become moribund." More recently, Joshua Muravchik argued: "We are better off without that UN resolution,"[55] and he asserted categorically, "We [neoconservatives] hate the United Nations."[56]

Neoconservatives' historical disdain for the United Nations demonstrates their conviction that the United States can act outside international institutions in the service of its own interests. When U.S. interests are in opposition to those of the United Nations, American interests should prevail. Neoconservatives' disregard for the United Nations makes them indifferent to the judgments of the organization, and helps explain their critical position against the United Nations in the aftermath of September 11.

The neoconservative notion of preemption was born during the time of the Gulf War in 1991. Neoconservatives had been disturbed by Saddam Hussein's regime for a long time, not only for his repressive domestic measures but also because he represented a threat to the region's stability. Neoconservatives were particularly worried about the safety of Israel and the protection of American interests in the region. Many neoconservatives were against Hussein's regime before the Gulf War, but others supported President George H. W. Bush and were critical of a possible American occupation of Iraq. In 1990, Irving Kristol argued that the idea of sending American troops to Baghdad would be wrong. Such a decision, he argued, "could end up committing us to govern Iraq. And no civilized person in his right mind wants to govern Iraq."[57]

Throughout the 1990s, the second generation promoted the removal of Hussein from power. As early as 1997, *The Weekly Standard* had advocated concluding what President George H. W. Bush had left unfinished: "American policy toward Iraq should aim at removing Saddam Hussein from power."[58] In a subsequent issue of *The Standard*, Zalmay Khalilzad and Wolfowitz argued in favor of American military intervention in Iraq. They stressed that "military force alone is not enough. It must be part of an overall strategy that sets as its goal not merely the containment of Saddam, but the liberation of Iraq from his tyranny." This broader strategy had six components: (1) "coordinat[ing] with regional allies, especially Turkey"; (2) promoting the resurgence of Iraqi opposition forces; (3) working to "delegitimize Saddam and his regime"; (4) collaborating with friends and regional allies—"we should arm and train opposition forces"; (5) restoring Radio Free Iraq and resuming support for Iraqi opposition radio programming; and (6) granting military security to "Iraqi units defecting from Saddam to the resistance movement." Finally, Khalilzad and Wolfowitz affirmed that there were no guarantees that the United States would succeed in its mission, but it needed to act before Hussein became even more powerful.[59]

In January 1998, neoconservatives wrote to President Clinton under the auspices of the PNAC criticizing his policy toward Iraq and suggesting concrete measures to remove Hussein from power. The letter's signatories mobilized the arguments that the George W. Bush administration would later present to the American people to justify the invasion of Iraq. They stressed their belief that Hussein possessed weapons of mass destruction. "Our ability to ensure that Saddam Hussein is not producing weapons of mass destruction," they wrote, "has substantially diminished." Consequently, they argued that "[the] only acceptable strategy is one that eliminates the possibility that Iraq will be able to use or threaten to use weapons of mass destruction." They also declared that the time had come to take military action against Iraq. In their view, the administration's current policy was "dangerously inadequate; . . . diplomacy is clearly failing." The United States, they wrote, has the "authority under existing UN resolutions to take military steps to protect our vital interest in the Gulf. In any case, American policy cannot continue to be crippled by a misguided insistence on unanimity in the United Nations Security Council."[60] In sum, they argued that Saddam Hussein had weapons of mass destruction, his regime should be removed, and the United States had the authority under UN resolutions to take military action against Iraq. Neoconservatives wanted a new, democratic Iraq, an Iraq in harmony with American principles and values and a supporter of American interests in the region. Only with the substitution of a pro-American government for Hussein's regime would the United States' interests be secure and the region become stable.

## Unilateralism

The notion of preemptive attack is closely related to two other core neoconservative principles, unilateralism and regime change. From the beginning, the Bush administration adopted a range of positions in relation to international organizations. On the one hand, Bush demonstrated his inclination toward unilateralism by repudiating global agreements such as the Kyoto Protocol on global warming and the International Criminal

Court. On the other hand, he supported multilateral arrangements like NATO and the North American Free Trade Agreement. Hours after the terrorist attacks on September 11, the United States obtained the backing of the international community. On September 12, the United Nations passed a resolution condemning the attack, and NATO, for the first time in its history, called upon Article V to defend the United States. But the Bush administration's early cooperation with multilateral, international organizations fell apart as neoconservatives in the administration persuaded the president that multilateral institutions would restrain American efforts to fight international terrorism.

The neoconservative notion of unilateralism evolved out of a more widespread conception of America's role in the world after the downfall of communism. Since the early 1990s, international relations scholars have enthusiastically debated three interconnected questions: (1) the meaning of unipolarity; (2) the role of the United Sates in the current, unipolar world; and (3) the connection between unipolar power and unilateralism.[61] According to Jonathan Monten, there are two schools of thought about the relationship between unipolar power and unilateralism. The first, represented by Robert Jarvis, asserts that unilateralism is the logical outcome of the United States' dominant global position. The second, represented by Thomas Rissen, emphasizes domestic variables to explain the United States' shift toward unilateralism. Neoconservatives tend to side with Jarvis, while also incorporating other ideas such as liberal exceptionalism.[62]

Also since the early 1990s, neoconservatives have debated what role the United States should play in the post–Cold War era. The movement is divided into two main camps on this point. In the first group, we find some members of the first generation like Glazer, Kristol, and Kirkpatrick, who supported the return to normal times. In the second, we find prominent members of the second generation and a few from the first, such as Podhoretz, Muravchik, and Novak.

For obvious historical reasons, the first generation never envisioned a unipolar world, at least before the collapse of the Berlin Wall. The founders of the neoconservative movement were politically active during the years of confrontation between the United States and the Soviet Union. The struggle against the Soviet Union imposed a particular mission on the United States: to contain the spread of communism. With the vanishing of communism, some neoconservatives questioned the role the United States should play on the international scene. They recognized that the United States was the sole superpower and the importance of defining national

interests. Irving Kristol asserted that the United States had no role to play
in international conflicts. "Many of the world's problems," maintained the
godfather of neoconservatism, "seem awfully distant from the U.S.—and
no longer particularly interesting for the point of view of American foreign
policy." He was not concerned about what happened in Liberia, Ethiopia,
or Cambodia. He argued in favor of "reviving the idea of 'national interest' and giving it national substance."[63] Kirkpatrick and Glazer held similar viewpoints.

From Glazer's perspective, the rise of Nazism and communism were
significant events that propelled the United States to face the threat represented by these ideologies. In his view, different American governments
devoted to democracy and military development had the duty of defending
the world against communism. "Whatever our commitment to governments of freedom and democracy," he asserted, "it would never have justified the enormous expansion of American military power were it not for
the threat of communism." He maintained that during the postwar era "the
United States needed allies to fight the Cold War." In his view, the support
of allies was necessary not only strategically but also to address domestic
policy concerns. "Public opinion," he said in 2007, "tends to be so critical
of sending soldiers overseas, so even a small war like Iraq produces tremendous strains. So you need the multilateral perspective and the allies
that might support that cause overseas."[64] With the downfall of communism, he argued, there was no need to maintain certain international agreements created in the immediate postwar years. "One must ask," he in-
quired, "why there is need any longer for a military alliance called NATO?
One concludes that the only reason we seem committed is inertia." Moreover, in his view, the perspective of Charles Krauthammer—an advocate
of the second generation of neoconservatives—that the United States
should play a role in the maintenance of global stability is "mystifying."[65]

Kirkpatrick, likewise, considered that with the collapse of communism
and the return of normality, the United States should "become again a normal nation."[66] From her perspective, the Cold War had demanded special
action on the part of the United States, which devoted significant resources
to international affairs. In her view, this was "unnatural" conduct, imposed
by particular historical circumstances. A good society, she argued, is defined by its domestic policies. Therefore, the "end of the Cold War frees
time, attention, and resources for American needs." She believed that there
is no "mystical American 'mission' or purpose to be found independent of
U.S. constitutional government." Rather, the United States has two impor-

tant tasks to fulfill in the post–Cold War years: support the U.S. economy, and work to strengthen democracy.[67]

Kirkpatrick's views were criticized directly by Robert Kagan and William Kristol in the pages of the *Washington Post*. There they wrote that her perspective was "at odds [with] the assumption embraced by the leaders who established the guiding principles of American foreign policy at the end of World War II." Kagan and Kristol expressed their belief that the United States should "shape the international environment to prevent such a threat [the next great threat] from arising in the first place."[68] Thus, neoconservatives of the first generation tended to be against the unipolar views of Krauthammer and the second generation of neoconservatives. These disagreements were both strong and open, clearly indicating the different positions and ideological orientations of some members of the first and second generations.

Other neoconservatives, mainly—but not exclusively—from the second generation, believe that the planet remains a dangerous place. This risky situation requires that the United States remain active in international affairs. "The world is still sufficiently dangerous," declared Paul Wolfowitz in 1994, "that it requires leadership to maintain peace, leadership that only the United States can provide and from which the United States benefits along with most other nations."[69] A few years later, Kristol and Kagan maintained that the "present danger is that the United States, the world's dominant power on whom the maintenance of the international peace and the support of liberal democratic depends, will shrink its responsibilities and . . . allow the international order that it created and sustains to collapse." According to these authors, the United States should not "return to normalcy."[70] Finally, in 2003 Max Boot argued, "As long as evil exists, someone will have to protect peaceful people from predators." [71] The only option for the United States, according to this school of thought, is to become a global police force.

Neoconservative advocates of this tendency perceive the world pessimistically—even during the periods of American predominance in the world, when the United States is indisputably the planet's most powerful military force. They perceive the world in Manichean terms, as a struggle between the forces of good and evil, in which the forces of good will always triumph. These neoconservatives place the United States on the side of good, with the authority, moral obligation, and military means to confront malevolent powers. The United States has a duty to spread American democracy and political and moral values, which they believe are superior to other principles and political ideologies. According to this logic, neoconservatives believe that the United States must prevail because the forces of good are on its side. The spread of American democratic values is merely a vehicle for reinforcing the forces of good.

These neoconservatives' Manichean worldview is rife with symbolism. Classifying terrorists, Saddam Hussein, or negative views of the United States as evil shifts the discourse from a rational debate to a moral and emotional cause. It is categorically impossible to negotiate with evil, because its behavior is part of its essence. What is more, Satan and God do not carry on dialogue or negotiate. "In a Christian political culture," argue Ronald Krebs and Jennifer Lobasz, "which sees itself as uniquely blessed by God, it is hardly a surprise that the villains of the moment would be portrayed as the personification of evil and of Satan's meddling in the world; . . . one may seek only to eradicate evil in a potential apocalyptic struggle. The power of Bush's post–September 11 rhetoric," they continue, "derived in part from the way in which it effectively tapped into this tradition."[72]

The neoconservatives also appeal to historical symbolism. Saddam Hussein and Osama bin Laden are often portrayed as the Hitlers of the twenty-first century. For some neoconservatives, the United States is engaged in a struggle with Islamofascists. Norman Podhoretz refers to this struggle as World War IV. According to him, contemporary Islamofascism has been influenced by previous American enemies, Nazism and Soviet communism. Islamofascists, he writes, "like the Nazis and the Communists before them, are dedicated to the destruction of freedom we cherish and for which America stands."[73] His choice of analogies has particular resonance in the United States, where the collective memory casts Hitler and fascism as the epitome of malevolence, intolerable political ideology, and tyrannical dictatorship. "Hitler," writes Lance Morrow, "is the 20th [sic] century's term for [the] Great Satan, and to invoke Hitler is to evoke evil's icon."[74] Podhoretz is not alone in placing Saddam Hussein, Osama bin Laden, and Hitler in the same category. Charles Krauthammer, Richard Perle, and Paul Wolfowitz have used similar rhetoric.[75]

In the domain of foreign policy, the views of the second-generation neoconservatives have prevailed over those of thinkers such as Kristol and Kirkpatrick. The younger generation considers previous foreign policy strategies like containment and deterrence useless against international terrorism, for reasons obvious to them. Terrorist organizations do not have a home address, and terrorists are willing to die to defend their cause. They cannot be persuaded. "Deterrence no longer works to defeat" terrorist networks and terrorist states, asserted Kenneth Adelman in 2002.[76] Similarly, Lawrence Kaplan and William Kristol maintain that "the notion that containment is working is wishful; . . . [a] realistic argument for deterrence is weak."[77] Finally, Gary Schmitt writes that "the strategic concept of deterrence in all of its mad manifestations has lost its half-century hold on American security posture."[78]

The United States, according to neoconservatives, should use its power to deploy a new strategy in accord with current events and in harmony with its interests. That is, the United States should define its foreign policy based on the powerful position it occupies in the international system. As the dominant power in the world, it has the flexibility and freedom to conduct its foreign affairs according to its preferences, independent of the normal constraints imposed by the international system. Finally, under certain circumstances—defined by the United States—America can behave outside the norms established by international, multilateral institutions. In the words of Kagan, "multilateralism is a weapon of the weak."[79] In the voice of Donald Rumsfeld, "weakness is provocative."[80] For Krauthammer, "America is no mere international citizen. It is the dominant power in the world, more dominant than any since Rome. Accordingly, America is in a position to reshape norms, alter expectations and create new realities. How? By unapologetic and implacable demonstration of will."[81]

For John Ikenberry, from a neoconservative perspective, "America is powerful; it should move toward a power-based rather than rule-based international order."[82] In the view of John Mearsheimer, American military power "explain[s] in large part, why the Bush administration and the neoconservatives favor unilateralism over multilateralism." He considers diplomacy a "multilateral enterprise," but a country that depends heavily on its military power "will not often need allies; . . . it can rely almost exclusively on its military might to achieve its goal."[83] Finally, for Robert Jarvis, unilateralism is the natural consequence of the predominance of the United States in the current unipolar world. "The forceful and unilateralist exercise of U.S. power," asserted Jarvis, "is not simply the by-product of September 11; . . . it is the logical outcome of the current unrivaled U.S. position in the international system."[84] American unilateralism, therefore, has a structural component derived from the nation's hegemonic position in world affairs. Sharing the perspective of Mearsheimer and Jarvis, neoconservatives judge that America should use its structural position as the unrivaled power to impose its will. "The core of the problem," asserted Kagan, "lies in the unique structural realities of the present international system.

The overwhelming power of the United States and the lack of any plausible peer competitor are naturally unnerving, certainly to those who do not benefit from American dominance, and perhaps even to some of America's allies, who do."[85]

For Kagan, the dominant position of the United States in the international system, in particular its military strength, "has produced a propensity to use that strength."[86] It is, thus, the United States' position in the world system that creates incentives to act both unilaterally and militarily. According to this logic, because the United States has the means to prevail in the international system—the power of weapons—it has no constraints on its exercise of power.

Highly ambitious neoconservatives predict that unipolarism will dominate the international scene in coming years. Among neoconservatives, Krauthammer has been the main intellectual architect of this perspective. In 1990–91, he published "The Unipolar Moment" in *Foreign Affairs*. He asserted that after the collapse of the Soviet Union, the world had entered a "unipolar moment" that should be dominated by the United States. Since those early days, he has refined his ideas. He wrote: "The history of paper treaties [international agreements] is a history of naïveté and cynicism." According to him, the United States must follow a "New Unilateralism," a position that "seeks to strengthen American power and unashamedly deploy it on behalf of self-defined global ends."[87]

Intervention in global affairs, according to Krauthammer, is a generous demonstration of American power because its interests are defined as "far beyond narrow self-defense. In particular it identifies two other major interests, both global: extending the peace by advancing democracy and preserving the peace by acting as a balancer of last resort."[88] The United States, in his view, dominates the unipolar world in which we live today, and it practices its unilateralism in a different way than previous world powers. America is benevolent, is concerned for the well-being of the world, is eager to advance peace and promote democracy, and is indispensable for the stability of the world. For Krauthammer and other neoconservatives like Kristol and Kagan, the goal of American foreign policy should be to turn a "unipolar moment into a unipolar era."[89]

Neoconservative ideas resonated with the first George W. Bush administration. In the *National Security Strategy* released on September 17, 2002, President Bush argued, "We do not use our strength to press for unilateral advantages." On the contrary, he asserted that the United States will only use its power in the service of noble causes. "We will defend the peace," he declared, "by fighting terrorism and tyrants. . . . We will extend the peace by encouraging free and open societies on every continent."[90] From the perspective of Bush and many neoconservatives, the American values of freedom and democracy are universal and can be sown and grown in any society. "When freedom takes hold," asserted President Bush in 2003, "hatred gives away to hope. When freedom takes hold, men and women turn to the peaceful pursuit of a better life. American values and American interests lead in the same direction: We stand for human liberty."[91] Thus, for Bush and his supporters, the pursuit of American national interests is structurally linked to the spread of freedom and democracy throughout the world.

Neoconservatives and Bush advocated for a comprehensive system that includes an economic, political, cultural, and moral perspective. In their opinion, the United States has proven that free enterprise works; that democracy, with all its problems, is the best political system ever created; and that freedom is better than tyranny. According to them, this can be seen throughout American history. As a consequence, the United States has a moral obligation to spread these valued gifts to the world. As Ivo Daalder and James Lindsay wrote in 2003, the "essence of the Bush strategy . . . was to use America's unprecedented power to remake the world in America's image."[92]

## *The Promotion of Democracy*

Historically, neoconservatives have been advocates of the promotion of democracy around the world. Since the Ronald Reagan years, and even before, the spread of democracy was a central component of their policy views. Neoconservatives, however, advocate a particular type of democracy that emphasizes procedures over substance. For them, the presence of free elections, basic civil liberties, and a market economy are sufficient to consider any country democratic. This conception fails to incorporate social and economic justice, endorsing the adoption of a democratic system that merely resembles American democracy. "We ought to wage democracy generally, and democracy American-style specifically," Ben Wattenberg asserted.[93]

This is so because neoconservatives are true believers in the supremacy of American democracy and values. They are convinced that the United States should spread democratic principles all over the world, a standpoint consistent with the opinion of a large portion of the country's population. According to the 2005 findings of the Pew Global Attitudes Project, 79 percent of Americans consider it positive that "American ideas and customs are spreading around the world."[94] Neoconservative views, therefore, are in step with the opinions of many American citizens. The promotion of democracy did not, of course, originate with neoconservatives. It has deep roots in American history and has been used by different American administrations to advance U.S. interests abroad. Neoconservatives merely integrated an old notion into a new, comprehensive framework.

To understand the promotion of democracy in neoconservative political thought, it is necessary to comprehend the main features of American exceptionalism. The first generation of neoconservatives dedicated a significant amount of time to exploring this topic from an academic standpoint. Following the work of Alexis de Tocqueville, Louis Hartz, and Gunnar Myrdal, scholars like Daniel Bell, Samuel Huntington, and Seymour Martin Lipset tried to answer the question of why socialism had never made significant inroads in the United States. In their explanations, they highlighted the distinctiveness of American democracy. The United States, the argument runs, was the "city upon the hill," a place selected by God to construct an exemplary democratic and political system. Likewise, the United States has never experienced either feudalism or socialism. Instead it has been governed by the twin ideologies of democracy and capitalism. This unique feature made it possible for the United States to break free from the European past. In Lipset's understanding, the United States was the "First New Nation" that emerged after breaking with a colonial power.[95]

Scholars of American exceptionalism argue that the United States has been defined in ideological terms, the primary elements of which can be summarized in five words: "liberty, egalitarianism, individualism, populism, and laissez-faire."[96] First-generation neoconservatives such as Lipset do not see American exceptionalism as leading to the assumption that "America is better than other countries, or has a superior culture. Rather, [it] simply suggests that it is qualitatively different, that is an outlier."[97] The notion that the United States possesses a superior political system and culture and that it needs to promote its values worldwide is basically a view of the second generation.

Americans, likewise, are one of the most religious people in the Western world. Many Americans' religious beliefs emphasize their identity as "chosen people" selected by Providence to spread God's blessings. Many

Americans, and many American leaders, perceive themselves as pastors to the world, whose mission is to show other nations the path to democracy. "Promoting liberal values abroad," asserted Joseph Lepgold and Timothy McKeown fifteen years ago, "has thus been seen as a principal U.S. value."[98]

Both the first and second generations of neoconservatives supported the promotion of democracy. The first generation promoted democracy as example, whereas the second, in contrast, saw the promotion of democracy as a mission. The first generation's stance toward the promotion of democracy represents what Jonathan Monten has called exemplarism, while the second's can be more readily understood as vindicationism.[99] Of course these classifications do not represent absolutes. We can find a member of the first generation who at a particular time favored the vindicationist perspective. For example, in the early 1980s, Samuel Huntington repeated the arguments expressed by Jeane Kirkpatrick in "Dictatorships and Double Standards." At the same time, he clearly expressed a vindicationist view: "Any increase in the power or influence of the United States in world affairs generally results not inevitably, but far more often than not, in the promotion of human rights in the world. The expansion of American power is not synonymous with the expansion of liberty, but a significant correlation exists between the rise and fall of American power in the world, and the rise and fall of liberty and democracy in the world."[100] Huntington expressed both these perspectives during the Cold War years, when the United States wanted to expand its reach on the international stage. Later, Huntington adopted a different position, more consistent with that of the first generation.

Three main frameworks for understanding global politics generally guide the study of international relations. The first is the realist perspective, represented by Henry Kissinger. The second is the "clash of civilizations" perspective, articulated by Huntington. And the third is Francis Fukuyama's "end of history" thesis.[101] Among these three analytic frameworks, distinguished neoconservative scholars have articulated the last two.[102] The academic and global debate about international policy, particularly since the end of the Cold War, has a significant neoconservative bent. In general terms, members of the first generation sympathize with Huntington's notion of the "clash of civilizations," and members of the second generation tend to agree with Fukuyama's perspective.

According to Huntington, the world is composed of eight major civilizations with differing cultural characteristics. The incompatibility of these cultures provokes imminent struggles between nations and groups of nations that constitute distinct civilizations. This is a pessimistic view that forecasts battles in global politics. As Gary Dorrien has asserted, with the "clash of civilizations," Huntington was "warning that Western intervention in the affairs of other civilizations is perhaps the most dangerous source of conflict in the world."[103] In contrast, Fukuyama brings a highly optimistic perspective to global politics. He argues that with the collapse of communism, ideological debates are over, and the world will follow just one trend, that of liberal democracy. Many have interpreted his perspective as legitimating the neoconservative promotion of democracy. Although he has asserted that this view is a misreading of his argument,[104] it is evident that neoconservatives of the second generation have privileged this reading over others. After criticizing Huntington's perspective on the "clash of civilizations," Robert Kagan used Fukuyama's argument in *The End of History and the Last Man* as a counterexample. Quoting Fukuyama, Kagan maintained that with the collapse of communism, Fukuyama "augured nothing less than the end point of mankind's ideological evolution and the universalization of Western liberal democracy as the final form of human government."[105]

Two themes are crucial to understanding the differences between the two neoconservative generations' perspectives on the promotion of democracy. The first is the historical context in which these two neoconservative expressions emerged. The members of the first generation of neoconservatives were fundamentally antitotalitarian. As I have shown, they were influenced by Hannah Arendt's views on totalitarianism; affected by the rise of fascism and communism, some as Jews, substantially moved by the events of the Holocaust; and extremely concerned about the violations of human rights in the world, especially in communist countries. Their main struggle was against communism and the Soviet Union. "The conflict between the United States and the Soviet Union," asserted Norman Podhoretz in 1981, "is a clash between two civilizations. More accurately, it is a clash between civilization and barbarism." He perceived communism as even more dangerous than Nazism because it had seduced many Western intellectuals.[106] Douglas Feith framed the issue in the following way: "We [the United States and the Soviet Union] were not rivals because we were powers; we were rivals because they had an aggressive, inhuman idea that threatened us."[107]

The second generation of neoconservatives became intellectually and politically active after the collapse of the Berlin Wall,[108] after the downfall of communism, when many countries started moving toward democracy. These are the same years designated the "end of history" by Fukuyama. During this period, many countries in Eastern Europe and Latin America began democratizing their political systems. This phenomenon was so evident and exciting that numerous scholars began to study what they called "transitions to democracy," creating a sort of subfield in political science and a new breed of political scientist, the transitologist. These were the days of the exaltation of the West by the West, of the discrediting of communism and Marxism, and of euphoria about the spread of democracy.

The second important theme is that of cultural difference. The first generation of neoconservatives believed that cultural differences among peoples and countries imposed barriers that are difficult to penetrate. In 1956, Irving Kristol wrote "Not One World," asserting that the "West would never come together in common cause because their values, goals and visions are diametrically different."[109] Furthermore, in 1987 he openly rejected the promotion of democracy as a U.S. foreign policy goal. In clear disagreement with Joshua Muravchik—an active member in both generations of neoconservatives—Kristol asserted that democracy would not conquer the world. "I am not one of those who is thrilled by the success of democracy in Argentina, or in the Philippines or, imminently, in Korea," Kristol declared. He continued, "Democracy will not survive in those countries." He believed that democracy requires certain cultural preconditions that "those countries do not have; . . . therefore, a democracy in any of them would shortly be discredited, and be replaced by some sort of authoritarian regime of either the left or the right."[110] Democracy cannot grow in just any place; it requires certain conditions that make its development possible. Here, Kristol followed the judgment of Seymour Martin Lipset, who argued in 1959 that some countries were more likely to achieve democracy than others.[111]

Huntington would take this argument further when he argued that unrecognizable cultural differences would provoke a "clash of civilizations between the 'West and the rest.'" International conflicts, in his perspective, were the result of cultural incompatibility. In his view, democracy is not an exportable product. In contrast, many members of the second generation of neoconservatives believe that liberal and democratic principles are universal and transfer easily to other countries. Neoconservatives of this breed frequently point to the fact that democracy has flourished in countries as diverse as Germany, Japan, Chile, and India. The world can be made more democratic. "The premise," argued Muravchik almost twenty years ago, "must be that our way of life is right and good, that it is accessible to others as well, that we do indeed believe that all men are endowed with 'undeniable rights,' and that we are prepared, and even eager, to do what we can to help people everywhere to vindicate those rights through the development of the democratic political institutions."[112]

Shaped by historical circumstances, the forerunners of neoconservatives were convinced that the United States should be an example for the undemocratic world, but they were against America taking the role of hegemon. In direct response to Charles Krauthammer's celebration of a unipolar world, Jeane Kirkpatrick maintained that "it is not the American purpose to establish 'universal dominance,' in the provocative formulation of Charles Krauthammer—not even the universal dominance of democracy—it is enormously desirable for the U.S. and others to encourage democratic institutions wherever possible. . . . It is not within the United States' power to democratize the world, but we can and should make clear our view about the consequences of freedom and unfreedom. We can and should encourage other to adopt democratic practices."[113]

In 1990, Nathan Glazer argued that the United States had become involved in unnecessary small wars. He believed that the country should be committed to democracy and free government, following the principles established by the Founding Fathers, but the United States should not be "the policeman of the world." In his view, America should play a limited role in "making democracy and free economy attractive" to the world. Clearly expressing the exemplarist perspective, he affirmed that "our example has played a larger role. And this was all the Founding Fathers intended," he concluded, "in favor of promoting and recommending those universal principles to which the United States was attached. . . . It is now time to withdraw to something closer to the modest role that the Founding Fathers intended."[114]

A year later, talking about American exceptionalism, Daniel Bell also clearly expressed an exemplarist point of view. He maintained that all nations have their own peculiarities. Consequently, uniqueness is not a distinctive feature of the United States. "But the idea of exceptionalism as it has been used to describe American history and institutions, assumes not only that the United States has been unlike other nations, but that it is exceptional in the sense of being exemplary."[115] Finally, in 2005, Samuel Huntington, changing his previous stance, affirmed, "I think that for the United States to export democracy or free markets to other countries is something to be avoided. We can certainly support the groups in those countries which want to move in that direction, but the idea that we're going to be able to impose our rather peculiar view of democracy and economic liberalism on other countries seems to me a very dangerous fallacy."[116] Thus, many of the leaders of the first generation of the neoconservative movement advocated the promotion of democracy by example.

The second generation of neoconservatives considers the promotion a moral duty that the United States is beholden to perform. "The United States," asserted Paula J. Dobriansky, a neoconservative politician affiliated with the Project for the New American Century and former undersecretary of state for global affairs, "has a moral imperative to advocate that individuals around the world have the freedom to pursue their dreams in a secure, prosperous and peaceful environment."[117] This sense of mission is based on a particular interpretation of American exceptionalism. Some features of American exceptionalism have no barriers; they can be transported to any place. Thus, Lawrence Kaplan and William Kristol think that the Bush Doctrine, or what they called American internationalism, "follows from 'American Exceptionalism'—a belief in the uniqueness and virtue of the American political system that, when translated into foreign policy terms, offers the United States as a model for the world."[118] In the view of Robert Kagan, this has been possible because the genius of American democracy has convinced people all around the planet to "adopt our model of government." Second-generation neoconservatives in general, and Kagan in particular, think the United States has played an "indispensable part in spurring and supporting this global transition to democracy." Thus, the United States has been able to influence the world because it has a mission: to promote universal principles that can be implemented in any nation.[119]

For the second generation of neoconservatives, the promotion of democracy is not only a moral mission but also crucial to American national security. "Most neoconservatives," asserts Richard Perle, "believe that democracy is a good thing. . . . If the world were democratic, it would be a safer place for everyone, because in a democracy it is very difficult for small revolutionaries to move people toward war."[120] Similarly, Reuel Marc Gerecht argues that the "spread of democracy in the Muslim Middle East remains the only cure for the sacred terror of 9/11."[121] The United States, neoconservatives believe, is both the most powerful country in the world and the most benevolent hegemonic power in the history of humankind.[122] As the sole superpower, the United States can and should transform the world in which we live. Among the different options that super-powers have to modify the world, America has taken the most gentle. The United States, in their perspective, is perceived as a compassionate nation. America does not attempt to dominate the world, as previous powers did, but rather to transform it in ways that encourage stability and peace. "U.S. imperialism," argues Max Boot, "has been the greatest force for good in the world during the past century."[123] According to this view, the over-whelming presence of the United States in certain areas of the world has had no negative effects.

Likewise, second-generation neoconservatives consider the United States the most powerful country on the planet, especially in military terms. America wields military power unmatched since "Rome dominated the Mediterranean world."[124] For neoconservatives, the collapse of the Soviet Union was a direct consequence of their ideas and the implementation of their views by Ronald Reagan. For years, neoconservatives had advo-cated the increase in military spending in the face of the challenges im-posed by the Cold War. Following neoconservative advice, President Rea-gan increased the military budget on a scale unprecedented in peacetime. From a neoconservative point of view, this and other measures helped strangle the Soviet economy and contributed to the breakdown of the So-viet Union. For example, Douglas Feith believes that Reagan's radical idea was not stabilizing relations with the Soviet Union but "putting commu-nism in the ashcan of history." According to Feith, "the United States and its allies were able to defeat the Soviet Union without war and that was a gigantic vindication of the Reagan approach." He believes that one of the "things that generated interest in the neocons was the fact that they scored an element of this great victory and argued for the great strategic victory in the history of the war. To defeat a power as great as the Soviet Union, without war, was a terrific victory."[125] Likewise, Paul Wolfowitz notes, "It is striking how many of Russia's new democrats give Ronald Reagan much of the credit for the Soviet collapse."[126]

For neoconservatives, advancing democracy is a means of modifying the hostile international environment and strengthening American national interests. In the eyes of Joshua Muravchik, "advancing the democratic cause can be America's most effective foreign policy in terms not merely of good deeds but of self-interests as well."[127] This idea is based on the principle that democracies do not fight among each other.[128] Although po-litical scientists have shown that this premise is questionable, neoconser-vatives have tried to promote the notion in the media and in political circles. For them, American national security is strengthened when the world embraces democracy. "What is good for democracy," declared Muravchik in 1991, "is good for America. . . . The more democratic the world becomes, the more likely it is to be both peaceful and friendly to America."[129]

Neoconservatives believe that the spread of democracy would produce a chain reaction. In the 1980s, they understood that the establishment of communism in one country would provoke a domino effect. Neoconservatives have adopted that formula with regard to democracy promotion, giving it a positive angle. The adoption of democracy in one country, neoconservatives think, will nurture the embrace of democracy by other nations in the same region. "Change toward democratic regimes in Tehran and Baghdad," asserted Muravchik before the American invasion of Iraq, "would unleash a tsunami across the Islamic world, just as changes in China will transform Asia."[130] Echoing this contention at the commemoration of the twentieth anniversary of the National Endowment for Democracy, President George W. Bush declared, "Iraqi democracy will succeed—and that success will send forth the news from Damascus to Teheran—that freedom can be the future of every nation."[131]

The spread of democracy has become one of the most enduring themes for neoconservatives. With the discrediting of the arguments of both President Bush and neoconservatives for the invasion of Iraq, in particular the absence of weapons of mass destruction, the promotion of democracy has become the only justification for the United States' presence. Thus, for neoconservatives, the advance of democracy is a basic principle of American exceptionalism and part of the fundamental character of American society and politics. The promotion of democracy assumes that American liberal and democratic values are the finest principles that can be conceived and implemented in the world. These principles are universal, and they can be transmitted easily to other countries. From a neoconservative perspective, America's commitment to democracy is a moral mission, an honorable obligation that the United States has with the world, and a way to defend U.S. strategic interests.

Neoconservatives argue that the United States can and should use different methods to establish democracy in the world. Among the most cited are (1) covert operations, (2) foreign aid, (3) support for opposition forces in nondemocratic countries, and (4) the use of force.[132] Another primary strategy is the promotion of cultural activities, including education and propaganda, aimed at transforming the way of thinking in diverse countries. In the view of neoconservatives, each country is different; therefore, it is imperative for the American authorities to evaluate what particular methods are suitable in each situation. Neoconservatives tend to agree that the United States should not launch a democratic crusade all over the world. Rather, the United States should privilege those regions and countries that are strategically relevant.

In recent years, neoconservatives and the Bush administration considered the Middle East and Iraq in particular one of the key regions for American national interests. The arguments presented by neoconservatives to justify the invasion of Iraq were used to the fullest by the White House to validate its policy toward Iraq. The implementation of neoconservative views by the Bush administration has been the clearest example of the fusion between the promotion of democracy and national security. It is also an unambiguous case of the influence of neoconservatives on American foreign policy during the Bush administration.

This theme has been fully explored by other scholars.[133] Therefore, in the next chapter, I focus on comparing the views of the first generation of neoconservatives on the Vietnam War with those of the second generation on the war in Iraq. This comparison will allow me to delineate the current neoconservative perspective on American foreign policy and evaluate how neoconservatives' perspectives on war have changed.

# 8

# Neoconservatives at War

One of the primary differences between the first and second generations of neoconservatives is their view of and involvement in armed conflicts. First-generation neoconservatives have witnessed many international conflagrations over their lifetimes—World War II, the Korean War, the Vietnam War, the 1991 Gulf War, and the war in Iraq—but for they most part, they were not direct participants. Nathan Glazer and Daniel Bell did not serve during World War II because of health issues. Irving Kristol was perhaps the only neoconservative to enlist. Thus, their opinions about war have tended to be intellectually motivated rather than based on personal experience. It is unsurprising that neoconservatives have framed armed conflicts as part of the conflict between the East and the West, or between the United States and the Soviet Union, its satellite states, or countries that seemed to be teetering on the brink of communism. What is more, during the apex of the first neoconservative movement, the Ronald Reagan years, there was no major military conflict for the movement to develop an intellectual position about.[1]

In contrast, the first generation of neoconservatives was deeply affected by the Vietnam War, which would prove a defining moment in the history of the neoconservative movement. Vietnam generated intense debate in virtually all sectors of American society and political circles. It took place at a critical point in U.S. history, a decade when social upheaval motivated many neoconservatives to move from liberalism to neoconservatism. It was during those tense years that neoconservatives developed their arguments against the student revolt, anti-Americanism, and the new liberal intellectual class. It was also during that decade that neoconservatives established their name as reputable intellectuals.

Like other intellectuals, neoconservatives turned their attention to the war in Vietnam during the 1960s and early 1970s. Several important neoconservatives were, in general terms, against American involvement in Southeast Asia. Kristol, for example, argued that the United States was "supporting and sustaining a regime whose legitimacy we doubt, whose practice we deplore, and whose ineffectuality is becoming every day more evident." He saved his sharpest criticism for containment policy. He argued that containment, born in Europe during the postwar years, "worked reasonably well" but might not be appropriate for Southeast Asia.[2] In fact, Vietnam illustrated containment's potential for failure when not applied to broad regions. Kristol came to the conclusion that containment had become more than a policy; it had become an ideology.

Kristol also worried that the implementation of containment policies could turn the United States into a colonial state, in direct opposition to American tradition and principles. In 1968 he declared,

> It is now clear that, in practicing the policy of "containment" we cannot intervene in a situation where such intervention might put us, for any length of time, in a colonialist position. We started out in Vietnam, with what seemed to be traditional "intervention"—limited in scope, intention and time. We have found ourselves involved in a minor (if bloody) war which we could not win, since in order even to have a chance to win we would, in effect, have had to transform South Vietnam into an American colony.[3]

For Kristol, the United States' history as a noncolonizing state should have constrained the implementation of containment.

Kristol applied the same logic to earlier conflicts. He compared the situation in South Vietnam with South Korea:

> South Vietnam, like South Korea, is barely capable of decent self-government under the very best of conditions. It lacks the political tradition, the educated classes, and the civic spirit that make safe government workable. This is an exceedingly fragile polity. . . . The most we can hope for in South Vietnam is what we have achieved in South Korea: That is, to have removed this little, backward nation from the front line of the Cold War so that it can stew quietly in its own political juice.[4]

For Kristol, there are places where the United States has no national interest and thus should not intervene.

Nathan Glazer was also a strong opponent of the Vietnam War. In the early 1970s, when the United States faced serious problems in Southeast Asia, he advocated an immediate withdrawal of U.S. armed forces. He thought the war was senseless, cruel, and unnecessary. According to him, antiwar forces had been unsuccessful because the conflict had left the United States "relatively unharmed in a physical sense." "Our territory," he continued, "has never been touched by the war, our economy has not been seriously damaged, and even our casualties from six years of large-scale ground combat have amounted to no more than the number of Americans killed in automobile accidents in the course of an ordinary year. Morally, the effect of Vietnam has been enormous, greater in some ways than the impact of any war in the history of the nation. But the moral damage was not enough in itself to get us out of the war."[5]

Glazer strongly opposed the use of extreme force, advocating instead the use of diplomacy to end the war. He suggested that Congress refuse to authorize the resources needed to conduct the war. Perhaps more important, he was convinced that the president had obtained too much power and that Congress had given over its power to the chief executive. The war would end, he declared, when "men decided that, whatever the costs of ending it, they [would be] exceeded by those of continuing it."[6]

Daniel Bell joined Glazer's opposition to the Vietnam War. Concerned about Soviet expansionist tendencies, he had supported containment in the 1940s and 1950s. In the 1960s, he reversed his views. For example, in 1967 he declared: "I oppose . . . on moral grounds many of the repressive features of the Tito regime, but I would not favor taking political measures against Yugoslavia." He believed that the solution to the Vietnam conflict was to "reduce great-power involvement and to let the political character of South Vietnam be determined by a free competition of political forces." The American presence in Vietnam, he believed, was only justified if it would facilitate the democratic process—competition among different political groups—but not to promote or "maintain a specific regime." He condemned the bombing of North Vietnam by Southern Vietnamese forces and admitted that the United States had political reasons to be in Vietnam, but he condemned policies that had "moved beyond the original intentions of a limited war."[7] Thus, he came out against the escalation of American involvement rather than the war itself.

Norman Podhoretz was the neoconservative who addressed the Vietnam War most extensively. His position combined two seemingly opposing ideas. First, he rejected American involvement in Southeast Asia. Second, he opposed American antiwar forces. His first position was supported by his exposition of certain pacifist tendencies in American history. He argued that Americans have always judged war "as at best a hideous necessity, not a continuation of policy by other means; . . . the sooner it can be gotten over the better."[8]

Podhoretz opposed U.S. intervention in Vietnam from the beginning. In contrast to Bell, he opposed the American presence in Southeast Asia on a strategic basis. He categorically asserted that the United States had gone into Vietnam because it was "trying to save the Southern half of that country from the evils of communism."[9] The problem with the war in Vietnam was that the United States did not have any chance of prevailing. "The United States demonstrated," he asserted, "that saving South Vietnam from communism was not only beyond its reasonable military, political, and intellectual capability, but that [it] was ultimately beyond its moral capability as well."[10] Like Glazer, Podhoretz called for the immediate withdrawal of American forces from Vietnam.[11]

At the same time, Podhoretz emphatically rejected the position of antiwar activists. As Mark Gerson writes, "While Podhoretz opposed the war, his opposition to the anti-war movement was more intense, and ultimately more important."[12] Podhoretz criticized American radicals, who in his word "gave the anti-war movement its dynamic, its energy, and most of all its visibility."[13] He dismissed the frequent comparison expressed by radical organizations of Nazism with the United States, rejecting the position of procommunists, groups opposed to anticommunists, and critics of the United States, whom he deemed anti-American. He opposed organizations like the DuBois Group, the Maoist Progressive Labor Party, and the Trotskyist Social Workers Party. In his view, "All American communists (and indeed communists everywhere in the world including the Soviet Union and China) were united in supporting the Vietcong and the North Vietnamese against the South Vietnamese and the Americans."[14]

According to Podhoretz, Communists worked closely with other, noncommunist radical expressions such as the New Left. Although he recognized the difference between these types of organizations, he believed that they were united in their work in the antiwar movement. These, in his view, ideologically biased organizations held a Manichean view of the conflict, in which "the Vietcong and Hanoi represented good, and the South Vietnamese represented evil."[15]

Podhoretz believed that these were weak groups with no chance of success, but he acknowledged that they had the support of well-respected intellectuals who shared their position. He highlighted the activities of Susan Sontag, Mary McCarthy, and Frances Fitzgerald. They were all, he wrote, "apologists for the communist side in the Vietnam War."[16] He was also critical of the views of liberal anticommunists such as Arthur M. Schlesinger Jr. and so-called anti-Americans such as Noam Chomsky. These writers were intent on portraying only the horrors of war, without recognizing that the United States was doing the right thing by fighting the spread of communism in South Vietnam.

In general, first-generation neoconservative intellectuals were opposed to armed conflict. They conceived of war as a last resort. During the 1960s and 1970s, at precisely the moment when their views were receiving public recognition, they opposed the Vietnam War.[17] Though they differed in the rationale for this opposition, they were united in their antagonism toward large-scale American military action in Southeast Asia and their opposition to containment as a foreign policy principle.

During the Reagan administration's first term, when these intellectuals were at the height of their influence and power, the United States was not involved in any major international conflicts. Although some neoconservatives supported the so-called Freedom Fighters in Nicaragua, these were not conflicts that involved the United States in a significant way. Some of these first-generation neoconservatives—including Glazer, Jeane Kirkpatrick, Bea Himmelfarb, and Irving Kristol—opposed the deployment of American armed forces in Iraq. Others—such as Podhoretz, Michael Novak, Joshua Muravchik, Richard Perle, and Elliott Abrams—supported American intervention there. In contrast to their position on Vietnam, first-generation neoconservatives demonstrated significant divisions on the issue of Iraq.

The second generation of neoconservatives has encouraged American intervention in global conflicts. They, along with some first-generation neoconservatives, played a central role in persuading President George W. Bush to attack Iraq. Indeed, they were considered the architects of the United States' intervention in Iraq. Despite the American fiasco in Iraq, they continue to advocate American military action against Iran. Neoconservatives have kept close tabs on politics and economics in the Middle East. Many have been, whether for political or personal reasons, ardent promoters of the alliance between Israel and the United States. In the 1970s and 1980s, there were disagreements among neoconservatives about American foreign policy toward Israel; for example, Podhoretz and Glazer had significant differences over this issue. Kristol and Glazer also disagreed on

Israel. "I always felt that there were possibilities of peace with the Arabs," asserted Glazer, "and Irving was convinced that it [*sic*] was not."[18]

James Mann reports that in the mid-1970s, Paul Wolfowitz was closely involved in studying the strategic relevance of Middle Eastern oil for the United States.[19] Later on, neoconservatives were extremely disturbed by the Soviet invasion of Afghanistan and the Iranian revolution of 1979. These two events and the Sandinista uprising in Nicaragua were on Kirkpatrick's mind when she wrote "Dictatorships and Double Standards." The main link between neoconservative political thought and Iraq came, however, during the 1991 Gulf War.

Before the beginning of Operation Desert Storm, several neoconservatives opposed U.S. foreign policy toward Iraq. In their eyes, it was a mistake to restrain the assignments of the armed forces only to pull American troops out of Kuwait. In their view, the United States was losing a golden opportunity not only to depose a ruthless tyrant but also to modify the political geography in the Middle East, and in doing so preserve American interest in the region. As early as 1990, Perle was presenting the arguments that George W. Bush would later provide to justify the invasion of Iraq in 2003. In the eyes of Perle, the United States was losing the war even before engaging Iraqi troops. The reason was simple. President George H. W. Bush had established the wrong goals. "Our objectives," Perle declared, "must be dismantling or destroying Saddam Hussein's military power. Nothing less will suffice. . . . Only by crushing Saddam Hussein and his war machine can we begin to build a stable political order in the Middle East."[20]

Perle went further. He argued that Hussein was untrustworthy—as President George W. Bush said after the September 11, 2001, terrorist attacks—and consequently, any compromise with him "would prove disastrous for the West." As President Bush asserted many years later, Perle believed that Hussein had chemical weapons and was working hard to obtain nuclear arms.[21] It was, therefore, a logical conclusion that Hussein must be stopped. Perle believed the way to do so was to launch "massive air strikes to destroy Iraq's chemical and nuclear facilities and its missiles and aircraft." Attacking Hussein would prove useful to the United States, according to Perle, because the Arab world would be thankful to the United States if American armed forces destroyed "Hussein's military power."[22]

Neoconservatives like Perle believed that Hussein had to be confronted for seven primary reasons. First, Hussein was a threat not only to the Middle East but also to the Western world. Second, he was untrustworthy. Third, he possessed weapons of mass destruction. Fourth, he was close to obtaining nuclear arms. Fifth, removing him from power would be consistent with American interests in the region. Sixth, removing him from power was necessary for the stability of the region. Seventh, the Arab world would be grateful if the United States rid them of Hussein. Initially, Perle did not address the nexus between Hussein and terrorist organizations like Al Qaeda. Neoconservatives would incorporate that issue into their thinking a few years later.

During the 1990s, neoconservatives' anxiety about Iraq never disappeared. On the contrary, they continued to highlight the international danger represented by Hussein. Wolfowitz, in the now-famous Defense Planning Guidance, advocated the use of "military forces, if necessary, to prevent the proliferation of nuclear weapons and other weapons of mass destruction in such countries as North Korea, Iraq."[23] For George W. Bush, after September 11, these countries, with the addition of Iran, would constitute the "axis of evil." In 1994, Wolfowitz, no longer a government official, criticized Bill Clinton's foreign policy during his first term. From his point of view, the Democratic "administration has done virtually nothing to call Iraq to account for its renewed claim on Kuwait, its border incursions, its oppression of Shia in the south, or its war crimes in Kuwait."[24]

In 1996, the notion of terrorism was incorporated into neoconservative thinking. Zalmay Khalilzad declared that the United States needed a different approach to confront terrorism. He sounded the alarm that the terrorist war against America would become "deadlier, with future attacks including biological and nuclear weapons, even strikes against American information infrastructure." He presented a frightening picture, a portrait of a vulnerable America, of a country facing an imminent threat. His language exploited the fear of his readers. His arguments created an image of catastrophe that he hoped would remain in the minds of American citizens. He also suggested that the United States needed to fight not only terrorist organizations but also the states that sponsored them. The American response, he wrote, should be "disproportionate—a response that strikes at the foundations of the sponsor regime by targeting its security forces, its economic infrastructure, its communications, and other sources of support." This campaign, "by missiles and attack aircraft," he went on, "should continue until the state renounces terrorism and cooperates with U.S. officials in bringing the guilty terrorist groups to justice." He proposed that in order to confront this problem, the United States needed to

1. Know the enemy.
2. Build American defenses to face terrorism.
3. "Confront states that sponsor, promote, or facilitate terrorism against the United States and do so proactively." In his view, only four weak governments—Iran, Iraq, Libya, and Syria—made terrorist actions against the United States possible. He suggested a regime change in these nations and maintained that the "citizens of these countries want better economic and political conditions. We should help them achieve those objectives."
4. Use all the United States' military power against these countries.
5. "Shrink the zone of chaos that fosters terrorism." In particular, Khalilzad asked the United States to pay attention to Afghanistan and work with Afghans to promote stability in the region.
6. Lead American allies in the fight against terrorism.[25]

Khalilzad was troubled by the possibility of a nuclear attack, at a time when neither Iraq nor Iran appeared to be building nuclear weapons. In his view—as many had argued during the George W. Bush administration's first term—the United States should confront not only terrorist groups but also the states that sponsored them. After September 11, Khalilzad only addressed issues related to international terrorism. Domestic terrorism in other countries and revolutionary terrorism were absent from his analysis. Finally, he never questioned whether the United States had the right to attack those countries, or if America's actions would be constrained by the United Nations.

Similarly, in 1996 Joshua Muravchik argued that Iraq was very close to obtaining nuclear weapons capabilities, and the acquisition by Hussein of nuclear arms was, to Muravchik, a serious threat to countries near Iraq, and a way to "deter American intervention against local aggression." Consequently, he also believed that the United States should use all the resources at hand to counter nuclear proliferation. He suggested a range of measures to stop Hussein, such as diplomacy, economic sanctions, control and transfer of technology, and "even through preemptive military strikes."[26] Other neoconservatives, like William Kristol and Robert Kagan, also advocated removing Hussein from power.[27]

In 1997, Kristol founded the Project for the New American Century. From the beginning, the project became another source against the deposition of Hussein from power. In some ways, the project consolidated the arguments of the second generation of neoconservatives. This view was clearly expressed in the project's Statement of Principles and in a letter its members sent to President Bill Clinton in 1998. At this stage, these neoconservatives were far less radical than they would become in the 2000s. In their letter to Clinton, the members argued that United Nations resolutions should authorize the United States to "take the necessary steps, including military steps, to protect our vital interest in the Gulf." They recognized the authority of the UN, though in their estimation the organization had allowed the attack. This position is consistent with the fact that neoconservatives never talked about Hussein's possession of nuclear weapons or that he was close to obtaining them. They referred to weapons of mass destruction in general and to chemical and biological arms in particular. Individual neoconservatives such as Perle, Wolfowitz, Khalilzad, and Muravchik asserted that Hussein did not in fact have nuclear arms, but no statement of this kind was offered by neoconservative organizations.

In the final years of the twentieth century, neoconservatives tirelessly endorsed the idea of removing Hussein from power. They criticized Jack Kemp for not supporting the bombing of Iraq in 1996.[28] In 1998, they alerted their readers that the Middle East would soon become unstable unless the United States took action.[29] They judged that containment would not be sufficient to control Hussein.[30] John Bolton condemned the United Nations for rewarding Hussein and maintained "the suffering of the Iraqi people since 1990 has not been the result of sanctions . . . but of the policy choices of Saddam Hussein."[31] They suggested overthrowing Hussein, using air strikes and the deployment of ground troops.[32] They argued that Hussein's administration was in crisis and that "a serious bombing campaign could be the first step in a strategy to remove him."[33] Long before September 11, these neoconservatives had disseminated the arguments that would constitute George W. Bush's foreign policy toward Iraq after the terrorist attacks on American soil.

At the time, these ideas did not resonate far beyond these neoconservatives' political and journalistic circles. With Clinton in power, neoconservative politicians were on the bench, waiting for a political leader to put them back in the game. The 1990s were also a period of transition for neoconservatism itself. The members of the first generation were publishing less frequently than in the 1970s or 1980s, and the lack of an international enemy made their arguments on international affairs less appealing. At the same time, the second generation of neoconservative thinkers was emerging with a clear view on foreign affairs that frequently collided with their predecessors' perspectives.

With George W. Bush's installation in the White House, neoconservatives began to be appointed to important positions in the new administration. Now they had the ideas, the positions, and the power to implement their policy views. They only had to wait for the right moment to arrive to justify the implementation of their views. And thus the September 11, 2001, terrorist attacks made neoconservative ideas resonate in American political circles. To a significant degree, September 11 changed the political fortunes of neoconservatives.

# 9

# Neoconservatism and American Foreign Policy after September 11

The terrorist attacks on New York and Washington on September 11, 2001, were, inarguably, a watershed moment in American history and the history of neoconservatism. On that tragic day, the United States was attacked within its territorial boundaries, something that had not happened since 1814, when British forces burned Capitol Hill. Almost two centuries later, U.S. citizens and the entire world witnessed the collapse of the Twin Towers and the damage to the Pentagon on television. In a few hours, two important symbols of American economic and military power had either vanished or been severely damaged. Since those events, the United States, and to a certain extent the world, have never been the same. To an unprecedented extent, national security, now called homeland security, has become the American government's highest priority.

The neoconservatives joined most of the Western world in energetically condemning the terrorist attacks. They began, almost immediately, to try to understand the assault and to present their views on terrorism, the Middle East, and ways to confront the enemy. In contrast to the immediate past, when their ideas on these matters had been theoretical, the neoconservatives now had an enemy to fight and a concrete case to which to apply their views. The events of September 11 generated fear and anxiety in the American population and obviously preoccupied government officials. Under these circumstances, neoconservative ideas resonated in both the media and circles of power.

## Identifying the Enemy

Immediately after the September 11 terrorist attacks, the neoconservatives identified the enemy as radical Islam. Placing foes at the extreme of the ideological spectrum has long been a tendency in the United States. At the beginning of the twentieth century, for example, extremist organizations like the Ku Klux Klan considered people and organizations that did not meet their definition of 100 percent American as adversaries of the United States. During the Cold War era, many in the United States were anticommunist without making distinctions between the different forms of communism found in countries such as Poland, Cuba, China, and the Soviet Union. Similarly, neoconservative members of George W. Bush's administration and others—conservatives and liberals alike—lumped together a range of groups under the rubric "radical Islam."

The neoconservatives have been some of the strongest advocates of this perspective. Daniel Pipes—the son of Richard Pipes, emeritus professor at Harvard University and a member of the Committee on the Present Danger—believes that militant Islam or Islamism had historically tried to dominate the United States. To support his assertion, he referred to a document written by Islamic missionaries upon their arrival in the United States in the 1920s. According to Pipes, these missionaries stated, "Our plan is, we are going to conquer America."[1] According this conspiratorial perspective, Muslims in the United States aspire to overthrow the U.S. government and transform the United States into an Islamic country. Pipes believes that the U.S. government has to recognize that "the enemy is not a featureless 'terrorism' but a militant Islam."[2] However, Pipes never properly evaluates if militant Islam has the means to conquer America. He takes any assertion expressed by radical Islamists as fact. The real possibility that militant Islam might conquer the United States is, of course, negligible.

Norman Podhoretz goes much further—he criticizes the basic features of the Islamic faith. He argues that there is something intrinsic to Islam that has caused it to "become an especially fertile breeding-ground of terrorism in our time." The actions of figures like Osama bin Laden are legitimated by the "obligation imposed by the Koran to wage the Holy War, or jihad, against the infidels." In his view, to preserve America's existing order and institutions, Islam should be confronted. "The United States," he asserts, "has entered World War IV, a war that will reshape the entire world."[3] Likewise, in Pipes's estimation, Islamism threatens the United States because it is a political ideology that aspires to erode America's "social and legal arrangements, including the separation of church and state."[4]

The neoconservatives tend to view Islam as a "monolithic bloc, static and unresponsive to change." From their perspective, Islam is a doctrine or creed that "does not have values in common with other cultures, is not affected by them, and does not influence them; . . . is . . . inferior to the West; . . . barbaric, irrational, primitive, and sexist; . . . violent, aggressive, threatening, supportive of terrorists, and engaged in a clash of civilizations."[5] Thus, the neoconservatives fail to differentiate between Islamic religious fundamentalists and secular modernists.[6] In assuming that American democratic values are not only universal and superior, they affirm their belief that "civilized" countries should pursue American democratic principles.

This promotion of democracy has a national security component. The more democratic the world, the less the likelihood that there will be terrorism or regimes that harbor terrorists and possess weapons of mass destruction. The current political situation in the Middle East makes this position untenable. Hamas, which is considered a terrorist organization by neoconservatives, is both a protest movement and a political party that holds the majority in the Palestinian Authority Council. It would seem that Islamist parties can come to power and maintain a strong opposition to the United States. Nations with different attitudes and ideologies will, however, continue to be considered hostile to the United States. Terrorists and countries that harbor terrorist organizations, in the neoconservative view, hate the United States and its values. President Bush encapsulated this perspective when he asserted in 2005 that terrorists "want to end American and Western influence in the broad Middle East, because we stand for democracy and peace and stand in the way of their ambitions."[7]

To strengthen their ideological position and reinforce the urgency of confronting radial Islam, neoconservatives have constructed analogies between previous dictators and totalitarian regimes with radical Islamic forces. For some neoconservatives, such as Podhoretz, terrorists and states that harbor them are similar to socialist, communist, and fascist regimes. Recalling the beginning of World War II, Podhoretz has likened Saddam Hussein and Iranian President Mahmoud Ahmadinejad to Hitler. He asserts that the United States is at war with Islamofascism—an ideology that is a "mutation of the totalitarian disease we defeated first in the shape of Nazism and Fascism and then in the shape of Communism. Like Hitler," Podhoretz has said, "he [Ahmadinejad] is a revolutionary whose objective is to overturn the going international system and to replace it in the fullness of time with a new order dominated by Iran and ruled by the religious political culture of Islamofascism." Podhoretz sees only one response to Iranian ambitions to develop nuclear weapons: the United States needs to bomb Iran.[8]

In April 2007, Queens College of the City University of New York organized a conference titled "Is It 1938 Again?" Podhoretz and other neoconservative thinkers participated in the two-day event organized to analyze the state of world Jewry. The main conceit of the conference was a
comparison between the beginning of Adolf Hitler's march to power and
his plans for the destruction of the Jewish people, and with current events,
particularly the rise of radical Islam and the present Iranian regime.[9] Podhoretz has expressed quite clearly, in print and at conferences as well as
directly to President Bush, his view that if Ahmadinejad obtains nuclear
weapons, the possibility of another Holocaust is imminent. After a private
meeting with Bush and his adviser Karl Rove in late September 2007,
Podhoretz proclaimed that "Bush is going to hit Iran before the end of his
presidency."[10] Whether or not this was probable, Podhoretz had direct access to the president to discuss his views on the issue.

Many scholars and journalists alike consider the concept of Islamofascism misleading. As policy experts Anatol Lieven and John Hulsman assert, "During the Cold War, Podhoretz continually refer[red] to 'the Communists' as if they were all the same. Today he refers to radical Islam and
the states breeding, sheltering, or financing terrorist armory—as wildly
varied a bunch as one could well imagine—as 'the enemy.'"[11] Paul Krugman maintains that there is no such thing as Islamofascism, that it is not an
ideology but rather a figment of the neoconservative imagination.[12] According to Krugman, the term was useful to neoconservatives in arguing
for the transition from combating Al Qaeda to targeting Saddam Hussein.
The historian Niall Ferguson describes the analogies between the leaders
and regimes of World War II and current Middle Eastern political leaders
as a caricature. "Islamofascism is a completely misleading concept," he
says. "In fact, there is virtually no overlap between the ideology of Al
Qaeda and fascism, . . . so 9/11 becomes Pearl Harbor and then you go after the bad guys who are fascists, and if you don't support us, then you
must be an appeaser."[13] Finally, Katha Pollitt maintains that the term "Islamofascism" is "a terrible historical analogy . . . [that] conflates a wide
variety of disparate states, movements and organizations, as if, like the
fascists, they all want similar things and are working together to achieve
them." "Islamofascism looks like an analytical term," she writes, "but really it's an emotional one, intended to get us to think less and fear more."[14]

Framing the conflict in ideological terms has the advantage of allowing
the identification of a powerful enemy and the states that harbor them as a
global threat. But naming a rival that is impossible to clearly identify is a

vague way to frame the problem. "Radical Islam" becomes a general term to embrace the many difficulties currently faced by the United States. Casting the problem this way gives the American population the inaccurate perception that the enemy includes everything and anyone that comes from an Arab state or the Middle East. Turbans, long beards, and the Arabic language become symbols of radical Islam. In the wake of September 11, some American Muslims were attacked on the streets because of their appearance. Others faced discrimination in the workplace. This kind of Islamophobia has become a problem in both Europe and the United States.

This collapsing of the categories "terrorism" and "Islam" has made it very difficult to distinguish the major differences among terrorist organizations, Muslim associations, Middle Eastern states (Syria, Iran, Iraq, or Saudi Arabia), and Arab nationalists and Islamists. As Lieven and Hulsman assert, "The most dangerous aspect of the Bush administration's approach to the war on terror is the desire to lump together radically different elements in the Muslim world into a homogenous enemy camp."[15] Framing the war on terror in ideological terms was useful in advancing neoconservative political aims but problematic for American foreign policy.

## Getting Ready for War

The reaction of neoconservatives to the September 11 terrorist attacks was harsh and instantaneous. A day after the assault, Charles Krauthammer declared: "This is not crime. This is war." He argued that long before September 11, the enemies of the United States had declared war on America without generating a reaction. "Until we declare war in return," he asserted, "we will have thousands of innocent victims." He emphatically declared that the United States was living in an "age of terror" and that the enemy's name was "Radical Islam." In his view, "Any country that harbors and protects [bin Laden] is also our [the United States'] enemy. If bin Laden was behind this, then Afghanistan is our enemy."[16] As Krauthammer's comments suggest, neoconservatives immediately began articulating three primary points. First, the United States must react violently to the assault by declaring war on the perpetrators. Second, the enemy is radical Islam. Finally, the United States needs to declare war not only on terrorists but also on countries that harbor and protect terrorists. These three ideas would become central components of the Bush administration's justification for the attacks on Afghanistan and Iraq.

In the same issue of the *Washington Post* where Krauthammer's op-ed essay appeared, Robert Kagan offered similar arguments. Kagan rejected any possibility of negotiating with the perpetrators, whom he spoke of as "soldiers." He demanded that the United States "go to war with those who have launched this awful war against us" and urged the U.S. government to undertake a global effort to capture or kill the terrorists. Like Krauthammer, he asserted that terrorist organizations were incapable of functioning without the support of "governments with a long record of hostility to the United States and an equally long record of support of terrorism." He argued that with the end of the Cold War, the United States had all the resources it needed to fight the war against international terrorism.[17] Neoconservatives like Krauthammer and Kagan were remarkably in accord in their assessment of the post–September 11 situation, and publications like the *Post* gave them ample opportunities to air their views.

The declarations of high-ranking political officials immediately after the terrorist attacks echoed the neoconservatives' response. Just a few hours after the publication of Krauthammer's and Kagan's articles, President Bush declared the attacks on the United States more than "mere acts of terror." Bush predicted that the struggle against international terrorism would be a long campaign, "a monumental struggle of good versus evil," in which "good [would] prevail."[18] The next day, September 13, Secretary of State Colin Powell asserted that not only would the campaign begin but that the United States "among other measures had to isolate those countries that gave them [terrorists] support and serve as their host."[19]

Statements by both the neoconservatives and government officials that the United States was at war with terrorists and countries that harbor terrorists was critical to the way the war on terror was conceptualized. From the beginning, both the administration and the neoconservatives privileged military over legal action. As a consequence, they believed that the United States had to focus on crafting a military strategy and prepare for an international confrontation. This meant taking an offensive position: discussing the appropriate strategy, generating a domestic consensus about how the United States should conduct its international affairs, organizing an international coalition, obtaining congressional support for the war effort, and securing the budget needed to deploy U.S. armed forces abroad. President Bush and his closest collaborators were convinced that this approach would generate results. "President Bush," Douglas Feith recalled in a recent interview, "understood that there were major risks of going to war— we talked a lot about that—but he also understood that there were major risks [in] not going to war. . . . I think that he rationally decided that as risky as war was, it was [a] lower risk than leaving Saddam in power."[20]

Top government officials persistently asked what the war on terror should look like. Some of the president's closest advisers advocated a restricted war, which would be limited to confronting Al Qaeda and the government of Mullah Omar in Afghanistan. Others felt the war should be broader and should include deposing governments that harbor terrorists or might provide weapons of mass destruction to terrorist organizations. This was precisely the issue taken up in a meeting of the National Security Council on September 13, 2001. According to Feith, in that meeting President Bush asked if Iraq had been involved in the terrorist attacks or had any relationship with Al Qaeda. The secretary of defense, Donald Rumsfeld, responded that Saddam Hussein was a threat to both the region and the United States. He added that the Iraqi dictator was a supporter of terrorism and might himself use weapons of mass destruction against the United States.[21] The White House press secretary, Scott McClellan, would later write that in his view, for Vice President Dick Cheney, Rumsfeld, and Wolfowitz, September 11 was "an opportunity to go after Saddam Hussein, take out his regime, eliminate a threat, and make the Middle East more secure."[22] Immediately after September 11, the consensus was reached that the United States should first take care of Al Qaeda and the Taliban and wait to depose Saddam Hussein.[23]

The neoconservatives were intimately involved in the formation of post–September 11 policy. The weekend of September 15, President Bush called a meeting of the National Security Council, including Rumsfeld and Wolfowitz, at Camp David. Rumsfeld had asked Feith, a prominent neoconservative, to prepare a memo for the meeting. Feith and Peter Rodman, a foreign policy expert, collaborated on the memo. "We considered identifying the enemy," Feith recalled, "as an ideology and using the term 'Radical Islam' or 'Islamist extremism.'" Feith and Rodman admitted that the enemy was not monolithic. Feith noted that Rumsfeld was concerned about incorporating a coalition because that could put the mission at risk. He and Wolfowitz asked Feith to make a case for "acting soon . . . against the threat from Iraq." Accordingly, in the memo Feith and Rodman proposed that the "immediate priority target for initial action should be Al Qaeda, the Taliban, and Iraq." They offered three primary justifications for this recommendation: "Saddam Hussein had weapons of mass destruction that might be used by terrorist organizations; Hussein refused to comply with United Nations resolutions; and he had supported terrorist organizations in the past."[24] This memo, presented by neoconservative members of the Defense Department, reiterated neoconservative ideas that had been circulating in the media for a number of years. These views corresponded to those of neoconservatives outside government circles. September 11 had provided an opportunity for neoconservative ideas to be both heard and incorporated into the Bush administration's policy.

These neoconservatives' ideas were part of the discussion at the Camp David meeting. The meeting's agenda included such topics as the nature of Al Qaeda and its terrorist network; the best way to pressure the Taliban regime to turn over bin Laden and the other terrorists in their territory; how to conduct operations in Afghanistan; the possibility of instability in Afghanistan rebounding in Pakistan; and investigations related to the hijackings of September 11. Two different views were offered during the reunion. One perspective maintained that the United States should invade only Afghanistan. The other, presented by Rumsfeld and Wolfowitz, argued that the United States also needed to invade Iraq. Feith asserted that Rumsfeld left "to Wolfowitz the responsibility to present the case for action against Saddam Hussein."[25] In George Tenet's view, "Wolfowitz genuinely believed that there was a connection between Iraq and 9/11."[26] According to Bob Woodward's account of the meeting, Wolfowitz argued that it was easier to break Iraq than Afghanistan and that there was a "ten to fifty percent chance that Saddam Hussein was involved in the September 11 terrorist attacks."[27] Wolfowitz was clearly convinced that Iraq had to be included in the war against terror. Though he offered no evidence, he seriously considered that Hussein might have been involved in the terrorist attacks.

The neoconservative position articulated at Camp David represented the beginning of an institutional conflict between the Department of State and the Department of Defense on the question of Iraq. This conflict stemmed from the characteristics and duties of each department, as well as the views of those in charge of foreign and defense policy during the George W. Bush administration's first term. Though not going into depth about the structural and institutional differences between the two departments, here I would like to emphasize two points. The Department of State is in charge of diplomatic relations and must consider other countries in making policy. The Department of Defense, in contrast, is in charge of American military affairs—the defense of U.S. territory and citizens. The tensions inherent in these different missions increase during periods of military conflict.

After September 11, this structural interbureaucratic struggle was exacerbated by President Bush's appointment of Rumsfeld and Powell as, respectively, the secretary of defense and the secretary of state. Since the 1970s, Rumsfeld has been very sympathetic to neoconservative views. He was quite close to members of the Committee on the Present Danger, became an honorary member of the Committee for the Free World, and was involved in the Project for the New American Century. In contrast, Powell is a moderate, lifetime military man who worked for President George H. W. Bush and conducted the Gulf War in 1991. Powell was key in persuading the first President Bush not to send ground forces into Baghdad during the Gulf War. After September 11, he argued that the United States should only go to war with the support of the United Nations. Now, in the Department of State, Powell appointed liberals and conservative establishment professionals. In contrast, Rumsfeld filled some of the most important positions in the Defense Department with neoconservatives or people sympathetic to neoconservative views, such as Wolfowitz and Feith.

During those difficult mid-September days, one question pressed on the minds of American citizens: Why was the United States attacked? Some thought that the attacks were the result of the United States' unconditional support of Israel. Norman Podhoretz immediately rejected this idea. According to Podhoretz, Arabs hate the United States because it was "an embodiment that most of the Arabs consider evil, . . . because of who and what we are." "Their enmity," he argued, "is not [because] of what we have done wrong, but what we have done right. To them, our democratic polity and the freedom that go with it are as corrupting as our economic system. They want to destroy all this."[28] Feith believed that the terrorists had the potential to affect the essence of the United States, "a way of life that embodies an idea—the idea of individual freedom."[29]

Nine days after the attacks, a number of prominent neoconservatives wrote an open letter to President Bush. In this missive, they offered strong support for the president's war against "the terrorist organizations and those who harbor and support them." They also listed the five steps that they believed were necessary to succeed in the "first war of the 21st century." First, the United States needed to start an active campaign to capture Osama bin Laden, which included the deployment of American military forces and the support of anti-Taliban groups. Second, they identified Saddam Hussein as one of the main terrorists worldwide, arguing that the Iraqi government may have "provided assistance in some form to the recent attack on the United States." Moreover, even if Hussein had not been involved in the attacks, it was necessary to remove him from power. Thus, the United States needed to "provide full military and financial support to the Iraqi opposition, American forces should be used to provide a 'safer zone' in Iraq from which the opposition can operate, and American forces must be prepared to back up our commitment to the Iraqi opposition by all necessary means." Third, the neoconservatives believed that the government should work to stop the terrorist activities of Hezbollah and contended that the Bush administration "should demand that Iran and Syria immediately cease all military, financial, and political support for Hezbollah and its operations." If these governments declined to obey these demands, the Bush administration should take whatever necessary actions against "these known state sponsors of terrorism." Fourth, the United States should support Israel in fighting terrorism and stop any assistance to the Palestinian Authority. Fifth and finally, to be successful in the war against international terrorism, the United States should increase its defense spending.[30] The letter was signed by, among others, William Kristol, William Bennett, Midge Decter, Francis Fukuyama, Frank Gaffney, Reuel Marc Gerecht, Donald Kagan, Robert Kagan, Jeane Kirkpatrick, Charles Krauthammer, Richard Perle, Norman Podhoretz, and Gary Schmitt.

The ideas presented by these neoconservatives in this letter reinforced the viewpoints that had been expressed by neoconservative politicians to President Bush and other high-ranking officials at Camp David. The neoconservatives, therefore, were able to offer to Bush, his top advisers, and the population in general a policy alternative to confront America's new enemy: international terrorism. However, to adopt this neoconservative perspective, Bush had to be persuaded. He was influenced by neoconservative ideas, because some of his beliefs, even before September 11, were in harmony with neoconservative views. According to McClellan, the president seriously believed in the right of every single human being to live in freedom. Bush also disrespected tyrants and believed that dictators never renounce their ambition to obtain weapons of mass destruction. Saddam Hussein—like many other tyrants—represented a clear example of what Bush really detested. Consequently, the president's perspective constituted a sort of predisposition that facilitated his receptivity to the initiative of deposing Hussein from power. "This alone [Bush's belief] put Iraq on the President's radar screen from the start of his administration."[31]

A few hours after the publication of the neoconservatives' letter, Bush officially endorsed neoconservative ideas. On September 20, he addressed a joint session of Congress, making his first major speech since September

11. The entire country was waiting impatiently to hear his speech, as was the world. In an emotional speech, he presented some of the same arguments that had been made by the neoconservatives. He declared that terrorists hate America because of "what we see right here in this chamber, a democratically elected government. . . . They hate our freedom—our freedom of religion, our freedom of speech, our freedom to vote and assemble and disagree with each other." He echoed Krauthammer's characterization of the unipolarity of the world system. "Freedom and fear are at war," he claimed. As he went on, he mobilized virtually the same words that had been employed by the neoconservative signers of the letter.[32]

In his speech, Bush offered his first public reaction to the events of September 11. He made clear that he wanted not only to confront Osama bin Laden and his terrorist organization but also to take on governments that were believed to harbor terrorists, whether or not they were connected with bin Laden. The war on terror must be much broader; the United States would have to fight on many fronts and with a variety of weapons. Bush's speech contained many of the arguments that would form the basis for a new foreign policy strategy. As Michael Boyle asserted, "[The] declaration of a global war on terror . . . constituted the single most ambitious reordering of America's foreign policy objectives since the Second World War."[33]

The most polished version of these new American foreign policy goals came in the form a National Security Strategy document published in September 2002. However it was clear, a year earlier, that the United States' foreign policy strategy would be constructed according to neoconservative principles. Over the course of the following months, additional elements, such as a focus on weapons of mass destruction, would be added to this general foreign policy framework.

In the course of his post–September 11 speech, Bush's public persona underwent a significant transformation. He became not only the president but also the father figure who knew what to do in difficult times, the psychologist who knew how to reduce fear and provide comfort, and the doctor who knew how to heal wounds. Only a few months earlier, he had assumed the presidency amid serious questions about the legitimacy of his election, to a degree previously only associated with nineteenth-century Presidents John Quincy Adams, Rutherford B. Hayes, and Benjamin Harrison. But now, eight months later, the contingency of history had made Bush a popular leader and statesman.

Although Bush did not mention his intentions to invade Iraq in his speech, the neoconservatives were writing openly about the need to depose Hussein. Krauthammer argued that the "overriding aim of the war on terror [is] regime change." He suggested that the Bush administration should proceed by destroying the Taliban, transforming the Syrian government, and sponsoring regime change in Iran and Iraq. He believed that in Iran change "might come from within," but that in Iraq the United States would have to "confront the most dangerous terrorist regime in the world."[34]

At the Pentagon, military officials and neoconservative politicians were also considering military options against Hussein. According to Feith, on September 29, 2001, Rumsfeld asked General Richard Myers to "begin preparing military options for Iraq." Feith asserted that Rumsfeld had two basic ideas in mind: finding Iraqi weapons of mass destruction, destroying them, and locating the people that had built them; and a quick regime change.[35]

Almost simultaneously, another concern captured the attention of politicians and the general population. A week after September 11, five letters containing deadly anthrax spores were sent to news organizations in New York and Florida. The disclosure of the first anthrax case in Florida frightened government officials and magnified the perception that the United States might be attacked again at any moment. "The anthrax attack," a former government official recalled in a conversation, "really changed the way we think. We had been attacked with weapons of mass destruction." The Bush administration feared that the attacks could be "something massive; . . . somebody could get to the top of one of our highest buildings and drop anthrax that could kill three or four thousand people immediately." The anthrax attack temporarily paralyzed congressional mail, increased fears of a massive biochemical strike, and made the general population hypersensitive to the possibility of a chemical attack.

In his speech, Bush sketched certain unilateralist tendencies that were later reinforced by the neoconservatives. Robert Kagan and William Kristol argued that the Bush administration was falling into a "coalition trap." For these neoconservatives, the idea of building a large coalition to destroy Al Qaeda was a mistake. The administration had made so many concessions that it risked the United States' main goals in the war on terror. Kagan and Kristol seriously criticized Powell for making the formation of the coalition the "new strategy." They believed this was a huge mistake, because "in pursuit of the coalition, we have averted our eyes from Iranian-backed terrorism. . . . We have allowed our Arab allies to conclude that we will not target Iraq." They believed that Hussein's development of weapons of mass destruction might soon pose an even greater threat than bin Laden. "In pursuit of the coalition," they wrote, "we have encouraged Palestinians and Arab radicals to believe that terrorism works." If Powell's ideas became the prevailing policy, Kristol and Kagan feared that "the war against terrorism [would] be brief, limited, and ineffectual."[36]

Krauthammer also argued that the idea of establishing a vast coalition was a mistake. He thought that the United States should make an arrangement with the countries bordering Afghanistan, but the plan to just add partners to the coalition would "simply paralyze decisionmaking and prevent us from doing what we have to do: defeat our enemy." He initially favored what Rumsfeld called "shifting" or "floating" coalitions.[37] Later, he would assert that he was in favor of unilateralism. Restating his old position, he contended that conflicts like the 1991 Gulf War and the war in Afghanistan were unilateral confrontations "dressed up as multilateralism." He was not opposed to other countries' supporting American goals, but he did not want them to be in a position to object to American decisions. He believed that American military might justified unilateral action. The essence of unilateralism, he concluded, "is that we do not allow others to deter us from pursuing the fundamental security interests of the United States and the free world."[38]

A few days before Bush's State of the Union Address in January 2002, Kagan and Kristol were openly encouraging the Bush administration to remove Hussein from power. They argued that capturing bin Laden, destroying Al Qaeda, and stabilizing Afghanistan, though fundamental, would not mean that the United States could afford to overlook Iraq. They argued that because Iraqi intelligence had been in contact with Mohamed Atta, the leader of the September 11 attacks, Hussein's regime was most likely in contact with Al Qaeda as well. From their point of view, "failure to remove Saddam would mean that despite all that happened on September 11, we as a nation [were] unwilling to shoulder the responsibility of global leadership, even to protect ourselves."[39]

In his State of the Union Address, President Bush offered compassionate words to the families of the victims of September 11. He said that the war in Afghanistan had helped to confirm America's "worst fears." The troops had found information detailing how to construct chemical weapons, along with diagrams of American nuclear power plants and public water facilities. He announced that his administration would pursue two primary objectives: combating terrorism, and preventing terrorists from obtaining weapons of mass destruction. He identified three regimes hostile to the United States—North Korea, Iran, and Iraq, calling them an "axis of evil." Finally, in accord with neoconservative thinking, he argued for the need for a preemptive strike. "I will not wait on events," he said, "while dangers gather. I will not stand by as peril draws closer and closer."[40]

Bush's speech provoked a strong reaction around the world. Politicians in Iran, Iraq, and North Korea reacted with anger, and they vehemently denied that they harbored terrorists. Iran's foreign minister, Kamal Kharazi, demanded that President Bush "back up his assertions with evidence." Other leaders, such as Dimitri Rogozin, a very well-known figure in Russia, observed that the speech "seemed to indicate that ultra-conservatives in the administration had gotten the upper hand."[41] In the United States, Ari Fleischer, then the White House press secretary, promptly said that the president's words were not "sending the signal that military action was imminent."[42]

Senior officials in the State Department seemed shocked by the president's words. They had not heard the term "axis of evil" until the president used it in his speech.[43] From that point forward, Powell publicly supported Bush's foreign policy while privately he became the voice of moderation within the administration. Before the House International Relations Committee, Powell maintained that "Bush was committed to 'regime change' in Iraq, that he firmly supported Bush's position and that overthrowing Saddam was something that the United States might have to do alone."[44] The neoconservatives applauded Powell's public position; his reputation as a moderate would make him an effective salesman for the war.[45]

In his speech, an emphatic defense of American unilateralism, Bush introduced the notion of weapons of mass destruction as a central component of his foreign policy design. He now faced the challenge of creating a coherent policy out of the views he had articulated. In doing so, he was openly following neoconservative views and declaring the United States' intention to overthrow Saddam Hussein.

Days after Bush's speech, William Kristol congratulated him on articulating a new foreign policy for the United States. Kristol believed that Bush had uttered the most significant sentence in almost twenty years when he said, "The United States of America will not permit the world's dangerous regimes to threaten us with the world's most destructive weapons." Kristol was convinced that Bush had moved in the right direction when he declared the main task of American foreign policy to be "[acting] decisively to remove these threats to our liberty, and to our civilization." He argued that with this speech Bush, whom he compared with Truman and Reagan, had put an end to a "decade of temporizing and timidity and committed the nation to removing the threat of hostile tyrannies seeking weapons of mass destruction."[46]

Unsurprisingly, Krauthammer also applauded Bush's speech, saying that Bush had "redefined the war." According to Krauthammer, Bush had prevented the "next September 11, . . . in particular a nuclear, chemical, or biological September 11." He particularly approved of Bush's choice to focus on Iraq, Iran, and North Korea. In a highly questionable comparison, he declared, "North Korea is more Stalinist than Stalin, Iran is the Soviet Union in a pre-Gorbachevian foment, and Iraq is a Hitlerian Germany, a truly mad police state with external ambition and a menacing arsenal." Approvingly, he noted that Bush's speech was "just short of a declaration of war" against Iraq, and he called Bush a "president on a mission."[47] He thus used language that resonated with the politics of fear developed by the Bush administration.

Meanwhile, the neoconservatives were busy defending the doctrine of preemptive strikes against European critiques. Countries such as France called the United States' analysis of the situation simplistic and rejected a preemptive strike as an appropriate response. Krauthammer called Europeans the "ultimate free riders [*sic*] on American power." He also argued that the United States must remain constantly vigilant. Therefore, the U.S. government would "let them [Europeans] hold our coats, but not our hands."[48]

Bush rearticulated his foreign policy position in a June 2002 speech at West Point. He maintained that in some cases the doctrines of containment and deterrence still applied, but that "new threats require new thinking." It was in this speech that Bush declared that terrorists had no home address and were insensitive to massive retaliation, and thus there was nothing to contain. Instead, the United States needed to turn its attention to dictators who might provide terrorists with weapons of mass destruction. Reiterating his call for an offensive rather than defensive posture, Bush argued that the twentieth century had ended with a "single surviving model of human progress, based on no negotiable demands on human dignity, the rule of law, limits on the power of state, respect for women and private property, and free speech and equal justice and religious tolerance"—that is, the values Bush considered fundamental to American democracy. He acknowledged that the United States could not impose these values on other countries, but it could "support and reward governments that make the right choice for their own people."[49]

Each of these speeches by Bush contained the main elements of the United States' new foreign policy strategy: the struggle against terrorists and the countries that harbor them, the need to combat dictators with weapons of mass destruction, the decision to be offensive and use a preemptive strike if necessary, and the primacy of American values over other principles. The National Security Strategy (NSS) document published in September 2002 set out this policy in official form. This document stressed American dominance as a central component of the new strategy, promoted the view that American values are universal, and declared that the United States should "reward nations moving toward democracy." The document also explicitly set out the United States' intention to "exercise our right of self-defense by acting preemptively against such terrorist[s]."[50] The document officially endorsed fundamental neoconservative principles as the framework for the United States' new foreign policy strategy. "This document [the NSS]," asserted Max Boot, "builds on more than a decade of hard work by many thinkers associated with the administration [the Bush administration] (and this magazine)."[51] The neoconservatives clearly saw the publication of the NSS as a victory. The policies prescribed in the NSS document did not alter the balance of international power, but they did substantially modify American foreign policy.[52] Yet those changes needed to be sold to the American public.

## Selling the War

Arguably, the George W. Bush administration had been selling the idea of war to the world and the American public since the days immediately following the September 11 attacks. The American citizenry was terrified by the possibility of another attack. Terrorists had not only killed almost three thousand people in just a few hours and temporarily paralyzed the country; they had also created a deep sense of vulnerability. Bush's approval ratings soared to 86 percent at the beginning of 2002. Bush and his top advisers took advantage of this climate to sell the war to the public. Using incendiary language, the administration worked hard to convince Americans that removing Saddam Hussein from power was central to winning the war on terror and ensuring American security.

Domestically, Bush used the politics of fear to advance his political career and keep the Republican Party in power. He emphasized over and over again that the nation would only be secure under a Republican administration. The possibility of the Democratic Party winning the 2004 presidential election was framed as the path to increased insecurity. For example, in September 2004, Dick Cheney declared that if Americans voted for John Kerry, the country would assuredly face another terrorist assault. "It's absolutely essential," Cheney told a crowd in Iowa City, "that on November 2, we make the right choice, because if we make the wrong choice the danger is that we'll get hit again and we'll be hit in a way that will be devastating from the standpoint of the United States."[53] Cheney seemed to be saying that the terrorists considered Democrats weak and that Americans should take this into consideration when they cast their votes.

During this phase of the war on terror—when the war was being sold to the public—the neoconservatives found themselves in a new position. Before the terrorist attack, the neoconservatives had conceived and designed a post–Cold War era foreign policy. After September 11, they worked to make their ideas resonate in American circles of power. Once Bush embraced their ideas, they took on a new role. They became the source of "intellectual legitimacy" behind presidential initiatives. They also took on the role of critiquing the president and his advisers for what they perceived as mistakes or deviations from neoconservative principles. Above all, they pushed to make neoconservative policy a permanent feature of American foreign policy.

The neoconservatives had made four primary arguments to justify the invasion of Iraq. Iraq, they argued, simply could not be contained. The United States had pursued a policy of containment, warning Hussein to abandon the development of weapons of mass destruction, periodically bombing Iraq, and promoting the implementation of economic sanctions. The neoconservatives saw containment as a deficient policy. Hussein had, they argued, demonstrated a desire to kill Americans and expand his control in the Middle East. In the words of Max Boot, "Traditional theories of containment and deterrence are insufficient to deal with the shadowy foes we now confront."[54] Douglas Feith concurred: "The main pillars of containment were crumbling—weapons inspection, which Saddam ended in 1998; economic [sanctions], there was diminishing international support for preserving them; there were no-fly zones; and Saddam [had] started to shoot at the British and American planes patrolling the no-fly zones."[55]

The United States, he declared, had to change its policy from one of containment to one of active confrontation with terrorists and the countries that harbored them.

The neoconservatives also stressed that there was evidence that Iraq was involved in terrorist activities. According to Feith, one of the rationales for going to war against Hussein was that he had "supported various terrorist groups; key terrorist leaders were getting safe haven in Iraq; he was offering rewards [to] Palestinian suicide bombers; he was giving training to terrorists in Iraq; and thousands of foreign terrorists were being trained by the Fedayins, of which we learned more after we overthrew Saddam."[56] The neoconservatives pushed this point further. They tried to establish a connection between Hussein and the terrorist attacks on September 11. To do so, they mobilized two different arguments.

First, they maintained that there was a strategic connection between bin Laden and Hussein. Despite the fact that bin Laden is a religious fanatic and Hussein had established a secular regime, the neoconservatives believed that they shared a desire to "expel the United States from the Middle East." Gary Schmitt, for example, argued that high-ranking Iraqi officials had met with bin Laden and Iraqi defectors in Afghanistan and claimed to "have seen radical Muslims at the special terrorist training site in Iraq."[57] Similarly, William Kristol argued that Hussein maintained secret terrorist training camps for Islamic radicals.[58] Second, they alleged that Mohamed Atta—the lead hijacker on the first plane that crashed into the Twin Towers—had met with Iraqi intelligence officials in Europe in June 2002. According to Schmitt, "Atta would never have met with an Iraqi intelligence officer unless the Iraqis had been in some way in on the operation."[59] The neoconservatives repeated this allegation as conclusive proof of the relationship between Al Qaeda and Iraq.[60]

The neoconservatives emphasized that Hussein possessed weapons of mass destruction. They offered his use of such weapons on Kurdish Iraqis as incontrovertible evidence of this claim. Hussein had "already gassed 5,000 Kurds," asserted Krauthammer, "[and] used chemical weapons against Iran."[61] Hussein, they reasoned, was thus perfectly willing to use those weapons against the United States and its allies. From the point of view of Kagan and Kristol, nothing could be worse for the world than the "disease of Saddam with weapons of mass destruction."[62]

The neoconservatives magnified these fears by asserting that Hussein was in the process of obtaining nuclear weapons. They argued that the Iraqis had a very well-developed program to build nuclear arms. Hussein,

Richard Perle had asserted in 2002, had a "clandestine program spread over many sites to enrich Iraqi natural Uranium to weapons grade. We know he has the designs and technical staff to fabricate nuclear weapons once he obtained the materials. . . . Intelligence sources know he is in the market with plenty of money, for both weapons material and components as well as finished nuclear weapons."[63] Lawrence Kaplan and William Kristol joined in, claiming that after Operation Desert Storm, United Nations inspectors "found that Iraq was only months away from producing a nuclear bomb."[64] They asserted that the Federation of American Scientists affirmed that even with an intrusive inspections regime, "Iraq might be able to construct a nuclear explosive before it was detected."[65] The neoconservatives argued that the United States had made a grave mistake in not stopping Hussein's nuclear ambitions, and that the United States must act immediately.

These arguments in favor of deposing Hussein were complemented by a deep distrust of Hussein and a sense that U.S. security was at stake. The neoconservatives emphasized Hussein's record. Perle wrote, "He invade[d] two countries, and kill[ed] with impunity. His brutal rule includes slaughter, rape, mutilation, and the destruction of families."[66] Michael Ledeen called Hussein a "terrible evil."[67] And Krauthammer declared Iraq "the most dangerous terrorist regime in the world."[68] Kristol and Kaplan went even further, calling Hussein a "pathological risk-taker," a "tyrant," and a "threat to civilization."[69] After September 11, they judged Hussein "probably the most dangerous individual in the world."[70]

The primary arguments offered by the neoconservatives to justify the invasion of Iraq resonated with Bush's politics of fear. The neoconservatives reiterated the urgency of toppling Hussein. Krauthammer said the United States was in a "race against time."[71] The neoconservatives recommended that the United States take action against Hussein before Hussein took action against the United States.

History has shown that both the neoconservatives and the Bush administration were wrong. Experts, nongovernmental organizations, and others have proved conclusively that the threat was overstated. Today we know that Saddam Hussein had no connection to Osama bin Laden and Al Qaeda, nor was he involved in the September 11 attacks. He did not have weapons of mass destruction, nor was he on the verge of obtaining nuclear weapons. In January 2004, the declaration of David Kay, former head of the Iraqi Survey Group, resonated around the world. Before the Senate Armed Service Committee, Kay admitted, "It turns out we were all wrong,

... and that is most disturbing."[72] Later, some of Bush's closest collaborators revealed a more perplexing truth. The president had been aware—before the invasion of Iraq—that Hussein did not have weapons of mass destruction. Nevertheless, he persistently presented the case that Hussein had stockpiles of weapons of mass destruction. He was able to convince Congress, intellectuals, and the population in general that the United States needed to attack Iraq.[73]

How did President Bush and his collaborators convince an entire nation of their claims? According to Chaim Kaufman, there are five possible explanations. First, democratic systems might be "inherently vulnerable to issue manipulations." Second, President Bush, like other American presidents, had significant control over the nation's intelligence apparatus. This control allowed the chief executive to selectively present information to the public. Third, the Office of the President has been a dominant force in American foreign affairs, giving its occupant more credibility than other sources of information. Fourth, those organizations that traditionally provide a counterpoint or check on presidential power—the press, political parties, nongovernmental organizations, and intellectuals—did not execute their charge. The voices of protest of distinguished scholars such as G. John Ikenberry, John Mearsheimer, Robert Jarvis, Stephen Walt, and John Lewis Gaddis were ignored. And the complaints of former realist politicians such as Brent Scowcroft and James Baker were not taken into account. Fifth and finally, the terrorist attacks on September 11 created a "crisis atmosphere" that may have limited public skepticism.[74] In sum, historical circumstances, combined with the institutional structure of the American political system and the manipulation of information by the Bush administration, merged to successfully sell the war.

Perhaps the most dramatic truth is that not a single argument offered by the neoconservatives since the 1990s, nor the sole justification they offered for the invasion of Iraq, has turned out to have merit. The invasion of Iraq will remain in the annals of American history as an example of the ways in which manipulation and untruths became central to persuading the American public to support a misguided policy.

# 10

# The Iraqi Debacle and the Partial Decline of Neoconservatism

The implementation of neoconservative views by the George W. Bush administration is an example of a policy failure with devastating consequences. Before he left office, President Bush's popularity had declined to a low of 22 percent. The Republican Party had lost control of Congress, and the former allies of the United States in the invasion of Iraq had withdrawn their troops. As of the time of writing, more than 4,000 American troops have died in Iraq, and more than 100,000 have been wounded. More than 86,000 Iraqi civilians have been killed since the beginning of the American invasion. For a long time, Baghdad and other Iraqi cities were in complete chaos, although the conditions currently seem to be improving. Violence has gone down considerably, but attacks by suicide bombers and car bombers are still killing people. Notwithstanding, President Barack Obama has declared that most U.S. troops will leave Iraq by August 2010, with only between 35,000 and 50,000 troops remaining to train and support the Iraqi security forces until the end of 2011. Meanwhile, the American fiscal deficit has reached more than $40 billion and is severely affecting the nation's economy. In 2006, the cost of the war in Iraq was "$2.2 trillion, not counting interest," and in September 2007, the cost was $720 million a day.[1]

Despite the serious problems the Obama administration is still facing in Iraq, the neoconservatives were convinced that the invasion was necessary and that their foreign policy design was adequate. At the end of the Bush administration, their opinions varied according to their position inside or outside the government, from neoconservative politicians to intellectuals. For the former members of the Bush administration, the Iraq policy was not a failure. "I do not agree that the foreign policy in Iraq is a failure," Richard Perle maintained. "The cost is much higher than it needed to be."[2] By the same token, Elliott Abrams asserted: "I do not think that the president believes that the Iraq war is lost. I think that he believes that the Iraqi war was a necessary war and we are doing a lot better in 2008." For Abrams, the neoconservatives' foreign policy was a combination of two basic elements: one was a strong military position against regimes like that of Saddam Hussein; and the other was ideological, the freedom agenda fundamentally used against Islamic extremism. Abrams considered that the great challenge of Islamic extremism could only be beat with the implementation of both, the ideological and the military strategies. In his view, "People can say, well this theory has been disproved. I would say come back in five years and I will see the next president of either party pursuing essentially the same policy, or if not, you do not have a foreign policy." For Abrams, all these arguments about the death of neoconservatism were "largely a product of the opposition to the war in Iraq."[3] Neoconservatism, is in his view, was the only game in town.

In a similar vein, Douglas Feith considered neoconservative ideas and policy prescriptions as correct. He stated that there were some mistakes in the policy implementation of neoconservative ideas, but those problems did not come from neoconservative thinking: "I do not think that the important things that were done wrong derive from the essential ideas of neoconservatism." The errors, from his perspective, were errors of policy but not of conception and not mistakes related to the basic policy design: "The administration created more problems than were necessary." Among the most important was "setting up the occupation." Finally, he stressed that the failure was not inevitable: "We had a plan of doing things differently, but the plan got [tossed] aside because of some complicated bureaucratic politics."[4]

Perhaps the most severe criticism of a former Bush collaborator was expressed by David Frum. For him, as well as for many neoconservatives, the theory was correct but the implementation was erroneous. In his view, the Bush administration made many mistakes, and Bush was unwilling to recognize the problems and modify the route. Frum maintained that any countries engaged in war make errors, but rarely "have so many and such lethal mistakes been made as in Iraq, and probably never in American history have war leaders so stubbornly refused to correct mistakes when exposed."[5] For Frum, Bush's incapacity to change course provoked, among other things, the path of events that resulted in Republicans losing their advantage as the dominant party in security matters.

Frum's critique may stem from the nature of his former job. His position as speechwriter was in many ways a flexible one. Speechwriters are not involved in the decisionmaking process. They write, but then they very rarely see their words or ideas reflected in the president's discourse. This allows them, at least partially, to see presidential decisions from the outside world, from the perspective of observers who seek with their words to reflect the president's interests and ideas but who have their own judgments, which are not necessarily constrained by the policies or decisions of the chief executive or his administration. Therefore, Frum's position was closer to that of those neoconservative intellectuals outside the government than those inside the administration.

The views of the neoconservatives outside the Bush administration were different. Contrary to the neoconservative politicians, who defended their performance in the Bush administration, the neoconservatives outside the government had more freedom and flexibility to express their criticisms. They fundamentally judged that Bush's foreign policy toward Iraq was in trouble because of the erroneous implementation of neoconservative foreign policy views. "We were very critical here at *The [Weekly] Standard*, of the failures to send more troops, very early, even right away," asserted William Kristol. "We were critical of Rumsfeld; I called for him to be fired in December 2004. So I wish that what we were doing now with [General David] Petraeus, we had done three years earlier." Kristol judged that the problem with the Bush foreign policy in Iraq "was not that it was too neoconservative; it was not neoconservative enough," and thus the difficulties faced by the Bush administration had nothing to do with neoconservative thought. "I am pretty doubtful," argued Kristol, "that [neoconservative] ideas are collapsing." For him, if the Iraqi policy of Bush was facing problems, it had "nothing to do with the virtues of anything I write or the cleverness of Bob Kagan or Max Boot or all of my friends."[6]

Gary Schmitt followed the same kind of reasoning as Kristol. He argued that the problem was not neoconservative ideas but that the Bush administration did not correctly apply neoconservative views. This was like saying, "You know how to fix your car, but you do not have the right tools." In his view, the failures in Iraq were not inevitable, but a combination of factors came "together in a perfect storm. You have a president that was not very experienced in foreign policy, you have a national security structure that was design to be inactive in foreign policy, and you have Donald Rumsfeld, who consistently was not on board in the president's own policy." In Schmitt's view, Bush made a big mistake in security matters in that his administration did not have a counterinsurgency strategy.

The United States also made several institutional errors that seriously affected the outcome of the war. "We gave them a crappy constitutional system, we gave them a system with a weak president; you need a strong executive to get things done." The party system was, for him, another serious problem: "If anyone wants to design a party system that kept sectarian violence and tension high, it is the one that we designed."[7] For Schmitt, in a nutshell, bad decisions, inferior institutional structure, and poor constitutional and party design came together to cause the failure of U.S. policy in Iraq.

Joshua Muravchik emphasized that those people who judged that neoconservatism was collapsing because of American problems in Iraq were wrong. However, he recognized that the problems faced by the Bush administration in Iraq were a "big embarrassment to us." Muravchik stated that what distinguished neoconservative thinking after the September 11, 2001, terrorist attacks was not the war on Iraq but the war on terrorism. For him, the war on terrorism meant "the Bush doctrine, the feeling, on the one hand, that we have to fight very hard, . . . to be very tough, have a lot of military strength to use sometimes. To be very tough on the governments to support terrorists like Iran and so on; . . . and on the other hand, that the key to the strategy was to try to change the psychology of the Middle East and the politics of the Middle East. That is the neoconservative idea that also becomes Bush's idea."

Thus, Muravchik, like most neoconservatives outside the government, differentiated neoconservative thinking and the performance of the Bush administration in Iraq. He consequently pointed out that "even though the war in Iraq has been a debacle, that idea is still right. . . . I think that the basic idea is still correct and no one has a better idea." In his view, these ideas were adopted by the Bush administration because they were "the only ideas on the table." Neoconservatives' views and explanations, he maintained, "might be wrong, but at least they were an answer. And I think that is still true, still the only answer out there."[8]

Muravchik affirmed that the Bush administration made many mistakes—especially "not sending enough troops" to Iraq. He blamed Rumsfeld as well as Bush for this error. In his view, Rumsfeld and Paul Wolfowitz believed that the entire enterprise in Iraq could be done with a small number of forces: "Rumsfeld came and said, 25,000. This was really a disastrous mistake." Muravchik expressed the opinion that neoconservatives like William Kristol and Robert Kagan complained immediately about the lack of sufficient troops, but the administration ignored them. Muravchik was recently especially critical of the way things were conducted in Iraq. His views positioned him as the neoconservatives' severest critic of the war. He even had reservations about the invasion itself, stating that "I think it is very questionable whether it was the right idea to invade Iraq." For him, it was not obvious that Iraq should be the target after Afghanistan, but he encouraged the invasion "because I supported the war on terror." In his view, Iran was the next target and not Iraq, but that does not necessarily mean that "we should invade Iran in the way that we invaded Iraq." He supported different measures against Iran, such as a "strategy of economic warfare, trying to foment a rebellion inside Iran, trying to isolate Iran in a more serious way." Finally, he stated his belief that despite the fact that neoconservative ideas have been discredited, neoconservatism will survive as an important foreign policy framework.[9]

In short, at the end of the George W. Bush administration, the neoconservatives had fundamentally two different viewpoints on the situation in Iraq. From one perspective, those neoconservative politicians who had been involved in the administration did not consider the invasion of Iraq to be a fiasco. The Iraq war was a necessary war, and, sooner or later, America will prevail. But from the other perspective, those neoconservative intellectuals outside the government considered that the failure in Iraq was not inevitable. Their external position gave them more freedom to judge Bush's performance. They regarded their principles and views as accurate, but they judged the Bush administration as having wrongly implemented their policy. Whatever the case may be, all these neoconservatives did agree on one point: The principles were reasonable, and neoconservatism will endure as the most relevant alternative—perhaps even the only alternative—for conducting American foreign policy.

One point is unquestionable: The foreign policy that the neoconservatives and the George W. Bush administration developed and implemented in Iraq will have a long-term impact on the United States and the world. We will live for years to come with the consequences of America's decision to go to war in Iraq. In very few episodes of American history have ideas so decisively changed the course of the nation's politics and of world affairs. No doubt, the neoconservatives—this small group of politicians, journalists, and intellectuals—will be thought of as members of one of the most influential intellectual and political movements in American history. The implementation of neoconservative ideas will also be remembered as one of the most destructive episodes in contemporary American politics.

# Epilogue

Throughout this study of neoconservatism, I have shown that it is possible to combine realignment theory with historical institutionalism. The blending of these two approaches is important for two main reasons. First, through realignment theory, we are able not only to place our analysis in the proper historical context but also to understand the main features of the particular historical period that saw the growth of neoconservative thought. Second, historical institutionalism offers us a way to understand the intricacies of American politics by advising us to carefully evaluate the internal dynamics of institutions, to observe institutional trajectories, and to assess whether institutions allow or obstruct the free flow of ideas. I consider realignment theory my general framework and historical institutionalism my guide to the details of my subject of inquiry. As this study has shown, it is not only possible but also fruitful to combine realignment theory and historical institutionalism.

This book has revealed that neither interests nor ideas were the sole protagonists of political change. Neoconservative ideas penetrated economic interests, and economic interests supported and in some cases shaped ideas. Large corporations understood the relevance of investing in think tanks, research institutions, or journals to create a political climate suitable for them. To assign policy changes to one variable is to obscure rather than illuminate the issue. A more satisfactory answer to the question of how to explain policy shifts is to say that they were the result of a "complex interaction of interests and ideas" in a particular historical context, in "which institutional factors played a critical mediating role."[1]

What accounted for the convergence of ideas and interests during this period? What accounted for the growth and development of neoconservatism? As I have shown, this marriage of ideas and economic interests became possible in the historical context provided by the nonpartisan realignment of the late 1960s. Realignment periods are times of structural change, in which the system is open to modifications and political actors redefine their roles to fit new circumstances. Realignment eras, therefore, are ideal moments to explore the behavior of different political actors and their influence on policy changes. As I have demonstrated, the nonpartisan realignment of the late 1960s and early 1970s opened space for the interaction of ideas, institutions, and interests in the promotion and implementation of neoconservative policies.

Although essential, these conditions are not sufficient to explain the emergence and influence of the second generation of neoconservatives. In that case, at least three additional issues need to be considered. First, the long-term work of neoconservatives on American foreign policy issues needs to be taken into account. Neoconservatives have been participants in the American political debate on foreign policy for more than fifty years. In the last three decades, they have been a permanent point of reference for American foreign policy. Their thinking on this topic constitutes a political view—for John Mearsheimer, "Wilsonianism with teeth"[2]; and for some scholars, even a theory of international relations.[3] Neoconservatives have invested in building a foreign policy view with an appeal to some sectors of the population and to politicians, especially, but not exclusively, in the Republican Party. This investment has shown its dividends.

Second, over the years, neoconservatives have constructed strong relationships with politicians and elected officials. They have established important connections to people like Richard Cheney, Donald Rumsfeld, Condoleezza Rice, George Shultz, Richard Allen, John McCain, and many others. These relationships have been central to the influence of neoconservative ideas. Many conservative politicians are familiar with neoconservatives' thinking, with their magazines, and with their op-ed columns in newspapers. Politicians also sympathize with neoconservatives' opinions and consider their ideas important in shaping public opinion and promoting policy measures. Neoconservatives have formed—sometimes officially, other times unofficially—a sort of neoconservative coalition to promote and implement neoconservative perspectives.

This permanent collaboration between politicians and neoconservatives has activated an implicit political agreement: When the right moment arrives, politicians recruit neoconservatives for political posts or implement neoconservative views. This was exactly what happened with the re-

cruitment of neoconservatives by the Ronald Reagan administration. Richard Allen—a close associate of Reagan, a founding member of the
Committee on the Present Danger, and a politician very acquainted with
neoconservative ideas—established the linkage between neoconservatives
and Reagan. Allen therefore was instrumental in bringing neoconservatives into the Reagan government.

In a similar vein, neoconservatives of both the first and second generations were recruited by the George W. Bush administration. Rumsfeld and
Cheney were very familiar with neoconservatives like Elliott Abrams, Paul
Wolfowitz, Richard Perle, and Scooter Libby. Cheney promoted the appointment of neoconservatives to different positions within the Republican
administration. At the same time, neoconservatives outside the government
performed two basic functions. First, they advised high-ranking administration officials. Second, they continued disseminating neoconservative
views, sometimes reinforcing and at other times criticizing the decisions
made by the Bush administration. The work of neoconservative politicians, their relationship with important political figures, the impact of neoconservative views on the shaping of public opinion, and the relevance of
neoconservative ideas for some conservative politicians—all have facilitated the influence of neoconservative views on American foreign policy.

Finally, the September 11, 2001, terrorist attacks were a key event not
only in American history but also for the trajectory of neoconservatism.
Obviously, at the time of the terrorist attacks, neoconservatives held important positions in the government, and they aired their views in the media. However, the historical context was not quite right for the implementation of their ideas. After September 11, these neoconservatives had an
enemy to fight and an excuse for advocating regime change in Iraq. Neoconservative politicians like Douglas Feith, Richard Perle, John Bolton,
and especially Paul Wolfowitz were instrumental in persuading President
Bush to invade Iraq. Their intellectual counterparts helped shape public
opinion in favor of the overthrow of Saddam Hussein. September 11 changed
these neoconservatives' political fortunes by giving them the opportunity
to influence American foreign policy.

In this work, I have tried to draw a detailed picture—perhaps unsuc-
cessfully—of one of the most important political and intellectual phenomena in recent American politics. This type of study requires bridging disciplinary boundaries and absorbing different modes of knowledge—what
Richard Bensel has called an "intellectual insurgency," an effort to destroy
disciplinary boundaries with the goal of making sense of our object of

study.[4] In a way, this book has attempted to show that political science can be nourished by other disciplines. Perhaps only interdisciplinary approaches will allow us to take a closer look at the political reality we are trying to understand.

In this book, I have sought to account for change and continuity in American politics—in particular, for change and permanence in the primary characteristics of neoconservatism. It is evident that the United States of the 1980s was very different from the nation of the early twenty-first century. Clearly, the neoconservative expression that emerged in each historical period varied. The first generation of neoconservatives was more academically oriented than the second, which was more politically determined. Likewise, in general terms, the second generation is more conservative than the first. These are substantial modifications in the long-term historical trajectory of the neoconservative movement. What accounted for these changes? The first change is related to the transformation experienced by American society in the 1980s. The second is connected to the historical journey taken by neoconservatism in roughly the last fifteen years.

The historical period during which the first generation of neoconservatives emerged as an important intellectual force—the 1950s and 1960s—was a moment of transition in American intellectual life. From the 1910s to the 1940s, American intellectuals were people with a broad knowledge of politics, society, and culture. They were primarily leftists and liberal thinkers—contrary to the liberal and conservative tendencies of today—who were able to address a large educated audience and make a living, although sometimes with serious difficulty, writing for magazines. These were the years when bimonthly and monthly publications were the primary arena for political and cultural debate. During these decades, intellectuals' opinions were highly valued by members of a society in constant change.

These were also the days of *Partisan Review, The New Masses, The New Leader, The New Republic,* and *The Nation,* as well as the emergence of the group of thinkers who would become known as the New York intellectuals. In their youth, neoconservatives were to some extent part of the bohemian world of Greenwich Village and of American leftist organizations. The first decades of the twentieth century possessed an incredible political and cultural dynamism. Daniel Bell, Irving Kristol, Nathan Glazer, Seymour Martin Lipset, Norman Podhoretz, and other future neoconservative figures absorbed and shared in this intellectual environment.

They enjoyed debating daily events, they started writing for magazines to express their opinions and share their views with the public, and they felt compelled to transform the world with their ideas.

By the late 1940s through the 1960s, another important phenomenon took place in American cultural life. Intellectuals found employment, often with tenure, in universities. They brought to the universities their habits of reading, writing for, and editing magazines aimed at the general public. In these university settings, the new scholars never lost contact with the public sphere. In the university, they were able to be both academics and "public intellectuals."

Neoconservatives like Bell, Kristol, and Glazer exemplify this phenomenon. Primarily essayists and editors, they had expressed their opinions about a variety of topics and had been involved in the publication of various magazines before becoming distinguished academics. Bell was involved with *The New Leader*, *Common Sense*, and *Fortune* before joining the faculty of Columbia University and later Harvard University.[5] Kristol was the least academic of the three. His books are collections of articles that appeared in magazines like *Commentary* and *The Reporter*, and he was a cofounder of *Encounter* before becoming professor of social thought at New York University in the 1960s. Glazer worked on the staff of *Commentary* before his appointments as a professor of sociology at the University of California, Berkeley, and later as a professor of education at Harvard.

When these neoconservatives entered American universities, they not only taught and wrote books but also created magazines—Bell and Kristol created *The Public Interest*, and Kristol organized *The National Interest*. Also they edited magazines—Bell and Kristol, *The Public Interest*, where Glazer later took Bell's place. They wrote for other publications, like *Dissent*, *The New Republic*, and *Commentary*. Kristol published frequently in the *Wall Street Journal*. Of course, other neoconservatives like Podhoretz spent their entire professional careers as journalists. Moreover, in some cases, universities recognized the work of neoconservatives engaged outside academia. According to Russell Jacoby, Bell never wrote a dissertation, but Columbia granted him a PhD for his work on his book *The End of Ideology*. Kristol received a BA in history from the City College of New York, and he ended up becoming a professor at New York University without a higher degree.

In the 1950s and 1960s, at the time that these public intellectuals were moving to the university campuses, being both an academic and a public intellectual was a feasible project. Today, the worlds of academia and public intellectuals are quite separate. Scholars very rarely appear on news talk shows or write newspaper articles.⁶ The world of public debate left by intellectuals of the 1910s to the 1950s has been relocated to a significant degree to think tanks. Since the 1970s, think tanks have become the home of contemporary "public intellectuals,"⁷ the institution in which they can spread out their ideas to an educated audience and political and business elites. At the same time, to achieve prestige, and thus authority, think tanks like the American Enterprise Institute purposefully employed university professors during the 1970s. Neoconservative scholars like Seymour Martin Lipset and James Q. Wilson found in the American Enterprise Institute a way to continue practicing their activities as public intellectuals. Today, however, think tanks' reputations are not tied to those of the university professoriate.⁸

The transformation of neoconservatism is related to these political changes but also to an internal process of change within the neoconservative movement. Five primary factors explain the radicalization of the second generation of neoconservatism. Although these themes have been addressed in this book, it is useful to briefly summarize them. First, contrary to their predecessors, the members of the second generation of neoconservatives have never affiliated with socialist or Democratic politics. Rather, they have been committed, lifelong Republicans. Thus, whereas the first generation of neoconservatives accepted the Welfare State, the second generation's members adamantly reject it.

Second, the second generation of neoconservatives, thanks in a significant degree to the work of their forerunners, came of age in a country where conservative thinking was a respectable viewpoint. The history of American conservatism is an old and complex tale, with intellectuals, politicians, organizations, and business groups as some of the main protagonists. It is fair to say, however, that contemporary American conservatism started in the early 1950s with the publication of Russell Kirk's *The Conservative Mind* (1953) and the start-up of the *National Review* (1955). Since then, conservative views have been publicly expressed in a systematic and permanent fashion.

Third, at least since the mid-1960s, conservatism has predominated in American politics. According to responses to an American National Election Studies feeling thermometer poll from 1964 to 2004, most Americans identified with conservativism. In 1964, 53 percent of the electorate thought favorably toward liberals, and 57 toward conservatives. By 2004, the sympathy of the American public for conservatism increased. Fifty-five percent of the electorate felt favorably toward liberals and 61 percent toward conservatives.[9] Many people were expecting that these proportions might change because of the questionable performance of George W. Bush and the arrival of Barack Obama in the White House. However, a Gallup Poll published on June 15, 2009, reported that 40 percent of the people interviewed defined themselves as conservatives, 35 percent as moderates, and 21 percent as liberals. Conservatism, therefore, remains the most popular political ideology in the United States. What is more, the Republican Party itself has become increasingly conservative. A 2005 Harris Poll reported that 82 percent of Republicans favor conservative candidates.[10] And self-identified liberals constitute less than 5 percent of the party's membership.

Since the 1950s, different conservative expressions have emerged on the American political scene, some of them with a significant audience and constituency. Many Americans sympathize with the causes of single-issue groups like the Eagle Forum, the National Rifle Association, or the Minutemen. Others identify with the social conservatism of the Christian Right. As Leo Ribuffo asserts, "In 2003 hardly anyone denies that political and cultural conservatism has been an important part of contemporary U.S. history."[11]

Fourth, in a historical context replete with conservative political expressions—and many radical-right organizations—it is natural that conservative tendencies have not only emerged but are also heeded. Second-generation neoconservatives expressed their opinion on Iraq beginning in the 1990s, but their words found neither a leader nor a constituency. It was not until the arrival of the George W. Bush administration to power and the events of September 11 that neoconservative thought achieved its highest level of political relevance. The terrorist attacks on U.S. soil changed many aspects of American political life. Terrorism became a central topic for Americans; fear became a fundamental tool for the government to manipulate the American population; the invasions of Afghanistan and Iraq led to a significant waste of money and an enormous loss of human lives; and the Department of Homeland Security became the institutional reaction to international and domestic terrorism. The Bush administration's responses to the terrorist attacks were perceived by the public as "acceptable," under the circumstances. Extremist assaults thus facilitated the introduction and implementation of extremist views.

Finally, many neoconservatives have adopted a pragmatic approach to influencing politics. For example, although William Kristol finished a PhD in political science at Harvard and had a brief experience in academia, he basically developed his professional career, first as chief staff for Vice President Dan Quayle and later as a journalist and commentator. It is evident that Kristol wants to be in the political arena as either an adviser or a policy intellectual. He wants his thinking to have an impact on daily politics.

The transition of neoconservatism from an intellectual to a more pragmatic political expression is, in Kristol's view, part of the natural developmental process for any intellectual movement. "What it means to be a movement," he asserted to me in 1993, "is that it is a great effort to create a line of thought, which then is implemented and developed and refined." "Any movement," he continued, "like Marxism, various forms of English conservatism, or liberation theology," follows this trend. First, these people are important scholars with a line of thought, and then "their views become more practical in the second or third generation."[12] Neoconservatism, in his view, has thus followed the traditional route of other intellectual expressions, traveling a long journey from the academy to politics, and neoconservatives thus have moved from being academic public intellectuals to being public intellectuals–politicians. The views of many neoconservatives of the first generation now coincide with the views of the second, which suggests that another transition is in the making.

It is quite evident that neoconservatives' strategic views were wrong. The rationale offered by neoconservatives and President George W. Bush for the invasion of Iraq has been shown to be misguided, if not false. In particular, regime change in Iraq has been a failure.[13] The invasion provoked strong resistance from diverse sectors of Iraqi society who, despite their differences, have in common their desire to see the United States leave Iraq. The invasion exacerbated hostilities between Sunni and Shiite groups in Iraq, engendering chaos across the country. There is no simple solution to this ancient ethnic conflict. But the American presence in Iraq has done little to alleviate tension in Iraqi society or eliminate terrorism.

During the last years of the George W. Bush administration, the majority of Americans recognized that the invasion of Iraq was a mistake and asked for the immediate withdrawal of American troops. According to a poll conducted by *Newsweek* on March 28 and 29, 2007, 65 percent of those responding disapproved of the way President Bush was handling the situation in Iraq, and only 28 percent approved. A total of 57 percent of the people polled supported legislation passed by the Senate calling for the withdrawal of U.S. troops from Iraq by March 2008, and only 36 percent opposed such legislation.

Despite evidence that Congress was voicing the opinion of the majority of the population, the Bush administration clung to neoconservative views. For a long time, neoconservatives criticized Donald Rumsfeld for not increasing the number of armed forces in Baghdad. President Bush's solution to the Iraqi turmoil was to send even more troops into Baghdad. Moreover, the president declared that he would veto any congressional initiative to remove American armed forces from Iraq. The position adopted and defended by Bush typifies what Walter Dean Burnham calls the *interregnum state*, in which public policy is disassociated from any base of popular support. In this case, President Bush repeatedly ignored the demands of the American population. Under the claim that he was the commander in chief of the armed forces, he pursued his own path. Now that President Obama is in the White House, we are starting to see some changes in the conduct of American foreign policy. He started his presidency by pledging to close the Guantánamo Bay prison—although he did not say anything about Bagram Prison in Afghanistan, where many people have been tortured and some even killed—and by reversing some policies defended by the Bush administration. In the case of Iraq, Obama has promised to begin withdrawing American troops by August 2010. However, we will have to wait some time to see if the changes announced by Obama early in his administration represent a significant departure from Bush's foreign policy or just symbolic measures. At least in his announcement of American foreign policy toward Afghanistan, his policy highly resembles that of Bush.

However, for many neoconservatives, the arrival of Obama in the White House and the appointment of Hillary Clinton as secretary of state—and of many other diplomats, such as Susan Rice, Dennis Ross, and Richard Holbrooke—do not reflect change but the continuity of neoconservative foreign policy views. Richard Perle has asserted: "On all the main issues—Iraq, Iran, Russia, China, Islamist terrorism, Syria, the Israel-Palestine dispute, relations with allies—Obama's first term is likely to look like Bush's second."[14] In an interview with Justine Rosenthal, editor of *The National Interest*, Perle maintained that "Condi sounded a lot like Hillary toward the end. I do not expect a lot of changes in substance. . . . I think there will be a change in tone."[15] Perle is not alone in this view. In January 2009, William Kristol asserted that Obama has moved to the center and that the "new President will govern as a centrist."[16] With regard to foreign policy, some neoconservatives are pleased with the foreign policy team of the Obama administration.

Despite the failure of the American invasion of Iraq and the popular rejection of neoconservative ideas, it is quite probable that neoconservatism will languish but not disappear. I base this prediction on three factors. First, the neoconservative movement is deeply rooted in the Republican Party. Many Republicans—though, of course, not all—are in favor of the fundamental bases of neoconservative foreign policy: the preservation of American military power, the opposition to international institutions, the belief that peace is best achieved through strength, and the promotion of democracy as the best antidote to anti-Americanism.

The Republican Party is not a homogenous entity. There are people within the organization who disagree with neoconservative thinkers. For a long time, neoconservatives have had significant disagreements with "paleoconservatives." Likewise, we have only to remember that one of the main opponents to the invasion of Iraq was Brent Scowcroft—a former national security adviser under presidents Gerald Ford and George H. W. Bush—to realize that there are anti-neoconservative perspectives within the Republican Party.[17]

The episodes of neoconservative ascendancy studied in this book reveal that at particular political moments, neoconservatives have formed alliances with Republican presidential candidates, becoming an important political and intellectual group supporting a presidential aspirant who may later become the chief executive. There is no reason to believe that this arrangement will change in the future. Under the proper historical circumstances, neoconservatism will reemerge as a powerful political force.

Second, neoconservatism promises to remain important in both American politics and the Republican Party due to the continued polarization of American society. Various scholars of American politics have demonstrated the polarization of the electorate and the deep divide between the country's two main political parties. According to these scholars, the ideological and party polarization is a trend that is not likely to disappear in the foreseeable future. Some academics have even discussed a new ideological realignment among the electorate. "More than 90 percent of the Republican identifiers," assert Kyle Saunders and Alan Abramowitz, "and almost 90 percent of the Democratic identifiers voted for their own party's presidential candidate in 2000 and 2004. By 2004, liberal Democrats and conservative Republicans made up 59 percent of all white party identifiers, while conservative Democrats and liberal Republicans were down to 9 percent."[18] In other words, there is a growing consistency between ideological preference and party affinity.

The increasing polarization of American voters suggests a great deal about the future of the neoconservative movement. In the current political environment, both political parties and society will tolerate extremist positions[19]—especially from the right—in general. Today, significant numbers of business organizations, interest groups, religious associations, conservative foundations, think tanks, pundits, magazines, newspapers, electronic media, lobby firms, and so on are in agreement with conservative and neoconservative principles. This vast universe of conservative politics will not disappear or diminish in the years to come. On the contrary, the trend will most likely be reinforced. Neoconservatives now and in the future have an audience willing to listen to their words and accept their ideas.

The third reason that neoconservatives' influence will persist is because their views serve the interests of some corporations, in particular those in the defense industry. Since September 11, the defense industry has substantially benefited from the rhetoric of the neoconservative movement. Neoconservatives and the Bush administration developed a political discourse that highlighted the threat of international terrorism. To confront this new menace, the United States needs not only sophisticated technologies to protect it from another terrorist attack but also weapons to fight wars in the Middle East that seem to have no clear end date.[20]

Some might argue that the profits of military-related corporations, not neoconservative views, were boosted by September 11. To some degree, this is true. The Bush administration demanded the development of new technologies to make the United States safe from international terrorism. However, it is quite possible that without neoconservatism, the Bush administration would never have launched an attack on Iraq in the first place. Before the invasion, many scholars argued that the war with Iraq would not advance U.S. national interests and would only distract the United States from the main threat, Al Qaeda. Distinguished scholars of international security like Robert Art, Alexander George, Robert Jarvis, John Mearsheimer, Stephen Walt, and Kenneth Waltz expressed their belief that "the United States should maintain vigilant containment of Iraq and be prepared to invade Iraq if it threatens to attack America or its allies"—a set of conditions not met in 2002.[21] At that time, it was evident to these scholars, some politicians, and many civil society advocates that an attack to Iraq was not required.

Neoconservatives had a different perspective. They were convinced that Saddam Hussein represented a menace not only to the United States but also to the maintenance of peace around the world. Their convictions moved them to exploit the fears of everyday Americans and politicians alike. They fabricated a nonexistent threat. They persuaded a poorly informed president of the benefits of an invasion. They helped turn a questionable chief executive into an international dignitary.

This does not necessarily mean that neoconservatives signed a contract with military-related corporations to promote their interests—although the Center for Security Policy received money from defense contractors—but that a structural nexus exists between neoconservatives and these corporations. Since September 11, but particularly since the invasion of Iraq, these corporations have increased their profits substantially. According to the official figures of the Department of Defense, the Bush budget provided "$439.3 billions for the Department of Defense's base budget—a 7 percent increase over 2006 and 48 percent increase over 2001—to maintain a high level of military readiness, develop and procure new weapons systems. . . . This figure does not include the $50 billions request to maintain the war in Afghanistan and Iraq, and $173.3 billions for nuclear forces and missile defense."[22] A significant portion of this enormous budget has ended up in the hands of military-related corporations.

Finally, neoconservatism will survive, thanks to a well-established network of institutions that have been built up around the movement. During its history, the second generation has created think tanks, journals, and important relationships with conservative media outlets, such as Fox News. Neoconservatives seem well equipped to navigate the turbulent waters of the years to come. The members of the new generation have maintained the relationships established by their predecessors with conservative foundations and newspapers like the *Wall Street Journal*. They continue to cultivate strong connections to the American Enterprise Institute,[23] which guarantees their access to the most important conservatives on the political scene, and they have found in the media magnate Rupert Murdoch a source of seemingly unlimited financial support. Thus, it is unlikely that neoconservative institutions and networks will vanish in the near future. I would remind all those claiming that neoconservatism is dead of the words of that great American philosopher, Yogi Berra: "Predictions are risky, especially when they're about the future."

# Notes

## Preface and Acknowledgments

1. Many years later, in October 2004, when I was in Washington at the Woodrow Wilson International Center for Scholars finishing the first draft of this book, I had an opportunity to attend another gathering with neoconservatives. The National Endowment for Democracy presented an award to professor Seymour Martin Lipset at the Canadian Embassy in Washington. That night the keynote speaker was former president and scholar Fernando Enrique Cardozo, but Larry Diamond and Carl Gershman also spoke. After a very moving ceremony, at the cocktail party, I saw Jeane Kirkpatrick, Max Kampelman, Joshua Muravchik, Ben Wattenberg, Irving Kristol, Gertrude Himmelfarb, and many others. The event was full of neoconservatives who got together to celebrate Martin Lipset's academic achievements.

2. Dietrich Rueschemeyer, Evelyne Huber Stephens, and John D. Stephens, *Capitalist Development and Democracy* (Chicago: University of Chicago Press, 1992), 4.

3. Margaret Levi, "A Model, a Method and a Map: Rational Choice in Comparative and Historical Analysis," in *Comparative Politics: Rationality, Culture and Structure*, ed. Mark Irving Lichbach and Alan S. Zuckerman (New York: Cambridge University Press, 1997), 21.

4. Lionel Gossman, "Anecdote and History," *History and Theory* 42 (May 2003): 155.

5. It is important to highlight that many social scientists work with interviews. In the particular case of historians, they have a general area of work called oral history, in which they try to preserve and analyze oral testimonies.

6. Andrew Rich, *Think Tanks, Public Policy and the Politics of Expertise* (New York: Cambridge University Press, 2004), 10.

## Chapter 1. Introduction: An Analytical Framework

1. E.g., the *Christian Science Monitor*'s electronic edition features a special section, "Empire Builders: Neoconservatives and Their Blueprint for US Power," with

links to articles on neoconservatism; see http://www.csmonitor.com/specials/neocon/index.html.

2. There are four fundamental studies of the first neoconservative movement: Peter Steinfels, *The Neoconservatives: The Men Who Are Changing America's Politics* (New York: Simon & Schuster, 1979); Gary Dorrien, *The Neoconservative Mind: Politics, Culture, and the War of Ideology* (Philadelphia: Temple University Press, 1993); John Ehrman, *The Rise of Neoconservatives: Intellectuals and Foreign Policy* (New Haven, Conn.: Yale University Press, 1995); and Mark Gerson, *The Neoconservative Vision: From the Cold War to the Cultural Wars* (Lanham, Md.: Madison Books, 1995). The authors of these studies—especially Steinfels and Ehrman—make insightful observations on the influence of neoconservatism on American politics, but their books do not fully explore this theme.

3. Ehrman, *Rise of Neoconservatives*, vii.

4. Dorrien, *Neoconservative Mind*, x.

5. See Stefan Halper and Jonathan Clarke, *America Alone: The Neo-Conservatives and the Global Order* (New York: Cambridge University Press, 2004).

6. Although these questions are addressed with regard to a particular political and intellectual movement, they are also relevant queries for scholars working in the field of American political development and in the field of American contemporary history. For the relevance of these sorts of questions to the subfield of American political development, see Karen Orren and Stephen Skerownek, *The Search for American Political Development* (New York: Cambridge University Press, 2004).

7. Laurence G. McMichael and Richard J. Trilling, "The Structure and Meaning of Critical Realignment: The Case of Pennsylvania, 1928–1932," in *Realignment in American Politics: Toward a Theory*, ed. Bruce A. Campbell and Richard J. Trilling (Austin: University of Texas Press, 1980), 25.

8. Walter Dean Burnham, "Critical Realignment Dead or Alive?" in *The End of Realignment? Interpreting American Electoral Eras*, ed. Bayron E. Shafer (Madison: University of Wisconsin Press, 1991), 116.

9. Eldon Eisenach, "Reconstructing American Political Thought from a Regime Change Perspective," *Studies in American Political Development* 4 (1990): 171–72.

10. Ibid., 224–27.

11. Since its early days, realignment theory has been subject to criticisms. Campbell and Trilling slammed the work of Burnham for being an "immature theory, which articulates the often vague links among the social and economic environment, mass and elite political behavior, and governmental policy." See Richard J. Trilling and Bruce A. Campbell, "Toward a Theory of Realignment: An Introduction," in *Realignment in American Politics*, ed. Campbell and Trilling, 4.

12. Everett Carl Ladd's critique is twofold. First, the notion of realignment is so vague that it is fundamentally useless. Second, realignment theory failed to predict the 1968 realignment. Joel Silbey agrees with Ladd, and suggests a different periodization scheme to study American political history. Finally, David Mayhew shares the views of both Silbey and Ladd, and contends that realignment theory does not explain the last two centuries of American electoral politics, party politics, and political history. He argues that the "genre has evolved from a source of vibrant ideas into an impediment to understanding." After presenting fifteen classical claims of realignment theory and criticizing them from an empirical standpoint, he argues that the claims of realignment theory regarding the notions such as the dichotomy realignment/nonrealigning

elections, periodicity, and dynamics are untenable. See Everett Carl Ladd, "Like Waiting for Godot," in *End of Realignment?* ed. Shafer, 24–36; Joel H. Silbey, "Beyond Realignment and Realignment Theory: American Political Eras, 1789–1989," in *End of Realignment?* ed. Shafer, 3; and David Mayhew, *Electoral Realignments: A Critique of an American Genre* (New Haven, Conn.: Yale University Press, 2002), 5, 165.

13. For Orren and Skowroneck, politics is a permanent flow of events that can neither be fully captured nor explained by an inflexible model. One needs a "paradigm that engages several periodization schemes at once." From their perspective, the "overall view of politics is no longer that of an integrated order punctuated periodically by a radical change [as realignment does]. Rather, it is one of multiple and disjointed ordering that overlay one another, with the interplay among them breaking down the period-bound distinction between order and change." Karen Orren and Stephen Skowronek, "Institutions and Intercurrence: Theory Building in the Fullness of Time," in *Political Order: Nomos XXXVIII*, ed. Ian Shapiro and Russell Hardin (New York: New York University Press, 1996), 117.

14. Orren and Skowronek, *Search for American Political Development*, 108, 112.

15. On this perspective, see James E. Campbell, "Party Systems and Realignments in the United States, 1868–2004," *Social Science History* 30, no. 3 (Fall 2006): 359–86. I chose Burnham's notion of nonpartisan realignment because it has helped me to explain the particular historical-political features that facilitate the influence of neoconservative ideas on certain policy issues.

16. Charles S. Bullock et al., "Regional Variations in the Realignment of American Politics, 1944–2004," *Social Science Quarterly* 87, no. 3 (September 2006): 495.

17. See Daniel Bell, *The Cultural Contradictions of Capitalism* (New York: Basic Books, 1978); Jürgen Habermas, *Legitimation Crisis* (Boston: Beacon Press, 1973); Samuel P. Huntington, Michael J. Crozier, and Joji Watanuki, *The Crisis of Democracy* (New York: New York University Press, 1975); Irving Kristol, "New Left, New Right," *The Public Interest*, Summer 1966; Joyce Kolko, *America and the Crisis of World Capitalism* (Boston: Beacon Press, 1974); James O'Connor, *The Fiscal Crisis of the State* (New York: St. Martin's Press, 1973).

18. As Thomas Ferguson and Jie Chen have asserted, "There is simply no reason in realignment theory why major departures in public policy should only occur during realignment. For instance, there were critical elections in 1856 and 1932, but not necessarily complete policy realignment." Thomas Ferguson and Jie Chen, "Investor Blocs and Party Realignment in American History," unpublished paper, 6. Policy realignments do not always occur during the same span of time than critical elections. Bruce Ackerman has spoken of 1937 as an "American constitutional moment," when the New Deal legitimated the activist state and fundamentally altered American constitutional politics.

19. On the notion of nonpartisan realignment, see Burnham, "Critical Realignment"; and Walter Dean Burnham, "The Reagan Heritage," in *The Election of 1988: Reports and Interpretations*, ed. Gerald M. Pomper (Chatham, N.J.: Chatham House, 1989). John Aldrich and Richard Niemi agree with different emphases and perspectives on the notion of a post–New Deal realignment. See John Aldrich and Richard Niemi, "The Six American Party Systems: Electoral Change, 1952–1992," in *Broken Contract? Changing Relationships between Americans and Their Government*, ed. Stephen C. Craig (Boulder, Colo.: Westview Press, 1996). See also John Aldrich, *Why*

*Parties? The Origins and Transformation of Party Politics in America* (Chicago: University of Chicago Press, 1995).

20. Burnham's realignment theory is a macrosystemic model of American political development, whereas Orren-Skowronek's framework is a middle-range theory of historical institutionalism. To consider historical institutionalism a middle-range theory is not an arbitrary decision. Most scholars working on historical institutionalism will accept this classification. On this topic, see Kathleen Thelen, "Historical Institutionalism in Comparative Perspective," *Annual Review of Political Science* 2 (1999): 373.

21. John Lewis Gaddis, *Surprise, Security, and the American Experience* (Cambridge, Mass.: Harvard University Press, 2004), 107.

22. Edward Carmines and Michael Wagner have also tried to fuse realignment theory with other frameworks. These researchers combine realignment theory with their conception of issue evolution. In their view, realignment theory "can help us understand the circumstances under which issues become salient enough to foster gradual political change." Cf. Edward G. Carmines and Michael W. Wagner, "Political Issues and Party Alignments: Assessing the Issue Evolution Perspective," *Annual Review of Political Science* 9 (2006): 78. Evidently, my study is very different and less ambitious than the work of Carmines and Wagner. Here, I would just like to highlight that there are other scholars whose studies move in the same direction as mine.

23. Burnham, "Critical Realignment," 115–16.

24. Burnham has argued that the midterm election of 1994 reflects the beginning of the seventh realignment era. Cf. Walter Dean Burnham, "Realignment Lives: The 1994 Earthquake and Its Implications," in *The Clinton Presidency: First Appraisals*, ed. Colin Campbell and Bert A. Rockman (Chatham, N.J.: Chatham House, 1996). See also Walter Dean Burnham, "Punctuated Change and the System of 1996," paper prepared for at the Annual Meeting of the Southern Historical Association, Little Rock, October 30–November 2, 1996.

25. Here, Burnham detected the main features of political phenomena that were relevant until the current time. The characteristics of the nonpartisan realignment have continued, developed, or intensified, independent of the existence of another traditional partisan realignment in the middle 1990s. For example, the current role of the Internet and the social-networking Web site Facebook in political campaigns has, in a way, its origins in the relevance of the mass media, especially television, since the late 1960s.

26. Morris P. Fiorina, *Cultural Wars: The Myth of a Polarized America* (New York: Pearson Longman, 2005), 150.

27. Elizabeth Sanders, "In Defense of Realignment and Regimes: Why We Need Periodization," *Polity* 37, no. 4 (October 2005): 539.

28. In recent times, the literature on historical institutionalism has grown substantially. However, I found the following studies very useful for my analysis: Theda Skocpol, "Bringing the State Back In: Strategies for Analysis in Current Research," in *Bringing the State Back In*, ed. Peter Evans, Dietrich Rueschmeyer, and Theda Skocpol (New York: Cambridge University Press, 1985); Theda Skocpol, *Protecting Mothers and Soldiers: The Political Origins of Social Policy in the United States* (Cambridge, Mass.: Harvard University Press, 1992); Sven Steinmo, Kathleen Thelen, and Frank Longstreth, eds., *Structuring Politics: Historical Institutionalism in Comparative Perspective* (Cambridge: Cambridge University Press, 1992); Peter Hall and Rosemary C. R. Taylor, "Political Science and the Three New Institutionalisms," *Political Studies*

44, no. 5 (1996): 936–57; Ellen M. Immergunt, "The Theoretical Core of New Institutionalism," *Politics and Society* 26, no. 1 (1998): 5–34; Karren Orren and Stephen Skowronek, "Beyond the Iconography of Order: Note for a New Institutionalism," in *The Dynamics of American Politics: Approaches and Interpretations*, ed. Lawrence C. Dodd and Calvin Jillson (Boulder, Colo.: Westview Press, 1994), 311–30; and Sven Steinmo, "The Evolution of Policy Ideas: Tax Policy in the 20th Century," *British Journal of Politics and International Relations* 5, no. 2 (May 2003): 206–36.

29. Jeffrey K. Tulis, *The Rhetorical Presidency* (Princeton, N.J.: Princeton University Press, 1987), 17, 18.

30. The literature on ideas, institutions, and interests is vast. These are only some of the works that I have found most useful: Peter A. Hall, ed., *The Political Power of Economic Ideas: Keynesianism across Nations* (Princeton, N.J.: Princeton University Press, 1989); Evans, Rueschemeyer, and Skocpol, *Bringing the State Back In*; Judith Goldstein and Robert O. Keohane, eds., *Ideas and Foreign Policy: Beliefs, Institutions and Political Changes* (Ithaca, N.Y.: Cornell University Press, 1993); Mark Blyth, *Great Transformations: Economic Ideas and Institutional Change in the Twentieth Century* (New York: Cambridge University Press, 2002); and Steinmo, "Evolution of Policy Ideas."

31. See Joseph G. Peschek, *Policy-Planning Organizations: Elite Agendas and America's Rightward Turn* (Philadelphia: Temple University Press, 1987), 52; James T. Campen and Arthur MacEwen, "Crisis, Contradictions, and Conservative Controversies in Contemporary U.S. Capitalism," *Review of Radical Political Economy* 14 (Fall 1982): 5; and Thomas Ferguson and Joel Rogers, *Right Turn: The Decline of the Democrats and the Future of American Politics* (New York: Hill and Wang, 1986), 79.

32. Thomas Byrne Edsall, *The New Politics of Inequality* (New York: W. W. Norton, 1984), chap. 3, esp. 113–14; David Vogel, "The Power of Business in America: A Re-appraisal," *British Journal of Political Science* 13, no. 1 (January 1983): 24–25.

33. See Edsall, *New Politics*; and Vogel, "Power of Business." See also Jerome Himmelstein, *To the Right: The Transformation of American Conservatism* (Berkeley: University of California Press, 1990), 129–64.

34. In this study, I give special attention to the role of neoconservative organizations in the origin, development, and consolidation of this movement. Neoconservative ideas were filtered and diffused through the different organizations in which they operated. These organizations enhanced the formation of a prominent political and intellectual movement, facilitating the influence of neoconservatism on public policies. Neoconservative organizations had four main functions. They (1) promoted the dissemination of neoconservative ideas, (2) coordinated neoconservatism's political network, (3) operated as centers of political organization and advice for political and economic elites, and (4) were alcoves for political and intellectual deliberation. In short, they formed the structure that permitted interaction between neoconservatives and American political and economic elites, between neoconservatives and U.S. society, and among neoconservatives themselves.

35. Irving Kristol, "On Corporate Philanthropy," *Wall Street Journal*, March 21, 1978. A similar viewpoint is expressed by Michael Novak, *The American Vision: An Essay on the Future of Democratic Capitalism* (Washington, D.C.: American Enterprise Institute, 1978), 48; and Ernest W. Lefever et al., *Scholars, Dollars, and Public Policy: New Frontiers in Corporate Giving* (Washington, D.C.: Ethics and Public Policy Center, 1983).

36. Thomas Langston offers a similar idea; see Thomas S. Langston, *Ideologues and Presidents: From the New Deal to the Reagan Revolution* (Baltimore: Johns Hopkins University Press, 1992), 19–24. Langston recognizes that the decline of political parties has enabled the rise of ideas and ideologues as powerful political instruments of change. His study differs from mine on two grounds. First, he is not working within the framework of political realignment. Moreover, he does not recognize the existence of realignment in the 1960s, but rather a dealignment. For him, the absence of a critical partisan realignment is the "underlying cause" of the rise of people of ideas, because realignments "set the boundaries for ideological maneuvering and within those boundaries, allow the president a free hand to redirect the national agenda" (p. 18). Second, he is working basically at the presidential level, connecting people of ideas with presidents, particularly Roosevelt, Johnson, and Reagan. I am, on the contrary, working simultaneously at three levels: ideas, institutions, and interests. David Ricci also considers that the changes experienced by the United States since the late 1960s facilitated the growth of think tanks as organizations dedicated primarily to the dissemination of ideas; see David Ricci, *The Transformation of American Politics: The New Washington and the Rise of Think Tanks* (New Haven, Conn.: Yale University Press, 1993).

37. Sydney Blumenthal, *The Rise of a Counter-Establishment* (New York: Times Books, 1986), 313.

38. It is interesting to observe that four neoconservatives of the first generation were presidents of the American Political Science Association: Seymour Martin Lipset (who was also president of the American Sociological Association), Aaron B. Wildavsky, Samuel P. Huntington, and James Q. Wilson.

39. Russell Jacoby, *The Last Intellectuals: American Culture in the Age of the Academe* (New York: Basic Books, 1987).

40. Stephen Jay Gould, *The Panda's Thumb: More Reflections on Natural History* (New York: W. W. Norton, 1980), 28. For Gould, the central principle of all history is contingency. In his view, a "historical explanation does not rest on direct deductions from laws of nature, but an unpredictable sequence of antecedent states, where any major change in any step of the sequence would have altered the final result. The final result is dependent, or contingent, upon everything that came before—the unerasable and determining signature of history." His perspective on contingency is related to his conception of time in history. In his opinion, there are two main notions that are strictly related, which he metaphorically calls time's arrow and time's cycle. Time's arrow is history conceived as "irreversible sequence of unrepeatable events. Each moment occupies its own distinct position in a temporal series, and all moments, considered in proper sequence, tell a story of linked events moving in a direction. At the other end—time's cycle—events have no meaning as distinct episodes with causal impacts upon a contingent history. Fundamental states are immanent in time, always present and never changing. Apparent motions are parts of repeating cycles, and differences of the past will be realities of the future. Time has no direction." For Gould, time's arrow and time's cycle "do not blend, but dwell together in tension of fruitful interaction." Stephen Jay Gould, *Time's Arrow and Time's Cycle: Myth and Metaphor in the Discovery of Geological Time* (Cambridge, Mass.: Harvard University Press, 1988), 10, 11, 200.

41. John Lewis Gaddis, *The Landscape of History: How Historians Map the Past* (New York: Oxford University Press, 2002), 30, 31.

42. Huge Heclo, "Ideas, Interests, and Institutions," in *The Dynamics of American Politics: Approaches & Interpretations*, ed. Lawrence C. Dodd and Calvin Jillson (Boulder, Colo.: Westview Press, 1994), 382–83.

43. Judith Goldstein and Robert O. Keohane, "Ideas and Foreign Policy: An Analytical Framework," in *Ideas and Foreign Policy*, ed. Goldstein and Keohane, 27.

44. Isaiah Berlin, *Concepts and Categories* (New York: Viking Press, 1979), 135.

45. Ronald J. Grele, *Envelopes of Sound*, 2nd ed. (Chicago: Precedent Publishing, 1985), viii.

## Chapter 2. Who Is a Neoconservative?

1. Peter Steinfels, *The Neoconservatives: The Men Who Are Changing American Politics* (New York: Simon & Schuster, 1979), 49.

2. For a general view of American conservatism, see Seymour Martin Lipset, "U.S. Political Conservatism: Meaning and Origins," in *American Annual 1982 Yearbook of Encyclopedia Americana* (Danbury, Conn.: Grolier, 1982); and Jonathan M. Schoenwald, *A Time for Choosing: The Rise of Modern American Conservatism* (New York: Oxford University Press, 2001). Conservative and radical specialists coincide on the liberal matrix of American conservatism. For a conservative viewpoint, see Peter Viereck, "The Philosophical New Conservatism," in *The Radical Right, Expanded and Updated*, ed. Daniel Bell (Garden City, N.Y.: Doubleday, 1963), 167. Also see Daniel Bell, *Unadjusted Man: A New Hero from Americans* (Boston: Beacon Press, 1956), 246, 182, 183. For a left-wing perspective, see Alan Wolfe, "Sociology, Liberalism and the Radical Right," *New Left Review*, July–August 1981, 6.

3. Cf. Rob Kroes, ed., *Neo-Conservatism: Its Emergence in the USA and Europe* (Amsterdam: VU Uitgeverij / Free Press, 1984), especially the essay by Rhodri Jeffreys-Jones. In the United States, a similar kind of terminological confusion is evident in John B. Judis; cf. John B. Judis, "Conservatism and the Price of Success," in *The Reagan Legacy: Promise and Performance*, ed. Sidney Blumenthal and Thomas Byrne Edsall (New York: Pantheon, 1988), 135–71.

4. Mark Gerson, *Neoconservative Vision: From the Cold War to the Culture Wars* (Lanham, Md.: Madison Books, 1997), 4.

5. Seymour Martin Lipset, "Replies to His Critics," *Society*, January–February 1989, 8–9.

6. A similar view is presented by Steven Biel when he asserts that "professional communities maintain their identity and coherence through a variety of institutions: permanent associations, periodic conferences, specialized publications, a common discourse, jargon. Cf. Steven Biel, *Independent Intellectuals in the United States, 1910–1945* (New York: New York University Press, 1992), 85.

7. Daniel Bell, *The Cultural Contradictions of Capitalism* (New York: Basic Books, 1978), xi.

8. Letter from Daniel Bell to the author, December 16, 1993.

9. Letter from Daniel Bell to Sidney Hook, October 5, 1981, in Sidney Hook Papers, Hoover Institution on War, Revolution, and Peace, Stanford, Calif., box 6, folder 6.39.

10. Letter from Daniel Bell to Sidney Hook, June 10, 1984, ibid.

11. Norman Podhoretz, "The Neo-Conservative Anguish over Reagan's Foreign

Policy," *New York Times Magazine*, May 2, 1982, 30–33, 96–98; the quotation is on 30.

12. Seymour Martin Lipset, "Neoconservatism: Intellectuals on the Right?" unpublished paper, 1993, 2.

13. Charles Kadushin, "Networks and Circles in the Production of Culture," *American Behavioral Scientist* 19, no. 2 (July–August 1978): 770, 771.

14. The three articles are Seymour Martin Lipset, "Neoconservatism: Myth or Reality," *Society* 25, no. 5 (July–August 1988): 29–37; Podhoretz, "Neo-Conservative Anguish"; and Daniel Bell, "The Cultural Wars: American Intellectual Life, 1965–1992," *Wilson Quarterly* 16, no. 3 (Summer 1992): 74. Two criteria were used to select these articles. First, the authors were commonly identified as neoconservative; and second, in these articles, they broadly alluded to the advocates of this tendency.

15. Alexander Bloom, *Prodigal Sons: The New York Intellectuals and Their World* (New York: Oxford University Press, 1986), 369.

16. Robert Nisbet, "The Conservative Renaissance in Perspective," *The Public Interest*, Fall 1985, 128–41.

17. Steinfels, *Neoconservatives*; Isidore Silver, "Neoconservatism vs. Conservatism?" *The Commonwealth* 107, no. 14 (July 31, 1981).

18. Adam Wolfson, "Conservatives and Neoconservatives," *The Public Interest*, Winter 2004, 45.

19. Some readers would rightly ponder whether Bell, Moynihan, and Lipset classified themselves as neoconservatives. I have three answers to this question. First, other neoconservatives cited these individuals as part of their intellectual community. If their peers recognized them as members of this group, it is difficult for an external observer to reject their opinions. Second, as I will show in detail later in this book, they were members of at least one of the four neoconservative organizations of the first generation considered in this study: the Coalition for a Democratic Majority (CDM), the American Enterprise Institute (AEI), the Committee on the Present Danger (CPD), and the Committee for the Free World (CFW). Thus, although Bell did not participate actively, he was a member of the CDM, and he could be considered during the early years of the CDM part of this expression. Later on, Bell distanced himself from some of the main leaders of this movement. Moynihan was a founding member of the CDM and maintained constant and enthusiastic participation within the organization. Lipset was involved in the CDM, AEI, CPD, and CFW. Third, the main differences between these three and other neoconservatives revolved around domestic issues rather than foreign affairs. Although they disagreed with people like Podhoretz and Decter on topics such as Israel, in general they shared the neoconservatives' hardline view on foreign policy.

20. Conversation with Irving Kristol, May 27, 1993.

21. Conversation with Jeane J. Kirkpatrick, April 4, 1993.

22. Conversation with Charles Horner, August 4, 1993.

23. Conversation with Richard Schifter, August 13, 1993; conversation with Douglas J. Feith, July 22, 1993; conversation with Eugene Rostow, May 8, 1998.

24. For a good analysis of neoconservatism before the 1960s, see Hamilton Lawson Bowling III, "The New Party of Memory: Intellectual Origins of Neoconservatism, 1945–1960," PhD dissertation, Columbia University, 1990.

25. Alan M. Wald, *The New York Intellectual: The Rise and Decline of the Anti-*

*Stalinist Left from the 1930s to the 1980s* (Chapel Hill: University of North Carolina Press, 1987), 6.

26. Joseph Dorman, *Arguing the World: The New York Intellectuals in Their Own Words* (New York: Free Press, 2000), 46.

27. Ibid., 44.

28. Seymour Martin Lipset, "'It's the Final Conflict' . . . : The Stalinists and Anti-Stalinists—Comments Inspired by the Film *Arguing the World*," unpublished paper, n.d., 2, 3.

29. Irving Kristol, "Memoirs of a Trotskyist," in *Reflections of a Neoconservative*, by Irving Kristol (New York: Basic Books, 1983), 9.

30. Letter from Ronald Reagan to Sidney Hook, October 28, 1982, in Sidney Hook Papers, Hoover Institution on War, Revolution, and Peace, Stanford, Calif., box 24, folder 24.38.

31. Letter from Daniel Bell to Sidney Hook, December 23, 1984, ibid., box 6, folder 6.39.

32. Letter from Irving Kristol to Sidney Hook, July 25, 1961, ibid., box 18, folder 18.14. Also see "Proceedings of the Dinner in Honor of Norman Podhoretz on His Twenty-Fifth Anniversary as Editor of *Commentary*, New York: the Rainbow Grill, January 29, 1985," 11.

33. Letter from Midge Decter to Sidney Hook, n.d. (apparently written in 1980), in Sidney Hook Papers, Hoover Institution on War, Revolution, and Peace, Stanford, Calif., box 10, folder 21.39.

34. Telegram from Daniel Patrick Moynihan to Sidney Hook, October 26, 1982, ibid.

35. Gary Dorrien, *The Neoconservative Mind: Politics, Culture, and the War of Ideology* (Philadelphia: Temple University Press, 1993), 64.

36. For an example of neoconservatism's rejection of communism and fascism, see the opinions expressed by Nathan Glazer and quoted by Bowling, "New Party of Memory," 68.

37. Cf. Lipset, "'It's the Final Conflict,'" 10.

38. Conversation with Seymour Martin Lipset, March 18, 1993.

39. Conversation with Seymour Martin Lipset, March 2000.

40. Cf. Daniel Bell, *Marxian Socialism in the United States* (Princeton, N.J.: Princeton University Press, 1967).

41. Cf. American Committee for Cultural Freedom, *The American Committee for Cultural Freedom: Manifesto* (New York: American Committee for Cultural Freedom, n.d.), 8.

42. On the Committee for Cultural Freedom, see Peter Coleman, *The Liberal Conspiracy: The Congress for Cultural Freedom and the Struggle for the Mind of the Postwar Europe* (New York: Free Press, 1989), 247.

43. Quoted by Bloom, *Prodigal Sons*, 212.

44. Daniel Bell, ed., *The New American Right* (New York: Criterion Books, 1955).

45. Bell, *Radical Right.*

46. Cf. Daniel Bell, "Interpretations of American Politics," in *New American Right*, ed. Bell, 14; and see Seymour Martin Lipset, "The Sources of the Radical Right," ibid., 167.

47. Lipset, "Sources," 168.

48. Richard Hofstadter, "The Pseudo-Conservative Revolt," in *New American Right*, ed. Bell, 43–44. Similar concepts are used by Lipset, "Sources," 168.

49. Seymour Martin Lipset and Earl Raab, *The Politics of Unreason: Right-Wing Extremism in America, 1790–1977* (Chicago: University of Chicago Press, 1978), 29, 23.

50. Later, Lipset and Raab expanded the notion of status politics by using the concept of extremism. Their conceptual model is characterized by five basic elements. First, all extremist groups from the right and from the left share similar traits; they are antipluralist, which is to say, they are monists. Second, they are backlash organizations, and consequently antimodernist. Third, they are simplistic expressions, movements that offer simple remedies for multifactor phenomena. Fourth, they are moralist, with special emphasis in Christian morality. Fifth and finally, conspiracy theory is a central element of their ideology and political action. Cf. ibid. It is important to highlight that the notion of extremism was a clear concept for the contributors to *The Radical Right*. However, Lipset and Raab expanded and systematized this model. For a good critique of status politics theory, see Alan Wolfe, "Liberalism and the Radical Right," *New Left Review*, July–August 1981; and Jerome L. Himmelstein, *To the Right: The Transformation of American Conservatism* (Berkeley: University of California Press, 1990).

51. Conversation with Richard Schifter, August 13, 1993.

52. Melvyn P. Leffler, "9/11 and the Past and Future of American Foreign Policy," *International Affairs* 79, no. 5 (2003): 1052. For more on the NSC-68 report, see chapter 5 in this book.

53. See Peter A. Hall, ed., *The Political Power of Economic Ideas: Keynesianism across Nations* (Princeton, N.J.: Princeton University Press, 1989); Peter Evans, Dietrich Rueschemeyer, and Theda Skocpol, eds., *Bringing the State Back In* (New York: Cambridge University Press, 1985); Judith Goldstein and Robert O. Keohane, eds., *Ideas and Foreign Policy: Beliefs, Institutions and Political Changes* (Ithaca, N.Y.: Cornell University Press, 1993); Mark Blyth, *Great Transformations: Economic Ideas and Institutional Change in the Twentieth Century* (New York: Cambridge University Press, 2002); and Sven Steinmo, "The Evolution of Policy Ideas: Tax Policy in the 20th Century," *British Journal of Politics and International Relations* 5, no. 2 (May 2003): 206–36.

54. Daniel Bell, "Columbia and the New Left," in *Confrontation: The Students Rebellion and the University*, ed. Daniel Bell and Irving Kristol (New York: Basic Books, 1969), 106, 107.

55. Seymour Martin Lipset, "The Activist: A Profile," in *Confrontation*, ed. Bell and Kristol, 48.

56. Quoted by Wald, *New York Intellectual*, 356.

57. Daniel Bell and Irving Kristol, "Introduction," in *Confrontation*, ed. Bell and Kristol, xi.

58. Nathan Glazer, *Remembering the Answers: Essays on the American Student Revolt* (New York: Basic Books, 1970), 13.

59. Michael Novak, in the symposium article "The American 80's: Disaster or Triumph?" *Commentary*, September 1990, 35. It is interesting to observe that the emphasis on abortion and the statement in favor of the prolife movement come mainly from the Catholic sector of neoconservatism. Jews, the dominant group within neoconservatism, are not very concerned with this topic.

60. Hilton Kramer, ibid., 52.

61. Gillian Peele, *Revival & Reaction: The Right in Contemporary America* (New York: Oxford University Press, 1984), 5.

62. On the debate of the end of ideology, see Chaim I. Waxman, ed., *The End of Ideology Debate* (New York: Clarion Books, 1969).

63. Cf. Dean E. McHenry Jr., "Summary and Analysis of a Survey of Graduate Core Course in Comparative Politics," *Political Science Teacher* 1, no. 2 (Spring 1988): 5–6.

64. The exceptions were Daniel Bell and Nathan Glazer, who voted for McGovern.

65. Letter from Daniel Bell to Sidney Hook, June 10, 1984, in Sidney Hook Papers, Hoover Institution on War, Revolution, and Peace, Stanford, Calif., box 6, folder 6.39.

66. My account of these events comes fundamentally from two sources: Dorrien, *Neoconservative Mind*, 2–6; and Maurice Isserman, *"If I Had a Hammer": The Death of the Old Left and the Birth of the New Left* (Urbana: University of Illinois Press, 1993), esp. chap. 2.

67. Al Glotzer, "Max Shachtman," *New American*, November 15, 1972, 4; in the same issue, also see the article by Tom Kahn.

68. Cf. John Ehrman, *The Rise of Neoconservatism: Intellectuals and Foreign Affairs, 1945–1994* (New Haven, Conn.: Yale University Press, 1995).

69. Lipset, "Neoconservatism: Myth or Reality," 34.

70. On the Social Democrats and their connection with the neoconservative movement, see Michael Massing, "Trotsky's Orphans: From Bolshevism to Reaganism," *New Republic*, June 22, 1987, 18–22.

71. James Allen Smith, *The Idea Brokers* (New York: Free Press, 1991), 182.

72. Conversation with Jeane J. Kirkpatrick, April 13, 1993.

73. Francis Fukuyama, *America at the Crossroads: Democracy, Power, and the Neoconservative Legacy* (New Haven, Conn.: Yale University Press, 2006), 61.

74. Conversation with Gary Schmitt, January 29, 2008.

75. Conversation with Douglas Feith, January 30, 2008.

76. Conversation with William Kristol, November 2004.

77. Murray Friedman, *The Neoconservative Revolution: Jewish Intellectuals and the Shaping of Public Policy* (New York: Cambridge University Press, 2005), 1.

78. Stefan Halper and Jonathan Clarke, *American Alone: The Neo-Conservatives and the Global Order* (New York: Cambridge University Press, 2004), 99.

79. Gary Dorrien, "Consolidate the Empire: The Neoconservatives and the Politics of American Dominion," *Political Theology* 6, no. 4 (2005): 414.

80. Conversation with Joshua Muravchik, January 31, 2008.

## Chapter 3. Neoconservative Organizations as a Vehicle for an Ideological Crusade

1. Douglass C. North, *Institutions, Institutional Change and Economic Performance* (New York: Cambridge University Press, 1990), 4. North makes an important distinction between institutions and organizations. For him, there is a great similarity between both, but organizations are fundamentally influenced by an institutional framework. I adopt North's perspective on organizations because it more or less de-

scribes the type of entities that I am studying. For an overview of the institutional perspective, see James G. March and Johan P. Olsen, "The New Institutionalism: Organizational Factors in Political Life," *American Political Science Review* 78, no. 3 (September 1984); and James G. March and Johan P. Olsen, *Rediscovering Institutions: The Organizational Basis of Politics* (New York: Free Press, 1989).

2. It is important to emphasize that I obtained this information as a result of my conversations with different neoconservative figures. However, Peter Rosenblatt, who was president of the CDM, categorically rejects the suggestion that the CDM was a neoconservative organization.

3. Irving Kristol expressed a slightly different viewpoint, asserting that neoconservatives are very well represented at AEI. Conversation with Irving Kristol, May 27, 1993.

4. North, *Institutions*, 5. Besides political and educational organizations, North includes economic and social bodies. Economic bodies include firms, trade unions, family farms, and cooperatives. Social bodies include churches, clubs, and athletic associations.

5. Irving Kristol, *Neoconservatism: The Autobiography of an Idea* (New York: Free Press, 1995), 233.

6. Benjamin Ginsberg and Martin Shefter, "A Critical Realignment? The New Politics, the Reconstituted Right, and the 1984 Election," in *The Election of 1984,* ed. Michael Nelson (Washington, D.C.: Congressional Quarterly, 1985), 1–25.

7. Quoted in "A Report on the Institute on Religion and Democracy," *International IDOC Bulletin,* nos. 8–9 (1982): 17. Also see Peter R. Rosenblatt, "Statement of Ambassador Peter R. Rosenblatt, President of the Coalition for a Democratic Majority, before the 1984 Democratic Platform Committee," New York City, April 9, 1984," in Peter Rosenblatt Personal Papers, LBJ Library and Museum, Austin, container 51, 1. A similar assertion is made by Jay Winik, *On the Brink* (New York: Simon & Schuster, 1996), 81.

8. Conversation with Peter Rosenblatt, August 19, 1993.

9. Jeane J. Kirkpatrick, "Why We Don't Become Republicans," *Commonsense,* 1979, 30. This article is an explanation of the basic political principles of the CDM in a Republican journal.

10. A. James Reichley, "The Rise of National Parties," in *New Directions on American Politics,* ed. John E. Chubb and Paul Peterson (Washington, D.C.: Brookings Institution Press, 1985), 184, 185.

11. Interview with Peter Rosenblatt, August 19, 1993.

12. Quoted by Sidney Blumenthal, *The Rise of the Counter-Establishment: From Conservative Ideology to Political Power* (New York: Times Books, 1986), 128. The person appointed to this post was Peter Rosenblatt.

13. Kirkpatrick, "Why We Don't Become Republicans," 29.

14. Cf. The 1984 CDM Advisory Task Force on Foreign and National Defense, *Democratic Solidarity: Proposal for the 1984 Democratic Party Platform on Foreign Policy and National Defense* (Washington, D.C.: Coalition for a Democratic Majority, 1984).

15. Interview with Peter Rosenblatt, August 19, 1993.

16. Cf. Letter from Peter R. Rosenblatt to Ben Wattenberg, November 15, 1978, in Peter Rosenblatt Personal Papers, LBJ Library and Museum, Austin, container 22.

17. Alan Wolfe and Jerry Sanders, "Resurgent Cold War Ideology: The Case of the Committee on the Present Danger," in *Capitalism and U.S.-Latin American Relations,* ed. Richard Fagen (Stanford, Calif.: Stanford University Press, 1979), 41–75.

18. Letter from Penn Kemble to Charles McGuire, February 27, 1993, in Peter Rosenblatt Personal Papers, LBJ Library and Museum, Austin, container 3.

19. On the DLC, see Nicol C. Rae, *Southern Democrats* (New York: Oxford University Press, 1994), esp. chap. 5. Also see James A. Barnes. "Regrouping," *National Journal,* June 1993.

20. Conversation with Peter Rosenblatt, August 19, 1993.

21. Ibid.

22. John Ehrman, *The Rise of Neoconservatism: Intellectuals and Foreign Affairs, 1945–1994* (New Haven, Conn.: Yale University Press, 1995), 61.

23. Interview with Peter Rosenblatt, August 13, 1998.

24. It is important to note that Kirkpatrick and Abrams moved to the Republican Party at the end of Reagan's first term.

25. Telephone interview with Ben Wattenberg, December 2004.

26. James Allen Smith, *The Idea Brokers* (New York: Free Press, 1991), xiv.

27. *AEI Memorandum,* no, 2, May 22, 1972, 4.

28. *AEI Memorandum,* no. 4, December 15, 1972, 3.

29. *American Enterprise Institute for Public Policy Research, 1973–1974* (Washington, D.C.: American Enterprise Institute, 1974), 1. This was the equivalent of an annual report for the organization.

30. In the Lecture Series on the American Bicentennial, Irving Kristol presented "The American Revolution as a Successful Revolution," Seymour Martin Lipset presented "Opportunity and Welfare in the First New Nation," and Peter L. Berger presented "Religion in Revolutionary Society." The excerpts from Lipset's work were published in *AEI Memorandum,* no. 7, Fall 1973, 11.

31. *American Enterprise Institute for Public Policy Research, 1978* (Washington, D.C.: American Enterprise Institute, 1978), 28.

32. Ibid., 30–31.

33. Martha Derthick and Paul J. Quirk, *The Politics of Deregulation* (Washington, D.C.: Brookings Institution Press, 1985), 36–37.

34. Cf. *AEI Memorandum,* no. 19, Spring 1977, 4.

35. Letter from Richard V. Allen to Eugene V. Rostow, June 7, 1976, in Papers on the Committee on the Present Danger, Hoover Institution on War, Revolution, and Peace, Stanford, Calif., box 447.

36. *AEI Memorandum,* no. 9, Spring–Summer 1974, 11.

37. *AEI Memorandum,* no. 14, Fall 1975, 6.

38. *AEI Memorandum,* no. 9, Spring–Summer 1974, 1, 3, 7.

39. Peter H. Stone, "Conservative Brain Trust," *New York Times Magazine,* May 10, 1981, 18.

40. Conversation with Irving Kristol, May 27, 1993.

41. Ibid.

42. Conversation with Peter Skerry, July 20, 1993. For a similar viewpoint, see Robert Landers, "Think Tanks: The New Partisans?" *Editorial Research Report* 1, no 23 (June 20, 1986): 463.

43. Conversation with Irving Kristol, May 27, 1993.

44. William E. Simon, "A Tribute to Irving Kristol," in *The Neoconservative Imagi-*

*nation: Essays in Honor of Irving Kristol,* ed. Christopher DeMuth and William Kristol (Washington, D.C.: AEI Press, 1995), 86.

45. Irving Kristol, "On Corporate Philanthropy," *Wall Street Journal,* March 21, 1978. A similar viewpoint is expressed by Michael Novak, *The American Vision: An Essay on the Future of Democratic Capitalism* (Washington, D.C.: AEI Press, 1978), 48; and Ernest W. Lefever et al., *Scholars, Dollars, and Public Policy: New Frontiers in Corporate Giving* (Washington, D.C.: Ethics and Public Policy Center, 1983).

46. Irving Kristol, "Why I Left," *New Republic,* April 11, 1988, 25.

47. "Annual Dinner Honoring Allan H. Meltzer and Featuring an Address by President George W. Bush," http://www.aei.org/include/events_print.asp?eventID=88.

48. Ibid., 5.

49. *AEI Memorandum,* no. 41, Winter 1984.

50. For a view of the Team B chairman, cf. Richard Pipes, "Team B: The Reality behind the Myth," *Commentary,* October 1986.

51. David Callahan, *Dangerous Capabilities: Paul Nitze and the Cold War* (New York: HarperCollins, 1990), 378.

52. Jerry W. Sanders, *Peddlers of Crisis: The Committee on the Present Danger and the Politics of Containment* (Boston: South End Press, 1983), 200.

53. Anne Hessing Cahn, "Team B: The Trillion Dollar Experiment," *Bulletin of the Atomic Scientists* 49, no. 3 (April 1993): 27.

54. Conversation with Eugene Rostow, May 8, 1998.

55. The same idea is presented by Callahan, *Dangerous Capabilities,* 371, 374. A detailed description of the CDM's Task Force report and the controversy between Rostow and Kissinger are presented in chapter 5.

56. Callahan, *Dangerous Capabilities,* 374, 375.

57. Letter from Eugene Rostow to Donald Rumsfeld, April 5, 1976, in Papers on the Committee on the Present Danger, Hoover Institution on War, Revolution, and Peace, Stanford, Calif., box 019.

58. "Draft Strictly Confidential Signed by John B. Connally and James A. Elkins, July 7, 1976," ibid., box 447.

59. Callahan, *Dangerous Capabilities,* 375.

60. Committee on the Present Danger, "Original Houston Contributors," in Papers on the Committee on the Present Danger, Hoover Institution on War, Revolution, and Peace, Stanford, Calif., box 447.

61. Letter from Charls Walker to Donald H. Rumsfeld, January 31, 1977, ibid.

62. From Eugene V. Rostow, to the Board of Directors of the Committee on the Present Danger, "Report No. 1: Our Debut," December 7, 1976, ibid.

63. Cf. the drafts of September 21, 1976, ibid., box 275.

64. Simon Dalby, *Creating the Second Cold War: The Discourse of Politics* (New York: Guilford, 1990), 46, 47.

65. Letter from Eugene V. Rostow to the Board of Directors of the Committee on the Present Danger, December 7, 1976, in Papers on the Committee on the Present Danger, Hoover Institution on War, Revolution, and Peace, Stanford, Calif., box 447.

66. "Common Sense and the Common Danger: Policy Statement of the Committee on the Present Danger," ibid., 3–5.

67. Max Kampelman, "Introduction," in *Alerting America: The Papers of the Committee on the Present Danger,* ed. Charles Tyroler II (Washington, D.C.: Pergamon-Brassey's, 1984), xv, xvi.

68. Cf. Pipes, "Team B," 39–40.

69. Kampelman, "Introduction," xvi, xvii.

70. Paul H. Nitze, *From Hiroshima to Glasnost: At the Center of Decision—A Memoir* (New York: Grove Weidenfeld, 1989), 354.

71. Ibid., xvii.

72. Dan Caldwell, *The Dynamics of Domestic Politics and Arms Control* (Columbia: University of South Carolina Press, 1991), 103.

73. Memorandum written by Eugene V. Rostov for the files, n.d., in Papers on the Committee on the Present Danger, Hoover Institution on War, Revolution, and Peace, Stanford, Calif., box 288.

74. Confidential letter from Eugene V. Rostow to the Executive Committee of CPD, August 10, 1977, ibid., box 266.

75. Letter from Eugene V. Rostow to the Board of Directors, August 23, 1977, in Papers of the Committee on the Present Danger, Stanford, Calif., Hoover Institution, box 441.

76. Letter from Eugene V. Rostow to the Board of Directors, August 23, 1977, ibid., box 441.

77. Eugene Rostow, Memoranda for the File, n.d., ibid., box 288.

78. Walter J. Stone, Ronald B. Rapoport, and Alan I. Abramowitz, "The Reagan Revolution and Party Polarization in the 1980s," in *The Parties Respond: Changes in the American Party System*, ed. L. Sandy Maisel (Boulder, Colo.: Westview Press, 1990), 73–74.

79. Cf. David Vogel, "The Power of Business in America: A Re-appraisal," *British Journal of Political Science* 13, part 1 (January 1983).

80. John L. Boies, "Buying for Armageddon: Factors Influencing Post–World War II Weapons Purchases since the Cuban Missile Crisis," PhD dissertation, University of Michigan, 1991, 47–48.

81. Caldwell, *Dynamics of Domestic Politics,* 106.

82. Richard Pipes, "Why the Soviet Union Thinks It Could Fight and Win a Nuclear War," *Commentary* 64 (July 1977); Jeane J. Kirkpatrick, "Dictatorships and Double Standards," *Commentary* 68, no. 5 (November 1979).

83. Interview with Joshua Muravchik, July 28, 1993. It is commonly accepted that this memo was written by Penn Kemble and Muravchik, but the only author given was Muravchik. At the time that the memo became public, the CDM was basically collapsing and its leaders had decided to rebuild the organization, designating Senator Henry Jackson and Daniel Patrick Moynihan as cochairmen. In this new, reconstituted association, Muravchik would be the director. However, because of the CDM's serious financial problems, Senator Moynihan decided to temporarily add Muravchik to his staff. When the memo hit the press, Muravchik was working for Moynihan, and the senator from New York did not want to be connected to it. To save Moynihan from embarrassment, Penn Kemble called the press and revealed that the note had been written by him and Muravchik.

84. Quoted by Beth Ann Ingold, "The Committee on the Present Danger: A Study of Elite and Public Influence," PhD dissertation, University of Pittsburgh, 1989, 211.

85. Conversation with Joshua Muravchik, July 28, 1993.

86. Sanders, *Peddlers of Crisis,* 264.

87. Peter Coleman, *The Liberal Conspiracy: The Congress for Cultural Freedom and the Struggle for the Mind of the Postwar Europe* (New York: Free Press, 1989), 247.

88. Cf. "Founding Statement of the Committee for the Free World," in Committee for the Free World Collection, Hoover Institution on War, Revolution, and Peace, Stanford, Calif., box 37, 1981, 1, 2.

89. Cf. *Committee for the Free World* (brochure), ibid., box 25, 1.

90. Ibid.

91. Cf. "Founding Statement," 2.

92. Cf. "Interview with Midge Decter," *Review of the News*, January 20, 1982, 43.

93. Committee for the Free World, "Request for Funds, 1988," in Committee for the Free World Collection, Hoover Institution on War, Revolution, and Peace, Stanford, Calif., box 55, 3.

94. Decter especially had relationships with Richard M. Scaife and Richard Larry of the Carthage and Sarah Scaife foundations, with Joseph Coors of the Coors Foundation, with Randolph Richardson and Leslie Lenkowsky (Lenkowsky was often associated with the neoconservative movement) of the Smith Richardson Foundation, and with William Simon and Michael Joyce of the Olin Foundation.

95. Letter from Leslie Lenkowsky to Midge Decter, CFW Archives, Hoover Institution.

96. Inter-Departmental Memo from A. D. Gaffney to R. R. Richardson, July 22, 1986, in Committee for the Free World Collection, Hoover Institution on War, Revolution, and Peace, Stanford, Calif., box 60.

97. Letter from Jack Brauntuch to Midge Decter, September 14, 1984, ibid.

98. Letter from William Simon to Midge Decter, January 31, 1989, ibid., box 55.

99. Letter from Midge Decter to Michael Joyce, September 16, 1988, ibid.

100. Letter from Midge Decter to Richard Larry, January 19, 1987, ibid., box 58.

101. Letter from Richard Allen to Midge Decter, July 10, 1984, ibid., box 1.

102. Letter from Stanley Ebner to Donald Rumsfeld, November 21, 1983, ibid., box 7.

103. *The Committee for the Free World: Contentions*, August 1981, 1.

104. Committee for the Free World Collection, Hoover Institution on War, Revolution, and Peace, Stanford, Calif., boxes 37 and 58.

105. "Request for Funds for 1988," ibid., box 55.

106. The titles of the conferences were "Our Country and Our Culture," "The United States and the World," "Thinking about East/West," "The Transatlantic Crisis," and "Does the West Still Exist?"

107. Letter from Midge Decter to Richard Larry, October 12, 1988, Committee for the Free World Collection, Hoover Institution on War, Revolution, and Peace, Stanford, Calif., box 58. Cf. Ehrman, *Rise of Neoconservatism,* 141.

108. Decter, more than any other neoconservative thinker of the first generation, maintained friendly relationships with the members of the New Right. This placed her on the extreme right wing of the neoconservative movement, and illustrates the kinds of divisions within neoconservatism. She was the only neoconservative who participated on the board of trustees of the Heritage Foundation. She was invited (although she declined the offer) to be a permanent columnist for *Conservative Digest*, Richard Viguerie's journal, and she supported and advocated for Howard Phillips and the *Howard Phillips Issue and Strategy Bulletin.* For more details, see "Memo from Midge Decter to Ed Feulner, Burton Pines," in Committee for the Free World Collection, Hoover Institution on War, Revolution, and Peace, Stanford, Calif., box 2; also see

box 6 for her rejection of the offer to contribute in *Conservative Digest,* and box 3 for her relations with Phillips. It is also interesting to observe that, in 1985, the CDM established contact with groups of the New Right, in particular with the Heritage Foundation. In a memorandum sent to Penn Kemble and Ben Wattenberg on November 22, 1985, a leader of the CDM (whose name is not in the text) informed them of a meeting he held at Heritage with Burton Yale Pines and Gordon Jones. In this memo, the author asserted that Heritage was interested in maintaining some contact with the CDM as a way of getting some "access to Democrats who can subscribe to at least some of their positions." He disagreed with the view of many Democrats, who refused to talk to the Heritage Foundation, and he asserted that the "quality of much of their work is so high that they cannot simply be written off as a bunch of ideological kooks who represent a political extreme. Are we going to refuse," he added," to have anything to do with the people who one issue after another, agree with us?" He concludes his letter by saying that the CDM's contacts with Heritage were harmless and therefore should be maintained. He endorsed "occasional exchanges of views and, in appropriate cases, mutual assistance." Cf. "Memorandum for Penn Kemble and Ben Wattenberg," in Peter Rosenblatt Personal Papers, LBJ Library and Museum, Austin, container 58.

109. *American Enterprise Institute Annual Report, 1983–1984* (Washington, D.C.: American Enterprise Institute, 1984), 34.

110. *American Enterprise Institute Annual Report, 1982–1983*, 5.

111. Irving Kristol, "On Corporate Capitalism," in *The New American Commonwealth*, ed. Irving Kristol and Nathan Glazer (New York: Basic Books, 1973).

112. Quoted by Sydney Blumenthal, *The Rise of the Counter-Establishment: From Conservative Ideology to Political Power* (New York: Times Books, 1986), 42.

113. Leon Howell, "Funding the War of Ideas," *Christian Century*, July 19–26, 1995, 701. On the support by the Olin Foundation for neoconservatism until the early 1990s, see Jon Wiener, "Dollars for Neocon Scholars," *The Nation*, January 1, 1990, 12–14. On the Scaife Family Foundation and its economic support for the conservative movement in the late 1970s early 1980s, see Karen Rothmyer, "Citizen Scaife," *Columbia Journalism Review*, July–August 1981, 41–50. On the Scaife Family Foundation in a more contemporary period, see the series of articles by Ira Chinoy and Robert G. Kaiser, "Decade of Contributions to Conservatism," *Washington Post*, May 2, 1999; "How Scaife's Money Powered a Movement," ibid.; Robert G. Kaiser, "An Enigmatic Heir's Paradoxical World," *Washington Post*, May 3, 1993; and Robert G. Kaiser, "Two Plans for Newspapers Never Took Off," ibid.

114. Beth Schulman, "Foundations for a Movement: How the Right Wing Subsidizes Its Press," *Extra* 8, no. 2 (1995): 11.

115. Cf. "CDM Contributors $250.00 and Up," January 1977, LBJ Library and Museum, Austin, container 46.

116. Stanley Ebner, senior vice president for governmental relations of the Northrop Corporation, was instrumental in providing a list of business executives of the arms industry that would be invited to the dinner for Penn Kemble. Ebner, who had permanent contact with CDM officials and was sympathetic to the CDM's views, not only supplied the list but also asserted that he would make telephone calls and send his own letters to representatives of these industries. The people suggested by Ebner included, among others, Robert Andrews, director of congressional relations for

Rockwell International Corporation; Bruce Benefield, vice president, electronics and defense sector, TRW, Inc.; Richard K. Cook, vice president, Lockheed Corporation; John Ford, vice president, government affairs, AVACO Corporation; Thomas M. Gunn, staff vice president–Washington, McDonnell Douglas Corporation; and Gus Kinnear, vice president, Grumman Corporation. Cf. Letter from Stanley Ebner to Penn Kemble, May 30, 1985, in Peter Rosenblatt Personal Papers, LBJ Library and Museum, Austin, container 58. It is important to stress that for several years, Ebner was close to neoconservative organizations such as the CDM and the CFW and helped to establish linkages between the neoconservative movement and organizations and the defense industry.

117. Conversation with Ben Wattenberg, July 9, 1998.

118. Ibid.

119. Boies, "Buying for Armageddon." According to Boies, resources related to the "Olin family include a $50 million foundation, $300 million family fortune, and a significant interest in $1.6 billion Olin Corporation. Richard Mellon Scaife is the director of the $200 million Sarah Scaife Foundation and is linked to the Mellon fortune, worth at least $6 billion in 1984. David Packard and his family were reported to be worth at least $2.1 billion in 1986. John M. Cabot is a member of the Cabot family worth over $350 million in 1979" (p. 46).

120. The CPD asserted early on that it would not accept money from military corporations. While working in the CPD's archives, I found that Edward Teller had donated 200 common shares of stock in Helionetics, a military contractor. However, his contribution could be classified as a personal donation from his own Helionetics stock rather than as an official donation from the corporation. This theory is supported by further research in the CPD's uncataloged archive that made it clear that it did not receive significant donations from U.S. military-related corporations.

121. E.g., Decter glorified the life and work of Rumsfeld; see Midge Decter, *Rumsfeld: A Personal Portrait* (New York: Regan Books, 2003).

122. Conversation with Joshua Muravchik, American Enterprise Institute, Washington, January 31, 2008.

123. In 1983, Ebner, Northrop's senior vice president for governmental relations, wrote in reply to a letter from Rumsfeld, "There is a real need for an organization such as CFW to wage a war of ideas in defense of the United States against false political arguments and misrepresentation of facts. . . . I would certainly recommend careful consideration by Northrop of a formal proposal of its support." Though there is no indication that Northrop financially supported the CFW, it was willing to consider possible economic contributions to the organization based on ideological agreement. Letter from Stanley Ebner to Donald Rumsfeld, November 21, 1983, in Committee for the Free World Collection, Hoover Institution on War, Revolution, and Peace, Stanford, Calif., box 7.

124. William Kristol and Robert Kagan, "Toward a Neo-Reaganite Foreign Policy," *Foreign Affairs*, July–August 1996.

125. Conversation with Gary Schmitt, Washington, D.C., October 2004.

126. Ibid.

127. Ibid.

128. See "Memorandum from E. V. Rostow to Fowler, Packard, Rusk, Kirkland, Nitze, Kampelman, Allen, Gullion, Marshall, Walker, Tyroler, and Mrs. Hauser, September 21, 1976," in Papers on the Committee on the Present Danger, Hoover Institu-

tion on War, Revolution, and Peace, Stanford, Calif., box 275. See also "Draft Strictly Confidential, July 7, 1976," ibid., box 447.

129. Conversation with Schmitt, October 2004.

130. The exception was Irving Kristol, who wrote on a permanent basis for the *Wall Street Journal*, and, to a lesser extent, Michael Novak, Jeane Kirkpatrick, and Joshua Muravchik, who sometimes wrote for different newspapers.

131. See Center for Security Policy, "Mission of the Center for Security Policy," http://www.centerforsecurity policy.org/index.jasp.

132. Gaffney was an associate of Richard Perle during the Reagan years.

133. Donald F. Kettl, *Team Bush: Leadership Lessons from the Bush White House* (New York: McGraw-Hill, 2003), 59, 60.

134. "Richard Perle: The Making of a Neoconservative," Ben Wattenberg interview with Richard Perle on his television program *Think Tank*, http://www.pbs.org/thinktank/transcript1017.html.

135. John W. Kingdon, *Agendas, Alternatives and Public Policies* (Boston: Little, Brown, 1984), 214.

136. Center for Security Policy, "Editor's Desk: Occasional Papers Series by the Center for Security Policy," http://www.centerforsecuritypolicy.org/index.jsp?.

137. William Hartung was cited by Maria Ryan, "The Rumsfeld Commission: Filling in the 'Unknown Unknowns,'" http://www.nthposition.com/fillingtheunknown.php. The Strategic Defense Initiative, popularly known as Star Wars, was a defense plan introduced by President Reagan in 1983. The idea was to create a system to protect the United States from an attack by strategic ballistic missiles.

138. Center for Security Policy, "Mission."

139. Ibid.

140. I heard this joke from William Kristol. Conversation with William Kristol, Washington, D.C., November 2004.

141. Tim Russert interviews with Fred Barnes and William Kristol, CNBC Transcripts, September 10, 2005.

142. Conversation with William Kristol, November 2004.

143. Conversation with Jeane J. Kirkpatrick, Washington, D.C., November 2004.

144. Conversation with William Kristol, November 2004.

145. Conversation with William Kristol, January 31, 2008.

146. Murdoch is the owner of News Corporation, a multibillion-dollar company. Among the main assets of Murdoch are Fox News, Fox Sports, 20th Century Fox Studios, and the *New York Post*. On Murdoch, see James Fallows, "The Age of Murdoch," *Atlantic Monthly*, September 2003, 81–98.

147. Cited by Margaret Carlson, "Political Junkies, Rejoice," *Time*, May 15, 1995, 66.

148. Midge Decter, "Remarks," May 2, 1994. These remarks were made during a dinner honoring Norman Podhoretz on his retirement as editor of *Commentary*; see *National Review*, January 12, 1995, 22.

149. Nina J. Easton, "Thunder on the Right," *American Journalism Review*, December 2001, 35.

150. These figures were found in Wikipedia; see www.wikipedia.org.

151. Russert interviews with Barnes and Kristol.

152. Ibid.

153. See Joannie M. Schorof, " Seeking the Right Word," *U.S. News & World Re-*

*port*, September 18, 1995, 98; William F. Buckley, "Come on In," *National Review*, September 25, 1995, 18; and Carlson, "Political Junkies."

154. "Behind Bush's Drive to War," *The Humanist*, November–December 2003, 21.

155. Scott Sherman, "Kristol's War," *The Nation*, August 30–September 6, 2004, 7.

156. Conversation with Irving Kristol, November 2004.

157. See Zalmay M. Khalilzad and Paul Wolfowitz, "Overthrow Him," *The Weekly Standard*, December 1, 1997.

## Chapter 4. Ideas, Institutions, and Interests: The Influence of Neoconservatism on Reagan's Human Rights Policy

1. This article was reprinted in her book: Jeane Kirkpatrick, "Dictatorships and Double Standards," in *Dictatorships and Double Standards: Rationalism & Reason in Politics* (New York: Simon & Schuster for the American Enterprise Institute, 1982), 32, 49.

2. Conversation with Jeane J. Kirkpatrick, May 15, 1998.

3. Telephone conversation with Richard Allen, August 10, 1998.

4. The same story is narrated in a more detail version by Jay Winik; see Jay Winik, *On the Brink: The Dramatic Behind the Scenes Saga of the Reagan Era and the Men and Women Who Won the Cold War* (New York: Simon & Schuster, 1996), 106–8.

5. Conversation with Kirkpatrick, May 15, 1998.

6. Allan Gerson, *The Kirkpatrick Mission: Diplomacy without Apology—America at the United Nations 1981–1985* (New York: Free Press, 1991), xv.

7. Arthur M. Schlesinger Jr., *The Vital Center: The Politics of Freedom* (Boston: Houghton Mifflin), 1949.

8. Neil Jumonville, *Critical Crossings: The New York Intellectuals in Postwar America* (Berkeley: University of California Press, 1991), 222.

9. Daniel Bell, ed., *The New American Right* (New York: Criterion Books, 1955).

10. Irving Kristol, *Reflections of a Neoconservative* (New York: Basic Books, 1983), 80.

11. Norman Podhoretz, "Right about Everything, Wrong about Nothing," *Encounter* 75, no. 1 (1990): 10. Also Cf. Norman Podhoretz, "Why *The God That Failed* . . . ," *Encounter* 60, no. 1 (1983): 28. In the second essay, Podhoretz asserts that into the "intellectual darkness" of the Cold War, a "series of flares was fired," of which the brightest were *The God That Failed*, edited by Richard H. Crossman; Hannah Arendt's *Origins of Totalitarianism*; and Whittaker Chambers's *Witness*.

12. Norman Podhoretz, *Ex Friends: Falling Out with Allen Ginsberg, Lionel & Diana Trilling, Lillian Hellman, Hannah Arendt, and Norman Mailer* (New York: Free Press, 1999), 143. Later on, Podhoretz became critical of some of Arendt's viewpoints, finally breaking with her.

13. Conversation with Kirkpatrick, May 15, 1998.

14. Alexander Bloom, *Prodigal Sons: The New York Intellectuals and Their World* (New York: Oxford University Press, 1986), 329–30.

15. Michael Novak, "A Conversation with Michael Novak and Richard Schifter," in *Human Rights and the United Nations* (Washington, D.C.: American Enterprise Institute, 1981), 17.

16. Michael Novak, "Human Rights and Whited Sepulchres," in *Human Rights*

and *U.S. Foreign Policy: Theoretical Approaches and Some Perspectives on Latin America*, ed. Howard J. Wiarda (Washington, D.C.: American Enterprise Institute, 1982), 82.

17. It is important to highlight that Kissinger also used this distinction before Kirkpatrick. Cf. Henry A. Kissinger, "Continuity and Change in American Foreign Policy," in *Human Rights and World Order*, ed. Abdul Aziz Said (New York: Praeger, 1978).

18. "Memorandum from Joshua Muravchik to CDM Executive Committee and Members," August 17, 1977, LBJ Library and Museum, Austin, container 20; emphasis added.

19. Penn Kemble, "Launching the 'Liberty Party,'" August 17, 1977, ibid., pp. 2, 3, 4.

20. Coalition for a Democratic Majority, "Beyond Détente: Toward a Foreign Policy of Human Rights," August 17, 1977, LBJ Library and Museum, Austin, container 20, 29. I do not have the precise date on which this document was distributed. I found it in the same clipping of Muravchik's memo and Kemble's proposal. Therefore, I assume that it was presented to the CDM's Executive Committee the same day. Seven months later, on March 31, 1978, I found a proofread draft under the same title and basically with the same ideas. I decided to use the first draft because it reveals the CDM's initial approach to this subject.

21. Ibid., 21.

22. Robert Conquest, "Draft Statement on Human Rights and American Foreign Policy," LBJ Library and Museum, Austin, container 34, p. 6, 9, 11, 15. It is interesting to observe that I found this document in the CDM papers, which indicates an exchange of information among neoconservative organizations.

23. Memorandum from Dick Olson to Josh Muravchik, January 25, 1978, LBJ Library and Museum, Austin, container 20, 3.

24. Letter from Penn Kemble to Senator Daniel Patrick Moynihan, Attention Charles Horner, April 3, 1978, ibid., container 34.

25. Letter from Daniel V. Flanagan Jr. to Mr. Thomas V. Beard, January 31, 1980, ibid., container 51.

26. Letter from the Coalition for a Democratic Majority to the President, ibid. The letter does not have a date, but because of the political context and its place within the CDM file, it appears to have been sent between December 1979 and January 1980.

27. On the reascendance of Congress, see James L. Sundquist, *The Decline and Resurgence of Congress* (Washington, D.C.: Brookings Institution Press, 1981).

28. A. Glenn Mower Jr., *Human Rights and American Foreign Policy: The Carter and Reagan Experiences* (New York: Greenwood Press, 1987), 61.

29. Stephen B. Cohen, "Conditioning U.S. Security Assistance to Human Practice," *American Journal of International Law* 76 (1982): 271.

30. Quoted by David Carlton and Michael Stohl, "The Foreign Policy of Human Rights: Rhetoric and Reality from Jimmy Carter to Ronald Reagan," *Human Rights Quarterly* 7, no. 2 (May 1985): 210.

31. Advisory Task Force, Coalition for a Democratic Majority, *Democratic Solidarity: Proposal for the 1984 Democratic Party Platform on Foreign Policy and National Defense* (Washington, D.C.: Coalition for a Democratic Majority, 1984), 8.

32. David P. Forsythe, "Congress and Human Rights in U.S. Foreign Policy: The Fate of General Legislation," *Human Rights Quarterly* 9, no. 3 (1987): 385. Also see David P. Forsythe, *Human Rights and U.S. Foreign Policy: Congress Reconsidered* (Gainesville: University of Florida Press, 1988), 54–55.

33. Cf. Cohen, "Conditioning U.S. Security Assistance."

34. Forsythe, "Congress and Human Rights," 391, 392.

35. Ibid.

36. On the Jackson-Vanik Amendment, see Dan Caldwell, "The Jackson-Vanik Amendment," in *Congress, the Presidency and American Foreign Policy*, ed. John Spanier and Joseph Nogee (New York: Pergamon Press, 1981), 1–21; and Michael S. McMahon, "From the Jackson-Vanik Amendment to the Trade Act of 1974: An Assessment after Five Years," *Columbia Journal of Transnational Law* 18 (1979): 525–56.

37. Quoted by President's Commission on Organized Crime, *America's Habit: Drug Abuse, Drug Trafficking and Organized Crime* (Washington, D.C.: U.S. Government Printing Office, 1986), 263.

38. Cf. Cecil V. Crabb Jr. and Kevin V. Mulcahy, *Presidents and Foreign Policymaking* (Baton Rouge: Louisiana State University Press, 1986), 43.

39. Ibid., 55–57. The ideological bias of the State Department has varied according to the particular historical moment. In the 1940s and 1950s, the State Department was accused of being procommunist; in the 1970s, it was accused of being overly anticommunist.

40. Cf. Cohen, "Conditioning U.S. Security Assistance," esp. 257–61.

41. Howard Warshawsky, "The Department of State and Human Rights: A Case Study of the Human Rights Bureau," *World Affairs* 142 (1980): 195, 196.

42. Edwin S. Maynard, "The Bureaucracy and Implementation of U.S. Human Rights Policy," *Human Rights Quarterly* 11, no. 2 (May 1989): 185, 186.

43. Ibid., 187.

44. Elliott Abrams. "Speech before the Council on Foreign Relations," New York City, February 10, 1982, in Shattan Papers, Hoover Institution on War, Revolution, and Peace, Stanford, Calif., box 10. A similar citation can be found in Mower, *Human Rights*, 26. Also Cf. Christopher Madison, "Abrams, State's Human Rights Chief, Tries to Tailor a Policy to Suit Reagan," *National Journal*, April 1, 1982, 763.

45. It is interesting to highlight that in the 1990s, when the Bill Clinton administration was in power and therefore neoconservative politicians were out of the government, Elliott Abrams became the head of the Ethics and Public Policy Center.

46. Letter from Ernest W. Lefever to Midge Decter, December 20, 1984, in Committee for the Free World Collection, Hoover Institution on War, Revolution, and Peace, Stanford, Calif., box 5.

47. Ernest W. Lefever, "The Trivialization of Human Rights," *Policy Review*, Winter 1978, 12, 14, 16, 20, 22.

48. Letter from Ronald Reagan to Ernest W. Lefever, June 15, 1981, in Committee for the Free World Collection, Hoover Institution on War, Revolution, and Peace, Stanford, Calif., box 5.

49. Cf. Letter from Ernest W. Lefever to Charles Tyroler II, November 5, 1982, in Papers of the Committee on the Present Danger, Hoover Institution on War, Revolution, and Peace, Stanford, Calif., box 290.

50. On Elliott Abrams, see Eric Alterman, "Elliott Abrams: The Teflon Assistant Secretary," *Washington Monthly* 19, no. 4 (1987).

51. Irving Kristol, "The Common Sense of 'Human Rights,'" *Wall Street Journal*, April 8, 1981.

52. Michael Novak, "The Reagan Approach to Human Rights Policy," *Wall Street Journal*, April 28, 1981.

53. "Human Rights and American Foreign Policy: A Symposium," *Commentary*, November 1981.

54. The disagreements between Jeane Kirkpatrick and Elliott Abrams are well known. Abrams suggests that these difficulties were the result of the overlapping of functions in these two offices. Obviously, neoconservatism was not immune to conflict or ideological discrepancies.

55. Conversation with Elliott Abrams, April 28, 1998.

56. Tamar Jacoby, "The Reagan Turnaround on Human Rights," *Foreign Affairs*, Summer 1986, 1066–86; the quotation is on 1071.

57. Conversation with Elliott Abrams, April 28, 1998.

58. Maynard, "Bureaucracy and Implementation," 184.

59. Forsythe, *Human Rights and U.S. Foreign Policy*, 124. It is also important to stress that Reagan's anticommunist crusade was reinforced by a careful selection of political appointees and by the use of career bureaucrats, who functioned as team players. On this topic, see Linda L. Fischer, "Fifty Years of Presidential Appointments," in *The In and Outers: Presidential Appointees and Transient Government in Washington*, ed. G. Calvin Mackenzie (Baltimore: Johns Hopkins University Press, 1987), 11, 12; Dick Kirschten, "Wanted: 275 Reagan Team Players; Empire Builders Need Not Apply," *National Journal*, November 29, 1980, 2077; and Dom Bonafede, "Reagan and His Kitchen Cabinet Are Bounded by Friendship and Ideology," *National Journal*, April 11, 1981, 608.

60. Fischer, "Fifty Years of Presidential Appointments," in *The In and Outers*, ed. Mackenzie, 11, 12.

61. Kirschten, "Wanted."

62. Bonafede, "Reagan and His Kitchen Cabinet."

63. John H. Kessel, "The Structure of the Reagan White House," *American Journal of Political Science* 28, no. 2 (May 1984): 235.

64. In fact, the CDM often gave its Friend of Freedom Award to people who had been politically persecuted, such as Huber Matos, Andrei Sakharov, and Alexander Solzhenitsyn.

65. Quoted by Paul Y. Hammond et al., *The Reluctant Supplier: U.S. Decision-making for Arms Sales* (Cambridge, Mass.: Oegschlage, Gunn & Hain, 1983), 75. Also see "Hearing on HR 15628: To Amend the Foreign Military Sale Act," 2.

66. William P. Avery, "The United States and Conventional Arms Transfers: Who Gets What and Why," in *American Foreign Policy in an Uncertain World*, ed. David P. Forsythe (Lincoln: University of Nebraska Press, 1984), 170.

67. Ibid., 191.

68. Cf. Andrew J. Pierre, "Arms Sale: The New Diplomacy," *Foreign Affairs*, Winter 1981–982, 276–77.

69. Hammond et al., *Reluctant Supplier*, 32. Also see James L. Buckley, "Arms Transfer and the National Interests," address to the meeting of the Board of Governors of the Aerospace Industries Association, Williamsburg, Va., May 29, 1981.

70. Roger P. Labrie et al., *U.S. Arms Sales Policy: Background and Issues*, Studies in Defense Policy 359 (Washington, D.C.: American Enterprise Institute, 1982), 15.

71. Conversation with Elliott Abrams, April 28, 1998.

72. Many H. Cooper, "The Defense Economy," *Editorial Research Report* 1, no. 18 (May 17, 1985): 362.

73. Hammond et al., *Reluctant Supplier*, 35, 36. Also see "U.S. Arms Sales Abroad: A Policy of Restraint?" *American Enterprise Institute Defense Review* 2 (1987): 10.

74. George P. Shultz, *Turmoil and Triumph: My Years as a Secretary of State* (New York: Charles Scribner's Sons, 1993), 970.

## Chapter 5. Ideas, Institutions, and Interests: The Influence of Neoconservatism on the U.S. Military Buildup

1. Cf. "Republican Party Platform of 1980, Adopted by the Republican National Convention, July 15, 1980, Detroit," http://www.presidency.ucsb.edu/showplatforms .php?platindex=R1980.

2. William Schneider, "Conservatism, Not Interventionism: Trends in Foreign Policy Opinion, 1974–1982," in *Eagle Defiant: United States Foreign Policy in the 1980s,* ed. Kenneth A. Oye, Robert Lieber, and Donald Rothchild (Boston: Little, Brown, 1983), 36.

3. Robert B. Reich, "Reagan's Hidden 'Industrial Policy,'" *New York Times*, August 4, 1985.

4. Cf. Schneider. "Conservatism," 40–41; and Michael Mandelbaum and William Schneider, "The New Internationalism: Public Opinion and American Foreign Policy," in *Eagle Entangled: U.S. Foreign Policy in a Complex World*, ed. Kenneth A. Oye, Robert Lieber, and Donald Rothchild (New York: Longman, 1979), 42, 63–65.

5. Conversation with Max Kampelman, August 27, 1993.

6. Letter from Ronald Reagan to the Members and Friends of the Committee on the Present Danger, November 7, 1980, in Papers on the Committee on the Present Danger, Hoover Institution on War, Revolution, and Peace, Stanford, Calif., box 002.

7. Irving Kristol was perhaps the only exception. In 1958, he defended the "maintenance of a very large, well-equipped, well-trained military establishment based on non-nuclear armaments." Irving Kristol, "Thoughts on the Bomb," *The New Leader*, June 30, 1958, 13, 15.

8. This report was titled "United States Objectives and Programs for National Security"; see U.S. Department of State, "NSC-68, 1950," http://www.state.gov/r/pa/ho/time/cwr/82209.htm.

9. Michael Nacht, *The Age of Vulnerability: Threats to the Nuclear Stalemate* (Washington, D.C.: Brookings Institution Press, 1985), 170.

10. Samuel F. Wells Jr., "Sounding the Tocsin: NSC 68 and the Soviet Threat," in *American Cold War Strategy: Interpreting NSC 68*, ed. Ernest R. May (Boston: Bedford Books/St. Martin Press, 1993), 137.

11. Zara Steiner, "The United Kingdom," in *American Cold War Strategy*, ed. May, 181.

12. Daniel Yergin, *Shattered Peace: The Origins of the Cold War and the National Security State* (Boston: Houghton Mifflin, 1977), 401.

13. Jerry W. Sanders, *Peddlers of Crisis: The Committee on the Present Danger and the Politics of Containment* (Boston: South End Press, 1983), 24.

14. It is important to emphasize that at this time American history registered the emergence of the first CPD. Cofounded by Harvard University President James Conant, former Undersecretary of the Army Tracy Voorhees, and atomic scientist Vannevar Bush, the CPD rose out of the notion of the Soviet threat. In the 1970s, the second CPD had as an important source of inspiration the first CPD. On the first CPD, see ibid., esp. chaps. 2 and 3.

15. Henry Jackson, "How Shall We Forge a Strategy for Survival?" Address, National War College, Washington, D.C., April 16, 1959. Cited by Samuel P. Huntington, *The Common Defense: Strategic Programs in National Politics* (New York: Columbia University Press, 1961), 51.

16. Douglas Brinkley, *Dean Acheson: The Cold War Years* (New Haven, Conn.: Yale University Press, 1992), 17.

17. *AEI Memorandum*, no. 4, December 15, 1972, 1, 4.

18. *American Enterprise Institute for Public Policy Research, 1973–1974* (Washington, D.C.: American Enterprise Institute, 1974), 18.

19. Ibid., 5.

20. *AEI Memorandum*, no. 9, Spring–Summer 1974, 1, 3, 7.

21. Cf. Eugene V. Rostow, "For an Adequate Defense," *Wall Street Journal*, May 12, 1975. My comments on this document are taken from this piece.

22. Ibid.

23. Letter from Henry Kissinger to Eugene V. Rostow, August 19, 1974, LBJ Library and Museum, Austin, container 52, 1, 2.

24. Letter from Eugene V. Rostow to Henry Kissinger, September 4, 1974, ibid., container 52, 1, 2, 4.

25. Cf. House of Representatives, *Congressional Record*, November 18, 1975, H11394–95.

26. Norman Podhoretz, "The Culture of Appeasement," *Harper's Magazine*, October 1977, 25.

27. Richard Pipes, "Why the Soviet Union Thinks It Could Fight and Win a Nuclear War," *Commentary*, July 1977, 26–31.

28. Gary Dorrien, *The Neoconservative Mind: Politics, Culture, and the War of Ideology* (Philadelphia: Temple University Press, 1993), 182.

29. Sanders, *Peddlers of Crisis*, 165.

30. Coalition for a Democratic Majority, "The Platform of the Democratic Party," July 1976, LBJ Library and Museum, Austin, containers 14, 71, 73, 75, 76.

31. Stephen S. Rosenfeld, "Secretary of State Scoop Jackson?" *Washington Post*, June 18, 1976.

32. On Carter's views on foreign affairs, cf. Jimmy Carter, "Commencement Address at the University of Notre Dame," in *A Reader in American Foreign Policy*, ed. James M. McCormick (Itasca, Ill.: F. E. Peacock, 1986), 150–55. Here, Carter declared that the "unifying threat of conflict with the Soviet Union has become less intensive even though the competition has become more extensive."

33. *AEI Memorandum*, no. 17, Fall 1976, 3.

34. Ibid., 9.

35. Max M. Kampelman, "Introduction," in *Alerting America: The Papers of the Committee on the Present Danger*, ed. Charles Tyroler II (Washington, D.C.: Pergamon-Brassey's, 1984), xv.

36. Committee on the Present Danger, "Common Sense and the Common Danger: Policy Statement of the Committee on the Present Danger," in Papers on the Committee on the Present Danger, Hoover Institution on War, Revolution, and Peace, Stanford, Calif., box 447, 3, 5.

37. Beth Ann Inglod, "The Committee on the Present Danger: A Study of Elite and Public Influence, 1976–1980," PhD dissertation, University of Pittsburgh, 1989, 2.

38. Podhoretz, "Culture of Appeasement."

39. My description of the Jackson-Perle memo is based on Strobe Talbott, *Endgame: The Inside Story of SALT II* (New York: Harper & Row, 1980), 52–57.

40. Ibid., 53.

41. Committee on the Present Danger, "Where We Stand on SALT," in *Alerting America*, ed. Tyroler, 17, 19.

42. Kampelman, "Introduction," xix.

43. Committee on the Present Danger, "Where We Stand on SALT."

44. Ibid.

45. Committee on the Present Danger, "Is America Becoming Number 2?" in *Alerting America*, ed. Tyroler, 41, 87.

46. Eugene V. Rostow, "The Case against SALT II," *Commentary*, February 1979, 32.

47. Ibid., 264.

48. Institutionally speaking, the project revealed a significant recognition within AEI of the relevance of military matters and a fundamental shift in its main areas of concern. By the mid-1970s, AEI had evolved from being a think tank merely involved in the study of economics to an organization highly interested in domestic and foreign policy issues.

49. *AEI Memorandum*, no. 19, Spring 1977, 4. Also cf. *American Enterprise Institute for Public Policy Research, 1978* (Washington, D.C.: American Enterprise Institute, 1978), 48.

50. Cf. *AEI Memorandum*, no. 23, Summer 1978, 3, 5.

51. *AEI Memorandum*, no. 34, September–October 1980, 1, 8.

52. *AEI Memorandum*, no. 33, July–August 1980, 3, 5.

53. Norman Podhoretz, "The Present Danger," *Commentary*, March 1980, 39, 40.

54. Quoted by Sanders, *Peddlers of Crisis*, 236.

55. Although some neoconservatives did not change their Democratic affiliation, they were more sympathetic to Reagan's viewpoint. This was the case for Jeane Kirkpatrick, who remained a Democrat until 1984 but participated in the first term of the Reagan administration. Something similar happened with several associates of the CDM and the CPD.

56. Norman Podhoretz, "The Neo-Conservative Anguish over Reagan's Foreign Policy," *New York Times Magazine*, May 2, 1982, 30–33, 96–98; the quotation is on 30.

57. Telephone conversation with Richard Allen, August 10, 1998.

58. Cf. Working Groups, in Papers on the Committee on the Present Danger, Hoover Institution on War, Revolution, and Peace, Stanford, Calif., box 016.

59. Ibid.

60. Letter from Paul Nitze to Charles Tyroler, November 19, 1980, ibid.

61. Letter from Fred C. Iklé to Anne Armstrong, December 18, 1980, in Fred C. Iklé Papers, Hoover Institution on War, Revolution, and Peace, Stanford, Calif., box 11, file: Staffing the Ronald Reagan Administration.

62. Letter from Ronald Reagan to Charls E. Walker, July 12, 1982, in Papers on the Committee on the Present Danger, Hoover Institution on War, Revolution, and Peace, Stanford, Calif., box 018.

63. Letter from Ronald Reagan to Charls E. Walker, February 16, 1984, ibid.

64. Richard E. Neustadt, *Presidential Power: The Politics of Leadership* (New York: John Wiley & Sons, 1960), 33.

65. Hugh Heclo, *A Government of Strangers: Executive Politics in Washington* (Washington, D.C.: Brookings Institution Press, 1977), 154.

66. Edward S. Crowin, *The President: Office and Power* (New York: New York University Press, 1967), 171.

67. Harold Hongju Koh, *The National Security Constitution: Sharing Power after the Iran-Contra Affair* (New Haven, Conn.: Yale University Press, 1990), chaps. 5 and 6, esp. 148.

68. Cf. Allan Ides, "Congress, Constitutional Responsibility and the War Powers," *Loyola of Los Angeles Law Review* 17, no. 3 (1984); and Michael Glennon, "The War Powers Resolution Ten Years Later: More Politics Than Law," *American Journal of International Law* 77, no. 3 (July 1984). Also see Louis Fisher, *Congressional Abdication on War and Spending* (College Station: Texas A&M University Press, 2000).

69. Louis W. Koenig, "The Modern Presidency and the Constitution: Foreign Policy," in *The Constitution and the American Presidency*, ed. Martin L. Fausold and Alan Shank (Albany: State University of New York Press, 1991), 181.

70. F. S. Northedge, "Elements of U.S. State Policy," in *The Foreign Policy of the Powers,* ed. F. S. Northedge (New York: Free Press, 1975), 44.

71. John E. Endicott, "The National Security Council: Formalized Coordination and Policy Planning," in *The National Security Policy: The Decision-Making Process,* ed. Robert L. Pfaltzgraff Jr. and Uri Ra'anan (Hamden, Conn.: Archon Books, 1984), 179.

72. Cecil V. Crabb and Kevin V. Mulcahy, *American National Security: A Presidential Perspective* (Pacific Grove, Calif.: Brooks/Cole, 1991), 13.

73. William P. Bundy, "The National Security Process: Plus Ça Change . . . ," *International Security* 7, no. 3 (Winter 1982–83): 95, 96.

74. Endicott, "National Security Council," 179.

75. Frederick H. Hartmann and Robert L. Wendzel, *Defending America's Security* (New York: Pergamon-Brassey's, 1988), 103.

76. Samuel P. Huntington, "Organization and Strategy," in *Reorganizing America's Defense: Leadership in War and Peace*, ed. Robert J. Art, Vincent Davis, and Samuel P. Huntington (New York: Pergamon-Brassey's, 1985), 232.

77. Ibid.

78. Quoted by Michel Hobkirk, "Policy Planning and Resources Allocation in the U.S. Department of Defense: An Outsider's View," in *National Security Policy*, ed. Pfaltzgraff and Ra'anan, 203, 204.

79. Norman J. Ornstein, "The Open Congress Meets the President," in *Both Ends of the Avenue: The Presidency, the Executive Branch, and Congress in the 1980s*, ed. Anthony King (Washington, D.C.: American Enterprise Institute, 1983), 189–90.

80. Ibid., 195.

81. Henry A. Kissinger, "Institutionalized Stalemate," *Washington Quarterly*, New Year's 1988, 138.

82. James M. Lindsay, "Congress and Defense Policy: 1961 to 1986," *Armed Forces and Society* 13, no. 3 (Spring 1987): 381.

83. Steven S. Smith and Christopher J. Deering, *Committees in Congress* (Washington, D.C.: Congressional Quarterly, 1984), 134, 135. The same figures are quoted in Lindsay, "Congress."

84. Lindsay, "Congress," 131.

85. Smith and Deering, *Committees*, 116.

86. Ibid., 107. Also see House Armed Services Committee, U.S. Congress, no. 91-14, March 27, 1969, 170–72; emphasis added.

87. Letter from Edmund S. Muskie to Eugene V. Rostow, May 26, 1978, in Papers on the Committee on the Present Danger, Hoover Institution on War, Revolution, and Peace, Stanford, Calif., box 226; Letter from Eugene Rostow to Edmund S. Muskie, July 19, 1978, ibid.

88. Cf. Hartmann and Wendzel, *Defending America's Security,* 127.

89. On the Office of International Security Affairs, see Geoffrey Piller, "DOD's Office of International Security Affairs: The Brief Ascendancy of an Advisory System," *Political Science Quarterly* 98, no. 1 (Spring 1983): 59–78.

90. Barry M. Blechman and Janne E. Nolan, "Reorganizing for More Effective Arms Negotiation," *Foreign Affairs,* Summer 1983, 1157–82; the quotation is on 1164.

91. Cf. I. M. Destler, "The Evolution of Reagan Foreign Policy," in *The Reagan Presidency: An Early Assessment,* ed. Fred I. Greenstein (Baltimore: Johns Hopkins University Press, 1983), 122.

92. Strobe Talbott, *Deadly Gambits: The Reagan Administration and the Stalemate in Nuclear Arms Control* (New York: Alfred A. Knopf, 1984), 11.

93. Conversation with Eugene V. Rostow, May 8, 1998.

94. Ibid.

95. Christopher M. Lehman, "National Security Decision Making: The State Department's Role in Developing Arms Control Policy," in *National Security Policy,* ed. Pfaltzgraff and Ra'anan, 212.

96. Johanna McGeary, "Into the 'Evil Empire': Richard Perle, an Old Kremlin Foe, Finally Gets to Moscow," *Time,* August 25, 1986, 22.

97. Russell Watson, "The Battle for Reagan's Mind: A Fictional Account of the Bureaucratic Wars," *Newsweek,* May 4, 1992, 42.

98. Conversation with Douglas J. Feith, July 22, 1993.

99. Ibid.

100. Tamar Jacoby, "The 'Prince of Darkness' Calls It Quits," *Newsweek,* March 23, 1987, 27.

101. Daniel Wirls, *Buildup: The Politics of Defense in the Reagan Era* (Ithaca, N.Y.: Cornell University Press, 1992), 35.

102. Thomas Ferguson and Joel Rogers, "The Empire Strikes Back," *The Nation,* November 1, 1980, 436–40.

103. Sanders, *Peddlers of Crisis,* 179; also see Sanders's interview with Norman Podhoretz in the same volume.

104. Ferguson and Rogers, "Empire Strikes Back," 438.

105. Gordon Adams, *The Politics of Defense Contracting: The Iron Triangles* (New Brunswick, N.J.: Transaction Books, 1982), 114.

106. Ibid.

107. *New York Times.* April 9, 1985.

108. Cf. Richard L. Berke, "Military PAC's Led Donations in '86 Campaigns," *New York Times,* August 28, 1987.

109. Larry J. Sabato, *PAC Power: Inside the World of Political Action Committees* (New York: W. W. Norton, 1984), 78.

110. Cf. CDM invitation to 1985 Henry M. Jackson Friend of Freedom Award Dinner, CDM papers, LBJ Library and Museum, Austin. The awards were granted on

April 17, 1985. It is interesting to observe that the recipients were Max Kampelman and two members of the Armed Services Committee, Senator Sam Nunn and Representative Les Aspin.

111. See the section on the CPD in chapter 3 of this book.

112. John Boies, "Buying for Armageddon: Factors Influencing Post–World War II Weapons Purchases since the Cuban Missile Crisis," PhD dissertation, University of Michigan, 1991, 46.

113. Conversation with Douglas J. Feith, July 22, 1993.

## Chapter 6. The Second Neoconservative Movement

1. Norman Podhoretz, "Neoconservatism: A Eulogy," *Commentary*, March 1996.

2. See Stefan Halper and Jonathan Clarke, *America Alone: The Neo-Conservatives and the Global Order* (New York: Cambridge University Press, 2004); Gary Dorrien, *Neoconservatism and the New Pax America* (New York: Routledge, 2004); and Murray Friedman, *The Neoconservative Revolution: Jewish Intellectuals and the Shaping of Public Policy* (New York: Cambridge University Press, 2005).

3. Stephen Skowronek, *The Politics Presidents Make: Leadership from John Adams to George Bush* (Cambridge, Mass.: Harvard University Press, 1993).

4. George W. Bush's final approval rating was 25 or 22 percent, depending on the polling.

5. Cf. James L. Sundquist, *The Decline and Resurgence of Congress* (Washington, D.C.: Brookings Institution Press, 1981); James L. Sundquist, "The Crisis of Competence in Governance," in *Political Economy and Constitutional Reform: Hearing before the Joint Economic Committee, Congress of the United States, Ninety-Seventh Congress* (Washington, D.C.: U.S. Government Printing Office, 1983), pt. 2, 531–63; Michael L. Mezey, *Congress, the President and Public Policy* (Boulder, Colo.: Westview Press, 1989); Lloyd N. Cutler, "To Form a Government," in *Separation of Powers. Does It Still Work?* ed. Robert A. Goldwin and Art Kaufman (Washington, D.C.: American Enterprise Institute, 1986); and C. Douglas Dillon, "Speech Given at Fletcher School of Diplomacy, Tufts University, May 30, 1982," in *Political Economy and Constitutional Reform*.

6. Walter Dean Burnham, "The Reagan Heritage," in *The Election of 1988: Reports and Interpretations*, ed. Gerald M. Pomper (Chatham, N.J.: Chatham House, 1989), 8.

7. Alonzo L. Hamby, *Liberalism and Its Challengers: FDR to Reagan* (New York: Oxford University Press, 1985), 352.

8. Kenneth Waltz, "Structural Realism after the Cold War," *International Security* 25, no. 1 (Summer 2000): 29.

9. Stephen M. Walt, "Two Cheers for Clinton's Foreign Policy," *Foreign Affairs*, March–April 2000, 79. This description of Clinton's foreign policy has been mainly based on Walt's article but also on these articles: The Editors of *Foreign Policy*, "Clinton's Foreign Policy," *Foreign Policy*, November–December 2000; and Josef Joffe, "Clinton's World Purpose, Policy and Weltanschauung," *Washington Quarterly* 24, no. 1 (Winter 2001): 141–54.

10. Norman Ornstein, "The Legacy of 2000," *Washington Quarterly* 24, no. 2. (Spring 2001): 99–105.

11. Marjorie Random Hershey, "The Campaign and the Media," in *The Election of 2000*, ed. Gerald M. Pomper (Chatham, N.J.: Chatham House, 2001), 46–72. Also see Charles Babington, "Campaign Matter: The Proof of 2000," in *Overtime! The Election 2000 Thriller*, ed. Larry J. Sabato (New York: Longman, 2001).

12. Cited by Stefan Halper and Jonathan Clarke, *America Alone: The Neo-Conservatives and the Global Order* (New York: Cambridge University Press, 2004), 112.

13. Conversation with Joshua Muravchik, January 31, 2003.

14. Quoted by Jacob Weisberg, "The Misunderestimated Man: How Bush Chose Stupidity," *Vanity Fair*, July 2003.

15. Ibid.

16. Conversation with Gary Schmitt, January 29, 2008.

17. Some neoconservatives of the second generation, such as Gary Schmitt, worked for Daniel Patrick Moynihan, but these would prove to be minor episodes in their political and journalistic careers.

18. Max Boot, "American Conservatism: What the Heck Is a 'Neocon'?" *Wall Street Journal*, December 30, 2002.

## Chapter 7. Second-Generation Neoconservatives and Foreign Policy

1. Seymour Martin Lipset, "Neoconservatives: Intellectuals on the Right," unpublished paper, 1993.

2. Nathan Glazer recently asserted that domestic concerns were central in the birth and development of *The Public Interest*. Contrary to his opinion, I think that neoconservatism was, from the beginning, concerned not only with domestic social issues but also with foreign affairs. As I have tried to show, since the birth of the Coalition for a Democratic Majority—the first neoconservative organization—foreign policy has been a central concern. The theme became quite visible with the founding of the Committee on the Present Danger. On Glazer's opinion, see Nathan Glazer, "Neoconservative from the Start," *The Public Interest*, Spring 2005, 17.

3. William Kristol and Robert Kagan, "Toward a Neo-Reaganite Foreign Policy," *Foreign Affairs*, July–August 1996, 22.

4. Samuel P. Huntington, "The Erosion of American National Interests," *Foreign Affairs*, September–October 1997, 32.

5. Irving Kristol, "A Post-Wilsonian Foreign Policy," *AEI Online*, August 2, 1996, http://www.aei.org/issue/17311.

6. See Samuel Huntington, *American Politics: The Promise of Disharmony* (Cambridge, Mass.: Harvard University Press, 1981), 4; and Samuel Huntington, *The Clash of Civilizations and the Remaking of the World Order* (New York: Simon & Schuster, 1996). Some of the interesting criticisms of *The Clash of Civilizations* are Robert Jarvis, "The Clash of Civilizations and the Remaking of the World Order," *Political Science Quarterly* 112, no. 2 (Summer 1997): 307–8; Peter Evans, "The Clash of Civilizations and the Remaking of the World Order," *Contemporary Sociology*, November 1997; Richard Rosecrance, "The Clash of Civilizations and the Remaking of the World Order," *American Political Science Review* 92, no. 4 (December 1998): 978–80; and Walter A. McDougall, "The Clash of Civilizations and the Remaking of the World Order," *Journal of Modern History*, June 1998.

7. Ervand Abrahamian, "The US Media, Huntington and September 11," *Third World Quarterly* 24, no. 3: 529.

8. Norman Podhoretz, "Israel Isn't the Issue," *Wall Street Journal*, September 20, 2001.

9. Samuel P. Huntington, "The Age of Muslim Wars," *Newsweek*, December 17, 2001), 4 (online version).

10. Catherine Zuckert and Michael Zuckert, *The Truth about Leo Strauss: Political Philosophy and American Democracy* (Chicago: University of Chicago Press, 2006), 22, 23.

11. See Seymour Hersh, "Selective Intelligence," *The New Yorker*, May 12, 2003, http://www.newyorker.com/archive/2003/05/12/030512fa_fact.

12. Ivan Kenneally, "The Use and Abuse of Utopianism: Leo Strauss's Philosophic Politics," *Perspectives on Political Science* 36, no. 3 (Summer 2007): 142.

13. Earl Shorris, "Ignoble Liars: Leo Strauss, George Bush, and the Philosophy of Mass Deception," *Harper's Magazine*, June 2004, 66.

14. Max Boot, "Neocons," *Foreign Policy*, January–February 2004, 26.

15. Paul Wolfowitz, interview with Sam Tanenhaus, *Vanity Fair*, May 9, 2003; reproduced in the transcripts of the Department of Defense, http://www.defenselink.mil/transcripts/2003/tr20030509-despsecdef0223.html.

16. See Anne Norton, *Leo Strauss and the Politics of American Empire* (New Haven, Conn.: Yale University Press, 2004).

17. Irving Kristol, *Neoconservatism: The Autobiography of an Idea* (Chicago: Elephant Paperbacks, 1997), 7.

18. Many journalistic articles maintain that people like Abraham Shulsky and Carnes Lord were second-generation neoconservatives influenced by Strauss. I have not included these people in my work, so I am not evaluating their perspective.

19. William Kristol, "Defending and Advancing Freedom: A Symposium," *Commentary*, November 2005, 44.

20. Steven Lenzner and William Kristol, "What Was Leo Strauss Up To?" *The Public Interest*, Fall 2003, 38.

21. Morton J. Frish, "Leo Strauss and the American Regime," *Publius* 17, no. 2 (Spring 1987): 4.

22. The notion that liberal democracy was an alternative to communism and fascism was a common argument during the Cold War years. One only has to remember that Arthur M. Schlesinger Jr. expressed a similar view in his book *The Vital Center* to realize that this was not an exclusive vision of Strauss. What is certainly different is the analysis and the way that Strauss reached his conclusions.

23. Lenzner and Kristol, "What Was Leo Strauss Up To?" 37.

24. James Mann, *The Rise of the Vulcans: The History of Bush's War Cabinet* (New York: Viking, 2004), 27.

25. Francis Fukuyama, *America at the Crossroads: Democracy, Power, and the Neoconservative Legacy* (New Haven, Conn.: Yale University Press, 2006), 3.

26. Robert Kagan, "Neocon Nation," *World Affairs*, Spring 2008, 24.

27. Conversation with Elliott Abrams, January 28, 2008.

28. E.g., see Kristol and Kagan, "Toward a Neo-Reaganite Foreign Policy."

29. Norman Podhoretz, "Strange Bedfellows: A Guide to the New Foreign-Policy Debates," *Commentary*, December 1999, 29.

30. Jeane J. Kirkpatrick, "A Steady and Strong Policy," *Human Events*, June 14, 2004, S13.

31. See Douglas Feith, "American Power—for What? A Symposium," *Commentary*, January 2000, 21–27.

32. Project for the New American Century, "Statement of Principles," available at www.newamericancentury.com.

33. William Kristol, "In 2008 It's Ronald Reagan vs. Bobby Kennedy," *Time*, April 9, 2007, 26.

34. Allen Buchanan and Robert O. Keohane, "The Preventive Use of Force: A Cosmopolitan Institutional Proposal," *Ethics & International Affairs* 18, no. 1 (2004): 1.

35. See John Lewis Gaddis, *Surprise, Security, and the American Experience* (Cambridge, Mass.: Harvard University Press, 2004).

36. Melvyn P. Leffler, "Bush's Foreign Policy," *Foreign Policy*, September–October 2004, 23.

37. Melvyn P. Leffler, "9/11 and American Foreign Policy," *Diplomatic History* 29, no.3 (June 2005): 398.

38. See Bob Woodward, *Bush at War* (New York: Simon & Schuster, 2002).

39. Robert Jarvis, *American Foreign Policy in a New Era* (New York: Routledge, 2005), 85.

40. John Gerald Ruggie, "Doctrinal Unilateralism and Its Limits: American and Global Governance in the New Century " in *American Foreign Policy in a Globalized World*, ed. David P. Forsyth, Patrice C. McHahon, and Andrew Wedeman (New York: Routledge, 2006), 40.

41. Richard Perle, "How America Could Lose," *U.S. News & World Report*, September 24, 1990, 45.

42. See also Richard Perle, "Why the Gulf Is Not Vietnam," *U.S. & World Report*, November 19, 1990.

43. See Paul Wolfowitz, "Rising Up," *New Republic*, December 7, 1998, 12.

44. Cited by Patrick E. Tyler, "U.S. Strategy Calls for Insuring No Rivals Develop," *New York Times*, March 8, 1992.

45. Project for the New American Century, "Statement of Principles."

46. Frank J. Gaffney Jr., "Defending and Advancing Freedom: A Symposium," *Commentary*, November 2005, 30.

47. Conversation with Douglas Feith, January 30, 2008.

48. Irving Kristol, "In Search of Our National Interest," *Wall Street Journal*, June 7, 1990.

49. Jeane J. Kirkpatrick, "The Case for Force," *Chronicle of Higher Education*, September 28, 2001. This article can also be found at the Web site of the American Enterprise Institute (www.aei.org).

50. Of course, Feith and Wolfowitz were already politically active during the Reagan administration, when the first neoconservative expression acquired relevance in American foreign policy. However, their reputation, position in the government, and public exposure increased substantially during the first term of the George W. Bush administration.

51. Conversation with Jeane J. Kirkpatrick, American Enterprise Institute, Washington, D.C., November 2004.

52. For Walzer, "the way to avoid the big war [the invasion of Iraq] [was] is to intensify the little war that the United States is already fighting." At the time, Walzer

conceived of the following strategy: First, "extend the northern and southern no-flight zones to include the whole country." Second, "impose smart sanctions . . . and insist that Iraq's standing partners commit themselves to enforcing them." Third, "the United States should expand the United Nations monitoring system." Fourth and finally, he believed that the United States "should challenge the French to make good on their claim that force is indeed a last resort by mobilizing troops of their own and sending them to the Gulf." Michael Walzer, "What a Little War in Iraq Could Do," *New York Times*, March 7, 2003.

53. See Michael Novak, "War to Topple Saddam Is a Moral Obligation," *The Times* (London), February 12, 2003. This article can also found at the Web site of the American Enterprise Institute (www.aei.org).

54. William Galston, "Perils of Preemptive War," *The American Prospect*, September 23, 2002, 32.

55. Daniel Patrick Moynihan, *A Dangerous Place* (Boston: Little, Brown, 1978); conversation with Jeane J. Kirkpatrick; Irving Kristol, "The Coming 'Conservative Century,'" *Wall Street Journal*, February 1, 1993; Joshua Muravchik, "We're Better Off without That U.N. Resolution," *Wall Street Journal*, March 18, 2003.

56. Conversation with Joshua Muravchik, January 31, 2008.

57. Irving Kristol, "Tongue-Tied in Washington," *Wall Street Journal*, April 15, 1991.

58. William Kristol and Robert Kagan, "Saddam Must Go," in *The Weekly Standard: A Reader, 1995–2005*, ed. William Kristol (New York: HarperPerennial, 2006), 220. This article was originally published in *The Weekly Standard*, November 17, 1997.

59. Zalmay M. Khalilzad and Paul Wolfowitz, "Overthrow Him," *The Weekly Standard*, December 1, 1997, 14.

60. "Letter to Honorable William J. Clinton, President of the United States, January 26, 1998," available at Project for the New American Century, www.newamericancentury.org. The same letter was published in the *Washington Times*, January 27, 1998.

61. See Samuel P. Huntington, "The Lonely Superpower," *Foreign Affairs*, March–April 1999; Charles Kupchean, *The End of the American Era: US Foreign Policy and Geopolitics of the 21st Century* (New York: Alfred A. Knopf, 2002); G. John Ikenberry, ed., *American Unrivaled: The Future of the Balance of Power* (Ithaca, N.Y.: Cornell University Press, 2003); and Jonathan Monten, "Primacy and Grand Strategic Beliefs in US Unilateralism," *Global Governance* 13 (2007): 119–38.

62. Monten, "Primacy and Grand Strategic Beliefs."

63. Kristol, "In Search of Our National Interest."

64. Conversation with Nathan Glazer, December 7, 2007.

65. Nathan Glazer. "A Time for Modesty," *The National Interest*, Fall 1990, 32.

66. Jeane J. Kirkpatrick, "A Normal Country in a Normal Time," *The National Interest*, Fall 1990, 25, 40–45.

67. Ibid., 40–41.

68. Robert Kagan and William Kristol, "The Look at America's Role; the Burden of Power Is Having to Wield It," *Washington Post*, March 19, 2000.

69. Paul Wolfowitz, "Clinton's First Year," *Foreign Affairs*, January–February 1994, 40.

70. Robert Kagan and William Kristol, "Introduction: National Interests and

Global Responsibility," in *Present Dangers: Crisis and Opportunity in American Foreign and Defense Policy*, ed. William Kristol and Robert Kagan (San Francisco: Encounter Books, 2000), 4, 9.

71. Max Boot, "American Destiny Is to Police the World," *Financial Times*, February 19, 2003. This article was taken from Boot's Web page at the Council on Foreign Relations Web site, available at www.cfr.org/publications.

72. Ronald R. Krebs and Jennifer K. Lobasz, "Fixing the Meaning of 9/11: Hegemony, Coercion, and the Road to War in Iraq," *Security Studies* 16, no. 3 (July–September 2007): 426.

73. Norman Podhoretz, *World War IV: The Long Struggle against Islamofascism* (New York: Doubleday, 2007), 14.

74. Lance Morrow, "Evil," *Time*, June 10, 1991, 48.

75. See Timothy Noah, "Father and Sons," *New York Times*, January 13, 2008.

76. Kenneth Adelman, "No, Let's Not Waste Any Time," *Time Europe*, October 14, 2002, 33.

77. Lawrence F. Kaplan and William Kristol, *The War over Iraq: Saddam's Tyranny and America's Mission* (San Francisco: Encounter Books, 2003), 80, 81.

78. Gary Schmitt, "A Case of Continuity," *The National Interest*, Fall 2002, 11.

79. Cited by G. John Ikenberry, "The End of the Neoconservative Moment," *Survival* 46, no. 1 (Spring 2004): 15. Also see Robert Kagan, *Of Paradise and Power* (New York: Alfred A. Knopf, 2003).

80. Cited by David Frum and Richard Perle, *An End to Evil: How to Win the War on Terror* (New York: Random House, 2003), 16.

81. Charles Krauthammer, "The Bush Doctrine," *Time*, March 5, 2001, 42.

82. Ikenberry, "End of the Neoconservative Moment."

83. John Mearsheimer, "Hans Morgenthau and the Iraq War: Realism versus Neo-Conservatism," *Open Democracy*, April 21, 2005; available at www.opendemocracy.net.

84. Robert Jarvis, "The Compulsive Empire," *Foreign Policy*, July–August 2003, 84.

85. Robert Kagan, "Looking for Legitimacy in the Wrong Places," *Foreign Policy*, July–August 2003, 70.

86. Robert Kagan, "Power and Weakness," *Policy Review*, June–July 2002, 10.

87. See Charles Krauthammer, "The Unipolar Moment," *Foreign Affairs*, Winter 1990–91, 23–33; and Charles Krauthammer, "The New Unilateralism," *Washington Post*, June 8, 2001.

88. Charles Krauthammer, "The Unipolar Moment Revisited," *The National Interest*, Winter 2002–3, 13–15.

89. Kristol and Kagan, "Introduction," 6.

90. George W. Bush, *The National Security Strategy of the United States of America* (Washington, D.C.: U.S. Government Printing Office, 2002), 1.

91. "President Bush Announces Major Combat Operations in Iraq Have Ended: Remarks by the President from the USS *Abraham Lincoln*," http://www.whitehouse.gov/news/releases/2003/05.

92. Ivo H. Daalder and James M. Lindsay, *America Unbound: The Bush Revolution in Foreign Policy* (Washington, D.C.: Brookings Institution Press, 2003), 123.

93. Ben J. Wattenberg, "Neo-Manifest Destinarianism," *The National Interest*, Fall 1990, 51.

94. Cited by Stephen Walt, "Taming American Power," *Foreign Affairs*, September–October, 2005, 22.

95. See Seymour Martin Lipset, *The First New Nation: The United States in Historical and Comparative Perspective* (New York: W. W. Norton, 1979); Samuel P. Huntington, *American Politics: The Promise of Disharmony* (Cambridge, Mass.: Harvard University Press, 1981); and Samuel P. Huntington, "The Erosion of American National Interest," *Foreign Affairs*, September–October 1997, 28–49.

96. Seymour Martin Lipset, *American Exceptionalism: A Double-Edged Sword* (New York: W. W. Norton, 1996), 19.

97. Ibid., 18.

98. Joseph Lepgold and Timothy McKeown, "Is American Foreign Policy Exceptional? An Empirical Analysis," *Political Science Quarterly* 110, no. 3 (1995): 372.

99. Jonathan Monten, "The Roots of the Bush Doctrine: Power, Nationalism, and Democracy Promotion in U.S. Strategy," *International Security* 29, no. 4 (Spring 2005): 112–56.

100. Samuel P. Huntington, "Human Rights and American Power," *Commentary*, September 1981, 38. Monten presents this same assertion; see Monten, "Roots of the Bush Doctrine," 125, where he places neoconservatives in a long tradition of vindicationism without recognizing that there are different voices within the first generation of neoconservatives that could correctly be placed within the vein of exemplarism.

101. See Francis Fukuyama, *The End of History and the Last Man*, reprint ed. (New York: Simon & Schuster, 2006); and Takashi Inoguchi, "US Democracy Promotion in the Asia-Pacific," in *American Democracy Promotion: Impulses, Strategies, and Impacts*, ed. Michael Cox, G. John Ikenberry, and Takashi Inoguchi (New York: Oxford University Press, 2000), 269.

102. Fukuyama recently departed from the neoconservative camp. However, neoconservatives took his arguments very well.

103. Gary Dorrien, *Imperial Designs: Neoconservatism and the New Pax Americana* (New York: Routledge, 2004), 216.

104. Fukuyama, *America at the Crossroads*, 54.

105. See Fukuyama, *End of History*; and Robert Kagan, "Democracies and Double Standards," *Commentary*, August 1997, 20.

106. Norman Podhoretz, "The Future Danger," *Commentary*, April 1981, 29–47.

107. Conversation with Douglas Feith, January 30, 2008.

108. Evidently, this is not a categorical assertion. Many neoconservatives of the second generation were highly active before the collapse of communism. Yet they became fully involved in intellectual and political activities during the 1990s.

109. Cited by Mark Gerson, *The Neoconservative Vision: From Cold War to the Culture Wars* (Lanham, Md.: Madison Books, 1996), 166.

110. Irving Kristol, "The Reagan Doctrine and Beyond," in *The Reagan Doctrine and Beyond*, ed. Christopher C. DeMuth et al. (Washington, D.C.: American Enterprise Institute, 1987), 25.

111. Seymour Martin Lipset, "Some Social Requisites of Democracy," *American Political Science Review* 53 (1959): 69–105.

112. Joshua Muravchik, "The Reagan Doctrine and Beyond," in *The Reagan Doctrine and Beyond*, ed. DeMuth et al., 6.

113. Kirkpatrick, "Normal Country," 42, 43.

114. Nathan Glazer, "A Time for Modesty," *The National Interest*, Fall 1990, 34–35.

115. Daniel Bell, "The 'Hegelian Secret': Civil Society and American Exceptionalism," in *Is America Different? A New Look at American Exceptionalism*, ed. Byron E. Shafer (New York: Oxford University Press, 1991), 50–51.

116. Samuel P. Huntington, "The Great American Myth," *Maclean's*, February 2005, 40–41; the quotation is on 41.

117. Paula J. Dobriansky, "Advancing Democracy," *The National Interest*, Fall 2004, 71.

118. Kaplan and Kristol, *War over Iraq*, 64.

119. Kagan, "Democracies and Double Standards," 19, 26.

120. Telephone conversation with Richard Perle, January 28, 2008.

121. Reuel Marc Gerecht, "Going Soft on Iran," *The Weekly Standard*, March 8, 2004, 26.

122. Kristol and Kagan, "Toward a Neo-Reaganite Foreign Policy."

123. Max Boot, "U.S. Imperialism: A Force for Good," *National Post*, May 13, 2003.

124. Kagan and Kristol, *Present Dangers*, 5.

125. Conversation with Douglas Feith, January 30, 2008.

126. Paul Wolfowitz, "How the West Won," *National Review*, September 6, 1993, 62.

127. Joshua Muravchik, *Exporting Democracy: Fulfilling America's Destiny* (Washington, D.C.: American Enterprise Institute, 1991), 6.

128. See Michael Doyle, "Liberalism and World Politics," *American Political Science Review* 80 (1986): 1151–69; and Zeev Maoz and Bruce Russett, "Normative and Structural Causes of Democratic Peace, 1946–1986," *American Political Science Review* 87 (1993): 624–38.

129. Muravchik, *Exporting Democracy*, 222.

130. Joshua Muravchik, "Democracy's Quiet Victory," *New York Times*, August 19, 2002.

131. George W. Bush, "Freedom in Iraq and the Middle East," in *The George W. Bush Foreign Policy Reader: Presidential Speeches with Commentary*, ed. John W. Dietrich (Armonk, N.Y.: M. E. Sharpe, 2005), 263.

132. It is important to stress that some neoconservatives reject the implementation of democracy through force. "One of the ideas that neoconservatives are attracted to is the idea that we should be encouraging the development of democratic institutions. I do not know anyone who argues that we should be attempting to impose democracy by force." Telephone conversation with Richard Perle, January 28, 2008.

133. Two examples are Stefan Halper and Jonathan Clarke, *America Alone: The Neo-Conservatives and the Global Order* (New York: Cambridge University Press, 2004); and Dorrien, *Imperial Designs*.

## Chapter 8. Neoconservatives at War

1. Evidently, some neoconservatives supported the Contras in Nicaragua, and even some of them—like Elliott Abrams—were involved in the Iran-Contra scandal. But

neither Nicaragua nor Lebanon, nor other conflagrations, had the dimension of the current Iraq war.

2. Irving Kristol, "Facing the Facts in Vietnam," *The New Leader*, September 30, 1963, 8.

3. Irving Kristol, "We Can't Resign as a 'Policeman of the World,'" *New York Times*, May 12, 1968.

4. Kristol, "Facing the Facts."

5. Nathan Glazer, "Vietnam: The Case for Immediate Withdrawal," *Commentary*, May 1971, 37.

6. Ibid.

7. Daniel Bell, "Liberal Anti-Communism Revisited: A Symposium," *Commentary*, September 1967, 38.

8. Norman Podhoretz, *The Present Danger* (New York: Simon & Schuster, 1980), 61.

9. Norman Podhoretz, *Why We Were in Vietnam* (New York: Simon & Schuster, 1982), 197.

10. Ibid., 173.

11. Norman Podhoretz, "A Note on Vietnamization," *Commentary*, May 1971, 9.

12. Mark Gerson, "Norman's Conquest," *Policy Review*, Fall 1995.

13. Podhoretz, *Why We Were in Vietnam*, 88.

14. Ibid., 89.

15. Ibid.

16. Ibid., 99.

17. James Atlas, "Ideas & Trends: Perspective/Changing Minds; What It Takes to Be a Neo-Conservative," *New York Times*, October 19, 2003.

18. Conversation with Nathan Glazer, December 7, 2007.

19. James Mann, *The Rise of the Vulcans: The History of Bush's War Cabinet* (New York: Viking, 2004), 80–82.

20. Richard Perle, "How America Could Lose," *U.S. News & World Report*, September 24, 1990, 45.

21. At that time, it was well known that Hussein had chemical weapons. Those arms were used against the Iranian troops during the Iraq-Iran war in the 1980s and against the Kurdish population in Iraq in March 1988. Perle's words were more consistent at that time than when they were expressed in the 2000s.

22. Perle, "How America Could Lose." See also Richard Perle, "Why the Gulf Is Not Vietnam," *U.S. News & World Report*, November 19, 1990, 53.

23. Patrick E. Tyler, "U.S. Strategy Calls for Insuring No Rivals Develop," *New York Times*, March 8, 1992.

24. Paul Wolfowitz, "Clinton's First Year," *Foreign Affairs*, January–February 1994, 40.

25. Zalmay Khalilzad, "Six Steps against Terror," *The Weekly Standard*, August 5, 1996, 16.

26. Joshua Muravchik, *The Imperative of American Leadership: A Challenge to Neo-Isolationism* (Washington, D.C.: AEI Press, 1996), 29.

27. William Kristol and Robert Kagan, "Saddam Must Go," in *The Weekly Standard: A Reader, 1995–2005*, ed. William Kristol (New York: HarperPerennial, 2006), 220. This article was originally published in *The Weekly Standard*, November 17, 1997.

28. Douglas Feith, "Jack Kemp, Saddam Hussein & Jude Wanniski," *The Weekly Standard*, October 14, 1996, 2. It is interesting to note that the economic perspectives of Wanniski were highly supported by Irving Kristol. The second generation of neo-conservatives disregarded Wanniski's foreign policy views.

29. "1998: Year of Foreign Policy," *The Weekly Standard*, December 29, 1997–January 5, 1998, 7.

30. "The End of Containment," *The Weekly Standard*, December 1, 1997, 13.

31. John R. Bolton, "The U.N. Rewards Saddam," *The Weekly Standard*, December 15, 1997, 14.

32. "No Substitute for Victory," *The Weekly Standard*, February 16, 1998, 9.

33. "Attack Iraq," *The Weekly Standard*, March 2, 1998, 7.

## Chapter 9. Neoconservatism and American Foreign Policy after September 11

1. Daniel Pipes, *Militant Islam Reaches America* (New York: W. W. Norton, 2002), 113. It is interesting to observe that Pipes does not use the original document as his source of information. Instead, he quotes from an article written by Andrew T. Hoffert and published in 1930 in *The Moslem World*.

2. Pipes, *Militant Islam*, xix.

3. Norman Podhoretz, "How to Win World War IV," *Commentary*, February 2002, 27, 28; Pipes, *Militant Islam*, 124–25. The same arguments are used by Daniel Pipes, "The Danger Within: Militant Islam in America," *Commentary*, November 2001.

4. Pipes, *Militant Islam*, 124.

5. Louay Safi, "Islamophobia: A Call to Confront a Creeping Disease," *Islamic Horizons* 35, no. 6 (November–December 2006): 9–19.

6. On the differences between Islamic fundamentalism and modernism, see Stephen A. Harmon, "Joseph and Pharaoh: Religious Fundamentalism and Secular Modernists in Contemporary Islam and Their Hostility toward Western Liberalism," *Midwest Quarterly* 49, no. 2 (Winter 2008), http://search.ebscohost.com/login.aspx?direct=true&db=aph&AN=28628168&site=ehost-live.

7. "President Bush War on Terror at National Endowment for Democracy," October 2, 2005, http://www.whitehouse.gov/releases/2005/10/20051006-3.html.

8. Norman Podhoretz, "The Case for Bombing Iran," *Commentary*, June 2007, available at www.commentarymagazine.com.

9. Allan C. Brownfeld, "Using Hitler Analogy to Promote War with Iran Dangerously Wrong—For U.S. and Israel," *Washington Report on the Middle East* 27, no. 1 (January–February 2008): 52.

10. David Paul Kuhn, "Podhoretz Secretly Urged Bush to Bomb Iran," *Politico*, September 24, 2007, http://www.dyn.politico.com/printstory.cfm?uuid.

11. Anatol Lieven and John C. Hulsman, "Neo-Conservatives, Liberal Hawks and the War on Terror: Lessons from the Cold War," *World Policy Journal*, Fall 2006, 69.

12. Paul Krugman, "Fearing Fear Itself," *New York Times*, October 29, 2007.

13. "The War of the World: Laurence A. Tisch Talks with Niall Ferguson," Institute for International Studies, University of California, Berkeley, http://www.globetrotter.berkeley.edu/people 6/Ferguson/ferguson/06-con.5.html.

14. Katha Pollitt, "The Trouble with 'Bush Islamofascism,'" *The Nation*, August 26, 2006.

15. Lieven and Hulsman, "Lessons from the Cold War," 71.

16. Charles Krauthammer, "To War, Not to Court," *Washington Post*, September 12, 2001.

17. Robert Kagan, "We Must Fight This War," *Washington Post*, September 12, 2001.

18. "Remarks by the President in Photo Opportunity with the National Security Team," September 12, 2001, http//www.whitehouse.gov/news/release/2001/09/20010912 -4.html.

19. "Jim Lehrer Interviews Secretary Colin Powell," September 12, 2001, http:// www.pbs.org/newshour/bb/military/july-dec01/powell_9-13.html.

20. Conversation with Douglas Feith, January 30, 2008.

21. Douglas Feith, *War and Decision: Inside the Pentagon at the End Dawn of the War on Terrorism* (New York: HarperCollins, 2008), 14, 15, 50–51.

22. Scott McClellan, *What Happened: Inside the Bush White House and Washington's Culture of Deception* (New York: PublicAffairs, 2008), 126.

23. According to Bob Woodward, President Bush and some of his top advisers were convinced that the United States should sponsor regime change in Iraq from the beginning of the Bush administration. Cf. Bob Woodward, *Plan of Attack* (New York: Simon & Schuster, 2005), esp. 21–25. The views of neoconservatives on Iraq have been broadly discussed before. Therefore, from here on, I basically deal with neoconservative views and the Bush administration's positions after September 11.

24. Ibid., 50, 51, 52.

25. Ibid., 52

26. George Tenet, *At the Center of the Storm: My Years at the CIA* (New York, HarpersCollins, 2007), p. 306.

27. Bob Woodward, *Bush at War* (New York: Simon & Schuster, 2002), 83.

28. Norman Podhoretz, "Israel Isn't the Issue," *Wall Street Journal*, September 20, 2001.

29. Feith, *War and Decision*, 6.

30. Open Letter to the President, "Foreign Policy Experts Call on George W. Bush to Take Terrorism Seriously," *The Weekly Standard*, September 20, 2001.

31. McClellan, *What Happened*, 128.

32. "Address of President George W. Bush to a Joint Session of Congress and the American People," U.S. Capitol, Washington, D.C., September 20, 2001, http://www .whitehouse.gov/news/release/2001/09/print/20010920-8.html.

33. Michael J. Boyle, "The War on Terror in American Grand Strategy," *International Affairs* 84, no. 2 (2008): 191.

34. Charles Krauthammer, "The War: A Road Map," *Washington Post*, September 28, 2001.

35. Feith, *War and Decision*, 218.

36. Robert Kagan and William Kristol, "The Coalition of the Trap," *The Weekly Standard*, October 15, 2001.

37. Charles Krauthammer, "Clear Thinking on Coalition," *Washington Post*, October 19, 2001.

38. Charles Krauthammer, "Unilateral? Yes, Indeed," *Washington Post*, December 14, 2001.

39. Robert Kagan and William Kristol, "What to Do about Iraq," *The Weekly Standard*, January 21, 2002.

40. George W. Bush, "The President's State of the Union Address," January 29, 2002, http://www.whitehouse.gov/news/releases/2002/01/print/20020129-11.html.

41. Suzanne Daley, "A Nation Challenged: The Allies; Many in Europe Voice Worry U.S. Will Not Consult Them," *New York Times*, January 31, 2002.

42. Fleischer was quoted by Alan Ciprés and Thomas E. Ricks, "No New Military Action 'Imminent'; U.S. to Continue Other Approaches to 3 Nations Cited, Bush Aides Say," *Washington Post*, January 31, 2002.

43. Elisabeth Bumiller, "The World; Axis of Debate: Hawkish Words," *New York Times*, February 3, 2002.

44. Gary Dorrien, *Imperial Designs: Neoconservatism and the New Pax Americana* (New York: Routledge, 2004), 158.

45. Robert Kagan, "Powell's Moment," *Washington Post*, February 10, 2002.

46. William Kristol, "Taking the War beyond Terrorism," *Washington Post*, January 31, 2002.

47. Charles Krauthammer, "Redefining War," *Washington Post*, February 1, 2002.

48. Charles Krauthammer, "The Axis of Petulance," *Washington Post*, March 1, 2002.

49. "President Bush Delivers Graduation Speech at West Point," June 1, 2002, http://www.whitehouse.gov/news/releases/2002/06/20020601-3.html.

50. National Security Council, "The National Security Strategy of the United States of America," http://www.whitehouse.gov/nsc/nss.html.

51. Max Boot, "What Next? The Foreign Policy Agenda beyond Iraq," *The Weekly Standard*, May 5, 2003.

52. Stephen Walt, "Beyond Bin Laden: Reshaping U.S. Foreign Policy, *International Security* 26 (Winter 2001–2).

53. Amy Lorentzen, "Cheney: Kerry Victory Will Lead to Another Terrorist Attack on US," Associated Press, September 7, 2004, available at http://www.commondreams.org/headlines04/0907-10.htm.

54. Boot, "What Next?"

55. Conversation with Feith, January 30, 2008.

56. Ibid.

57. Gary Schmitt, "Why Iraq? If Saddam Hussein Stays in Power, the War on Terrorism Will Have Failed," *The Weekly Standard*, October 29, 2001.

58. Robert Kagan and William Kristol, "Getting Serious," *The Weekly Standard*, November 19, 2001.

59. Schmitt, "Why Iraq?"

60. See William Kristol, "What's Next in the War on Terrorism: Prepared Testimony for the February 7, 2002, Hearing of the Senate Foreign Relations Committee," *The Weekly Standard*, February 7, 2002.

61. Charles Krauthammer, "Voices of Moral Obtuseness," *Washington Post*, September 21, 2001.

62. Kagan and Kristol, "What to Do about Iraq."

63. Richard Perle, "The U.S. Must Strike at Saddam Hussein," American Enterprise Institute, January 1, 2002, available at www.aei.org.

64. Lawrence F. Kaplan and William Kristol, *The War over Iraq: Saddam's Tyranny and America's Mission* (San Francisco: Encounter Books, 2003), 32.

65. Kagan and Kristol, "What to Do about Iraq."

66. Richard Perle, "Why the U.S. Must Strike at Saddam Hussein," American Enterprise Institute, August 1, 2002, available at www.aei.org.

67. Michael Ledeen, "The War Won't End in Bagdad," *Wall Street Journal*, September 4, 2002.

68. Krauthammer, "The War: A Road Map."

69. Kaplan and Kristol, *War over Iraq*.

70. "Richard Perle: The Making of Neoconservative," Ben Wattenberg interview with Richard Perle on his television program, *Think Tank*, http://www.pbs.org/think tank/transcript1017.html.

71. Charles Krauthammer, "Holiday from History," *Washington Post*, February 14, 2003.

72. David Kay, "Transcript of David Kay at Senate Hearing, January 28, 2004," http://www.cnn.com/2004/US/01/28/kay.transcript/.

73. Sydney Blumenthal, "Bush Knew Saddam Had No Weapons of Mass Destruction," http://www.salon.com/opinion/blumenthal/2007/09/06/bush_wmd/print.html. Cf. Randall Mikkelsen, "Bush Misused Iraq Intelligence: Senate Report," *Boston Globe*, June 5, 2008; Jonathan S. Landay, "Senate Committee: Bush Knew Iraq Claims Weren't True," McClatchy Washington Bureau, June 5, 2008, http://www.mcclatchyd.c .com/224/v-print/story/39963.html; Charles Lewis and Mark Reading-Smith, "False Pretenses," *Center for Public Integrity*, January 23, 2008, http://www.projects.public integrity.org/WarCard.

74. Chaim Kaufman, "The Inflation and the Failure of the Market Place of Ideas: The Selling of the Iraq War," *International Security* 29, no. 1 (Summer 2004): 7, 8.

## Chapter 10. The Iraqi Debacle and the Partial Decline of Neoconservatism

1. Kari Lydersen, "War Costing $720 Million Each Day, Group Says," *Washington Post*, September 22, 2007.

2. Telephone conversation with Richard Perle, January 28, 2008.

3. Conversation with Elliott Abrams, January 28, 2008.

4. Conversation with Douglas Feith, January 30, 2008.

5. David Frum, *Comeback: Conservatism That Can Win Again* (New York: Doubleday, 2008), 138.

6. Conversation with William Kristol, January 31, 2008.

7. Conversation with Gary Schmitt, January 29, 2008.

8. Conversation with Joshua Muravchik, January 31, 2008.

9. Ibid.

## Epilogue

1. Peter A. Hall, "The Movement from Keynesianism to Monetarism: Institutional Analysis and British Economic Policy in the 1970s," in *Structuring Politics: Historical Institutionalism in Comparative Analysis*, ed. Steven Steinmo, Kathleen Thelen, and Frank Longstreth (New York: Cambridge University Press, 1992), 104.

2. John Mearsheimer, "Hans Morgenthau and the Iraq War: Realism versus Neo-Conservatism," *Open Democracy*, available at www.opendemocracy.net.

3. Michael C. Williams, "What Is That National Interest? The Neoconservative Challenge to IR Theory," *European Journal of International Relations* 11, no. 3 (2005).

4. Richard Bensel, "The Tension between American Political Development as a Research Community and as a Disciplinary Subfield," *Studies in American Political Development* 17 (Spring 2003): 106.

5. There is an interesting recollection of Bell's participation in the *New Leader*. See the series of articles by Daniel Bell, "The Early Years," *The New Leader*, January–April 2006.

6. There are always exceptions like Paul Krugman, the winner of the Nobel Prize in Economics.

7. Evidently, there are different kinds of think tanks. Some of them are academically oriented, like the Hoover Institution and the Brookings Institution; others are more ideologically inclined, like the Heritage Foundation.

8. Today, think tanks stand on their own merits, for six primary reasons. First, they have been part of the American political scene long enough to be recognized by politicians, businesspeople, and the public in general. Second, throughout the years, think tanks have established important ties with the media that identify their researchers as an important source of information. Third, think tanks, particularly conservative ones, have created strong links with corporations and conservative foundations—since the 1970s, conservative foundations have constituted a major source of ongoing financial support. Fourth, conservative think tanks receive significant contributions from people that sympathize with their philosophy and work, and who obtain some benefit from the ideological position advanced by a particular think tank. Fifth, think tanks have become the new home of influential politicians who for different reasons have left active political life. To a significant degree, in the world of think tanks, the power of politicians has substituted for the prestige of academics. Sixth and finally, the decline of political parties has been another central component in the consolidation of think tanks. Historically, political parties were the main channel of education and therefore information for the general public. With the decline of parties, the mass media, think tanks, and intellectuals have assumed the task of educating the public. This does not mean that we do not have public intellectuals any more. Scholars like the late Stephen Jay Gould, Paul Krugman, and the late Carl Sagan have successfully performed the role of public intellectuals and scientists.

9. American National Election Studies, *The ANES Guide to Public Opinion and Electoral Behavior* (Ann Arbor: University of Michigan Center for Political Studies [produer and distributor]), available at www.electionstudies.org.

10. See Harris Poll 43, May 19, 2005.

11. Leo P. Ribuffo, "Conservatism and American Politics," *Journal of the Historical Society* (Boston) 3, no. 2 (Spring 2003): 164.

12. Conversation with William Kristol, July 15, 1993.

13. Neoconservatives never accepted that their views were wrong; they believed that the problem was the inadequate implementation of their perspective by President Bush.

14. Richard Perle, "Ambushed on the Potomac," *The National Interest Online*, January 21, 2009, available at www.nationalinterest.org.

15. See the interview conducted by Justine Rosenthal with Richard Perle, "*The National Interest* Interviews Richard Perle," on YouTube (www.youtube.com). Here Perle is establishing a distinction between the first and second terms of the George W.

Bush administration. In the first Bush term, neoconservatives were a very important group. In the second, their presence diminished substantially, due to scandals or serious criticism of their performance, in particular on the Iraq War.

16. Cf. Jessica de Mello, "Tale of Two Bills: Kristol and Brooks; Salon Speakers; Prostate Cancer," *National Post, Calgary Edition*, January 31, 2009. See also Kevin Libin, "Obama's Glimmers of Neo-Conservatism: From Left to Center between Election and Inauguration," *National Post National Edition*, January 24, 2009.

17. See Brent Scowcroft, "Don't Attack Saddam," *Wall Street Journal*, August 15, 2002. It is interesting to observe that some of the main arguments presented by Scowcroft to oppose the invasion were more in tune with the political facts of those years than the views expressed by neoconservatives. At that time, Scowcroft argued that there was not a clear nexus between Hussein and terrorist organizations; that no unambiguous links existed between Hussein and the terrorist attacks of September 11; that an invasion of Iraq would be economically expensive and would cause a significant number of casualties; and that such an offensive would provoke a "large-scale, long-term military occupation." After seven years of American attacks on Iraq, it is evident that Scowcroft was right.

18. Kyle L. Saunders and Alan I. Abramowitz, "The Rise of the Ideological Voter: The Changing Bases of Partisanship in the American Electorate," in *The State and the Parties: The Changing Role of Contemporary American Politics*, ed. John C. Green and Daniel J. Coffey (Boulder, Colo.: Rowman & Littlefield, 2007), 314; in the same volume, see the essay by David C. Kimball and Cassie A. Gross.

19. By "extremist positions," I mean the political tendencies of persons or groups outside the center of the American political spectrum. Leftist political tendencies have never played a major role in electoral politics. We have to remember that in 1912, Eugene Debs obtained 6 percent of the popular vote, the highest proportion ever obtained by a Socialist candidate. Moreover, after McCarthyism and the consolidation of the Soviet Bloc in the aftermath of World War II, leftist tendencies declined in the United States, but they reemerged in the 1960s and 1970s with the New Left. However, this important political and intellectual movement did not have a significant impact on the ballot box, becoming a marginal expression in current times.

20. Jonathan Karp, "Defense Reloads; Rising Pentagon Spending Quells Talk of Profit Plateau," *Wall Street Journal*, January 17, 2007.

21. See "War with Iraq Is Not in America's National Interest," paid advertisement, *New York Times*, September 26, 2002.

22. See Office of Management and Budget, "Department of Defense," http://www .whitehouse.gov/omb/budget/fy2007/defense.html.

23. Recently, some neoconservatives have faced problems at the American Enterprise Institute. At the end of 2008 and the beginning of 2009, Reuel Marc Gerecht, Michael Ledeen, and Joshua Muravchik left the institute. According to Jacob Heilbrunn, this "vicious purge" was conducted by the vice president for foreign and defense policy studies, Danielle Pletka. Others believe that these neoconservatives left the institute due to the declining economy and the institute's need to adjust its budget. They maintain that associates in other departments, not only foreign policy, have also left. Ledeen and Gerecht have joined the Foundation for the Defense of Democracy, another think tank full of neoconservatives. On this topic, see Jacob Heilbrunn, "Flight of the Neocons," *The National Interest Online,* December 19, 2008, available at www .nationalinterest.org.

# Index

*Notes are indicated by "n" following the page number.*